# WRIGHT TO FLY

## CELEBRATING 100 YEARS OF POWERED FLIGHT

Compiled by

PETER R MARCH

*The Dream Fulfilled* by Keith Ferris ASAA

# CONTENTS

# FOREWORD

A HUNDRED YEARS AGO at Kitty Hawk, in North Carolina, USA – after many trials and much patient and inspired endeavour – the brothers Wilbur and Orville Wright made history when they accomplished man's first powered flight. Today their legacy lives on, immensely embellished by successive pioneers of many nations – shrinking distances and carrying millions, while drawing the people of the world ever closer together.

Air power has been a vital element throughout, repeatedly used to defend worthy national interests. Through some of the darkest of days it has been marked by outstandingly gallant acts of self-sacrifice, many of which are deservedly remembered in this volume.

The Royal Air Force Benevolent Fund was formed in 1919 by Marshal of the Royal Air Force Lord Trenchard, to care for those members who fall on hard times. It represents the family ethos of the Service, which includes all serving and retired airmen and women and their dependants. A constant demand exists for its resources, especially now that so many veterans of the Second World War have attained old age.

This volume vividly records, in words and pictures, a number of aviation's most memorable events through the years. May I commend it, most warmly, to everyone who reads this brief Foreword. I trust that it will generate significant contributions to the Royal Air Force Benevolent Fund.

**Sir Peter G Masefield**

MA CEng(Hon) BSc(Hon) DTech(Hon) FRAeS FCIT(Hon) FAIAA(Hon) FCASI(Hon) FIRTE

# INTRODUCTION

*For I dipt into the future, far as human eye could see.*
*Saw the vision of the world, and all the wonder that would be;*
*Saw the heavens filled with commerce, argosies of magic spells,*
*Pilots of the purple twilight, dropping down with costly bales.....*

......from Locksley Hall, Tennyson

As far back as we can discover, mankind has dreamed of flying. Apart from physically attempting to emulate the birds, usually with dire consequences, the record of fable and myth, art, literature and primitive technology all testify to this goal. While the early pioneers like Leonardo da Vinci got close, it was not until the Montgolfier brothers built their successful hot-air balloon in 1783 that man got airborne for the first time, and more particularly, landed safely after the flight.

Once man had moved away from trying to 'fly like a bird', largely as a result of British scientist Sir George Cayley establishing the basic principles of heavier-than-air flight at the turn of the nineteenth century, the pathway to man getting airborne was set. The next key milestone was the invention of the internal combustion engine towards the end of the century. This was to provide the means to sustain a suitable flying machine in the air.

Many pioneers around the world were taking up the challenge but it was the vision, intellect and determination of two young Americans, Wilbur and Orville Wright, bicycle-makers at Dayton, Ohio, that transformed the dream into reality. After four years of experimentation with kites and gliders, the Wright Brothers opened a new era in travel at Kitty Hawk, North Carolina on 17 December 1903 when they made a series of powered flights. At 10:35am on the sandy, wind-swept Kill Devil Hills, Orville Wright made the world's first powered flight. Lasting just 12 seconds it covered a distance of some 120ft, rising to about ten feet above the ground. By the fourth and final flight that day, the Wright Flyer I, as it was named, flew 852ft in 59 seconds with Wilbur at the controls. Just a short hop – but man's long-held dream was fulfilled.

In the one hundred years since the Wright Brothers' first faltering powered flight, man has developed the technology to fly around the world, into space, faster than the speed of sound and carry over 500 people or many tons of cargo in a single aircraft. Developments in aviation have brought many social and economic benefits, but they have also brought death and destruction when used as a weapon of war or terrorism. Efficient and reliable air transport has become an essential part of world-wide travel and trade while at the same time the military use of aeroplanes through two World Wars and subsequent conflicts has put air power at the heart of military strategy. For good or ill, the aeroplane has affected the lives of almost everyone in the past century and will undoubtedly continue to do so.

*Wright to Fly* follows the development of powered flight year by year from the flimsy wood and canvas planes of the pioneers and the military applications of the opening decades, through the tentative start of air transport and its evolution into a global transportation system, to today's sophisticated and often high tech helicopters, airliners, fighters, bombers, business, sport, private and homebuilt aircraft. Many of the achievements and events of the first hundred years have been chronicled in this book and some of them highlighted in an introductory narrative, as space permits. No work of this kind can be all-embracing. For many of the items included there are others that are equally worthy of inclusion, but have been omitted or only briefly touched upon.

Like the narrative and chronology, the choice of paintings throughout *Wright to Fly* is very subjective and was inevitably restricted by availability, quality and budgetary considerations. Ten of the paintings have been specially commissioned and others have been donated for use in this book by leading aviation artists from around the world.

The preparation of this book has been very much a team effort. I am indebted to Ben Dunnell and Brian Strickland for their painstaking research and collation of the history of powered flight year by year. Bob Dixon had to track down a huge catalogue of paintings and assisted by art consultant Wilfred Hardy, obtain copies for a final selection to be made. The process of balancing the possible subjects for each year against the quality of the works available and briefing artists for newly commissioned paintings was in turn very demanding.

Few people at the turn of the last century could have realistically envisaged that manned flight would have progressed within 100 years from fragile flimsy single-seaters to streamlined supersonic airliners, from wood and canvas biplanes to stealthy sophisticated bombers and fighters, that there would be helicopters, space shuttles, vertical take-off and landing aircraft or that it would be quite normal to fly to your holiday destination in an aeroplane. What does the next 100 years hold? That will be for others to chronicle, although one thing is certain – mankind will continue its eternal dream to 'fly with the birds'.

**Peter R March**

Towards the end of the 19th century English, French and American pioneers were racing to be the first to achieve powered, heavier-than-air flight. At the centre of this were two little-known bicycle mechanics from Dayton, Ohio, Wilbur and Orville Wright. They perfected the design for the initial Flyer, culminating in the historic first flight on 17 December 1903 from Big Kill Devil Hill, Kitty Hawk, North Carolina. Some ten years later, Orville Wright wrote a concise description of what they had achieved: 'the first in a history of the world in which a machine carrying a man had raised itself by its own power into the air in full flight, and sailed forward without reduction in speed, and had finally landed at a point as high as that from which it had started'.

On 30 May 1899, Wilbur Wright wrote to the Smithsonian Institution, seeking the latest information available on the subject of flying and aeronautics. He received a number of papers and four pamphlets, and studied them in detail. At the end of July, the brothers completed a small model glider which used the 'wing-warping' control technique, in which pulley linkages 'warped' the wingtips up and down to increase or reduce the aerofoil section's available lift. When this glider worked quite well, the brothers commenced the design and construction of a man-carrying glider using the same basic principles (including the use of techniques described by Otto Lilienthal).

On 13 September 1900, they arrived at Kitty Hawk, North Carolina, which had been recommended to them by the US Weather Bureau as a suitable test site, in order to carry out flight trials. Between then and 23 October, the glider was flown both as a tethered kite and as a free-flying glider. Again the wing-warping mechanism proved satisfactory as a means of control. The Wrights decided to use the dunes at Kill Devil Hills for their next glider trials between July and August 1901, further refinements being made to the configuration. Later that year, the brothers began more detailed research into aerodynamics, constructing a wind tunnel to help them.

The Wright 1902 glider, which flew for the first time on 20 September, made good use of their research using the wind tunnel. Following a minor accident, the craft had to be rebuilt, and took to the air again on 8 October with a number of further modifications – including the use of a single rudder linked to the wing-warping mechanism. With the incorporation of elevators into the design, the glider was now a fully-controllable aeroplane. This success enabled the Wrights to press on with an initial progression into powered flight.

The previous year they had sent letters to a number of motor manufacturers, hoping to purchase a relatively vibrationless motor engine that weighed no more than 180lb. The response was not encouraging, so Wilbur and Orville decided to look closer to home. In December 1902, their friend and bicycle repair shop colleague, Charlie Taylor, produced a four-stroke engine for the aircraft, and two months later the brothers themselves began working on the propellers, an entirely new departure in aeronautical design, as no-one had ever had to make a propeller which was efficient enough to get an aircraft off the ground.

Work on the aeroplane itself commenced in February 1903 in the Wrights' bicycle workshop in Dayton. They named the powered version 'Flyer', to distinguish it from the previous machines, and its construction continued into the summer. The skids that had proved satisfactory for landing their glider in sand were retained, but were extended several feet forward and braced to withstand the impact of landing the much heavier Flyer.

There were, at this time, similar attempts being made by other pioneers to get airborne. Foremost among these was Samuel Langley who, long before any official help or recognition was offered to the Wright brothers, had been paid $25,000 by the US Army to develop his Great Aerodrome project. This had originated from a series of model steam-powered Aerodrome gliders launched by Langley from the Potomac River. These had taken the form of a 'dual monoplane' (with one wing directly in front of another) powered by a single 52hp gasoline-driven engine. It crashed on both of the first two launch attempts in October and December 1903. Langley escaped unhurt both times, but US Government backing was soon withdrawn.

With its much more advanced and appropriate methods of power and control, the first Wright Flyer was a much better proposition for controlled flight. The required techniques were further trialled using the 1902 glider while arrival of the Flyer was awaited at Kitty Hawk. The 12hp engine, which delivered some 9.5hp once the power had been transmitted to the propeller, was run up and some minor defects found. This delayed matters somewhat. Most notably, engine vibrations caused a propeller shaft to crack, and Orville had to return to Dayton to make a new one.

Three days after he returned, on 14 December, the two brothers removed the Flyer from its shed at Kill Devil Hills, and mounted it on the purpose-built 60ft-long track from which it would be launched into the air. A coin was tossed to determine who would make the first flight, and Wilbur won. Unfortunately, he pulled the elevator back too vigorously, whereupon the aircraft pitched up and stalled into the sand, causing minor damage. On 17 December, with Orville at the controls, a second attempt was made. The Flyer became airborne at 10.35am, and flew a distance of some 120 feet. This 12-second flight became recognised as the first sustained, controlled, powered flight made by a heavier-than-air craft.

The Wright Flyer got airborne four times that day, each of the brothers having two turns at the controls. Two days afterwards, they returned to Dayton once more, having completed their work for the year. This was not the end of the Wrights' work, as over the years that followed they strived to further develop their design into a viable commercial proposition. This eventually opened the world's eyes to the possibilities that could arise from the great achievement of that December day at Kitty Hawk.

*John Young's painting depicts Orville Wright making the first sustained, controlled, powered flight by a heavier-than-air craft at Kill Devil Hills on 17 December 1903, in the Wright Flyer I.*

*On the Wind* by John Young VPGAvA, VPASAA

# 1904

As the year 1904 opened, the world's first aviators had less than two minutes total flight time between them in their powered aircraft, and they wanted to build something that would stay up a little longer.

Following on from the triumphant initial flight of their Flyer on 17 December the previous year, Wilbur and Orville Wright continued to develop their flying machines during the course of 1904. The Flyer II, which took to the air in May for the first time from a new test location on Huffman Prairie near Dayton (and thereby much closer to the brothers' workshop), was a heavier development of the original pioneering design. It used an improved engine delivering 16hp, a 25% increase over the previous installation, that allowed more ambitious flights to be undertaken in spite of the higher altitude of Huffman Prairie, which restricted the power available. On 15 September, Wilbur made the first controlled turn to be carried out in a powered flying machine when he accomplished a half-circle, and five days later he managed to fly the aircraft around a complete circle. This flight of some 4,000ft was followed by an even more impressive feat on 9 November, when Wilbur carried out the first ever controlled powered flight lasting more than five minutes (circling the test site four times in succession).

With characteristic inventiveness, the Wright's designed a simple catapult launching device that would speed their plane down the launching rail fast enough to become airborne even in a dead calm. The starting device consisted of a tower, a 1,600lb weight and ropes and pulleys, rigged so that when the weight descended it exerted a strong pull on the launching car as it slid down the first 50ft of track. Now they could fly whenever they wanted to on a clear day. They began their uneven, halting efforts to make an aircraft turn by working the clumsy hip cradle that warped the wings into a bank and moved the vertical tail. All the flights during 1904 were conducted openly with no attempt to discourage visitors, although they were few.

While these significant events in the early history of flight represented important advances for the Wrights, the Flyer II still suffered from instability in turns, which made attempts at ever longer controlled flights somewhat uncertain affairs. In addition, the 16hp engine was prone to relatively early failure. It was therefore decided by the brothers to scrap the aircraft, retrieving only the engine components for use in the next Flyer. However, overseas interest in their work had already been forthcoming during 1904. Lt Col John P. Capper from the British Royal Aeronautical Society, a ballooning expert with the British Army, visited Ohio in October to discuss with the Wrights the possible future use of their designs by the service to which he belonged. In spite of the brothers proposing the building of a two-seat aeroplane with a 50-mile range, and the enthusiasm of Capper, the British Army remained unimpressed by the performance of the Wrights' existing designs. It was some time before powered heavier-than-air flight really started to appeal in terms of potential military use.

America's first significant airship flights also took place in 1904. During the summer Thomas S Baldwin, an extraordinary airman and showman, who specialised in parachute jumping from free balloons, assembled a 54ft airship powered by a gasoline engine that was built by Glenn Curtiss, then a rising young motor cycle racer and builder.

---

**Jan:** Samuel Franklin Cody began work on powered aeroplanes. He followed the style of the Wright brothers, for whom he had great admiration, rather than attempting to further develop his own kite designs.

**24 Mar:** The Wrights applied for a German patent for their aircraft.

**15 May:** Sir John French, in command at Aldershot, wrote to the War Office asking for authority to proceed with preparing the ground for the proposed airship shed, the 'Elongated Balloon Erecting House' at Farnborough. This was agreed on 17 June.

**23 May:** Wilbur and Orville Wright undertook the initial, albeit unsuccessful, flight trial of their Flyer II on Huffman Prairie, OH.

**26 May:** Flyer No II made the first of 105 successful flights.

**7-25 Jun:** Military flight trials of Samuel Cody's kiting system (which were remarkably successful) were undertaken at Aldershot at his own expense. During the trials, over 20 flights were made by eleven different people.

**Jun-Jul:** Throughout this period, the Wrights made a large number of short, generally unsatisfying flights. Three times they stayed aloft for more than 35 seconds with distances of up to 1,750ft. Already they were beginning to ponder their next problem, which was how to make a turn.

**3 Aug:** In the USA, the first circular flight, by a lumbering 56ft long dirigible airship, was made by Thomas Scott Baldwin in his California Arrow design, which made its début at the St Louis Fair. It was powered by Glen Curtiss's lightweight gasoline engine, that had been developed for his racing motor cycles.

**7 Sep:** At Huffman Field, the Wrights carried out the first assisted launch of an aircraft, using a purpose-built derrick arrangement of weighted pulleys attached to four vertically-mounted poles.

**20 Sep:** Wilbur Wright made the first ever circuit in an aeroplane around a large field owned by a dairy farmer, on Huffman Prairie. As the Wrights shunned publicity, they had no plans to fly any nearer to Dayton itself.

**Oct:** Frenchman Robert Esnault-Pelterie flew a glider with ailerons (which were mounted forward of the wing) for control, the first full-scale aeroplane to feature such an innovation. Wing warping had been added, but with downward movement only. Pilot weight-shift provided pitch control.

**Oct:** Artillery captain Ferdinand Ferber began trials with his glider #5 at Chalais-Meudon in France. Trying to achieve longitudinal stability, he made an important innovation in adding a forward stabiliser to the Chanute/Wright-type machine.

**9 Nov:** To celebrate Theodore Roosevelt's election, Wilbur Wright flew 4.43km (2.75 miles) at Dayton, the first aircraft flight in excess of five minutes' duration.

**9 Dec:** The Wrights ended trials of their Flyer II after some 80 flights in just over six months.

*This specially commissioned painting by Charles J Thompson shows the Wright Flyer II taking to the air for the first time at Huffman's Field, near Dayton, Ohio at dawn on 26 May 1904.*

*Prairie Dawn* by Charles J Thompson GAvA, ASAA, MGMA, EAA

This year marked a temporary halt to the Wrights' flight testing of their designs, of which the Flyer III was the latest development. Orville got airborne in the new machine for the first time on 23 June, and it immediately showed itself to be considerably more effective as a flying machine than its predecessors. An 18hp engine provided improved motive power, while the wing had been redesigned and the elevators enlarged. Unfortunately, the maiden air test culminated in an accident on landing, but repairs were soon effected. As part of this work, the engine was uprated to 20hp and made more reliable, allowing longer flights to be carried out around Huffman Prairie.

The brothers made continuous refinements to the Flyer III until its final test of the year on 16 October, by which time the machine had been made longer, thanks to repositioned control surfaces fore and aft. As a result, this gave better aerial handling characteristics than its configuration had allowed in June. It was then decided by Wilbur and Orville to stop flight testing, and instead concentrate their energies on advancing their design. This work took some three years, during which time neither of the brothers took to the air.

Even after two years of great progress, the Wrights had still received no backing from officialdom, and their achievements remained the subject of considerable scepticism from some quarters. During March, they were contacted by one Ernest Archdeacon, a French lawyer with his own aspirations in the field of aeronautics. He doubted the truth of the brothers' feats, a view that was shared by a great many Europeans at the time (largely, perhaps, out of a degree of jealousy that European attempts at controlled flight in a heavier-than-air flying machine had thus far not been as successful as those of the Wrights). Apart from that, the US Army still showed little or no interest in Wilbur and Orville's work, while a contract between the Wrights and the French businessman Arnold Fordyce for the production of a single aeroplane, which Fordyce's associate Ferdinand Ferber hoped to sell on to the French government, also fell through. The brothers, though, did earn around $5,000 out of the deal, which was their first payment related to their aeronautical activities.

However, there was an increased international realisation that aviation generally, if not perhaps the work of the Wrights in particular, was of growing importance. It was with this in mind that, on 10 June 1905, Count Henri de la Vaulx, Vice President of the Aero Club of France, Major Moedebeck of the German Airship League and Fernand Jacobs, President of the Aero Club of Belgium, gave a presentation to the Olympic Congress of Brussels on their proposal for a co-ordinating body for the new 'sport' of aviation, entitled the Fédération Aéronautique Internationale (FAI). It was well received, and the Congress adopted a resolution stating that "This Congress, recognising the special importance of aeronautics, expresses the desire that in each country, there be created an Association for regulating the sport of flying and that thereafter there be formed a Universal Aeronautical Federation to regulate the various aviation meetings and advance the science and sport of Aeronautics".

On 12 October, representatives of eight countries (Belgium, France, Germany, Great Britain, Italy, Spain, Switzerland and the USA) met in Paris and discussed the new organisation's creation in more detail. After two days of talks, the FAI was officially founded, and has remained in being ever since. Its primary role remains the ratification of aviation records, the administration of the classes into which these different records fall and an organiser of competitive events. However, the growth in recent years of air sports has seen an extension of the FAI's remit, to take in a new role as a representative of the interests of involved parties and a forum for discussion. Almost a century on, the Fédération continues to flourish and develop.

---

**3 Jan:** Wilbur Wright wrote to the US Board of Ordnance and Fortification with an offer of an aeroplane for potential military use as a scouting platform. However, the proposal was declined on 26 January.

**1 Feb:** Samuel F. Cody began a three-month contract as a kiting instructor at the British Army's Balloon factory.

**27 Apr:** Sapper Moreton of the British Army's Balloon Section reached a record height of 2,600ft in a pilot kite at Farnborough.

**29 Apr:** Daniel Maloney of America, an amateur inventor and self-publicist, made the first glider flight from a tethered balloon. He was killed in a third flight on 18 July.

**14 May:** The Swiss Dufax brothers demonstrated a model helicopter. Powered by a 3hp engine, the 37lb machine succeeded in lifting a load of 13lb.

**25 May:** Ferdinand Ferber made the first flight in his #6 *bis* glider, fitted with a 12hp Peugeot engine.

**6 Jun:** Frenchman Louis Seguin founded the Gnome rotary engine factory.

**23 Jun:** The maiden flight of the fully controllable Wright Flyer III, fitted with new propellers, ended in a heavy landing that damaged the aircraft's wings.

**4 Oct:** At the controls of the repaired and modified Flyer III, Orville Wright made the first ever controlled heavier-than-air powered flight of more than half an hour's duration at Simms Station, near Dayton.

**5 Oct:** Its wings now repaired, the Wright Flyer III flew a new record distance of 24.2 miles (39km) around Huffman Prairie in just over 38min.

**14 Oct:** Following a two-day conference in Paris, the Fédération Aéronautique Internationale (FAI) was established as an official body to ratify records and regulate the new 'sport' of aviation. It had eight founder members.

**16 Oct:** The Flyer III made its final flight, in the hands of Wilbur Wright. This was also the last venture into the air by either of the brothers for three years, while a new design was perfected.

**30 Nov:** The inauguration of the Aero Club of America took place in New York, which reflected a renewed interest in the science of aeronautics.

**30 Nov:** Zeppelin airship LZII was damaged during an aborted take-off attempt at Lake Constance. Further launch attempts were postponed.

*The first flight of the fully controllable Wright Flyer III, on 23 June 1905, is captured by Frank Munger in his painting entitled* First Practical Aeroplane.

*First Practical Aeroplane* by Frank Munger AMRAeS, GAvA, MGMA

# 1906

While the previous three years in the fledgling history of powered flight had belonged to the Wright brothers, 1906 saw Alberto Santos-Dumont come to the fore, and with his successes, the birth of aeroplane flight in Europe. Others had tried, notably Jacob C. Ellehammer in Denmark, whose 'flight' around a circular track, tethered to a centrally-mounted pole, was said by some to represent this historic milestone. However, Santos-Dumont is viewed, almost without doubt, as the first to accomplish the feat. His 14-*bis* biplane of cellular construction (originally intended to be launched from his No 14 balloon, hence the name) was initially fitted with a 24hp Antoinette engine and had a 37ft 8in wingspan, a little less than that of the previous year's Wright Flyer III. The powerplant proved insufficient to get the 14-*bis* airborne under its own power in early tests. Having replaced it with a 50hp unit, Santos-Dumont finally took off from the Bois de Bologne polo ground in Paris on 13 September, for a flight which was not officially measured, but which was reported as having been around the 20ft mark. After this initial 'hop', Santos-Dumont started making lengthier flights, of up to 722ft by mid-November. Frenchman Ernest Archdeacon, who in 1905 had written to the Wrights, doubting the validity of their pioneering flights, put up two cash prizes for new European distance and average speed records in conjunction with the French Aero Club. Over the course of October and November both were claimed by Santos-Dumont.

A great deal of pride swept across France after these achievements, as the country began to mount the first serious challenge to the aeronautical supremacy of the Wrights in the USA. Santos-Dumont had in fact been born in Brazil on 20 July 1873, but was sent to live in Paris by his father at the age of 18. While there he studied chemistry, physics, mechanics and astronomy, and developed an interest in the construction of balloons. His ability in this field was soon obvious: his second balloon, *America*, won an Aéro Club de Paris award for flying higher and for longer than any of the other eleven entered in the competition. His next major development was a successful steered balloon (his third design of this type) which he demonstrated around central Paris in November 1900. In total, Santos-Dumont built a total of nine steerable balloons, which illustrated that such lighter-than-air vehicles could be manoeuvred successfully. After that, he turned his hand to heavier-than-air flight, and the construction of the 14-*bis*.

Another European aeronautical figure of great importance during 1906 was Graf von Zeppelin, the German count who was becoming a pioneer in the field of airships. He had formed a company to finance the design and building of such craft in 1896, and the first to fly was the LZ I which took off from the Zeppelin facility on Lake Constance on 2 July 1900. The LZ II made its maiden flight on 17 January 1906, but was forced to make an early landing due to high winds and was then almost immediately destroyed in the storm which had set in. The LZ III (the initial flight of which took place on 9 October) was more successful. Financed by a specially-organised lottery in the German state of Württemberg), the design incorporated stabilising wings which significantly improved the machine's in-flight control. The LZ III in fact became the first airship to enter German military service, being purchased by the Army who re-designated it the Z I, and there followed a long line of significant Zeppelins for both military and civil purposes.

**17 Jan:** The second airship design by Graf von Zeppelin to take to the air, the LZ II, made its maiden (and, as it turned out, only) flight from Lake Constance and landed at Kissleg due to fuel system problems. It was destroyed in a gale the following day.
**8 Feb:** Negotiations between the Wright brothers and the British government over the sale of one of the Flyer IIIs finally broke down.
**15 Mar:** Rolls-Royce was registered as a public company.
**18 Mar:** Transylvanian Trajan Vuia 'hopped' his No 1 monoplane for the first time. It featured a tractor-mounted 25hp carbonic acid engine, variable-incidence wing and an undercarriage with pneumatic tyres.
**May:** The first powered aeroplane from the Blériot stable, the Blériot III floatplane, was tested on the River Seine but failed to get airborne due to a lack of power.
**May:** Count Zeppelin began building his third airship, funded by a gift of 100,000 marks from the Kaiser and a nationwide lottery that raised 250,000 marks.

**27 May:** Colonel J. L. B. Templer, first Superintendent of the Balloon Factory, retired and was replaced by Col J. E. Capper.
**12 Sep:** A tethered 'flight' of some 138ft was made by Danish inventor Jacob C. H. Ellehammer in a semi-biplane machine of his own design and construction, as was the engine.
**13 Sep:** Alberto Santos-Dumont, piloting his 14-*bis* biplane, made what is generally recognised as the first controlled flight by a heavier-than-air flying machine in Europe. The odd-looking machine was dubbed Canard (Duck).
**30 Sep:** The first international balloon race was started at Les Tuileries. A total of 16 entrants competed for the Gordon Bennett Trophy.
**9 Oct:** The third Zeppelin airship, the LZ III (later the military Z I), made its maiden flight that lasted two hours 17 minutes and carried 11 people.
**23 Oct:** Santos-Dumont and his 14-*bis* scooped the Ernest Archdeacon Cup and a 2,000-franc prize for making the first flight

in Europe to exceed a distance of 25 metres (82ft).
**1 Nov:** Gabriel and Charles Voisin founded the world's first aircraft factory to build aeroplanes commercially, in Paris.
**12 Nov:** Alberto Santos-Dumont was presented with another Ernest Archdeacon award of 1,500 francs and a further 1,500F from the French Aero Club when he flew the 14-*bis* for 220 metres (722ft) at an average speed of just over 25mph – the first record to be officially ratified by the Fédération Aéronautique Internationale, which had been established the previous year.
**14 Dec:** A 56ft wind tunnel for testing air resistance of aircraft and propellers was opened at the Balloon School, Farnborough.
**31 Dec:** Léon Levavasseur perfected his 24 and 50hp Antoinette engines, which proved ideal for aviation use.

*The Santos-Dumont 14-bis biplane in Frank Munger's painting 'We Have Lift Off' is recognised as the first controlled flight by a heavier-than-air flying machine in Europe.*

*We Have Lift Off* by Frank Munger AMRAeS, GAvA, MGMA

Glenn Curtiss started out building bicycles (as did the Wrights), then became a record-setting motorcycle racer and, most notably of all, a creator of powerful, lightweight engines. As early as 1907 he had some for sale to the Wrights. He drew closer to a personal involvement with aviation when Tom Baldwin requested him to build an engine for an airship and during the year he was most fortunately brought into an early day 'think tank', the Aerial Experiment Association (AEA). He possessed just the know-how required by Alexander Graham Bell to make his own early bid for flight.

Up to the end of 1907, the Wright brothers did not make a lot of progress, although they had built a few improved engines together with a small number of Flyer IIIs, known as the Model A, and 'stockpiled' these against the day that either the US government or commercial interests decided to consider the aeroplane more seriously. The brothers had offered their aircraft to both the American and British governments but were turned down. Although they were offering a machine with a guaranteed aerial performance, the US Department considered the offer as a request for assistance, which was not the case.

Blériot had experimented with various configurations, but in 1907 he adopted the 'tractor' monoplane. His 1907 design had an enclosed fuselage, 50hp Antoinette tractor engine, forward-mounted wings and an empennage at the rear of the fuselage. The early Blériot elevators were in fact elevons, and it was a time before it was realised that to make them efficient, ailerons needed to be fitted as far as possible from the fuselage centreline.

Also in 1907 other tractor monoplanes emerged, notably the Santos-Dumont and Esnault-Pelterie. Farman was still a biplane enthusiast and was developing his Voisin-Farman I (modified) with a 50hp Renault engine.

Lieutenant J. W. Dunne was one of the earliest British experimenters with aircraft, and he shared with S. F. Cody the distinction of having an aeronautical connection with the War Office, long before the Royal Flying Corps was formed. He worked at Farnborough from 1906-1909 and gave expression to his ideas on stability by designing a series of tailless biplanes with sharply swept-back wings. The craft, designated simply D1, was initially tested as a glider before fitting the propulsion system which had been designed for it by Capt Carden, a system comprising twin propellers mounted on outriggers and driven, via belts or chains, by two 12hp Buchet engines, one of which had previously powered Cody's kite.

On 10 September, *Nulli Secundus* ('second to none', a name it shared with one of King Edward VII's favourite racehorses) left its shed for the first time. A tubular-framework keel was suspended beneath the dirigible airship, suspended from four silk bands slung over the envelope supporting the long narrow car, which housed the engine and the crew. Fore and aft stability was initially far from satisfactory but a large horizontal surface was added at the tail in an attempt to remedy this. In October, with Capper and Cody aboard, it made a flight over London. Because of an increased south-westerly breeze the airship was unable to return to Farnborough and had to land on Clapham Common.

In December, Samuel Cody began constructing a biplane with a British Army grant of £50, using the 50hp Antoinette engine which powered the airship *Nulli Secundus*.

---

**Jan:** Henri Farman successfully flew the first circular flight in Europe.

**Jan:** The German Military Air Force was founded when the Army purchased its first Zeppelin dirigible. It was followed by the first eleven aeroplanes in 1910.

**13 Jan:** The US Army Signals Corps purchased a balloon from France and began a series of tests on 13 June.

**27 Mar:** Trajan Vuia began tests of his airplane in France, fitted with new steering surfaces, and made its first flight on 21 June.

**18 May:** Wilbur Wright sailed for Europe to discuss the sale of his Flyer III in London, Paris, Moscow and Berlin.

**11 Jul:** The Blériot Type VI Libellule, a tandem wing aircraft, made a short flight. It featured the first cantilever wings to be tested and had wingtip-type ailerons, and to control vertical movement the pilot had to slide to and fro on a wheeled seat.

**1 Aug:** Formation of the Aeronautical Division of the US Signals Corps. It was formed to oversee 'all matters pertaining to military ballooning, air machines and all kindred subjects', and the possibility of adaptation for military purposes.

**10 Sep:** First public flight of the British Army *Nulli Secundus* at Farnborough, the first British military airship.

**30 Sep:** Maiden flight of the Voisin-Farman I, after 225 failed attempts.

**Oct:** Count Zeppelin's German airship travelled 200 miles (320km), making a complete circuit around Lake Constance in a flight lasting nine hours.

**10 Oct:** First flight of the French REP1, the first aircraft to be piloted by the use of a single, broom-like lever which left the pilot a hand free to control the engine throttle. Its completely enclosed fuselage was made of welded steel covered in red muslin, which cut wind drag.

**12-13 Oct:** The first aerial crossing of the North Sea, albeit by balloon. The hydrogen-balloon *Mammoth* flew a distance of 721 miles (1,160km) from Crystal Palace, London to Lake Vänern in Sweden.

**26 Oct:** Henry Farman set the second officially (FAI) recognised distance record in a Voisin-Farman I. He achieved 2,530ft (771m).

**29 Oct:** The Breguet-Richet Gyroplane No 1 became the first manned rotary-wing aircraft to fly, but it still required manual support.

**10 Nov:** First flight of the Blériot Type VII monoplane in France. It was the first monoplane to combine a tractor engine, enclosed fuselage, rear-mounted tail unit, two-wheel undercarriage and tailwheel.

**13 Nov:** In France an Antoinette-powered twin-rotor aircraft made the first free flight by a manned helicopter. The 20-second flight attained a height of one foot.

**30 Nov:** Glenn Curtiss founded the Curtiss Aeroplane Company, the first US airplane manufacturing company.

*British airship* Nulli Secundus I *made a flight over London on 5 October 1907, circumnavigating the dome of St Pauls' at 12.20pm, an event illustrated here in a specially commissioned painting by Colin J Ashford.*

*Nulli Secundus I over London* by Colin J Ashford GAvA, FCIAD

# 1908

After a self-imposed absence of nearly three years, the Wright brothers resumed flying again. The Wright's had made their aircraft practical and were, at that stage, ahead of the rest of the world. By the watershed year of 1908, the world was forced to take notice. Orville made history's first flight of an hour's duration at Ft Myer, VA, and seemed just about to secure the military contract that hitherto had eluded the brothers. They had promised to deliver an aeroplane that would be able to carry two people with a combined weight of 350lb, with enough fuel to fly for 125 miles, at a maximum speed of at least 40mph in still air.

The aircraft was to have at least an hour in the air and to be able to land without causing any damage that would preclude another immediate flight. For this they were to receive $25,000, with a 10% incentive clause for each full mile an hour over the 40, and a matching penalty for each mile less. But tragedy struck on 17 September when Lt Thomas E. Selfridge, US Army Signals Corps, became the first fatality of powered aeroplane flight when a Wright biplane, piloted by Orville Wright, crashed at Ft Myer, after a guy rope on the Flyer broke, damaging a propeller and causing a control problem. Orville Wright was seriously injured in the accident. Selfridge was the first of many martyrs to powered flight. However, by July 1909, Orville was flying again and had developed an aircraft to meet all of the Army's requirements.

Meanwhile, across the Atlantic, the sceptical and doubting Europeans were suitably impressed when Wilbur attained record distances and durations, flying with great skill. However, the Wrights' belief that no-one could catch up with their invention, and their preoccupation with defending their patents, hurt not only themselves, but all American pioneers – especially Glenn Curtiss.

The Wright's forced Curtiss in the US, and a host of adventurers in Europe, to cast wide for ways to break their lock on patents. However, their competitors made enormous progress. On the other hand, the Wrights were content to improve their aircraft gradually, without radical departure from their successful 1905 machines. They tweaked their engines into a reliable powerplant that increased in power from 25hp to 30hp.

On 4 July, at Hammondsport, New York State, Glenn Curtiss won the Scientific American Trophy in his June Bug, powered by a 40hp Curtiss engine, collecting a $2,500 prize (plus $10,000 from the New York Aero Club) for a flight of one kilometre. It was the first time that an aircraft had been filmed by a motion-picture camera, and it propelled Curtiss onto the world stage alongside the Wright brothers.

Curtiss's flight had an enormous impact on the Wrights, who were becoming worried about the dangers of competition. Having previously quoted the US Army a price tag of $25,000 per aircraft, they were now prepared to accept $10,000, and they also began to pursue their European interests more assiduously. They had shipped an aircraft to France the previous year, but had been unable to make suitable arrangements for a demonstration flight. In August, Wilbur went to France and made a series of flights at Hunaudières racecourse near Le Mans that astounded the Europeans. Curtiss continued to build aircraft, leasing them to pilots rather than selling them to avoid the legal injunction against sales.

During 1908, the AEA built and tested three similar biplanes: the Red Wing, the White Wing and the June Bug. A succession of Europeans hammered out aircraft that could lurch off and onto the ground – Gabriel Voisin, Henri Farman, Louis Blériot, A. V. Roe, Léon Lavavasseur, Trajan Vuia, Victor Tatin, Capt Ferdinand Ferber, Robert Esault-Pelterie, Samuel F. Cody, Frederick Handley Page, all names which after 1908 would be writ large.

---

**13 Jan**: A Voisin-Farman I won the Deutsche-Archdeacon Prize of 50,000 francs for achieving an altitude of 262ft and the first recording of a steered one kilometre flight.

**6 May:** The Wright brothers resumed flying following a self-imposed absence of nearly three years. Wilbur piloted the 1905 Flyer III, modified so that the pilot and a passenger could sit erect, on a flight of just over 1,000ft.

**14 May:** Wilbur Wright took the first passenger to fly in an aircraft on a flight of 1,968ft (600m), with a duration of 28.6 seconds.

**19 May:** Lt Thomas E. Selfridge became the first US military officer to fly an aircraft, when he piloted White Wing, designed and built by Dr Alexander Graham Bell's Aerial Experimental Association (AEA).

**8 Jun:** A. V. Roe made a 'hop' in his full-size biplane at Brooklands.

**10 Jun:** The Aeronautical Society of the United States was established.

**28 Jun:** The first recorded flight by an aircraft in Germany. Jacob Ellehammer flew his No IV at Kiel. The flight lasted eleven seconds.

**4 Jul:** Glenn Curtiss made the first flight of the AEA June Bug.

**8 Jul:** Mme Thérèse Peltier became the first female passenger when she flew in a Voisin at Turin. Soon afterwards she became the first woman to fly solo.

**26 Jul:** First flight of *Nulli Secundus II* at Farnborough.

**25 Aug:** The French airship République burst in mid-air and crashed in flames after a piece of the wooden propeller tore a hole in the gas-filled envelope.

**16 Oct:** Samuel F Cody, in his British Army Aeroplane No 1, powered by a 50hp (37kW) Antoinette engine, made the first officially recognised flight in the UK. A flight of 1,390ft (424m) was made at Farnborough, but ended with a crash-landing.

**30 Oct:** Farman made the world's first true cross-country flight of almost 17 miles (27km) in 20 minutes.

**19 Dec:** Port-Avion, the world's first aerodrome, was opened on the outskirts of Paris.

**31 Dec:** Wilbur Wright made the year's longest flight at Camp d'Aouvours in France. He achieved a distance of 77 miles (124km) in two hours 20 minutes, and won the prize of 20,000 francs.

*In June 1908 A V Roe made a short hop in his biplane at Brooklands. As this aircraft could not sustain flight he produced a Triplane, depicted here in Colin J Ashford's painting, which made a successful flight in the following year.*

These pages generously donated by BAE SYSTEMS

*Roe Triplane* by Colin J Ashford GAvA, FCIAD

# 1909

Louis Blériot's cross-Channel exploit on 25 July was the highlight of the aviation calendar for 1909. He won the Daily Mail prize of £1,000 for the first aeroplane to fly the English Channel. His arrival meant that Great Britain was no longer protected by her water boundaries. Blériot set out in his Blériot Type XI monoplane from Les Barraques, near Calais at 04.35 hours, and despite being almost immediately lost in early morning fog over the Channel, his 25hp (18.60kW) Anzani engine began to overheat. Fortunately this was cooled by a squall and he successfully completed the 37-minute flight, landing at Northfall Meadow alongside Dover Castle at 05.12 hours. For this epic flight, Blériot also received £3,000 from the French Government, which represented an important contribution to the future of the Blériot Company. Blériot had poured his own fortune, and his wife's, into his experiments and by the beginning of 1909 had achieved some success using wingtip ailerons for control.

By July, Orville Wright was flying again and had developed an aircraft to meet all of the US Army's requirements. But during 1909 the patent fights of the Wright and Curtiss camps had a stagnating effect on aviation in the US, offset by the resilience and persistence of a few daring individuals. During 1909, the Wrights' insight into the requirements for three-axis control broke the Europeans away from their lemming-like devotion to the idea of automatic stability, clearing the way for further achievements over the following five years.

The incredible Reims meet, the 'Grande Semaine d'Aviation de la Champagne' on 22-29 August, which had large prizes, attracted 38 aircraft, of which 23 flew. The entries included nine Voisins, four Blériots, four Antoinettes, six Wrights, a Breguet, an REP and a Curtiss. The update of the Golden Flyer, flown by Glenn Curtiss, won the speed prize at 47.65mph, narrowly beating Blériot. Henri Farman set the distance record of 112 miles at an average speed of more than 45mph, and Hubert Latham in an Antoinette achieved an altitude record of 508ft. The outcome was clear, the aeroplane was no longer a toy and the US no longer possessed a monopoly.

Charles Willard, who at 26 learned to fly under Glenn Curtiss, made a flight on 3 August in the Curtiss Golden Flyer and almost immediately achieved fame. Fewer than ten days later, with only two hours solo time, Willard broke the newly established ten mile distance record established on 30 July by Orville Wright and Lt Benjamin Foulois, the first US Army aeroplane pilot. Willard was also instrumental in developing the arresting gear used by Eugene Ely in his famous, first-ever landing on the deck of a ship, the USS *Pennsylvania*.

By the autumn of 1909, the Henry Farman III had become the most popular and successful 'production line' aeroplane in the world, and it retained this enviable position until the end of 1911.

Horatio Barber was one of the true pioneers of aviation in Britain and in early 1909 he moved to Larkhill on Salisbury Plain, where he formed the Aeronautical Syndicate Ltd and began to build aircraft.

---

**28 Jan**: The British War Office published a report rejecting the usefulness of aircraft in time of war.
**23 Feb:** The first aircraft flight was made in Canada. It took place in Nova Scotia by a Silver Dart biplane, which had first flown in the US at the end of 1908, as a product of the Aerial Experiment Association.
**Feb:** Short Brothers Ltd and the Aero Club of Great Britain established the first aerodrome in England, Shellbeach at Leysdown on the Isle of Sheppey in Kent.
**20 Mar:** Glenn Curtiss went into partnership with the pioneer Augustus Herring to form the Herring-Curtiss Company.
**24 Mar:** Wright brothers founded a school in the USA to train pilots for exhibition flights. They had already set up the world's first flying school at Pau in France in January.
**30 Apr:** Claude Moore-Brabazon made the first flight in the UK by a resident Englishman. He covered a distance of 450ft (137m) at Leysdown, Isle of Sheppey in a Voisin.
**14 May:** Samuel F. Cody (an American who later became a naturalised English citizen) made the first aeroplane flight in the

UK to exceed one mile (1.6km) in his British Army Aeroplane No 1 over Laffan's Plain at Farnborough.
**14 May:** The Wright brothers paid a visit to the new Short Brothers factory, where they were constructing six replica Wright Type A biplanes for members of Britain's Aero Clubs.
**21 May:** First flight of the Blériot Type XII.
**17 Jun:** Frederick Handley-Page formed Handley Page Ltd at Woolwich in order to manufacture aeroplanes.
**Jun:** The Wright brothers returned to Fort Worth with an improved version of their Type A to demonstrate cross-country and endurance flights to the US Army.
**13 Jul:** Alliott Verdon Roe flew his paper-covered triplane *Yellow Peril* at Lea Marshes in Essex, thus becoming the first Briton to fly an aeroplane of British design and construction. It only had a 9hp JAP engine but proved the first airworthy machine in England designed and piloted by a Briton.
**Jul:** A Voisin biplane made the first powered flight in Russia. The French manufacturer sold sufficient aircraft to equip the embryonic Russian Air service.

**2 Aug:** The US Army finally placed a firm order for a Wright biplane.
**22 Aug:** Around half a million people braved wind, rain and mud for the world's first international aviation meeting at Reims in France.
**Sep:** The first great Aero Exhibition was staged in Paris. Some 30 aircraft were on display, including Blériot's famous Type XI monoplane. The event subsequently became the Paris Air Salon at Le Bourget.
**7 Oct:** Glenn Curtiss became the first American to hold an FAI Airplane Certificate.
**30 Oct:** Claude Moore-Brabazon won a £1,000 prize offered by the *Daily Mail* for a circular flight of one mile in his Short biplane No 2, fitted with a Gnome engine. The flight took two minutes 36 seconds.

*One of the highlights of aviation history is caught in John Young's painting of Louis Blériot landing his Type XI monoplane at Dover Castle, after making the first flight across the English Channel.*

These pages generously donated by the Air League, founded in 1909

*Bleriot Arriving at Dover* by John Young VPGAvA, VPASAA

Like the Wright Model A and the Henry Farman III, the Bristol Boxkite marked the apogee of development from the concept of the original Wright Flyer I, but it was an evolutionary dead end, despite its popularity. In its dimensions, geometry and aerodynamics, the Boxkite of 1910 was an unabashed copy of the contemporary Henry Farman III. Substantial numbers were built and flown with, by the standards of the time, considerable success. The basic, primitive Farman biplane was well-known to Britain's aviation world, especially as a notable exponent was Claude Grahame-White, who flew the Farman in spectacular fashion. The Type Militaire was simply a standard boxkite biplane of the classic Farman III type on which strut-braced extensions had been added to the upper wings, and a third (central) rudder fitted between the tailplanes.

Flying displays were becoming popular, and they financed the growth and development of aviation. Private money was invested in these ventures which allowed manufacturers to expand their businesses. This would not have been possible if their sole income was from the sale of aircraft. There were also special air races. In 1910, the *Daily Mail* offered a prize of £10,000 for a London-Manchester Race, that was won by Henry Farman.

Though a number of aircraft types were produced by Humber before WWI, none of them were actually designed by the company, whose principal interests lay in the motor industry. The first machine produced by Humber in 1910 was the Humber-Blériot Monoplane, a copy of the Bleriot XI, followed by the Humber-Le Blon Monoplane and the Humber-Lovelace Monoplane.

Generally at this time air travel was an erratic operation which required courage, favourable winds and also inspired mechanical flair. By 1910, Glen Curtiss had built several water-cooled aero engines and in this year the OX-5 appeared. It retained inclined overhead inlet and exhaust valves, arranged in a transverse plane instead of the axial one. Le Rhône produced its first rotary engine in France that year, and between then and the take-over by Gnome in 1914, established its products as being in many ways superior to the Gnome.

In 1910, Breguet had evolved a remarkable form of biplane, characterised by wings of unusual flexibility and by the extensive use of steel tubing in the airframe, which appeared in a remarkable profusion of shapes, sizes and variation, with widely differing power units.

The earliest aeroplanes built by Short Brothers to their own design showed a certain amount of Wright influence, perhaps inevitably in view of their initiation into heavier-than-air flying machines having been the building of six Wright biplanes in England. In 1910 they turned to the Farman configuration and the Short No 18 appeared.

The civilian pilot Eugene Ely, in a Curtiss aircraft powered by a 50hp pusher engine, made the first take-off from a ship, the cruiser USS *Birmingham* which was at anchor in Hampton Roads, Virginia. Provided with a wooden ramp at the bow, Ely took-off safely and landed at nearby Willoughby Spit, four miles away.

In September, the first aerial manouevres took place in France and it was concluded that military aeroplanes could be used in war, and that it was important to develop their use. As a result, the first regional schools for military aviation were formed.

---

**10 Jan**: The first aeroplane meeting in the USA was held at Doningrieg Field, Los Angeles, where the public witnessed the emergence of 'barnstorming'.

**15 Feb:** The Royal Aero Club was formed in England.

**10 Mar:** A French Blériot XI monoplane made the world's first successful night flight at Buenos Aries, Argentina.

**28 Mar:** Henri Faber made the world's first flight in a seaplane Hydravion near Marseilles, in a floatplane of his own design.

**Mar:** To encourage military aviation in England, Charles Rolls donated his Wright biplane to the British Army.

**1 Apr:** The French Army Air Force was formed as a separate command.

**27/28 Apr:** Claude Grahame-White made the first night flight in the UK during his attempt on the Daily Mail £10,000 London-Manchester air race.

**2 Jun:** The Hon Charles S. Rolls flew a Wright biplane across the English Channel and back in the same day.

**3 Jun:** The British dirigible *Beta 1* made its first flight. Basically the lengthened *Baby* (which had followed *Nulli Secundus*), it was the first British airship to be fitted with wireless telegraphy, and the first airship anywhere in the world to be moored by a mast.

**17 Jun:** A parasol monoplane, the Vlaicu I, designed by Aurel Vlaicu in Romania, made its first flight in Paris.

**30 Jun:** Glen Curtiss dropped dummy bombs on the outline of a battleship moored in Lake Keuka, New York.

**7 Jul:** The establishment of the Belgian Flying Corps.

**10 Jul:** A Wright biplane achieved an altitude in excess of a mile; Walter Brookins reaching a height of 6,234ft over Indianapolis.

**31 Jul:** First flight of the Bristol Boxkite.

**8 Aug:** The first use of an aircraft with a tricycle undercarriage when the US Army trialled a Wright so fitted.

**27 Aug:** An American pilot transmitted and received the first radio message whilst flying his Curtiss biplane.

**27 Sep:** Peruvian Georges Chavez crashed on completion of the first flight over the Alps, and died from his injuries.

**26 Oct:** A new French-built airship arrived at Aldershot, which had been purchased by the British Government.

**28 Oct:** A Maurice Farman biplane, flying from Étampes in France, established a distance in a closed circuit record of 289.38 miles (465.72km). This put an end to the dominance of the Wright brothers' Flyer design.

**26 Nov:** The War Office's first Farman arrived at Farnborough in December, making its first flight on 7 January 1911.

**18 Dec:** Thomas Sopwith made a flight from Eastchurch in Kent to Beamont in Belgium in a modified Howard Wright biplane. This was the longest straight-line flight into Europe by a British aircraft to date, a distance of 177 miles (285km).

**31 Dec:** Samuel Cody won the Michelin Cup for the longest closed-circuit flight when he flew for four hours and 47 minutes.

*In this painting by Charles J Thompson, Samuel Cody is waving to the crowd after winning the Michelin Cup in his Biplane. This award was given for the longest closed-circuit flight (of nearly five hours), undertaken by Cody on 31 December 1910.*

*Waving to the Crowd* by Charles J Thompson GAvA, ASAA, MGMA, EAA

By 1911, American aircraft were no longer competitive in European races. The first major long-distance air race started in Paris, ran across France, Belgium, Holland and on to London, and back to Paris. The race attracted 43 contestants, flying 12 different kinds of aircraft, but only one American, flying a Nieuport. Three aviators were killed and six badly injured, with only nine finalists out of a field of 19 who finished the first leg.

Well before the first battles of WWI, men were already trying to adopt the aeroplane to warfare around the world. The first combat flights occurred in Libya in 1911. Capt Carlo Piazza took off in a Nieuport at dawn on 23 October and discovered Turkish troops encamped along the road that led to Tripoli. On 19 November, four Cipelli bombs were dropped on Turkish tents. America flirted with air power when a group of American dare-devil pilots embarked on an aerial spying mission for the Mexican Government upon rebels and in the Philippines, but inadequate equipment and training afforded little success.

The place in aviation history of the otherwise unimportant Humber-Sommer biplane is assured by the fact that it was an aircraft of this type which undertook the world's first carriage of mail by aircraft. This event was held in Allalabad in India, as part of the Universal Postal Exhibition, during February 1911.

In France the Clerget precision engineering firm, inspired by the Gnome, produced what it claimed to be an improved rotary engine in 1911, with lower consumption of both fuel and castor-oil lubricant. The main difference was that the mixture was fed from the crankcase via normal external induction pipes to the cylinder heads. The 1911 engine had seven cylinders and produced 80hp. The Hispano-Suiza Company, which made cars of the highest quality, was formed near Paris in April to commence work on an aero engine.

On 28 February, an Army order was issued, creating the Air Battalion of the Royal Engineers. Its official existence began on 1 April, whereupon it stood to inherit seven aircraft purchased but not, at that date, delivered.

Naval flying began in 1911 when three Naval officers and a Royal Marines lieutenant were permitted by their Lordships of the Admiralty to draw full pay while being taught to fly at the Royal Aero Club ground at Eastchurch, on three Short biplanes which had been lent to the club.

British politicians assembled at Hendon Aerodrome on 1 May to witness a 100lb sandbag, simulating a bomb, being dropped from a Farman biplane.

The Royal Aircraft Factory (RAF), actually an Army Aircraft Factory, was established on 26 April as part of the general expansion of Britain's flying services and the shift towards heavier than air flight. The factory staff designed a great many aeroplanes used by the British Army, and later by the RFC, before and during WWI. It nurtured the careers of many men, such as Geoffrey de Havilland and Henry Folland, who went on to achieve fame as aircraft designers in private industry. Its creations, such as the SE5A and Sopwith Camel, became very successful Allied fighters. It must be remembered that at that time aeroplane factories were non-existent. Only a Government organisation was able to perform the academic investigation necessary to determine of what use the new science of aviation could be to military forces.

---

**18 Jan**: During a series of tests, Eugene Ely landed the Curtiss pusher aboard the cruiser USS *Pennsylvania* at anchor in San Francisco Bay.

**21 Jan:** Wireless telephone conversation took place for the first time from an aircraft flying over Selfridge Field, USA.

**5 Feb:** The first aeroplane flight in New Zealand was made at Auckland by a Howard-Wright type of biplane.

**1 Mar:** Formation of the Aeronáutica Militar Española with four French aircraft.

**14 Mar:** Four Bristol Boxkites were ordered by the British Army Air Battalion from the British & Colonial Aeroplane company.

**23 Mar:** A Breguet biplane flew with eleven passengers on board.

**11 Apr:** The US Army set up its first permanent flying school at College Park.

**12 Apr:** A French Blériot made the first non-stop flight from London to Paris.

**26 Apr:** First flight of the Handley Page E type two-seater.

**8 May:** Official birth of US Naval Aviation.

**16 May:** Zeppelin LZ8 Ersatz Deutschland was destroyed in an accident during a docking manoeuvre.

**8 Aug:** First flight of the Flanders F4, a single-seat monoplane powered by a 60hp Green engine. Four were ordered for the RFC's Military Wing.

**18 Aug:** Geoffrey de Havilland commenced test flights of the FE2 biplane manufactured by the Royal Aircraft Factory. He tested the BE1 on its first flight on 27 December.

**9 Sep:** The first official airmail was carried in a Blériot from Hendon, Middlesex to Windsor, Berkshire.

**18 Sep:** Short S39 'Triple Twin' made its first flight.

**23 Sep:** First recorded airmail flight in the US was undertaken by a Blériot monoplane for a distance of six miles (9.70km) between Nassau Boulevard in New York State to Mineola, Long Island.

**9 Oct:** Curtiss test pilot Eugene Ely was killed whilst performing at an air show at Macon.

**10 Oct:** Formation of La Société anonyme des Aéroplanes Morane-Saulnier, whose monoplanes of clean lines and advanced design, powered by rotary engines, were flown with considerable success in the following few years.

**25 Oct:** First flight of the Japanese Kai-1 Army biplane, powered by a 50hp Gnome engine.

**18 Nov:** An Avro Type D biplane fitted with floats was the first British seaplane to take-off from water, at Barrow in Furness.

*Stan Stokes' painting shows Eugene B Ely in a Curtiss Pusher about to make the first landing of an aircraft on a ship, the US Navy cruiser USS Pennsylvania. This historic landing, which took place on 18 January 1911 on a specially built 120ft platform, made Ely America's first naval aviator.*

*The Navy Earns its Wings* by Stan Stokes

Although the name Sikorsky is generally associated with the development of the helicopter as a practical flying machine, he was also notable as a great designer of flying-boats and the world's first four-engined aircraft. Igor Sikorsky produced a number of relatively successful biplanes for the Imperial Russian Air Service. In the summer of 1912 he commenced the design of the Bolshoi Baltiska or 'Great Baltic One'. This was a large twin-engined airliner that featured accommodation for seven passengers and crew in a fully enclosed cabin.

In the autumn of 1912, the Military Aeroplane Competition, that was open to the world, was held on Salisbury Plain, and the £5,000 prize was won by Samuel F. Cody in a machine of his own make, with an Austro-Daimler engine.

The Gnome Monosoupape (single-valve) engine appeared in 1912 in an attempt to solve the problem of the troublesome piston valves. Holes were simply cut in the cylinder walls uncovered by the piston near the bottom of the stroke, through which very rich mixture could be admitted. It had no throttle and the so-called adjustment lever gave very coarse control. Therefore a 'blip switch' on the control column enabled the pilot to cut the ignition in or out at all times on the ground and during the approach. Early in 1912 the French Salmson Company produced the first of a long series of constantly improved radial engines of novel design. They used a system in which all conrods drove a cage revolving on the crankpin on epicyclic gears.

In practice, Naval pilots assisted at Army Manoeuvres in 1912, but no Army pilots ever took part in Naval exercises. The Royal Flying Corps was formed from the old Air Battalion, and the Aircraft Factory became the Royal Aircraft Factory (RAF), ostensibly as an experimental workshop.

In Russia, at the end of the year, the total number of aircraft was about 280, of which some 150 were 'modern'. Most of the time aircraft had been built in Russia under licence. In October Russia purchased several Curtiss 'hydro-avions' after trials at Sevastapol. A Russian officer, Lieut Nestoroff, was actually the first aviator to 'loop the loop', doing so in a Nieuport monoplane, some months before the Frenchman Pégoud. For this action he was charged with endangering military property and placed under arrest for a month.

The fourth Farnborough airship, the *Delta*, intended to have a speed of at least 32mph, a ceiling of 6,000ft and a range of 300 miles, made its first flight in September. Head resistance was reduced as much as possible and the engines were chosen for reliability rather than extreme lightness. It took part in the Army manoeuvres in the autumn and its wireless transmissions were received as far afield as Thetford and Portsmouth. Like all Army airships it passed to Admiralty control on 1 January 1914.

Lt Cdr Charles Rumney Samson RN, became the first British pilot to take-off from a ship when he flew a Short S38 from a specially erected platform on the foredeck of the battleship HMS *Africa* at the Isle of Grain on 10 January. On 9 May Samson recorded the world's first take-off from a ship underway, flying from HMS *Hibernia* during the Royal Navy review off Portland.

---

**10 Jan**: Glen Curtiss made a first flight in a flying boat, a converted Curtiss A2.

**1 Feb:** First flight of the BE2. It was powered by a 70hp Renault engine, and featured mainplanes of unequal span. The BE3 flew on 3 May.

**17 Feb:** French military aircraft were deployed for the first time for operational use in Algeria.

**22 Feb:** Frenchman Jules Vedrines in his Gnome rotary-engined Deperdussin was the first pilot to exceed 100mph (161km/h).

**1 Mar:** The first parachute descent from a powered aeroplane (a Benoist flying at 1,500ft) by a military pilot was made at St Louis, Missouri.

**1 Mar:** A Naval Aeronautical Service was officially instituted in France.

**15 Mar:** The newly-formed Turkish Army Aviation Section received its first aircraft.

**Mar:** The first competition for seaplanes was held at Monaco.

**13 Apr:** By Royal Warrant the Royal Flying Corps (RFC) was constituted.

**22 Apr:** First crossing of the Irish Sea by an aeroplane.

**1 May:** With a fully-enclosed cockpit for the pilot, the Avro Type F monoplane made its first flight.

**13 May:** The Air Battalion and its reserve were assimilated into the Military Wing of the RFC.

**30 May:** Wilbur Wright, the pioneer aviator, died of typhoid fever.

**7 Jun:** First firing of a machine gun (a low recoil Lewis) from an aeroplane in flight, a Wright Model B biplane, in the US.

**1 Jul:** Formation of the Aviation Battalion of the Italian Army.

**2 Jul:** The Danish Army Air Corps was established with the formation of a flying school.

**9 Jul:** The RFC Military Wing acquired its first two Henry Farman biplanes. They made their public début on 17 August.

**Aug:** US Army Signals Corps aircraft were used for the first time during Army manoeuvres. A Curtiss F two-seat biplane became the Corps' first flying-boat in November.

**14 Sep:** After crashes during Military Trials in September, the War Office issued an instruction suspending the use of monoplanes by pilots of the Military Wing.

**1 Oct:** The Military Aviation Service was formed in Germany, the first step in the remodelling of German military aviation into what would become the German Air Service.

**5 Nov:** The first use of aircraft in the US to direct artillery fire took place in tests for the location of targets, when radio telephony was used to communicate information to the ground.

**12 Nov:** First successful launch by a US Navy seaplane by catapult, a Curtiss A3 pusher biplane.

*The flying display at Hendon in 1912 was the first of the annual events to be staged at this historic North London airfield. Kenneth McDonough's painting shows Farmans and Blériots at the popular air show.*

These pages generously donated by the Royal International Air Tattoo

*Hendon Air Show* by Kenneth McDonough GAvA

By 1913, the Deperdussin monoplane, with the whirling rotary engine, had gone far past the mythical 100mph mark, the 'speed barrier' of the first decade of flight. On 29 September a Deperdussin flew at 126.67mph. This signalled a victory for European technological prowess, and was a sure sign that America might be losing the momentum generated by the Wright invention.

In the US, Tom Benoist ran a successful flying school and manufactured some good aircraft. Late in 1913, he and his brother went to Florida to prepare for what is generally considered to be the world's first scheduled flights, made by the St Petersburg-Tampa Airboat Line. It was promised an operating subsidy by St Petersburg in Florida, and a contract was signed on 17 December 1913, ten years to the day after the Wright brothers made the first flight. The Benoist Type XIV flying-boat was a conventional pusher aircraft of slim and attractive lines based on the Curtiss formula. Its modest cockpit accommodated one passenger, who paid a surcharge if he weighed more than 200lb (91kg).

The first air-to-air combat occurred in Mexico in late November when two pilots exchanged about a dozen pistol shots, with inconclusive results. Similar tentative use of aircraft occurred in minor skirmishes rumbling through the Balkans as Europe braced itself for war. More importantly, major powers of the Old World (Britain, France, Germany and Russia) were actively using their small air forces in support of ground manoeuvres.

The giant Sikorsky Ilya Muromets was completed in 1913 and made its first flight the following year. The aircraft had a span of 113ft, and notable were auxiliary winglets behind the mainplanes, railed promenade deck on the rear fuselage, large cabin (with sofa, four arm chairs and table), wardrobe, lavatory and cabin lighting and heating.

By 1913, Anzani had seven types of aero engine on sale in France, though they were hand-built in small numbers, the biggest being ten-cylinder radials. Although the Fiat company in Italy built its first aero engine in 1908, its new upright water-cooled S55 V-8 with large cylinders appeared in 1913. Sunbeam commenced the manufacture of aero engines in 1913 and two emerged that year, a 150hp eight-cylinder and a 200hp 12-cylinder. Both were water-cooled V-format engines, the larger one intended for airships. By the outbreak of war, a 100hp six-in-line engine was in production. Also at this time Wolseley Motors began building water-cooled aero engines, which led to the successful W.4 Viper family of engines, derived from the Hispano.

By the beginning of 1913, the RFC possessed 13 aeroplanes in flying order, but by the time of the Army Manoeuvres in the autumn something approaching 50 aeroplanes had been mustered. In this year it was laid down that the establishment of the RFC was to consist of 12 machines and 12 pilots for each squadron with a new Headquarters at Farnborough. This was also the year in which the Aeronautics Inspection Department was formed. Seaplanes took part in the Royal Naval Manoeuvres of 1913 (in the North Sea) and many flights were made far out to sea.

---

**Jan**: The Australian Flying Corps was established.

**3 Feb:** Formation of the German Gotha aircraft works in Germany.

**8 Feb:** A Russian pilot, who was flying for the Greeks, became the first man to be shot down in combat when his aircraft was hit by ground fire during the First Balkan War.

**Feb:** The Chilean Air Force was formed with the establishment of a flying school at Lo Espejo.

**5 Mar:** 1st Aero Squadron, US Army was formed. Initially the squadron could only muster nine biplanes and six pilots.

**Mar:** First flight of the Sikorsky Bolshoi Baltiskii, nicknamed the 'Tramcar with wings'. The Type B, an improved version, made the world's first four-engined aircraft flight on 10 May.

**16 Apr:** The first Schneider Trophy contest for La Coupe d'Aviation Maritime Jacques Schneider was flown at Monaco over 28 circuits of a 6.20 mile course. The race was won for France by Maurice Prévost in a 160hp Gnome-powered Deperdussin at an average speed of 45.75mph.

**16 Apr:** An independent air force was set up in Belgium.

**May:** US Naval aircraft were called upon during the crisis in Mexico, when five aircraft were sent as detachments aboard USS *Birmingham* and USS *Mississippi* to support the Atlantic Fleet.

**23 Jul:** First flight of the Russkii Vityaz 'Russian Knight', with eight passengers on board.

**7 Aug:** Samuel F. Cody, one of Britain's earliest pioneers of aviation, was killed in a crash on Laffan's Plain at Farnborough.

**18 Aug:** The British airship *Eta* made its first flight, powered by two 80hp water-cooled Canton-Unné engines.

**19 Aug:** The first successful parachute jump from an aeroplane was made in Europe.

**20 Aug:** First flight of the BE8. The type saw service on the Western Front in the early days of WWI, but was regarded as underpowered and prone to spinning.

**18 Sep:** First flight of the Avro 504 biplane, one of the most successful British aircraft ever built, a total of 8,300 of the type being manufactured.

**23 Sep:** A Morane-Saulnier made the first crossing of the Mediterranean by air, from Saint-Raphaël to Bizerte in Tunisia.

**4 Nov:** The engineer Constanti patented his vented wing. This comprised of a blade placed before the leading edge to improve airflow over the wing.

**Nov:** A compact little biplane, the Sopwith Tabloid, made its first flight, with a 80hp Gnome engine.

**28 Dec:** For the first time, an altitude record above 20,000ft was achieved by a Nieuport Type IIN over Saint-Raphaël, France.

**Dec:** The first truly efficient aeroplane compass was produced by the Royal Aeroplane Factory, designated RAF Mk IV.

**Dec:** The RAF built its first indigenous aeroplane engine, an air-cooled V-8 loosely based on the Renault. It gave an output of 90hp from a swept volume of nine litres at 1,800rpm.

*John Pittaway's painting illustrates a Deperdussin making a cross-country flight to Edinburgh after the type had become the first aeroplane to achieve 100mph, the initial 'speed barrier' of the first decade of flight.*

These pages generously donated by Shell Aviation

*Cross-country to Edinburgh* by John Pittaway GAvA

The event that had the most profound effect on the whole world in the 20th Century was the outbreak of the First World War on 4 August. When war broke out, two dozen or more aircraft, a mixed bag of English Blériots, Henry Farmans, Avros, BE2s and BE8s, landed in France. The Germans had some 450 aircraft, a little more than half of which were ready for combat duty. The Germans could also muster eleven dirigible airships. The French were able to field about 300 first-line aircraft from an overall strength of 600 together with about 12 dirigibles. The British had, at home, and in France, about 160 aircraft, of which perhaps a third were of front-line quality.

German aircraft tended to depend upon the heavy but reliable six-cylinder 'automobile' water-cooled type of engine, which developed around 100hp. They liked strong, fast machines and appreciated streamlining. Both England and France placed equal dependence on rotary and stationary engines and throughout the war both countries manufactured many variations of each type.

The Gnome rotary engine, which developed 100hp, was regarded as being so unreliable that after less than every 20 flying hours it had to be removed and completely overhauled, including renewal of fatigued components. The castor oil it used was flung into the cylinder heads and choked them up. But the rotary engine did give a high power ratio and the engine was based on a stationary crankshaft bolted to the airframe, and a rotating assembly of cylinders to which was attached to the propeller.

By 1914, aircraft construction was in the hands of a select group, and their output was only a few aircraft a year. Only the large firms such as the Bristol Aeroplane Company, Short Brothers, Blériot, Morane-Saulnier, Albatros and Caproni could offer any form of quantity production.

Already an established motor engineer, Lt W. O. Bentley RNAS was sent to study the overheating problems in rotary engines. He decided that the best long-term answer was a new engine, and starting with an expensive Clerget, produced an engine with aluminium-alloy pistons designated AR1 (for Admiralty Rotary). Also in this year, the Siemens-Schuckert Werke developed the Sh1 contra-rotating rotary, the crankshaft rotating one way and the cylinders the other, both being geared to the engine mount and the propeller being on the crankshaft.

In August 1914, many people believed that airships were the most potent instruments of military flying. Few expected aeroplanes to prove of any value except as unarmed aerial cavalry, able to observe the movements of men on the ground and ships over the horizon. The advances in aviation over the course of the First World War represented one of the most significant periods in the history of aerial warfare.

The first de Havilland design, built by Airco, was the DH1. Work had started on a tractor biplane but this approach was abandoned when the War Office made it clear that what was wanted was a pusher aircraft, giving its gunner an unobstructed field of view. It emerged the following January powered by a 70hp Renault. At the outbreak of war the War Office and Admiralty ordered substantial numbers of BE2cs from many contractors.

---

**1 Jan**: Formation of the Chinese Air Arm with the establishment of the first Chinese flying schools at Nan Yuan, initially equipped with the Caudron biplane.

**20 Jan**: The first permanent US Navy 'Aeronautic Station' was established at Pensacola, Florida, intended to form the centre of naval aviation training.

**23 Feb**: First flight of the Bristol Scout biplane at Larkhill training centre.

**20 Apr**: US Naval aviation's first combat action began when three aircraft from the base detachment left Pensacola on the USS *Mississippi* to assist forces at Vera Cruz, Mexico where they flew observation and photographic sorties.

**20 Apr**: France hosted the Schneider Trophy at Monaco and the contest was won by Australian Howard Pixton in a Sopwith Tabloid floatplane, powered by a 100hp Gnome Monosoupape rotary engine. His average speed beat the previous record by 25mph (40km/h).

**28 May**: Glen Curtiss made a successful flight in Samuel Langley's Aerodrome, which he had rebuilt. He was attempting to prove that a machine could have flown before the Wright's first flight, thereby invalidating the brothers' valuable patent rights.

**27 Jun**: Formation of the Pemberton-Billing Aircraft Company (later Supermarine) on the banks of the Solent.

**1 Jul**: The naval wing of the RFC separated and became the Royal Naval Air Service.

**28 Jul**: Squadron Commander Arthur Longmore of the RNAS dropped a torpedo for the first time from a Short S121 seaplane.

**30 Jul**: A Norwegian Blériot recorded the first crossing of the North Sea by aeroplane.

**Jul**: Earl Haig dismissed air reconnaissance with his opinion that "there is only one way for a commander to get information by reconnaissance – and that is by the use of cavalry".

**4 Aug**: The British Government declared war on Germany.

**26 Aug**: An Imperial Russian Air Service pilot was the first in the world to destroy another aeroplane by ramming.

**30 Aug**: A German Rumpler Taube made the first bombing raid on Paris. A Taube made an attack on English soil on 21 December.

**3 Sep**: The RNAS was made responsible for British air defence.

**16 Sep**: Formation of the Canadian Aviation Corps.

**8 Oct**: The first successful air raid on Germany during WWI was accomplished by Sopwith Tabloids of the Eastchurch Squadron when Zeppelin Z IX was destroyed in an airship shed at Dusseldorf.

**21 Nov**: Three RNAS Avro 504Ks were used in a successful attack on the Zeppelin sheds at Friedrichshafen, when bombs destroyed a Zeppelin in its shed and a gasworks located alongside.

**4 Dec**: The Imperial German Navy formed its first seaplane squadron.

*Claus Friedl Wuefling's painting* Prinz-Heinrich-Flug *depicts Rumpler Taubes, the first German aircraft type to bomb England.*

*Prinz-Heinrich-Flug* by Claus Friedl Wuelfing

# 1915

By 1915, aerial reconnaissance, both by eye and with camera, had reached such a level of sophistication that all of the maps for the Battle of Neuve-Chapelle, which began in March, were based on aerial photos. For the first time, bombing raids in direct support of ground operations were conducted in an attempt to destroy the railheads through which German reinforcements had to come.

Machine guns had been mounted on aircraft from the start of the war. The effect of the extra weight was so detrimental to flight performance that often these arms were immediately removed, but everyone learned. The concept of height as conferring high speed in a dive and serving as a store of energy, bringing with it a distinct combat advantage, was being universally adopted.

The initial step towards the development of fighter types took place when Roland Garros of French Escadrille MS23 arranged for bullet deflection devices, invented by Raymond Saulnier, to be attached to the propeller blades of his Morane-Saulnier Type N in March 1915. The deflection wedges attached to the propeller blades enabled a Hotchkiss machine gun to be fired through the arc formed by the propeller, without shooting off the blade.

Copying the deflectors was easy, but making the devices work was not. Fokker developed a synchronising system for the Parabellum machine gun mounted on the new Fokker M5K monoplane. Fokker's invention enabled German pilots to fire directly ahead, assuring improved accuracy and more 'kills'. Known as Eindekkers, they became the object of much desire of able young pilots seeking medals. In such hands they became known as the 'Fokker

Scourge' by mid-1915, and they vastly affected not only the air war on the Western Front, but the subsequent development of aircraft.

The French employed military Blériots, Farmans, Morane-Saulnier parasols and Voisins, but none was capable of standing up to the Fokkers. The riposte to the 'Fokker scourge' came in the form of the FE2b and DH2, both pusher types, to obviate the need for a synchronising gun gear. The DH2 proved very manoeuvrable and had a fixed Lewis gun in front of the pilot.

Flying early WWI aircraft was demanding. Training was limited and pilots were generally supposed to be able to fly anything with wings immediately, and without specialist tuition. The aircraft of the period were very demanding and needed constant attention. Few had any trim devices at all, so control pressures varied constantly with variations in power and speed. Rotary engines could be deadly on take-off and demanded careful handling at all times. Teaching methods had been crude. No 1 (Reserve) Squadron was set up at Gosport to experiment with the training aspect. The Avro 504K was selected and 'Gosport tubes' were installed between the two cockpits so that the pupil and his instructor could speak to each other whilst in the air, a significant innovation at the time.

The Wright brothers had gradually refined their engines, arranging the cylinders vertical fashion and adding six-in-line and V-8 patterns. For various reasons the brothers (Orville alone after Wilbur's death from typhoid in 1912) failed to keep abreast of aeroplane and engine technology, and their last engine was made in 1915.

---

**6 Jan:** The German Navy successfully launched a Friedrichshafen FF29a seaplane from the deck of a submarine during trials to extend the aircraft's reconnaissance range.

**19 Jan:** Two Zeppelins operated by the German Navy made the first attack by an airship on Great Britain, when installations along the River Humber near Hull were bombed.

**19 Feb:** Ilya Muromets bombers of the Imperial Russian Air Service went into action for the first time on an attack on Willenburg in East Prussia.

**3 Mar:** NACA (The National Advisory Committee for Aeronautics) was set up in the US in order to study problems of flight.

**Mar:** First Curtiss aircraft to be supplied to either of Britain's flying services were six two-seat biplanes delivered to the RNAS.

**11 Apr:** First flight of the Zeppelin-Straaken VGO1 heavy bomber. It was fitted with one tractor and two pusher engines.

**25 Apr:** The first operational aeroplane mission by the US Navy, when a Curtiss AB-3 flying-boat made a visual reconnaissance of Vera Cruz, Mexico for detection of possible mines.

**26 Apr:** The first Victoria Cross to be awarded to an airman was won by the pilot of a BE2b, Lt W.B. Rhodes Moorhouse of No 2 Squadron, who carried out a bombing attack on the railway station at Coutrai. He received numerous wounds from enemy fire, and although he managed to bring his aircraft back, his injuries later proved fatal.

**21 May:** The Spad A2 biplane made its maiden flight in France.

**24 May:** The Italians broke their 'alliance' with Germany and entered the war on the side of the Allies, with a strength of around 100 aircraft. They went on to engage the Austrians in pinprick air battles, primarily with seaplanes.

**31 May:** Zeppelin L381 made the first bombing raid on London, when bombs were dropped on Stoke Newington.

**Jun:** First flight of the DH2 prototype, a compact little two-bay biplane of typical 'nacelle-and-tailbooms' configuration, giving the pilot an unobstructed field of view in most forward directions. It went to France for operational evaluation on 26 July.

**10 May:** Capt L. A. Strange of the RFC took-off carrying 150ft of cable to which he had attached a lead weight, in the hope of entangling the cable in a German aircraft's propeller

**6 Jun:** Harry Hawker set up a British altitude record of 18,393ft in a Sopwith 1½ Strutter.

**1 Aug:** The first victory by an aircraft fitted with a fixed forward firing gun, firing through the airscrew disc, was made by a German Fokker E3 monoplane over the Western Front.

**13 Oct:** The Wright Airplane Company was bought by a syndicate, but Orville Wright stayed on as a consulting engineer.

**15 Oct:** First flight of the FE8, the first two-seat fighter to be designed at the Royal Aircraft Factory, powered by a 100hp Gnome Monosoupape rotary driving a four-blade propeller.

**1 Dec:** The first US Navy flying school opened at Pensacola, FL.

**17 Dec:** Maiden flight of the Handley Page O/100 heavy bomber.

*Dogfights were a daily occurrence over the Western Front. In Robin Smith's painting an RFC DH2 is shown shooting down a German Eindekker.*

*The End of the Chase* by Robin Smith GAvA

To counter the 'Fokker Scourge', the French responded with the Nieuport 11 Bébé (Baby) sesquiplane, which was very manoeuvrable and fast, and armed with a Lewis gun mounted on the top wing to clear the propeller disc. But the Germans quickly gained the upper hand with the Albatros, the first aircraft planned purely as a fighter.

In view of the German occupation of parts of France and Belgium, the British doctrine called for an unremitting offensive military posture to force the Germans back to their own soil. Trenchard insisted that the air war be carried to the Germans under all circumstances, in spite of the survival statistics of pilots on the front.

German air superiority was again temporarily at an end by 18 June, when the plane of ace Max Immelmann, the 'Eagle of Lille', was shot down by an FE2b. Equipment available to the Germans, Fokker and Halberstadt fighters, was becoming inadequate. In desperation, the German High Command called for copies of the Nieuport to be made. This provided the Siemens-Schuckert D1, which turned out to be superior to the Nieuport. The German aircraft soon began to carry two Spandau machine guns, double the fire power of any Allied aircraft. The Albatros D1 regained aerial superiority for Germany for a time and at its introduction in 1916, it was clearly superior to all Allied fighters. It became the backbone of the German Air Force until the end of the war.

The Germans were inflicting casualties at such a rate that the expected life for Royal Flying Corps pilots was officially calculated at 17 hours. The Allies were quick to respond, with both new aircraft and better training and tactics. Schools for 'Special Flying' were established in England in May 1916. Here veterans back from the front passed on the facts of life and death to newly fledged pilots and the offensive spirit was encouraged.

Both sides routinely photographed the entire front twice a day. Ground attacks came into vogue on both sides. Fighters were used at first, but their vulnerability to the hornet's nest of machine-gun fire from the ground (both friendly and unfriendly) led to the development of special armoured types. In the second half of 1916 the Albatros CVII and LFG (Roland) CII entered service.

Allied flying-boats had established anti-submarine patrols, and twin-float fighters were developed to oppose them. The sea war extended from the Baltic in a large arc around Europe into the Black Sea. It was extended even further when the Germans equipped ships with scout aircraft for reconnaissance.

The use of British heavy bombers was at the instigation of the Admiralty, who had called for a 'bloody paralyser' of an aircraft in 1915. This resulted in the Handley Page O/100, which entered service in 1916. Able to carry 2,000lb (907kg) of bombs, it proved a success and led to the O/400, which came on line two years later.

The Sikorsky Ilya Muromets was in production for the Imperial Russian Army, but few of the production aircraft were identical. Shortages of engines meant that they were flown with a variety of different powerplants.

Napier had become famous for its cars, and in 1916 the firm began working on the water-cooled W-12 (or broad-arrow engines), the Lion. In 1916, the Wright-Martin Aircraft Corporation linked two major US aviation firms to make Hispano-Suiza engines under licence.

---

**9 Feb**: One of the most significant fighter aircraft of the war, the Sopwith Pup single-seat fighter, made its first flight.

**1 Apr:** The Japanese Naval Air Corps was formed.

**20 Apr:** The Escadrille Américans was established as an American volunteer flying unit flying on the Western Front, later becoming the famed Lafayette Escadrille.

**Apr:** The French Spad VII made its maiden flight, and was immediately recognised as a fighter of great potential.

**Apr:** French aircraft began carrying rockets to attack German captive balloons, which made their survival much less likely. Incendiary bullets later superseded rockets.

**26 May:** First flight of the Sopwith Triplane. It was a formidable opponent until superseded by the Sopwith Camel and SE5a.

**30 May:** The first of the Super-Zeppelin airships, the L30 powered by six engines, joined the German Navy. It made nine major raids on England.

**17 Jun:** The prototype RE8 tractor two-seat biplane made its maiden flight at the Royal Aircraft Factory at Farnborough.

**1 Jul:** The Battle of the Somme commenced in France and both sides fought to gain air superiority. It was the first land battle where aircraft made a significant difference to the progress of a large offensive.

**2 Jul:** First flight of the Airco DH 3, a twin-pusher biplane.

**Jul:** The Bristol M1A made its first flight, but the numbers of M1s in operational service were too small to make any significant impression on the campaign in any theatre of war.

**Aug:** First flight of the Airco DH4, one of the truly great aircraft that were designed and built during the 1914-18 War.

**16 Aug:** First flight of the Zeppelin-Staaken R IV bomber, which was later used alongside Gothas for raids on England.

**29 Aug:** The US Naval Flying Corps was formed.

**9 Sep:** First flight of the Bristol F2A, built as a Corps reconnaissance and artillery-spotting two-seater to supersede the BE2C. The F2B followed in 1917.

**23 Sep:** Eleven Zeppelin airships attacked England in one raid.

**1 Oct:** The Allies restructured the way aircraft would be used, clarifying the distinction between reconnaissance, bombing and fighter escort.

**21 Nov:** The French Breguet 14 bomber first flew, becoming one of the most effective bombers of WW1.

**22 Nov:** An impressive aircraft, the SE5, with a 150hp direct-drive Hispano-Suiza V-8 made its first flight.

**28 Nov:** First aeroplane raid over London by a seaplane.

**28 Nov:** The first aeroplane raid on London was made by a German Navy LVG CII when six bombs were dropped on Victoria station in broad daylight.

*Igor Sikorsky designed bombers before he left his native Russia to start his own aircraft company in the USA. Stan Stokes' painting depicts a giant Ilya Muromets used by EVK 'Squadron of Flying Ships' on the Russian Front in 1916.*

*Russian Giant* by Stan Stokes

America joined the combat in April 1917 and its greatest contribution to the air war was unquestionably its thousands of enthusiastic pilots. Between 1914 and 1917, the war's furious pace had forced aviation through a hothouse period of change, never again to be matched. During this era, virtually all the possibilities for the development and deployment of air power were explored: strategic bombing, guided missiles, reconnaissance and surveillance. Three types of military aircraft had emerged: fighters, observation types and bombers.

The Germans commenced high-altitude bombing, with its aircrew sucking on oxygen tubes, and their Gotha GV bombers brought a new dimension to destruction. They attacked England in early 1917, after the German high command had halted ineffective attacks by their Zeppelins.

An embarrassing multiplicity of aircraft types and engines began to emerge on the Allied side, creating chaotic supply and maintenance problems. Shortages forced the Germans to concentrate on a few basic makes of engines, and to design aircraft suited to them. Generally, the Allies produced engines of superior horsepower. Both sides produced rotary engines throughout WWI, though it was clear by 1917 that this type of engine had reached the end of its development path. German aircraft typically mounted the 160hp Mercedes or 185hp BMW engines, while the Allied counterparts were using the 235hp Hispano or 375hp Rolls-Royce Eagle, and the 400hp American Liberty engine was becoming available.

At the end of 1917, the Allies wrested air superiority from the Germans once and for all, mainly because of improved aircraft reaching the front. The Sopwith Camel was followed by the SE5a; the Camel was to kill more Germans (and more RFC pilots) than any other aircraft. The Bristol F2b Fighter (which remained in service until 1932) was coming into its own and was the finest two-seat fighter of WWI. It combined good performance and agility with the extra 'sting' of a flexible machine gun. The French were fielding the Spad VII and XIII. The Sopwith Snipe and Dolphin were just entering production, with the prospect of the Nieuport 29 from the French.

Towards the end of the war the Fokker DVII was entering production. This represented a true departure from all previous aircraft designs of WWI and set the standard for the rest of the next decade of aircraft development.

The German bombers had been notorious, but by late 1917 the Handley Page O/100 and O/400 were better aircraft. Italy was developing the Ansaldo series of fighters and reconnaissance aircraft. The French were producing the Breguet 14, which sired a generation of able descendants and the Salmson 2, which was liked by the Americans.

---

**Jan**: First flight of the SE5a, fitted with a 200hp geared Hispano-Suiza engine. By the Armistice, 5,205 SE5as had been completed.
**16 Feb:** First flight of the Fairey Campania, the first aircraft in the world to be designed and built specifically for operation from seaplane carriers at sea.
**Feb:** The Junkers J4 armoured close-support biplane made its first flight. It featured corrugated duralumin-skimming.
**6 Mar:** No 55 Squadron, RFC received the first aircraft fitted with the new Constantinesco machine gun with synchronising gear.
**21 Mar:** No 100 Squadron was formed, the first to go to France specifically for night bombing operations.
**4 Apr:** The British Air Offensive on the Western Front began – five days before the land engagement in the Battle of Arras.
**7 Apr:** The first SE5As went to France, where they equipped No 56 Squadron, RFC.
**30 Apr:** In what became known as 'Bloody Sunday' the RFC lost 139 aircraft in combat, more than in any other month of the war; the Germans lost 72 aircraft and the French (who were less involved) lost 33 aircraft.
**25 May:** The first large daylight raid by enemy aircraft when 21 Gotha G.IVs attacked targets in Kent.
**26 May:** The U-36 was attacked by an RNAS Curtiss H12 and became the first German submarine to be sunk by an aeroplane.
**5 Jun:** The US Army's First Aeronautic Detachment arrived in France and began training on Caudron biplanes.
**13 Jun:** Fourteen Gothas made the first heavy daylight raid on London, killing 162 and injuring 438.
**24 Jul:** The RAF deployed its first 1,650lb (748kg) bomb operationally, when a Handley Page O/400 dropped bombs on Middelkerke in Belgium.
**Jul:** The Airco DH9 bomber made its maiden flight, an aircraft designed to carry heavier loads over greater distances than the DH4 – although it was not a great success in its intended role.
**26 Jul:** Formation of the German 'Flying Circus' under the command of Baron von Richthofen, 'The Red Baron'.
**2 Aug:** A German airship was the first to be shot down by a ship-launched aircraft, when a Sopwith Pup flying from a temporary 20ft forward flying deck of HMS *Yarmouth*, operating off the Danish coast, made a successful attack.
**2 Aug:** A Sopwith Pup was successfully landed on the deck of HMS *Furious*, which was steaming at 26kt into a 21kt wind.
**18 Aug:** Though neutral in WWI, the Dutch increasingly became aware of the importance of aviation to national defence and formed the Luchtuaartdienst.
**30 Aug:** The German Fokker Dr1 Triplane went into action for the first time.
**30 Aug:** First raid on England by German Staaken RVI bombers, carrying the largest bombs used operationally in WWI.
**29 Oct:** First flight of a DH4 bomber, re-engined with an American Liberty engine. It became known as the 'Liberty Plane'.
**20 Nov:** At the Battle of Cambrai Allied aircraft were used for the first time for ground attack behind enemy lines supporting large-scale infantry assaults.
**30 Nov:** The Vickers Vimy twin-engined biplane bomber, with a bomb capacity of over 2,000lb, was flown.

*Frank Wootton's painting shows an encounter between SE5As of No 56 Squadron RFC and the legendary 'Red Baron' von Richthofen in a Fokker Dr1 Dreidekker triplane over the Western Front in 1917.*
© Mrs V Wootton

These pages generously donated by Mitsubishi Motors

*Encounter with the Red Baron* by Frank Wootton OBE FPGAvA

On 11 November, an armistice was declared which brought the First World War to an end after four years, three months and seven days. The conflict had wrought a terrible toll of lives on all its fronts, not least among its aviators. A total of 6,166 personnel of the Royal Flying Corps, Royal Naval Air Service and the Royal Air Force (established on 1 April 1918 as the first air arm in the world to be independent from a country's other armed forces) were killed in action, while 5,533 members of the French Air Service were either killed or wounded. German Air Service losses amounted to some 8,212 killed or missing.

The war was the greatest single spur to progress in the field of military aviation, thanks to the urgent and ever-changing needs of military commanders. This was clearly illustrated by the output from aircraft manufacturers during the four years of hostilities. The US Air Service took on 3,261 front-line aircraft (from various sources) over this time; military aircraft production in Britain totalled 55,093 units, while 3,051 aircraft were purchased from abroad for use by the RFC, RNAS and RAF; the French aircraft industry built 67,982 machines, over half of which came out of the factories in 1918 alone (and employed over 186,000 people in the process); and Germany produced 47,637 aircraft. Not only was there a massive increase in volume but the sophistication and capability of the aircraft designs progressed rapidly.

Some of the leading 'exponents' of military fighting aircraft lost their lives during the closing months of the war. On 21 April, Baron Manfred von Richthofen, who had scored 80 confirmed victories and was Germany's highest-scoring fighter pilot of the conflict, met his death when his Fokker Dr.1 Dreidekker was shot down over Sailly-le-Sec, France. Exactly who was responsible for the kill is still the subject of much debate: it was credited to Capt A. R. Brown, a Canadian flying with No 209 Squadron, RAF, but members of an Australian rifle artillery unit claim to have downed the Fokker with their machine gun fire.

His British counterpart, Maj Edward 'Mick' Mannock, was lost three months later. He had just left No 74 Squadron in order to command No 85 Squadron, still flying the SE5a, but on 26 July his aircraft took hits from German machine guns over Pacaut Wood, France. The fuel tank caught alight, and the aircraft flew into the ground and exploded. During his wartime career, Mannock had become the leading British ace with 73 aerial victories. Of these, 61 were confirmed kills, nine having been shared with other pilots (including his last, on the day of his death).

---

**15 Jan**: Col William 'Billy' Mitchell was appointed chief of the Air Service of the US Fifth Army Corps, and took command of American aviation units on the front line in France.

**28 Jan**: The heaviest German night bomber raid of the First World War, comprising some fifteen bombers took place.

**18 Feb**: The famous Escadrille Lafayette, manned entirely by American volunteers, cut its ties with the French Air Service and became part of the US Air Service, as the 103rd Aero Squadron.

**4 Mar**: Maiden flight of the Airco DH10 Amiens bomber.

**9 Mar**: Capt James E. Miller became the first American casualty of WWI, when his Spad was shot down behind enemy lines.

**10 Mar**: The German Navy's Zeppelin airship L59 dropped possibly the heaviest bomb load ever carried by a dirigible, some 6,364kg (14,000lb), during a raid on Naples.

**11 Mar**: Lt Paul F. Baer, from the 103rd Aero Squadron, became the first US Air Service squadron pilot to shoot down an enemy aircraft.

**15 Mar**: The first DH4 to be built in the USA (at Dayton, OH) started its sea journey to France.

**24 Mar**: A high point of the Allied air campaign against the German Air Service, when the Royal Flying Corps claimed 42 'kills' in a single day.

**1 Apr**: The Royal Flying Corps and Royal Naval Air Service were amalgamated as the Royal Air Force, the world's first independent air arm. The Women's Royal Air Force was also founded.

**21 Apr**: Cavalry Cpt Baron Manfred von Richthofen, known as the 'Red Baron', the highest-scoring German ace of World War I, was killed whilst flying his Fokker Dr1 triplane.

**23 Apr**: Lt Paul F. Baer became the first American ace of the war.

**15 May**: The US Post Office Department's Aerial Mail Service was established. Curtiss Standard J and JN aircraft were used six days a week on a service between Washington, DC and New York.

**22 May**: First flight of the largest British bomber to date, the Handley-Page V/1500.

**19 Jun**: The leading Italian ace of the war, Maggiore Francesco Baracca, died after his Spad was shot down over the Piave river.

**26 Jul**: Maj Edward 'Mick' Mannock, highest-scoring British ace of World War 1 was killed when his SE5a was shot down.

**1 Aug**: Flt Sub Lt Stuart Culley RN, flying a Sopwith Camel, achieved the first take-off by aeroplane from a moving barge under tow behind HMS *Redoubt*.

**5 Aug**: The last German raid against Britain was carried out by five Zeppelins.

**1 Nov**: France's top-scoring ace, René Paul Fonck, claimed his 75th and final victory.

**10 Nov**: Last major raid of World War I, carried out by eleven DH4s of the RAF's Independent Force under the command of Maj Gen Hugh Trenchard.

**11 Nov**: The Armistice with Germany was signed, ending hostilities on the Western Front.

**15 Nov**: A Handley-Page V/1500 took off from Cricklewood with 40 passengers aboard, and in so doing set a new record for the largest number of people carried in a commercial aircraft.

**27 Nov**: The record of twelve days earlier was eclipsed by a Curtiss NC-1 which flew with two crew and 51 passengers.

**18 Dec**: A quartet of Curtiss JN-4 'Jenny' training biplanes arrived at Jacksonville, FL, having taken eighteen days to reach there from San Diego, CA. This was the first cross-USA flight by US Army Air Service aircraft.

*Flight Sub-Lieutenant Stuart D Culley RN in his Sopwith 2F1 Camel is just airborne after a five-foot run on the deck of a barge being towed by HMS* Redoubt *in the North Sea. Keith Ferris captures the occasion of 11 August 1918 when Culley took off to destroy the Zeppelin L53.*
© 2001 keithferrisart.com

These pages generously donated by the Directorate of Recruitment (RAF) and the Directorate of Corporate Communications (RAF)

*Just Airborne, at Sea* by Keith Ferris ASAA

# 1919

The first direct, non-stop flight across the Atlantic, by John Alcock and Arthur Whitten Brown, in their modified Vickers Vimy bomber, was made in June. Flying in appalling conditions, the airspeed indicator failed less than halfway across, and they flew 'blind' for most of the way in the dark. They encountered seven hours of unbroken fog, but they covered the 1,890 miles (3,041km) from Newfoundland to Ireland on 14-15 June in just under 16½ hours flying time. For this feat they won the £10,000 offered by the *Daily Mail* for such a crossing.

The aircraft industry had grown rapidly during the four years of WWI and had been accustomed to lucrative contracts for military aircraft, in large quantities. Overnight, these contracts dried up and a completely new market, with entirely different needs, had to be sought. In addition, large numbers of existing military aircraft had become surplus to requirements. By 1919, thousands of aeroplanes were available as war surplus, with the long list of necessary support equipment and spare engines. At the time of the Armistice, the RAF had 188 combat squadrons but a year later this had been reduced to 30, two-thirds of which were overseas. France's Air Force did not suffer such a severe cutback.

By early 1919, plans had been laid down to build the USAAS into a post-war service of some 24,000 personnel and 5,000 aircraft, but by the end of the year the military aviation budget was cut by two-thirds and there was no provision for any new military aircraft.

The monoplane configuration still attracted the enthusiasm of only a small handful of aircraft designers, but the beginnings of change were to become apparent before the end of the 1920s. Handley Page took out a patent in 1919 for a low-speed control device, in the form of a 'slotted' wing, which consisted of a curved auxiliary aerofoil or slat normally forming part of the wing leading edge when retracted. This postponed the point at which the wing would stall and Handley Page continued to develop it through the 1920s.

The USA still had few aerodromes in 1919, and large numbers of war surplus flying-boats were adapted for commercial services. One of the first passenger services was between Palm Beach, Bimini and Nassau using a mixed fleet of Curtiss and Felixtowe types. The first commercial flying-boat service in the UK was between Southampton and Le Havre in July, for passengers and air mail.

Casual employment was afforded by air racing, which companies entered into because it stimulated interest in aviation. Britain's first Aerial Derby, flown from Hendon in June, attracted huge crowds.

**2 Jan**: An RAF DH4, fitted with the first production 430hp Napier Lion engine, flew to a record height of 30,500ft.
**8 Jan:** The German Air Ministry restored civil flying several months prior to the renewal of civil aviation operations by the British Air Navigation Regulations.
**16 Jan:** A Handley Page V/1500 flew from England, via Rome, to Baghdad and then on to India.
**21 Feb:** The first US-designed fighter to enter full-scale production, the Thomas Morse MB-3 biplane, made its first flight.
**1 Mar:** An Army airmail service commenced between Folkestone and Cologne in Germany.
**3 Mar:** A Boeing Model CL-4S flew the first US international airmail service between Seattle, Washington and Victoria, British Columbia.
**9 Mar:** The first flight from a gun platform on a US battleship was made by a Sopwith Pup, flying from the USS *Texas* anchored in Guantanamo Bay, Cuba, demonstrated both the platform and operational application of a shipboard fighter.
**24 Mar:** Igor Sikorsky, the pioneering Russian aircraft designer, left France for the USA after fleeing from the October Revolution in the Soviet Union. The French had previously rejected his claim for asylum.

**1 Apr:** The Imperial Japanese Army Air Division was established.
**10 May:** First flight of the Avro Baby, the first practical British light aircraft to be built after WWI.
**16 May:** Three US seaplanes left Trepassey Bay, Newfoundland in an attempt to fly the North Atlantic to England in stages.
**23 May:** Hounslow, west of London, opened for international flights and handled most London-Paris air traffic.
**13 Jun:** Alcock and Brown left Newfoundland in a Vickers Vimy for their epic flight that ended at Clifden, Ireland.
**14 Jun:** The US Army Air Service began patrol operations in California for fire detection and reporting, the first in a series of expanding commitments to the US Forest Service. Aircraft used were Curtiss JN-4 Jenny biplanes.
**14 Jun:** The prototype Nieuport Delage 29 biplane fighter attained an altitude record of 29,850ft. The French Air Force ordered the type into production and 25 escadrilles, as well as several foreign operators, went on to use the fighter.
**28 Jun:** The Treaty of Versailles was signed. One of its provisions forbade Germany from supporting any military air force and called for the destruction of all air material.
**1 Jul:** London's first airport at Hounslow Heath opened.
**6 Jul:** The British airship R34 arrived at Mineola, Long Island with 30 crew members aboard after the first airship crossing of the North Atlantic. It then completed the first double crossing.
**21 Jul:** The Dutch Aircraft Factory at Schipol was founded by Anthony Fokker.
**24 Sep:** The annual Schneider Trophy event ended in controversy after the only finisher, Italy's Savoia S13 was disqualified. Held in Bournemouth, the event was marred by heavy fog, which had seen the withdrawal of the French competition and Britain's Supermarine Sea Lion being damaged.
**29 Sep:** A fully integrated air force was formed in Poland, the Polskie Wojaka Lotnicze, which included US Army Air Service pilots, incensed by Soviet Bolshevik adventures.
**11 Oct:** Handley Page Transport offered the first in-flight meals aboard its airliners, on its London-Brussels flights.
**12 Nov:** Australian brothers Capt Ross Smith and Lt Keith Smith left Hounslow in a Vickers Vimy to become the first men to fly from England to Australia.

*The Vickers Vimy, shown here in Gerald Coulson's painting, was used by Alcock and Brown on their epic first direct flight across the Atlantic in June 1919.*
© Solomon & Whitehead Limited

These pages generously donated by the Royal Air Force Benevolent Fund, founded in 1919

*Atlantic Conquerors 1919* by Gerald Coulson VPGAvA

In 1920, the British Air Ministry's Advisory Committee for Aeronautics organised a competition for a new British amphibian design. The Vickers Viking, a neat two-seat single-engined biplane design, was the winner of the competition. Although not adopted by the Royal Air Force, the Viking was sold to the navies of France, Holland, Russia and the Argentine.

It was the Curtiss flying-boat designs of WWI which influenced RAF flying-boats for almost two decades. In Germany, the Staaken E-4250, built by the Zeppelin concern near Berlin, had the distinction of being the first truly 'modern' airliner in the world. It owed much to the all-metal giant bombers that were developed by Staaken during 1918. As an 18-seat airliner, it was conceived for the route from Friedrichshafen to Berlin. Powered by four 245hp Maybach MbIVa in-line engines it featured an unusual passenger entrance through the nose. It also carried a radio room and washroom. However, the Inter-Allied Control Commission decreed the airliner had potential as a military aircraft and could not be further developed.

Despite the success of the DH16, it was felt by Airco that mere conversions of wartime bombers could be nothing more than an expedient, pending the introduction of custom-designed civil transports. This resulted in the DH18 of 1920, which had a deep fuselage filling the interplane gap. It was powered by a single 450hp Napier Lion W-12 engine. The pilot sat in an open cockpit just aft of the passenger compartment, with the baggage hold underneath his position.

Scheduled airline services, apart from those operated by Zeppelin airships in Germany, had been non-existent before the war. In 1920, the emergence of air transport as a business led to the appearance of improvised 'airliners'. Many of these exhibited only the minimum of conversion from the wartime bombing and other roles for which they had been designed. In some of these, the passengers were as much at the mercy of the elements as the pilots. Even when enclosed cabins began to appear, the accommodation was often crude, cramped and uncomfotable.

As the war ended, it was generally acknowledged that the rotary engine, which had borne so much of the wartime powering of military aircraft, had reached the limit of its development. Both the USA and Britain were beginning to place their faith in a single type of aero engine for post-war military use. The war had also clearly demonstrated that cities, transportation, industry, workers and innocent civilians would be open to air attack in any future conflict.

In December 1920, the first Russian duralumin was obtained from the metallurgical plant at Kolchugino. It was called Kochugaluminium and with high tensile strength, it was used to produce the first moulded and extruded wing profiles.

---

**Jan:** First flight of the de Havilland DH18, the first Airco machine designed and built from the outset as a commercial airplane.

**Jan:** The RAF dispatched a squadron of DH 9A bombers to British Somaliland as the 'main instrument and factor' in the overthrow of the 'Mad Mullah'.

**1 Feb:** Vickers Vimy *Silver Queen* attempted a London-Cape Town flight.

**1 Feb:** Instone Air Lines commenced a commercial air service from England to Paris.

**7 Feb:** A French Nieuport-Delage 29 set the first post-war world speed record of 171mph (276km/h).

**18 Feb:** The Canadian Air Force was established.

**Feb:** The first operational unit, No 14 Squadron, was established in Palestine, operating Bristol F2Bs.

**29 Mar:** Official opening of Croydon Airport as London's air terminal following a boom in European civil aviation.

**29 Mar:** The Farman F60 Goliath airliner was introduced on the Le Bourget-Croydon service.

**8 Apr:** The DH18 commenced service on the Croydon-Paris route with Air Transport and Travel.

**16 May:** A KLM DH16 made the first service between Amsterdam and London.

**4 Jun:** The US Army Air Service was formed. The US Army Reorganisation Act made the air service a combatant arm of the US Army. This legislation deferred hopes of an independent air arm similar to the RAF.

**1 Jul:** Belgium launched an internal air service in the Belgian Congo, the first such service for a colony.

**3 Jul:** The first RAF tournament was held at Hendon to raise money for the RAF Memorial Fund. Intended as a one-off event it proved very popular, attracting 60,000 spectators, and was the forerunner of annual events.

**19 Aug:** Formation of the South African Air Force.

**20 Aug:** The prototype Fairey IIID, developed as a general purpose land or floatplane, made its first flight at Hamble, initially powered by a 575hp Rolls-Royce Eagle engine.

**27 Aug:** Juan de La Cierva received a patent for his autogiro.

**30 Sep:** First flight of the Zeppelin-Staaken E4/20 monoplane 18-seat airliner.

**Oct:** The first trans-Canada proving flight of 3,265 miles, in a flying time of 45 hours, was made by a Canadian Air Force Fairey seaplane.

**1 Nov:** A US international air passenger service was inaugurated by Aeromarine West Indies Airways between Key West, FL and Havana, Cuba.

**16 Nov:** The formation of QANTAS (Queensland and Northern Territories Aerial Service) by two ex-service Australian Flying Corps pilots.

**24 Nov:** Prototype Dornier Delphin III commercial flying-boat made its maiden flight.

**2 Dec:** The first east-west crossing of Australia was accomplished by a DH4, covering the 2,169 mile flight in a flying time of just over 18 hours.

**12 Dec:** First flight of the French Blériot-Spad 33 airliner.

*This painting by Terence Cuneo, commissioned to celebrate British Airways' 60th anniversary, depicts Airco DH4A airliner G-EAJC of Air Transport and Travel Limited loading its passengers at Hounslow Heath.*
Reproduced by kind permission of the Cuneo Estate.

*Hounslow Heath* by Terence Cuneo CVO, OBE, RGI

In 1921 aviation transport in the USSR was in its infancy, but the Soviet Government, and Lenin himself, wholeheartedly supported the development of the civilian aviation sector. In May the Moscow-Kharkov route was opened using the 'Ilya Muromets'. The German-Russian commercial air company Deruluft was set up in November for a route from Moscow to Koenigsberg in East Prussia, using Fokker FIIIs.

In September the Bristol Jupiter II, with auto-compensation for cylinder expansion on the valve pushrods, became the first aero engine to pass the severe new Air Ministry type-test, reaching 400hp at 1,625rpm. It became the first post-war engine for the RAF. Within ten years it had 17 foreign licenses and a total of 7,100 Jupiters were produced for at least 262 different types of aircraft. In America, the Wright R-1 nine-cylinder air-cooled radial engine was introduced, which produced 350hp.

The Dornier Do CIII Komet first flew in 1921 and was basically the landplane equivalent of the CsII Delphin transport flying-boat of 1920. The single engine was located at the top of the upswept nose. The passenger cabin was located in the deepest portion of the fuselage, under the strut-braced high-set monoplane wing. At the time that it was introduced on the Berlin-London route it was described as being 'as comfortable as an American railroad coach'.

During the year, European countries poured substantial amounts of money into their national airlines. The aeroplane provided Europeans with the means to overcome the routine obstacles of the English Channel and avoid the drudgery of border crossings. It also became fashionable to fly in airliners. Aviation centres were set up to establish requirements for the next generation of aircraft; new engines, higher speeds, greater altitude capabilities, longer range and additional safety. They then developed the rules by which manufacturers were to achieve the standards that had been set.

Post-war development of both engines and airframes was stifled by the surplus of WWI materials. America's single greatest contribution to aviation during the war had been the Liberty engine. It served US military aircraft well during the 1920s, and this changed only when engines like the Curtiss D-12 emerged. Radial air-cooled engines were pioneered by the Americans, though they were more difficult to streamline than the liquid-cooled counterparts with their in-line pistons, they dispensed with the expensive and difficult to maintain coolant systems and promised greater reliability.

In July, bombing trials were held off the coast of Virginia and the unmanned ex-German Dreadnought *Ostfriesland* of 22,800 tons was sunk by Glenn Martin MB-2 bombers, commanded by Brig Gen William Mitchell. The cruiser *Frankfurt* was also sunk as part of the same trial. This was an experiment to demonstrate the vulnerability of ships to air bombing. Due to America's remoteness, Mitchell suggested that the US Navy should cede to the airmen its role as defender of the US coastline. In September, the US battleship *Alabama* was bombed and sunk. Mitchell caused much controversy over his assertion that surface ships were doomed when faced with air power, and argued that to be safe a ship had to stay beyond the reach of land-based aircraft. His outspokenness led to his court martial.

The US Army began experiments with pressurised aircraft for use on high altitude photographic reconnaissance missions. The pressurised cabin with riveted steel plates was deemed essential in the upper atmosphere where the air pressure was too low for the human body to function adequately.

---

**1 Mar**: Orly airport, south of Paris, was opened for international flights from other European countries.

**12 Apr:** The Franco-Romanian airline CFRNA commenced a Paris-Prague and Paris-Warsaw service.

**15 May:** An American female pilot claimed a new woman's record for consecutive loops, when she looped 199 times in one hour and 20 mins.

**May:** The Boeing Model 10, a three-seat ground attack aircraft of triplane configuration, first flew. It received the US Army Air Service designation GA-1 and was the first armoured aircraft to enter production for the US Army.

**8 Jun:** First experiments with cabin pressurisation commenced with the US Army at Wright Field, LA using a DH 9A biplane. Its two open cockpits were replaced by a heavy oval compartment designed to be pressurised by a propeller-driven supercharger attached to the lower wing.

**23 Jun:** An air mail service began between Cairo and Baghdad.

**Jun:** Boeing was awarded a US Army Air Service contract to build 200 Thomas-Morse MB-3A pursuit aircraft. It enabled Boeing to discard its furniture-making business that it had started as a means to survive, following the post-war decline in military aircraft sales.

**30 Jul:** A Swiss pilot achieved a daring flight when he succeeded in landing his Caudron G III at 16,000ft on the slopes near to the summit of Mont Blanc.

**3 Aug:** An American pilot found a new use for the aeroplane, when he sprayed a patch of ground infested with caterpillars.

**10 Aug:** Formation of the United States Navy Bureau of Aeronautics.

**13 Aug:** Formation of the Royal Australian Air Force.

**Sept:** The veteran polar explorer, Sir Ernest Shackleton, obtained two Avro Baby biplane seaplanes for his expedition to the Antarctic.

**13 Sep:** In Germany, a sailplane flew for 21 minutes, beating the 1911 gliding record set by Orville Wright.

**5 Nov:** A US Navy Curtiss C-12 won the Pulitzer Trophy speed race, achieving 177mph at Omaha. The aircraft was developed into a successful Schneider Trophy contender.

**12 Nov:** The first attempt at in-flight refuelling was made when a man with a five-gallon can of petrol strapped to his back climbed from the wing of a Lincoln Standard onto a Curtiss JN-4 and filled its tank.

**30 Nov:** Japan's first aircraft carrier, the *Hosho* was launched.

**5 Dec:** First regular and scheduled airliner service was inaugurated by West Australian Airways. Its aircraft were six Bristol Tourers.

*The experiment to demonstrate the vulnerability of ships to bombing from the air is illustrated in Robert Lavin's painting of General Mitchell's Martin MB-2 bombers sinking the ex-German Dreadnought* Ostfriesland *off the American coast in July 1921.*

*Gen Mitchell's Bombers Sink the Ostfriesland* by Robert Lavin

In 1922, the Curtiss D-12 engine, with a seven-bearing crankshaft and direct drive, passed its US Navy test at 400hp. It then began a brilliant career not only as an engine for fighters but also for racers, gaining world speed records and Schneider victories.

The Air Clause of the Treaty of Versailles omitted to ban the production of civil aircraft in Germany, and although in 1922 limitations on the size and performance of such aircraft were imposed, these were withdrawn four years later under the terms of the Paris Air agreement, which also restricted the number of German service personnel who were allowed to fly as part of their duty.

The prototype Dornier Do 15 Wal made its début in 1922 and incorporated many features used in flying-boats designed by Claudius Dornier in WWI. It incorporated fuselage-mounted stabilising sponsons and a parasol wing. It also had a tandem push/pull pair of engines installed in the centre section.

In the critical first months of the existence of the Soviet Union, commanders of the air force sought to maintain fighter units at an acceptable military and technical level. Soviet designers did their utmost to catch up with the great advances made by the Western powers, but this was impossible. They did design a few fighters, but these were experiments rather than aircraft good enough to be put into production. The Soviet Government decided on a prompt, if expensive, solution to the problem by opting to buy foreign fighters. During 1922 they ordered 100 British Martinsyde F4s, 30 Italian Ansaldo A-1s and 200 Dutch Fokker D-XI fighters. Tupolev produced his sporting two-seat ANT-1 and the commercial high-wing monoplane ANT-2, completely all-metal with corrugated sheeting covering.

In September, Lieut James Doolittle made a great flight from Jacksonville, FL to San Diego in a journey of 21 hours, with one refuelling stop. His aircraft was an Airco DH4, built in the USA as a de Havilland DH4 Liberty Plane.

It was the two-seat deck-landing amphibian (which first flew in 1922) that marked the emergence of Supermarine (previously Pemberton-Billing) as a military constructor. The Seagull was continuously developed over the next decade, and successive designs remained in RAF and RAAF service until 1946.

Early commercial operation by types such as the DH18 showed that profitable airline operations would only be possible with aircraft that were faster and capable of carrying a greater payload, which led to the DH34 of 1922. Airline service soon confirmed the potential of the DH34 as an immensely sturdy and serviceable aircraft, and Imperial Airways used it on routes to Brussels and Amsterdam.

Britain was saddled with the 'Ten Year Rule', an artificial measure that required the Cabinet to look ten years into the future to assess if war was likely. If the Cabinet decided that no war was in view (and this situation prevailed for the next 15 years) military spending was kept at a low level. In the US, it was traditional that military spending should be kept at rock-bottom levels during times of peace.

---

**Jan:** De Havilland DH10 Amiens aircraft were used by No 10 Squadron, RAF to bomb rebel tribesmen on the North West frontier of India.

**10 Feb:** An experimental night flight was undertaken at Croydon when the aircraft was given its position by radio and made an approach with the aid of aviation light beacons.

**Feb:** DH10 Amiens were employed to police the North West Frontier and to carry desert air mail between Cairo and Baghdad.

**Feb:** First flight of the Avro 549 Aldershot, Avro's first entirely new post-war military aeroplane. It was the first Avro type to have a metal fuselage, and featured a capacious plywood-covered central cabin divided into two decks.

**20 Mar:** The US Navy's first aircraft carrier, the USS *Langley* was commissioned. As CV-1 it was converted from the collier *Jupiter* and had a flight deck of 533ft.

**22 Mar:** The Loening PA-1 biplane, the first US fighter equipped with an air-cooled radial engine made its initial flight.

**26 Mar:** First flight of the DH34, an eight seat passenger airliner which set new standards of luxury flight.

**16 May:** Amelia Eahart became the first woman to obtain a pilots certificate in the US.

**May:** First flight in France of the Bréguet 19 biplane reconnaissance bomber.

**29 Jul:** The first of 200 Thomas-Morse MB-3A fighters built by Boeing was delivered to the US Army Air Service. It was the first indigenous American fighter.

**12 Aug:** The fifth Schneider Trophy Race at Naples was won by a British Supermarine Sea Lion II at an average speed of 145.7mph (234km/h).

**12 Aug:** Aircraft were used for seeding inaccessible areas in Hawaii.

**22 Aug:** The Vickers Victoria military transport first flew. It could carry 25 soldiers and equipment 400 miles in four hours.

**3 Sep:** First flight of the USS *Shenandoah*, the US Navy's helium-filled rigid airship.

**4 Sep:** Lt James H. Doolittle flew coast to coast across America in a day in a DH4, with a flying time of just over 21 hours.

**8-9 Sep:** The first King's Cup Air Race was held. DH4A *City of York* on a return flight from Croydon to Glasgow set a record for the route with a flying time of six hours and 30 minutes.

**20 Sep:** A Nieuport-Delage 29 set the first world speed record over 200mph (322km/h) in France at 205.23mph (330.28km/h).

**17 Oct:** A Vought VE-7SF completed the first USN take-off from American aircraft carrier, the USS *Langley*. A first landing was achieved by an Aeromarine 39B on the 26th.

**20 Oct:** RAF aircraft were sent to the Dardanelles to face the Turks in the Chanak crisis.

**18 Nov:** First flight of the Dewoitine D1 parasol-wing fighter.

**24 Nov:** The Vickers Virginia made its maiden flight.

**25 Nov:** First flight of the Fairey Flycatcher fleet fighter. Few aeroplanes have been the subject of so much praise from pilots although it was aesthetically ugly, with its clumsy undercarriage, cocked-up rear fuselage and squared-off fin and rudder.

*The Fairey Flycatcher, which first flew in 1922, was a standard first-line fighter of the Fleet Air Arm for over a decade. James Cox's painting illustrates Flycatchers of No 403 Flight overflying the Royal Navy carrier HMS Eagle.*

*Lining Up* by James Cox

The Supermarine Aviation Works Ltd at Southampton (then as Pemberton-Billing Ltd) had considerable experience with naval aircraft during WWI. With the coming of peace and the end of lucrative military orders, Supermarine, as most other aircraft manufacturers, turned to civil aviation. The Sea Eagle, with amphibious capability, was a compact biplane powered by a 350hp Rolls-Royce Eagle IX located on two 'N' struts under the upper wing centre section and driving a four-blade pusher propeller. The wings were arranged to fold forwards to allow the aircraft to be hangared.

Juan de la Cierva has a unique place in aviation history. His use of a rotor to sustain lift for a flying machine resulted in the gyroplane, or to use Cierva's name for it, the autogiro. The first flight of the Cierva C4 on 9 January 1923 was a significant step forward, which led in turn to the development of the practical helicopter during WWII.

Finnair was established in 1923 and the Junkers F13 all-metal single-engined seaplane was used on flights between Helsinki and Tallin in Estonia and to Stockholm, Sweden, and flights continued with seaplanes until the early 1930s. Winter operations consisted mainly of emergency services within Finland.

It is said that the history of Soviet fighter aircraft began on 23 March, the day that a new fighter flew for the first time, N. N. Polikarpov's low-wing monoplane I1-400, which was built entirely of wood. Production aircraft were given the Soviet M-5 engines, a licensed production version of the American Liberty engine.

In the same year Polikarpov, working with the Moscow Dux plant, produced the R-1 reconnaissance aircraft, from a mixture of de Havilland DH4 and DH9 machines and 2,800 were built. The important role played by the R-1 aircraft in building up the Red Air Force in the 1920s is undeniable. In the early 1920s, Soviet agricultural aviation suffered from lack of suitable aircraft, mostly using the German Junkers F13. The light biplane Khioni No 5 (Konjok Gorbunok), with a 100hp Fiat engine flew in the spring and a number served in the agricultural sector for many years.

With the help of other Russian émigrés, Igor Sikorsky, who had arrived in the USA in 1919, founded his own air company and built a number of floatplanes, including a five-seater for a company exploring for oil in South America.

Vickers became involved in airline production in the early 1920s, with the Vimy Commercial derivative of the Vimy bomber. Unlike de Havilland and Handley Page, the Vickers designers did not merely modify the standard bomber by the elimination of internal cross-bracing to provide a passenger cabin, but instead produced a new fuselage design intended to supply generous seating room for the passengers.

The little de Havilland DH53 Humming Bird low-wing single-seat monoplane, built for the *Daily Mail* trials at Lympne in October, was the first light aeroplane produced by de Havilland. It was fitted with a 750cc Douglas motor-cycle engine. The RAF purchased eight for communications and inexpensive flying practice.

**9 Jan:** Designed by Cierva in Spain, the C4 autogiro made its first successful flight with a $2^1/2$ mile (4nm) circuit at Madrid. It marked an increased interest in gyroplanes.
**Feb:** First take-off and landing on Japanese aircraft carrier *Hosho* by an indigenous aircraft, a Mitsubishi 1MF biplane.
**5 Mar:** First use of a jettisonable fuel tank, on a Boeing MB-3A fighter, which enhanced the aircraft's flying range to 400 miles.
**1 Apr:** The de Havilland School of Flying began training RAF reservists at Stag Lane using Avro 548s and Hire Service DH9s.
**2-3 May:** A US Army Air Force Fokker T2 single-engined monoplane made the first non-stop flight across the North American continent. The aircraft averaged a speed of 88mph (142km/h) for the flight which lasted nearly 27 hours. It carried an overload of 593.41 gallons of fuel.
**3 May:** The Sikorsky Aero Engineering Co was set up in the US by Igor Sikorsky. Since the end of WWI he had been unable to find employment in the aviation industry and had opted for teaching maths and giving talks on the future of aviation.

**6 May:** Three Breguet 14 biplanes of the French airline Latécoère completed the first flight down the West African coast from Casablanca in Morocco to Dakar in Senegal.
**23 May:** The Belgian airline SABENA was formed to expand European routes and to the Belgian Congo.
**2 Jun:** The Boeing PW-9 biplane made its maiden flight, which paved the way for a series of Boeing aircraft to serve with the US forces into the 1930s.
**30 Jul:** The DH50 first flew, a four-seat aircraft which had eight square roof lights. The following month, flown by Alan Cobham, it won a reliability trial at Gothenburg International Aeronautical Exhibition.
**14 Aug:** British Maritime Air Navigation Company launched the first flying-boat airline service to the Channel Islands.
**22 Aug:** First flight of the triplane Barling XNBL-1, the first six-engined aircraft. Although underpowered for its size, it was the largest aircraft in the world at the time of its appearance.
**23 Aug:** The first Soviet fighter to achieve series production, the

Polikarpov I-1, took to the air for the first time.
**28 Aug:** A USAAS DH4B remained airborne for $37^1/4$ hours at Rockwell Field, CA, during which time it was refuelled no less than 15 times by a DH4B tanker aircraft.
**6 Oct:** Curtiss R2C-1 racers took the first two places at the Pulitzer prize contest at St Louis, with a new world speed record of 243mph (392km/h).
**23 Oct:** First flight of the Handley Page Hyderabad, a military derivative of the W8 airliner which went on to serve in four RAF squadrons until the early 1930s.

*The first flight of the Cierva C-4 on 9 January 1923 in Madrid, only 20 years after Kitty Hawk, marked a defining moment in rotorcraft development, from which the modern helicopter has subsequently evolved. This specially commissioned painting by Roger H Middlebrook depicts Don Juan de la Cierva's initial success with the world's first practical rotating wing, non-stalling aircraft, which he named 'autogiro'.*

These pages generously donated by AgustaWestland

*First Flight of the Autogiro* by Roger H Middlebrook GAvA, FSAI

On 6 April four Douglas World Cruisers of the US Army departed from Seattle on the first flight around the world. Two eventually returned to base after completing the journey in 175 days.

The US Navy flying-boats made many long-range flights, partly in the interest of setting records and earning prestige, but also because one of the real benefits of flying-boats during the 1920s was the ability to offer a longer over-water range than the landplane. Development of larger landplanes in the 1920s was somewhat inhibited because the undercarriage design was not able to cope with much heavier weights, whereas the flying-boat allowed designers to overcome this problem. At that time the flying-boat offered a better chance of survival than the landplane in the event of an engine failure during an over-water stage.

In 1924, a new Government-sponsored British airline, Imperial Airways, was formed. It absorbed the operations of the Handley Page Transport Company, Instone Air Line, Daimler Airways and the British Marine Air Navigation Company. Initially, all pilots had to be a member of the Royal Auxiliary Air Force or to have been members of the RAF. It was in Europe that commercial aviation gathered the most immediate momentum, two manufacturers swiftly gaining position of great dominance. These were Junkers in Germany and the Dutch firm of Fokker.

In Russia, D. P. Grigorovich designed the I-1 biplane, which made its first flight in January. It was fitted with the American Liberty engine of 400hp and was produced in the national aircraft plant No 1 in Moscow (the initial 'I' meaning Istrebital, a fighter). The AK-1 was the first successful passenger aircraft in Russia that completed its maiden flight on 8 February. It was a strut-braced, high-wing monoplane of composite construction with an open cockpit for the pilot and mechanic in front of the wing and an enclosed cabin for two passengers in the fuselage.

The Fokker F.VII airliner was one of the truly great aircraft of the 1920s that eventually ran to a series of eight sub-types, with widely differing powerplants and capabilities. It featured an excellent wide-span undercarriage. Operating costs were relatively low and airlines had a choice of engines that could be installed.

The Spanish Government advanced money for Cierva to build his single-seat C6A research machine. This was basically an Avro 504K, with a 110hp Le Rhône, without mainplanes and fitted instead with a four-bladed articulated rotor mounted on a pylon of steel tubes. The rotor was not engine-driven, but was kept in motion entirely by the forward speed of the machine. It made its first flight in May and was demonstrated to the British Air Ministry at Farnborough in October of the following year.

On 24 November, Alan Cobham and two passengers set off from London to Rangoon in a de Havilland DH.50, it being the first long-distance flight to be made with the intention of surveying the air route to India as a precursor to a commercial air route.

---

**4 Mar:** Two Martin and two de Havilland bombers finally succeeded in unblocking an ice jam in the Platte River at North Bend, Nebraska following six hours of bombardment.

**Mar:** The world's first crop-dusting company was established in Georgia in the US, and began to develop commercial air services during the winter when there were no crop-dusting requirements. This was the forerunner of Delta Air Lines.

**1 Apr:** The Fleet Air Arm (FAA) was established. Royal Navy aircrew were on detachment to the RAF, which retained overall control.

**28 Apr:** Imperial Airways began operations from London to Paris.

**2 May:** A Douglas DT-2 torpedo bomber was launched by catapult from the carrier USS *Langley* while the ship was at anchor at Pensacola.

**19 May:** RAAF pilots in a Fairey IIID floatplane made the first entire circumnavigation of the coastline of Australia.

**22 Jun:** A Curtiss PW-8 pursuit aircraft completed the first one-day, daylight crossing of the United States in just under 22 hours, intended to prove the rapid deployment potential of the latest generation of USAAS aircraft.

**23 Jun:** First flight of the Focke-Wulf A16 monoplane, the first product of the Focke-Wulf Airplane Construction Co.

**1 Jul:** Regular night airmail services began over the US transcontinental route, using route-marking beacons and floodlit airfields.

**8 Aug:** The US airship *Shenandoah* proved that dirigibles could operate at sea by mooring to a mast of a moving ship.

**Aug:** First flight of the Hawker Cygnet. Designed by Sydney Camm it was Hawker's entry for the Lympne competition.

**1 Jul:** First flight of the de Havilland DH 51. At a time when the 1923 Lympne trials were encouraging the construction of low-powered single-seat light planes, the de Havilland Co designed a larger, more practical touring vehicle. It was fitted with war-surplus 90hp RAF 1A eight-cylinder air-cooled engines.

**Aug:** The Savoia Marchetti S55 flying-boat made its maiden flight, one of the most successful flying-boats of the inter-war years.

**11 Sep:** Canada's first scheduled air service commenced when Laurentide Air Services opened a route between Haileybury, Ontario and Rouyn, Quebec.

**Sep:** First flight of the Aero A-24, a twin-engined (245hp Maybachs) that was Czechoslovakia's first heavy night bomber.

**4 Nov:** First flight of the Fiat CR1 single-seat biplane fighter for the Regia Aeronautica.

**21 Nov:** A KLM Fokker FVII flew from the Netherlands to Java in the Dutch East Indies, a 9,552 mile (15,369km) flight that took 127 hours.

**15 Dec:** The first successful 'hook on' parasite experiment between an airship and an aeroplane (a Sperry Messenger biplane) took place at Langley Field, VA.

*The first contact between an airship and an aeroplane in flight was established over Langley Field, Virginia in December 1924. Nixon Galloway's painting shows a Sperry Messenger biplane 'hooking on' in a parasite experiment with a US Army D-3 Blimp.*

*US Army D-3 Blimp* by Nixon Galloway ASAA

In 1925, the Armstrong Siddeley Company introduced the first production engine with a geared supercharger, and its 82hp Genet appeared the same year. The Hispano Suiza aero engine factory had improved its range and became amongst the most reliable of all aero engines, setting numerous speed and distance records. The most capable engines of the mid-1920s were its 60 degree V-12s.

Pratt & Whitney, now the world's biggest aero-engine company, was formed in July. It decided a 'superior' engine, a nine-cylinder air-cooled radial, should be created to develop 400hp within a weight of 650lb. The first Wasp was running in December and produced 425hp for a weight of just under 650lb. Rolls-Royce was also developing a new aero-engine, the Eagle XVI, an X-16 with four banks of small two-valve cylinders supercharged by a double-sided gear-driven blower. This was subsequently dropped in favour of the V-12.

In November, Alan Cobham flew 16,000 miles (25,750km) to Cape Town and back in a DH50, for which he was knighted. The first Schneider winner to exceed the 200mph barrier was the Curtiss R3C-2, which won the 1925 contest averaging 232.57mph, piloted by the US Army's Lt Jimmy Doolittle.

In April, the Defence Commissariat of the USSR decreed that outdated fighter models of foreign provenance were to be continuously replaced. Soviet aircraft designers were exhorted to create new, more effective aircraft for series production during the period of its First Five Year Plan. The first Soviet two-seat fighter appeared in 1925 under the designation 2I-N1, designed by the Polikarpov bureau, with a British Napier Lion engine but the Red Air Force had no immediate need for an aircraft like this. The Tupolev ANT-4 twin-engined, low-wing monoplane flew on 26 November. The Red Air Force took ANT-4s as its first heavy bombers, and throughout the 1920s heavy bombers of the TB class attracted particular attention throughout the world. The design and construction of all-metal aircraft was a source of pride to the Soviet Government and special commissions were set up for propaganda flights to be made to foreign countries.

R.J. Mitchell's second flying-boat design was the Southampton, which entered service in 1925. The early versions had wooden hulls, but the Mk II had a metal hull. A total of 78 was built. The type constantly made headlines after a series of long-distance cruises.

The tri-motor Fokker FVIIs, amongst the most important transport aircraft of the 1920s, also featured in a number of classic long-distance flights. These flights by the tri-motor, which had 399hp Wright Whirlwind J6 radials, were intended to promote reliability in aircraft in airline service, and the type was widely built under licence in Belgium, Czechoslovakia, France, Great Britain (as the Avro Ten), Italy, Poland and the USA.

In common with several other Russian aircraft of the mid-1920s the Tupolev ANT-3 showed marked signs of Junkers influence. It was designed as a sesquiplane and built of Kolchugalumin, am aluminium alloy developed by the Russians and claimed to be stronger than aluminium. The engine was the Russian-built version of the 400hp Liberty 12, the H-5. It soon received good press as a result of some excellent long-distance flights.

Short Brothers produced a metal-hulled version of the F5 in 1925, which was the first metal-hulled flying-boat in the world, in an attempt to overcome one of the persistent problems of the flying-boat hull, the lack of adequate watertightness.

---

**3 Jan:** Influenced by Curtiss racing seaplanes the prototype Fairey Fox high-speed day-bomber, designed around the 480hp Curtiss D-12 engine, made its maiden flight. It proved faster than contemporary RAF fighters.

**Jan:** First flight of the Potez 25 biplane light bomber, which proved to be one of the most successful French designs of the inter-war period.

**1 Feb:** With just three squadrons operational in India, the RAF successfully quelled tribal warfare in Wariristan, without the support of ground forces.

**2 Feb:** De Havilland's DH60 Moth made its maiden flight. It was delivered to the first flying club in July.

**3-4 Feb:** A French Bréguet 19 recorded a straight line aircraft distance record of 1,967 miles (3,166km).

**Feb:** The Gloster Gamecock first flew, the last biplane fighter of wooden construction to enter RAF service.

**10 Mar:** The first Supermarine Southampton biplane flying-boat, with two engines midway between the wings, made its maiden flight at Calshot. It remained in service for 12 years, longer than any other flying-boat before the Short Sunderland.

**12 Mar:** First flight of the Fokker FVIIa eight-passenger airliner, powered by a 400hp Liberty engine, one of the most widely used airliners of the 1920s.

**1 May:** Establishment of the Japanese Army Air Corps. Like other air-minded powers, Japan considered military aircraft an adjunct to ground forces rather than as an independent force.

**10 May:** The Armstrong Whitworth Atlas, the first aircraft to be designed from the outset as an Army Co-operation type for the RAF, made its first flight.

**29 May:** The DH60 Moth made headline news when Alan Cobham flew one from Croydon to Zurich and back in a day.

**10 Jun:** A number of Polikarpov R-1s flew from Moscow to Peking, one of the longest flights involving a number of aircraft.

**3 Sep:** The US Navy airship *Shenandoah* was wrecked in a storm over Ohio, after it was ordered into the air by the fleet commander against the advice of its captain.

**5 Sep:** For the first time, aircraft were used in a mass evacuation of civilians from a war zone when 27 aircraft evacuated 67 British citizens from Sulaimaniya in northern Iraq.

**26 Oct:** This year's Schneider Trophy was held at Chesapeake Bay and won by Lt Jimmy Doolittle in a Curtiss R3C-2 at an average speed of 232.56mph (374.26km/h).

**26 Nov:** First flight of the Tupolev TB-1 (ANT-4), Russia's first twin-engined all-metal monoplane bomber. It was one of the most important aircraft to appear from the Soviet Union.

*The double career of the Curtiss JN series, firstly as a World War I trainer and then as a popular private and barnstorming aeroplane, made the 'Jenny' very well known across the USA in the 1920s. Howard Gerrard's painting* Oklahoma Joy Ride *shows the biplane in a typical setting.*

*Oklahoma Joy Ride* by Howard Gerrard GAvA

In 1926, Major Frank Halford and the de Havilland Company decided that the Cirrus engine (which had derived from the old Renault engine) should be followed by a completely new design. This resulted in the Gipsy air-cooled four in-line engine of 5.23 litres giving 85hp. The final Gipsy engine was the Major, producing 222hp, and total Gipsy deliveries amounted to 27,654. The Fairchild Aeroplane Manufacturing Co launched the Ranger, a new in-line air-cooled engine. This was produced in the following year as the 6-370, this giving the number of cylinders and the capacity.

During the year Dr Geoffrey Hill, in conjunction with Westland Aircraft, became interested in aircraft with heavily swept wings, which avoided the need for a large fuselage with the attendant drag and weight. His Pteradactyl design provided useful data on the use of elevons, as dual purpose control surfaces, on swept wings. It also provided information on the feasibility of tail-less aircraft.

The Allison company got into aviation in Indianapolis in 1926 with the V-1410 engine, an inverted version of the WWI Liberty engine with air-cooled cylinders. The following year it produced the 765hp two-stroke diesel airship engine for the US Navy. The Bristol Mercury aero engine appeared in 1926, initially a short-stroke Jupiter designed for Schneider racing.

In 1926 N. N. Polikarpov started to design a new standard aircraft for the aviation schools that was easy to fly, stable and reliable. He built the U-2, which initially had upper and lower wings that were interchangeable (the Red Air Force had demanded really simple production technology with maximum interchangeability of parts). It used the 100hp five-cylinder M-11 radial, one of the best and most used aircraft engines in the USSR. The

prototype first flew on 7 January 1928 and 33,000 had been built when production ceased in 1943. All sorts of very diverse variants of the U-2 appeared, and during the course of their history they performed almost every task open to aircraft, apart from fighter operations.

The 1926 Schneider Trophy Race was won by the Italians with their streamlined Macchi M39 low-wing monoplane floatplane. Blackburn Aircraft entered the flying-boat market with the all-metal Iris. Powered by three Rolls-Royce Condor engines, it was christened 'Britain's Aerial Battleship' because of its armament.

The Argosy was the initial civil aircraft developed by Armstrong Whitworth, being produced in response to an Imperial Airways requirement for a multi-engined airliner, but it reflected the degree to which British airliner design had fallen behind that of other European countries. The three Jaguar III radial engines were uncowled and the fuselage was a blocky structure of steel tubes covered with fabric. Nevertheless, it was what Imperial Airways wanted, a 20-passenger aircraft with a high safety factor, and it proved very popular, remaining in service for ten years. The de Havilland DH66 Hercules biplane airliner appeared around the same time, but was a much lighter and more graceful design. It entered service in the Middle East and took over the RAF's mail route from Cairo to Karachi in India. The three-engined airliner featured an unusual biplane tail unit.

Amongst the classic airliners of the 1920s, the Ford TriMotor (Models 4-AT and 5-AT) has a definite place of importance in air transport. It served for more than 40 years as an effective transport, at first with the major US airlines and then gradually with more remote operators in less accessible parts of the world. In 1926 it was the largest civil aircraft produced in the US.

---

**15 Feb:** Billy Mitchell, who had resigned from the post of the Chief of the USAAS four days earlier, urged the House Committee on Military Affairs to base the Nation's defence on aircraft rather than ships.

**1 Mar:** The RAF's first official long-distance flight, comprising four Fairey IIIDs, left Cairo for Cape Town. They then returned to Lee-on-Solent in the UK, covering a distance of 14,800 miles (22,530km).

**11-14 Mar:** Flying from Spitzbergen to Alaska in Norge, explorer Roald Amundsen made the first airship flight over the North Pole.

**19 Mar:** First flight of the Fairey IIIF general purpose aircraft, which had a composite wood-metal fuselage and wooden wings.

**24 Mar:** Juan de La Cierva set up the Cierva Autogiro Co.

**25 Mar:** The Messerschmitt Flugzenbau GmbH was formed in Germany by Willie Messerschmitt.

**6 Apr:** Varney Speed Lines (which later became Continental Air

Lines) commenced the first commercial airmail flights in the US.

**9 May:** Lt Cdr Richard E.Byrd USN and Floyd Bennett made the first aircraft flight over the North Pole. In Fokker FVIIa-3m Josephine Ford they took off from Northern Norway at midnight.

**2 Jul:** The US Army Air Service (USAAS) became the US Army Air Corps (USAAC).

**28 Jul:** The US submarine S1, whilst on experimental exercises, surfaced and launched a seaplane, then recovered the aircraft and submerged again.

**1 Aug:** The US Army Air Training Corps Centre at San Antonio, TX was established, which would eventually provide nearly all Air Corps pilots.

**17 Aug:** The Short S5 Singapore I flying-boat was first flown at Rochester. It had an all-metal hull and was the first in a line of Singapore developments to emerge over a ten-year period.

**21 Oct:** A Gloster Grebe was successfully launched from under

the airship R-33 after it took off from Pulham, a test designed to demonstrate the use of aircraft for reconnaissance patrols from airships operating far beyond the range of small aircraft.

**29 Oct:** In 1926, DH Moth output was approx one a day as the demand for Cirrus engines had rapidly exhausted the once large stocks of war surplus Renault components, and work started on the DH60G Gipsy Moth with the Gipsy I engine.

**15 Nov:** Henry Ford opened a large new production line for the construction of the 4-AT TriMotor, which had made its first flight on 11 June. It proved to be a reliable and tough 'workhorse' on long-distance services.

*Roger H Middlebrook's evocative painting of a DH66 Hercules standing on the apron illustrates the pleasing lines of this three-engined biplane airliner at a time when international passenger travel had begun to increase.*

*Empire Trailblazer* by Roger H Middlebrook GAvA, FSAI

On 20/21 May, 25-year old Capt Charles A. Lindbergh flew across the North Atlantic from Long Island, NY to Paris. Lindbergh raised money from sponsors in St Louis, hence the name of his Ryan NYP NX-211 *Spirit of St Louis*, powered by a 220hp Wright Whirlwind. He carried only elementary small-scale maps and a comparatively primitive set of instruments. But he had memorised all the definite details of his route, and he won the $25,000 prize offered by Raymond Orteig for the first New York-Paris flight. Surprisingly, the Ryan had one very odd and potentially dangerous feature, namely the complete lack of direct forward vision from the cockpit.

In the 1927 Schneider race, held in Venice, the two British Supermarine S5s totally outclassed the opposition by finishing in first and second places. The S5, a development of the S4, had the well-tried and reliable 800hp Napier Lion engine. Its clean lines were enhanced by the exceptionally thin wings and float struts, which had to be braced with wires for added strength, all of which cut the drag to the minimum.

Like many other countries during the mid-to late 1920s Germany saw the growth of air transport through small airlines, and an increasing interest in air-mindedness through flying and gliding clubs. The manufacture of light aircraft and civil machines for use by such airlines and clubs, saw the German aircraft industry develop through companies whose products were to become household names, such as Heinkel, Dornier, Messerschmitt and Junkers.

The Bellanca CH-300 Pacemaker was a high-wing monoplane that featured bracing struts that were faired into aerofoil shapes to reduce drag, but also to provide a small and useful increment in lift. By 1927 bungee-type springing on landing gear was being phased out in favour of vertically coiled springs.

During 1927, the BMW Company broadened its engine range to embrace air-cooled radials. The Warner Scarab seven-cylinder ran in November and practically swept the board at the following year's US Nationals. The Wright J-5 Whirlwind engine was introduced and achieved sudden fame when it took Lindbergh to Paris in May.

The first prototype of Sukhoi's I-4 (ANT-5) flew in the summer. The I-4's one special quality was its durability, despite being exposed to variable terrain and weather conditions in the USSR. It went into service the following year and served until 1937. Production aircraft were powered by a licence-built Bristol Jupiter, designated M-22, of 480hp. The Polikarpov I-3 also emerged that year, basically a single-seat redesign of the two-seat 2I-NI fighter. It was a simple biplane of composite construction with a German BMW-VIz engine of 500hp and over 400 were produced. The I-3 and I-4 were the first fighter models to be built and found suitable for series production during the first years of the Five Year Plan.

Pan American Airways Inc was formed in 1927 and obtained exclusive landing rights in Havana, and its first aircraft were rented Fairchild FC-2 floatplanes. The Junkers S36 was produced ostensibly as a mailplane, but was a subterfuge for the development of a military aircraft, which was banned under the Treaty of Versailles. It featured three open cockpits along the upper surface of the typically Junkers fuselage with twin tailfins.

Sir Alan Cobham obtained the loan of the Rolls-Royce engined Short Singapore prototype for a survey flight of Africa, seeking landing places for both Imperial Airways and the RAF. The Avro 575 (Cierva C8L Mk1) bearing RAF roundels flew on 30 September. Cierva flew from Hamble to Farnborough, making the first cross-country flight by a rotary-winged aircraft in the UK in the process.

The Lockheed Vega appeared in 1927, a graceful design, at the limits of wooden technology. With four passengers and a pilot it clearly met the requirements of smaller airlines. It was also produced as a floatplane.

---

**27 Mar:** The Westland Wapiti, a two-seat general purpose aircraft for the RAF, made its first flight. Designed as a replacement for the DH9A, it served in the RAF until the early 1940s.
**17 May:** The prototype Bristol Bulldog single-seat fighter made its first flight. It became one of the most famous RAF Fighters of the 1930s, serving until 1937, when it was replaced by the Gloster Gladiator.
**27 May:** France's first aircraft carrier *Bearn* was completed, thirteen years after being laid down. When scrapped in 1967 it was the longest-served carrier of all time.
**24 Jun:** First flight of the de Havilland DH71 Tiger Moth, a diminutive low-wing monoplane, constructed in considerable secrecy at Stag Lane and intended for high speed research at reasonable cost, and to act as a flying testbed for Halford's prototype Cirrus-replacement engine.
**28 Jul:** A US Army Fokker C-2 monoplane completed the first successful non-stop flight from the continental USA to Hawaii, a distance of 2,407 mile in a flight of 25 hours 50 minutes.
**27 Aug:** Bert Hinkler flew the Avro Avian from Croydon to Latvia to demonstrate the aircraft as a trainer for the Latvian Air Force. It was the longest non-stop flight by a light aeroplane up to that time. The 1,200 mile flight took $10^3/4$ hours.
**1 Sep:** An ANT-3 Nash Otvet arrived in Tokyo after a flight from Moscow. On return it had completed 22,000km and required 153 hours of flying time.
**1 Nov:** The USS *Saratoga*, the US Navy's first fleet-sized aircraft carrier was commissioned on the east coast, followed soon afterwards by the USS *Lexington*.
**Dec:** First flight of the de Havilland DH61 Giant Moth, a large single-engined cabin biplane to meet an Australian requirement for a DH50J replacement. The undercarriage was not the usual split type, but each wheel had its own steel axle hinged to the opposite longeron so as to cross the other diagonally. To ensure adequate view for the pilot the open cockpit was offset to port.

*Capt Charles Lindbergh, flying the Ryan NYP monoplane* Spirit of St Louis, *made the first non-stop solo crossing of the Atlantic in May 1927. Roger H Middlebrook's painting captures Lindbergh's sighting of fishing boats near to land prior to approaching the French coast.*

*Hallelujah! Fishing Boats* by Roger H Middlebrook GAvA, FSAI

Charles Kingsford-Smith, in his Fokker *Southern Cross*, was the first airman to conquer the Pacific. Fitted with three Wright Whirlwind engines of 220hp, the Fokker's total fuel capacity amounted to a substantial 1,298 gallons. It carried three radio transmitters and two receivers with a wireless direction finder as well. With a crew of four *Southern Cross* left Oakland, San Fransisco on 31 May for the first hop of 2,400 miles to Honolulu in the Hawaiian Islands. The second stage to Suva Bay in Fiji achieved the longest non-stop ocean flight, 3,138 miles in 34$^1$/$_2$ hours. The final part of the flight, Fiji to Australia, was made in atrocious weather conditions and the crew fought their way to Brisbane, a total flight of 7,300 miles.

The Berlin-based Argus Co re-entered the aviation engine scene in 1928, and produced the As8, an inverted four-inline air-cooled engine of 110hp and this put the company on a firm footing. In 1928 Flight Cadet Frank Whittle wrote a thesis at the RAF College, Cranwell in which he described how gas turbines and jet propulsion would free aircraft from the existing limitations on flight performance.

During the 1920s, Renault had persisted with big V-12 engines, both air and water-cooled, but in 1928 opted for the low-power market with the 4P upright four in-line, developing 90hp. The Rolls-Royce F-10 engine appeared (later named Kestrel) which produced 490hp at 2,350rpm, eventually 4,750 were delivered. In the same year Rolls-Royce developed a Special F to use steam cooling, which became the Goshawk.

Geoffrey de Havilland had seen the implications of the lightplane's failure to become a commercial success. He designed the beautiful single-bay biplane combined with a reasonable performance and manoeuvrability together with good economy. Powered by a 60hp Cirrus engine it carried two people in tandem in open cockpits. The DH60 Moth was an immediate success and became the standard aeroplane to be found in the flying clubs that were springing up in the UK. The US, by contrast, showed little or no interest towards private flying during the decade and few light aircraft of any note were produced.

Throughout the 1920s, enormous advances were seen in the theory and practice of flight; speed, range and altitude increased at a commendable rate. It became possible to build longer-span cantilever wings out of light alloys. For long-distance aircraft, high aspect ratio wings proved an excellent feature. The various components of drag, and their relationship to each other, began to receive detailed attention from designers; consequently aircraft performance improved out of all proportion to the extra power of the newer aero engines.

In 1928, the Sperry Organisation perfected the artificial horizon. With a gyroscopically stabilised artificial horizon on the instrument panel the pilot could fly in cloud without having an external reference.

The Short Calcutta three-engined flying-boat appeared in 1928. Imperial Airways had to operate to many areas where there was no airfield and the flying-boat was required to ensure safety over inhospitable areas. It was needed for the rapid re-equipment of Imperial Airway's routes to the south east, towards India and Australasia and to the south to South Africa.

The Thomas-Morse Co had long been a proponent of all-metal aircraft construction, but only achieved success in 1928 when the military ordered 180 O-19s. These observation aircraft featured the type of metal construction that Thomas-Morse had been championing since 1919, wrap-around corrugated sheet metal. The flying surfaces were of metal construction with fabric covering.

---

**7 Jan:** The Soviet Union's Polikarpov U-2 (later PO-2) trainer was flown for the first time, the first in a long line of derivatives and variants that would maintain the single-engined biplane in service for more than 60 years.

**7 Jan:** First use of a military flying ambulance when a US Marine Vought Corsair biplane rescued a wounded colleague in British Somaliland.

**1 Feb:** The defence of Aden and surrounding territory was made the responsibility of the RAF, which formed the Aden Command specifically for this task.

**3 Feb:** The Boeing F3B-1 naval fighter first flew. Designed as a multi-capability naval fighter-bomber, it was able to operate with floats or fixed undercarriage.

**15 Feb:** First flight of the Short S8 Calcutta flying-boat.

**2 May:** London's re-vamped Croydon airport officially opened.

**15 May:** Inauguration of the 'Flying Doctor Service' in Australia, run by the Revd John Flynn's Island Mission using a DH50.

**3 Jun:** The Dewoitine D27 fighter made its maiden flight.

**Jun:** First flight of the Hawker Hart prototype. More aircraft of Hart origin were built between the wars than any other basic design in Britain.

**18 Jun:** Amelia Eahart became the first woman to fly across the Atlantic, albeit as a passenger in the Fokker FVIIb-3M Friendship.

**Jun:** Potez, the prolific aircraft company, formed an engine design laboratory, subsequently producing a range of three, six and nine-cylinder radials originally derived from the Anzani.

**15 Sep:** In France the Ministere de l'Air was created, thus paving the way for an independent air force.

**18 Sep:** Cierva flew his C8L-III autogiro, powered by a 180hp Lynx engine, across the English Channel with a passenger aboard.

**30 Oct:** Japan Air Lines formed from the merger of a number of smaller airlines.

**11 Nov:** Inter-Island Airways was formed in Hawaii to operate eight-passenger twin-engined Sikorsky S-38 amphibians for island hopping.

**Nov:** First flight of the Hawker Tomtit. The type represented an advance in the design of elementary service trainers, achieved by the use of such sophisticated features as all-metal construction.

**23 Dec:** The RAF undertook to evacuate civilians from Kabul, Afghanistan during tribal disturbances. The aircraft flew a total of 28,160 miles without loss of life despite severe weather conditions and operating from only basic landing strips.

*Theo Fraser's painting depicts the three-engined Fokker FVIIB-3m* Southern Cross *flying from San Fransisco to Honolulu, Suva (Fiji) and Brisbane, Australia to complete the first trans-Pacific flight, flown by Capt Charles Kingsford Smith and C T P Ulm in June 1928. © Theo Fraser GAvA*

*Southern Cross* by Theo Fraser GAvA

A Golden Age was on the way, a glorious decade when aviation came into its young maturity. But the Depression in 1929 only exacerbated the lack of funding from either governments or industry to further the development of aircraft technology.

In September, Great Britain retained the Schneider Trophy at an average speed of 328.63mph. Although the US did not participate, there was a strong Italian challenge. The new Supermarine S6 floatplane of the RAF High Speed Flight, designed by R. J. Mitchell, featured a supercharged 1,900hp Rolls-Royce 'R' engine.

Imperial Airways inaugurated its long-awaited London to India passenger/airmail service. Commencing in March it used Armstrong Whitworth Argosy *City of Glasgow* for the flight from Croydon to Basle in Switzerland. Passengers were then taken by train to the Mediterranean port of Genoa where they boarded a new Short Calcutta flying-boat to Alexandra (with six stops en route) and then by DH66 Hercules to Karachi.

In January, two US Army Air Corps pilots, Major Carl Spaatz and Captain Ira C. Eaker (both to achieve high ranking in WWII), achieved a world flight endurance record by staying aloft for 150 hours using Fokker C-2A *Question Mark*, refuelled in flight. The Link Trainer was patented by Ed Link of Binghampton, NY. Consisting of a cockpit fitted with the basic controls and instruments found in any aircraft, the Trainer was mounted on a joint, which allowed movement in any direction. This enabled trainee pilots to learn the basic skills before leaving the ground.

The first circumnavigation of the globe was undertaken by the German LZ *Graf Zeppelin*. It left Lakehurst, NY in August and the 21,150 mile journey took 21 days and five hours, being achieved at an average speed of 70.23mph. In October, the world's largest and heaviest flying-boat, and one of the most ambitious aircraft ever built, took to the air. The Dornier X had twelve Bristol Jupiter engines of 525hp, in push-pull pairs mounted above the wings. It featured a two-ship hull and large waterline sponsons. The giant Junkers G38 made its first flight in November. With enormous wings, which dwarfed the fuselage, it featured Junkers' pioneering use of metal in aircraft construction, especially the tough alloy Duralumin. Six of the 34 passengers were actually seated in the wings, their special windows built into the leading edge afforded excellent viability.

The Armstrong Siddeley Cheetah engine appeared in 1929 which delivered 295hp and went on to give 425hp in the last Avro Ansons in 1952, by which time over 37,500 had been delivered. The Lycoming Co emerged in 1929, as a subsidiary of the Cord car company, and produced its first engine, the R-680 nine-cylinder radial of 285hp. Pratt & Whitney merged with Curtiss during the year and launched the improved Cyclone.

The first flying-boat designed by Igor Sikorsky to be operated by PanAm was the S-38, a ten-passenger amphibian used on local routes from Miami in 1929. Long-range Consolidated Commodore flying-boats, able to carry 32 passengers, were introduced by Pan Am later in the year.

The Fokker FXI was developed to meet the requirements of small airlines operating over short routes with a relatively low density of traffic. Accommodation was provided for six passengers with two crew, power being provided by a 500hp Gnome-Rhône Jupiter VI radial. The last Fokker type to emerge from the US was the FXXXII.

---

**25 Jan:** PanAm Grace Airways was inaugurated to operate an airmail service between the Panama Canal and Argentina. It was jointly owned by PanAm and the shipping and banking corporation W. R. Grace & Co.

**24 Mar:** The first non-stop flight from England to India was made by a Royal Air Force Fairey Long-Range Monoplane, a flight of 4,130 miles (6,647km) in a flight time of 50 hours 37 minutes.

**30 Mar:** Imperial Airways inaugurated its first scheduled UK to India air service.

**9 Apr:** Air Union, a French airline, commenced a nightly service from Paris to London.

**8 May:** Bristol Bulldogs entered service with No 3 Squadron, RAF.

**3 Jul:** A Vought VO-1 observation biplane successfully hooked on to the airship *Los Angeles* during experiments with parasite aircraft.

**7 Jul:** Transcontinental Air Transport inaugurated a 48-hour air-rail trans-US passenger service, Ford TriMotors being used for the air sections.

**11 Jul:** A Cierva C12 autogiro flew non-stop over the 350 mile journey between Madrid and Lisbon.

**19 Aug:** ZMC-2, the first metal airship, with a length of 149ft 6in, built for the US Navy, made its first flight at Detroit, MI and operated for ten years.

**12 Sep:** KLM inaugurated an airmail service from Holland to Djakarta, using a Fokker FVII for the 12-day, 9,000 mile flight.

**24 Sep:** A USAAC Consolidated NY-2 Husky biplane completed the first successful blind take-off, circuit and landing at Mitchell Field, NY. This was achieved by use of the new Sperry artificial horizon and directional gyro.

**27-29 Sep:** Breguet 19 *Point d'Intérrogation* was flown from Le Bourget, Paris to Manchuria, setting a new world distance record of 4,912 miles (7,905km).

**2 Oct:** The 722ft long, diesel-powered Airship R-101, built under State management, was unveiled at RAF Cardington. It made its first flight on 14 October.

**21 Oct:** The world's first civil ambulance service was set up in the United States.

**6 Nov:** The first gigantic Junkers G38 four-engined airliner, specifically built for Luft Hansa, made its first flight.

**26 Nov:** A Fairey Flycatcher made the first night landing by the Fleet Air Arm on HMS *Courageous*, while at anchor in Valetta Harbour, Malta.

**28-29 Nov:** Operating from New Zealand Admiral Byrd in the Ford 4-AT TriMotor Floyd Bennett, powered by three 230hp Wright engines, made the first aircraft flight over the snowswept, ice-capped, gale-torn South Pole.

**20 Dec:** An extension of Imperial Airways, the Indian State Air Service began a passenger service between Karachi and Delhi.

*Keith McDonough's painting shows passengers waiting to board Dornier Do R Super-Wal I-RIDE of SA Navigazone Aerea at Naples, with Mount Vesuvius in the background.*

These pages generously donated by Marshall of Cambridge, established in 1929

*I Ride* by Kenneth McDonough GAvA

Probably the greatest public interest in civil aviation in 1930 occured when the populace took Amy Johnson to their hearts. It was because the first and most famous long-distance flight by Amy, a typist from Hull, was her solo trip to Australia in May. She had taken up flying in her spare time and had later given up her office job. She then borrowed £600 from her father for a second-hand de Havilland Gipsy Moth *Jason's Quest*, and calmly announced that she was going to try and fly to Australia and beat the existing solo record for the flight, Bert Hinkler's fifteen and a half days. At the age of only 22, Amy was not only a qualified pilot, but also the only woman to hold an Air Ministry licence as a ground engineer. Amy became the first woman to fly alone to Australia, and her time of 20 days for the 9,960 mile (16,029km) flight to Darwin was made in spite of two forced landings and an ignition fault corrected at Sourabaya.

The 1930s are commonly referred to as the 'Golden Age of Aviation', but this was not entirely the case, as many manufacturers scraped by on small government contracts. There was insufficient finance available for adequate research and development, or the re-equipment of military air forces. Airlines were beginning to expand and they sought larger and faster airliners which offered improved comfort and safety. This requirement was met by manufacturers such as Fokker, Farman, Handley Page, Curtiss, Junkers and Ford. Advanced all-metal aircraft were beginning to emerge from Boeing, Douglas, Lockheed and Northrop.

These new aircraft required more powerful piston engines with improved reliability. A higher standard of instrumentation was demanded. From 1930, the dated wood-and-fabric biplane slowly gave way to the monoplane, and during the year new military monoplanes began to emerge, such as the Douglas Y1B-7 for the USAAC and Fairey Hendon for the RAF.

The Handley Page HP42 *Hannibal* four-engined biplane airliner for the Empire routes made its first flight in November, and eight were ordered for Imperial Airways. They set new standards in passenger comforts, but were cumbersome and slow (cruising at only 100mph) and only carried 24 passengers. The HP45 Heracles class, having different engines, was used on the European routes and could accommodate 38 passengers.

The principal American aircraft manufacturers were in the vanguard with retractable undercarriages. The Lockheed Model 8D Altair of 1930 had a retractable landing gear and the Grumman FF-1 fighter's wheels retracted into the fuselage side. Stinson was remembered for its series of single-engined high-wing monoplanes, but the company also built a number of three-engined transport aircraft. The SM-6000 arrived in 1930, followed by the Model U two years later.

A patent for a new kind of aircraft engine was filed by Flying Officer Frank Whittle, a serving junior officer in the RAF, who believed that aircraft could be powered by a 'turbojet'. His gas turbine created a propulsive jet of hot gas, enabling aircraft to fly higher and faster. However, he received no interest or support to develop his idea.

The worst disaster in the history of British aviation occurred on 5 October when the Government-built airship R101 crashed in northern France with the loss of 48 passengers whilst bound for Egypt and India.

---

**1 Feb:** First operation of San Francisco's first air ferry service using Loening amphibians (before the building of the Golden Gate bridge)

**29 Apr:** Russia's Polikarpov VT-11 (I-5) biplane fighter first flew, the latest fighter so far developed for the Soviet Air Force.

**1 May:** Northrop flew an experimental aircraft of 35ft wingspan to test the theory that in the future aircraft would have no tails and no fuselages, but would just be composed of a 'flying wing'.

**4 May:** The Espenlaub/Sohldenhoff E15, a German rocket-powered tailless glider made its first flight.

**6 May:** The Boeing Model 200 Monomail made its maiden flight. A mail and cargo aircraft it had a cantilever low wing and a retractable undercarriage.

**15 May:** United Airlines became the first airline to introduce female flight attendants, all in white, on its passenger flights.

**18 May:** LZ 127 *Graf Zeppelin* made its first South Atlantic crossing.

**May:** Initial flight of the Northrop Alpha, an important aircraft

because it set the pattern for the modern all-metal stressed-skin low-wing cantilever transport monoplane.

**12 Jun:** First flight of the Handley Page HP38 Heyford, which was the last biplane bomber to enter RAF service. It remained in squadron service for the remainder of the 30s.

**24 Jul:** The American Research Laboratory succeeded in tracing the position of aircraft in flight by using wireless detection equipment.

**3 Sep:** The French Breguet 19 *Question Mark* made the first direct flight non-stop east/west crossing of the Atlantic.

**10 Sep:** The Taylor E2 light aircraft made its first flight.

**24 Sep:** The first Short Rangoon patrol flying-boat was flown. Many went on to see service in the Persian Gulf, and were widely used on anti-smuggling duties.

**13 Oct:** The prototype Junkers Ju 52 single-engined transport made its maiden flight. It was subsequently developed into the three-engined Ju 52/3m.

**25 Oct:** TWA inaugurated all-air coast-to-coast service with

simultaneous departures from Newark, NJ and Los Angeles, including a 12 hour stop over in Kansas City.

**14 Nov:** The Handley Page HP42 made its first flight. A large unequal span biplane of metal construction, its engines were arranged two on the upper centre section and two on the lower wings.

**20 Nov:** France's Dewoitine D33 single-engine long-range monoplane made its maiden flight.

**25 Nov:** First flight of the Fairey Hendon, the RAF's first monoplane heavy bomber, which saw only limited service with one squadron.

**22 Dec:** At the time the world's largest aircraft, the Tupolev ANT-6 heavy bomber made its first flight. Many became unarmed G-2 paratroop transports.

*This specially commissioned painting by Keith Woodcock features the de Havilland DH60G Gipsy Moth* Jason *flown by Amy Johnson, the first woman to fly solo from England to Australia in 1930.*

These pages generously donated by the Western Daily Press

*Amy Johnson – Moth to Australia* by Keith Woodcock GAvA, ASAA, GMA

In another year of great feats of record-breaking and endeavour, perhaps the most significant event took place at Stag Lane aerodrome in Edgware, north London, on 26 October when the first de Havilland DH82 Tiger Moth made its maiden flight – and in so doing marked the start of a long and illustrious career for this most famous member of the Moth family. The design was a development of the DH60 Moth series, featuring staggered, slightly swept-back wings and an inverted engine as the most prominent external changes. Tiger Moth Is, which entered service with the RAF Central Flying School in February 1932, were equipped with the DH Gipsy III powerplant which delivered 120hp (89kW), but this was quickly supplanted by the DH82A Tiger Moth II which utilised the 130hp (96kW) Gipsy Major, which was to become the standard production variant. The type gave sterling service with the RAF's Elementary and Reserve Flying Training Schools before and during WWII, was a mainstay of the British Commonwealth Air Training Plan, and continued in the RAF inventory until 1951.

They were also used by the University Air Squadrons and the Volunteer Reserve. Tiger Moths were sold to numerous overseas air arms, and went on to become almost standard equipment for early post-war British civil flying clubs. By the end of production in 1945, some 4,668 Tiger Moths had been built in Britain for the RAF, with an additional 2,751 produced in Canada, Australia and New Zealand.

Other de Havilland-built light aircraft were much in the news during 1931, including the DH60G Gipsy Moth of Jim Mollison, which set a new record time for a flight between Australia and England in either direction (including the longest flight ever made in a single 24-hour period by a light aircraft of some 1,730 miles (2,784km)) and Bert Hinkler's DH80A Puss Moth, which flew the South Atlantic. The full potential of such small sporting and touring aircraft was now clearly being explored.

So too were the wider possibilities for ever longer-distance air travel, as demonstrated by the likes of Wiley Post, who (in spite of only having one eye) easily beat the previous record for a circumnavigation of the world by undertaking this feat in only eight days, 15 hours and 51minutes, flying his Lockheed Vega 5B *Winnie Mae*. Many other significant route-proving flights were carried out, new commercial aircraft (such as the Handley Page HP42) entered service and new carriers such as Swissair and United Airlines were established.

Great Britain won the Schneider Trophy outright, having won three competitions in a row, the latest victory being achieved by Flt Lt J. N. Boothman.

---

**6 Jan:** Start of the famous trans-Atlantic flight of twelve Savoia Marchetti S.55 flying-boats between Portuguese Guinea and Natal, Brazil, under the command of the Italian aviation minister Gen Italo Balbo.

**28 Feb:** Imperial Airways inaugurated the first commercial service from England to Central Africa, carrying passengers from Croydon to Khartoum.

**25 Mar:** First flight of the RAF's Hawker Fury single-seat biplane fighter.

**26 Mar:** Founding of Swissair (Schweizerische Luftverkehr AG), which subsequently became Switzerland's national airline.

**Apr:** The prototype three-engined Junkers Ju 52/3m transport aircraft made its first flight in Germany.

**1-9 Apr:** C.W.Scott made a solo flight from Lympne, England to Darwin, Australia in a DH Moth.

**1 Jul:** End of Wiley Post and Harold Gatty's circumnavigation of the globe in their Lockheed Vega 5B *Winnie Mae*, which beat the previous record time for this flight that had been set by the *Graf Zeppelin* airship.

**1 Jul:** Establishment of United Airlines.

**27 Jul:** Charles Lindbergh, together with his wife Anne, departed the USA in a specially-built Lockheed Sirius high-performance monoplane for a proving flight to China, which was completed on 2 October.

**28 Jul-6 Aug:** Amy Johnson flew in a DH 80A Puss Moth from England to Tokyo, Japan in under nine days.

**6 Aug:** Jim Mollison set a new record (eight days, 19hr 25min) for flying between Australia and England, completing the flight in his DH60G Gipsy Moth.

**14 Aug:** Maiden flight of the Tupolev ANT-14 passenger transport in Russia, at the time the world's largest landplane with a length of 86ft 11in and a wingspan of 132ft 6in.

**13 Sep:** Great Britain won the Schneider Trophy outright, thanks to the unopposed victory of Flt Lt John Boothman flying the RAF High Speed Flight's Supermarine S6B.

**29 Sep:** Flt Lt G. H. Stainforth set a new world speed record, and the first of over 400mph (644km/h), in the Supermarine S.6B at 406mph (655km/h) at Ryde, Isle of Wight.

**26 Oct:** The DH82 Tiger Moth made its first flight from de Havilland's Stag Lane factory airfield.

**27 Oct:** The US Navy's new airship *Akron* entered service, and began 'hooking-up' trials with Curtiss XF9C-1 Sparrowhawk scout fighters specially designed for the purpose.

**28 Oct:** The RAF's second Fairey Long-Range Monoplane completed a 2,857-mile (4,600km) proving flight between RAF Cranwell in the UK and Abu Sueir, Egypt, in some 31 hours.

**9 Nov:** Inaugural operational flight of Imperial Airways' Handley Page HP42W biplane, *Hanno* departing from its Croydon base for Cairo.

**9 Nov:** C. A. Butler finished an epic flight (of some nine days) in a modified Comper Swift light sporting monoplane from Lympne, England to Darwin in Australia.

**14 Nov:** The Sikorsky S-40 amphibious flying-boat entered service with Pan American Airways.

**26 Nov:** The first solo flight across the South Atlantic, and the first to be undertaken west to east, was completed by Bert Hinkler in a DH80A Puss Moth.

**29 Dec:** First flight of the Grumman XFF-1, the initial prototype of a new two-seat US Navy fleet fighter. As the FF-1, which entered service in 1932, it was to start a long association between the company and the USN.

*Roger H Middlebrook's painting shows the Supermarine S6B seaplane powered by a Rolls-Royce 'R' engine in which Flight Lieutenant J N Boothman RAF won the Schneider Trophy outright on 12 September 1931.*

*Outright Winner* by Roger H Middlebrook GAvA, FSAI

By 1932, large civil aircraft accounted for over a quarter of the American market by value. During the year Germany, Japan, the UK, USA and USSR built a total of 4,360 military aircraft (in 1939 this total was to be 33,279). However, in 1932 the world's air forces were still largely equipped with fabric-covered biplanes.

In the previous year, a TWA Fokker FXA airliner crashed in Kansas, killing the whole of a well-known football team. On examination of the remains it was discovered that the plywood used in the wings had delaminated and split into layers. In 1932, TWA elected to replace its Fokkers with new airliners, and sent out a list of specifications for all-metal aircraft to several manufacturers. Douglas responded with the DC-1, the progenitor of perhaps the most successful airliner of all time, the DC-3. The new Douglas represented a quantum leap forward from the previous generation of airliners such as the Fokker and Ford Tri-Motor. The DC-1 incorporated many of the technologies of the day, including metal skin monocoque construction and internally braced monoplane wings instead of external bracing. The new NACA cowlings reduced the drag of the engine by almost completely enclosing it. The introduction of wing flaps made it possible to increase cruising speed without changing the landing speed. Two-pitch propellers, and later, variable-pitch metal propellers, were being introduced.

Jim Mollison, in his silver de Havilland Puss Moth *The Heart's Content* made the epic east-west Atlantic crossing in August. Mollison had married Amy Johnson shortly before the flight and she was there to see him off on the 18th. He carried no wireless and reckoned his fuel would last for a maximum of 32 hours, but possible headwinds were a problem. The Gipsy III engine, of lower power than any which had previously attempted the ocean flight, was being tested just as severely as Mollison. When he encountered the Newfoundland fog-belt, he prepared to divert to Halifax, Nova Scotia. Only ten gallons of fuel remained of the 152 taken onboard, and after 30hr 15mins he landed at Pennfield Ridge, New Brunswick.

The year saw Japan begin to pursue overtly aggressive expansion policies in China. With the last deliveries of biplane fighters to the USAAC in 1932, came the flight of a revolutionary new bomber, the twin-engined Martin 123, which featured internal bomb storage and an enclosed front gun turret. All the crew were enclosed under transparent canopies. The new US Army fighter of the year was the Boeing P-26A Peashooter, a low-wing monoplane but its wings still had external wire bracing and featured a fixed undercarriage with pronounced 'trousers' to reduce drag. The Northrop Gamma 2A was launched in 1932, a streamlined aircraft with a NACA-style cowl. It had a remarkable speed range and set many point-to-point speed records, being able to achieve 190mph on 450hp.

Former Schneider pilot Jimmy Doolittle captured the world landplane speed record in the Gee Bee Super Sportster, at 294.4mph – the aircraft being little more than an engine with a minute monoplane fixed behind it. During March, the *Graf Zeppelin* began revenue services between Germany and Brazil (Recife) and later to Rio de Janeiro. In May, Swissair introduced the Lockheed Model 9 Orion on its Zurich-Munich-Vienna service. This new aircraft, which had first flown the previous year, was a low-wing six-passenger aircraft.

---

**16 Jan:** A DH80A Puss Moth, flown by Wg Cdr R. H. McIntosh, completed a journey around Africa and accomplished the first flight over the Sahara desert in a light plane.

**23-26 Mar:** A Blériot 110 set a world distance record in a closed circuit at Oran in Algeria, achieving 6,587 miles (10,601km).

**24-28 Mar:** Jim Mollison, in a DH80 Puss Moth set a new record flying from Lympne, Kent to Cape Town in four days, 17 hours and 19 minutes.

**27 Apr:** Imperial Airways inaugurated the first passenger service between Croydon and Cape Town. The final leg of the route was flown by a DH66.

**1 May:** The General Aircraft Monospar ST4 first flew, a four-seat twin-engined monoplane with Pobjoy Niagara engines. It was the first aircraft to go into production with the 'Monospar' wing designed by H. J. Steiger in the 1920s. This was a cantilever metal-structured wing which combined adequate strength with acceptably low weight, and the main wing panels could fold aft.

**9 May:** At Dayton, Ohio a Consolidated NY-2 biplane trainer made the first blind solo flight, entirely on instruments.

**20 May:** Amelia Earhart, flying a Lockheed Vega monoplane, became the first woman to fly solo across the North Atlantic. Leaving Harbor Grace in Newfoundland, she landed at Londonderry in Northern Ireland.

**29 Jun:** The parasite fighter Curtiss F9C-2 hooked on to USS *Akron*, using the specially designed 'skyhook'.

**6 Jul:** First flight of the Armstrong Whitworth Atalanta, a four-engined airliner built for Imperial Airways to operate over the southern section of its planned route to South Africa.

**14-23 Aug:** In America, a woman's flight-refuelled endurance record of eight days, four hours and five minutes was achieved.

**16 Sep:** Bristol Aeroplane Company's chief test pilot, Cyril F. Uwins, achieved a new world altitude record in a Vickers Type 210 Vespa Mk VI, when he reached 43,976ft.

**25 Sep:** A Pitcairn PCA-2 autogyro established a world autogyro altitude record of 21,500ft at Boston, MA.

**14-18 Nov:** Amy Johnson in DH80A Puss Moth *Desert Cloud* established a new solo record from England to Cape Town in four days, six hours and 54 minutes. Her return journey the following month also set a record time of seven days, seven hours and five minutes.

**19 Nov:** A national monument was unveiled at the site of the famous flight on 17 December 1903 by Orville and Wilbur Wright at Kitty Hawk, North Carolina, dedicated to their momentous achievement of manned powered flight.

**4 Dec:** The Beech Model 17 Staggerwing made its first flight. It was capable of 200mph and remained in production until 1948.

**11 Dec:** First flight of the Heinkel He 70, created to meet Luft Hansa's requirement for a fast aircraft to match the Lockheed Orion. However, single-engined aircraft did not prove entirely suitable for scheduled airline operations in Europe.

*A majestic Handley Page HP42 landing at Croydon Airport during fading light, with the impressive terminal building in the background, is captured in Douglas A Swallow's painting.*

*Evening Arrival* by Douglas A Swallow GAvA

From early 1933, Imperial Airways introduced the Armstrong Whitworth AW15 Atalanta on the Africa routes and the routes east of Karachi, until the routes were subsequently taken over by 'C' Class flying-boats. This was the first mainline monoplane to be operated by a British national airline.

Boeing produced the first modern airliner when the Model 247 first flew on 8 February and entered airline service later in the year. A very clean, all-metal, low-wing cantilever monoplane it had two radial engines and retractable landing gear, and carried ten passengers. It proved up to 70mph faster than contemporary airliners in the US. The 247 cut the coast-to-coast flying time from the 'normal' 26 hours to under 20 hours. Being so advanced, it virtually made obsolete all other existing types.

The Douglas DC-1 first flew on 1 July, to meet a TWA specification. It had outstanding performance and was to prove a very significant aircraft, eventually going into production as the DC-2, having a fuselage stretch of two feet and seating for 14 passengers.

The French Wibault airliner went into service with CIDNA on its Paris-Istanbul route. It was soon introduced on the Paris-London route as the *Golden Clipper* and was used on Air France's main European routes until 1938. Dewoitine also introduced a three-engined, all metal low-wing monoplane airliner.

In April, the Airspeed AS5 Courier made its first flight. A single-engined five-passenger aircraft, it was the first British transport aircraft with a retractable undercarriage. Only a few were built, but it led to the development of the six-seat twin-engined Envoy.

Jim Mollison still hankered after the non-stop flight from London to New York and saw the de Havilland Dragon twin-engined aircraft, capable of seating ten passengers, as suitable for the venture. In August, Jim and Amy christened their new plane *Seafarer* and together they set off from Pendine Sands, South Wales, which gave a seven-mile expanse of firm sand for the overweight take-off. Forty hours later, without any sleep and fighting persistent headwinds, they were only 20 minutes short of New York when they ran out of fuel. Fortunately they were able to glide towards Bridgeport aerodrome, but landed short in a swamp adjoining the airfield. The Dragon somersaulted and spreadeagled into a wreck. But they had proved their point.

For many years, airmen had dreamed of looking down on Mount Everest, but until this year there had been no aircraft engine capable of carrying the necessary load to a height of some six miles above sea level. The new Bristol Pegasus nine-cylinder radial engine was a definite advance, and was light for its power output. Two aircraft were chosen for the task, Westland PV-3s, subsequently called the Wallace. Despite the extremely low temperatures forecast over Everest, the crews opted for open cockpits with windshields. Wearing electrically-heated clothing and having the benefit of oxygen, the two Westlands took-off in the early morning of 3 April. After reaching the summit, and making a circuit or two to take photographs, they landed back at Purnea after a 3½ hour flight.

**2 Jan:** Orville Wright was awarded the US Institute of Aeronautical Science's first Honorary Fellowship.

**6-8 Feb:** The Fairey Long-Range Monoplane Mk II flew from RAF Cranwell, Lincolnshire to Walvis Bay in southwest Africa. It established a new world distance record of 5,309 miles (8,544km), covered in a flight time of 57 hours 25 minutes.

**6-9 Feb:** Jim Mollison became the first pilot to achieve an England-South America solo flight, the first to fly the South Atlantic solo east-west and the first to have made solo flights across both the North Atlantic and South Atlantic. His aircraft was a Puss Moth named *The Heart's Content*.

**14 Feb:** First flight of the Short S16 Scion, aimed at the market for a five-passenger light transport. Powered by two small 80hp Pobjoy R radial engines. Some saw airline duties in the UK, whilst others went to Australia.

**Mar:** A forty-passenger Sikorsky S40 amphibian began a circular proving flight over the Atlantic as part of preparation for a trans-Pacific air service with PanAm.

**4 Apr:** The US Navy's USS *Akron* dirigible airship crashed into the sea during a violent storm off the New Jersey coast. Seventy three personnel were lost, including the Chief of the USN's Bureau of Aeronautics.

**29 May:** Armstrong Whitworth Atalantas began operating between Karachi and Calcutta, followed by Rangoon and Singapore by the end of the year.

**May:** First flight of the Northrop Delta, a larger fuselaged version of the Gamma. Most were delivered to private owners following constraints on the use of single-engined aircraft for passenger flight operations at night.

**1 Jul:** First flight of the Curtiss XF12C-1, a parasol monoplane, that was the first US Navy fighter to have folding wings, thereby saving valuable space on aircraft carriers.

**15-22 Jul:** Wiley Post in the Lockheed Vega *Winnie Mae* completed the first solo round-the-world flight from New York. His route covered a distance of 15,596 miles (25,099km).

**5-7 Aug:** The Blériot 110 Joseph le Brix flew from New York to Rasyak in Syria, and established a new world distance record of 5,657 miles (9,104km).

**4-11 Oct:** Sir Charles Kingsford Smith flew his Percival Gull Four *Miss Southern Cross* from Lympne, Kent to Western Australia in a new record time of seven days, four hours and 44 minutes.

**15 Oct:** The prototype Rolls-Royce PV-12 Merlin liquid-cooled engine ran for the first time. It became the UK's most important powerplant in WWII, powering both fighters and bombers.

**31 Oct:** Formation of Air France, created out of the merger of several small pioneering airline companies.

**4 Nov:** The Brazilian Airline VASP was formed.

**1 Dec:** Inauguration of Indian National Airways. DH84 Dragons opened up the first daily air service in India carrying airmail, freight and passengers between Calcutta and Dacca.

**31 Dec:** The Polikarpov TsKB-12 (I-16), the first monoplane fighter to feature an enclosed cockpit and fully retractable undercarriage, was flown.

*Vickers Victoria troop-carriers, which served with the RAF in the Middle East, are shown here in Ian Wilson-Dick's painting, flying Over the Citadel, Cairo.*

*Over the Citadel, Cairo* by Ian Wilson-Dick GAvA

In Germany during 1934, Wilhelm 'Willy' Messerschmitt and Walter Rethel first laid down the angular lines of the Messerschmitt Bf 109 fighter, hoping to cram a 'huge' engine of nearly 700hp into the smallest airframe possible. It was still in production 11 years later with a 1,800hp engine, and a total of 33,000 was to be built.

In Britain, two epic designs were created, both essentially in advance of official specification. Sidney Camm broke his design team away from a long series of beautiful biplane fighters to fashion the Hawker Hurricane, which, with the exception of its tubular metal construction and fabric covering, incorporated all the advances of its Messerschmitt counterpart. At Supermarine, Reginald J. Mitchell took the same 1,000hp Rolls-Royce Merlin that the Hurricane used, and built the eight-gun Spitfire around it.

On the civil side, the great era of British flying-boats began this year, when the Empire Air Mail Programme was announced, Short Bros received orders for 28 'C' Class Empire flying-boats. The Douglas DC-2 began US transcontinental services, to an 18-hour schedule in May. The new type was widely adopted by US airlines and was soon acquired in Europe by KLM and Swissair.

In February, Lockheed flew its Model 10 Electra, the first of its series of modern all-metal twin-engined transports. With accommodation for ten passengers, it was powered by 450hp Pratt & Whitney Wasp Junior radials. During October, the USA, having already banned wooden airliners, banned the carriage of passengers in single-engined aircraft at night or over hazardous terrain. This gave added impetus to sales of the DC-2 and Electra.

Designers had attempted to solve the problem of external radiators, which caused considerable drag. In 1934, the RAE produced a radiator in a duct to act as a type of 'ram jet' to offset the large proportion of duct drag. NACA had developed a family of related aerofoils with mathematically defined thickness forms and camber lines and created a matrix of consistent data. This data, a 'designers bible', was published and the 'four digit' aerofoils it described became instantly popular. Also in 1934, NACA designed a tricycle landing gear and hydraulics were beginning to be used for undercarriage retraction.

The England-Australia air race was made possible by generous prizes offered by Sir MacPherson Robertson. The total distance was 11,333 miles and to win the race, crews had to be prepared to fly at night for as much of the way as they could. The route to be taken was Mildenhall-Baghdad-Allalabad-Singapore-Darwin-Melbourne. Twenty aircraft lined up for the start on 20 October. The race was won by DH88 Comet *Grosvenor House*, flown by Scott and Black, in two days, 22 hours and 59 minutes. One of the most fascinating facts of the race was that new KLM DC-2 *Uiver*, which was actually carrying three paying passengers and airmail, came second (first on handicap).

Experiments with in-flight refuelling in the UK had begun in the early 1930s, and in 1934 trials were undertaken using the prototype Airspeed AS5 Courier and one of Sir Alan Cobham's Handley Page W10s. Experiments continued and a practical system was developed.

---

**14 Jan:** First flight of the de Havilland DH86 Express, successfully developed as a simple economic ten-passenger wood and fabric biplane with four engines. Many went to QANTAS Empire Airways for the Singapore-Darwin-Brisbane-Sydney route.

**17 Feb:** The first airmail service between New Zealand and Australia was undertaken by the Avro Ten *Faith* in Australia, the crossing of the Tasman Sea taking just on 14 hours.

**19 Feb:** The USAAC began flying commercial airmail routes after the Roosevelt Administration cancelled all civil contracts. The pilots were poorly trained and ill-equipped to cope with instrument flying in severe winter conditions. A number of pilot fatalities occurred before the scheme ended in May.

**23 Feb:** The Lockheed L10 Electra made its first flight. Of all-metal construction with monocoque fuselage and metal skinned wings, it carried two pilots and ten passengers and went into service with Northwest Airlines in August.

**26 Mar:** The Short Scylla made its maiden flight. Imperial Airways was short of aircraft on its European routes and the Scylla was basically a landplane version of the Short S.17 Kent flying-boat.

It was used on the London-Paris service.

**17 Apr:** First flight of the DH89 Dragon Rapide. It had finely tapered wings and streamlined undercarriage housing.

**17 Apr:** The prototype of the Fairey TSR2, better known as the Swordfish, made its first flight.

**8-23 May:** Jean Batten, flying a DH60M Moth, achieved a new women's solo flight from England to Australia in 14 days, 22 hours and 30 minutes.

**15 May:** Luft Hansa introduced the Heinkel He 70, a single-engined monoplane with streamlined form, on services between major German cities. It was built to meet competition from the Lockheed Orion.

**30 May:** First flight of the Sikorsky S42 four-engined flying-boat. It broke with the Sikorsky tradition in having a full-length two-step all-metal hull, with the strut-braced wing mounted above the hull on a shallow superstructure.

**26 Jun:** Maiden flight of the Airspeed AS6 Envoy twin-engined monoplane developed from the Courier. A total of 62 was built with a variety of engines, and it was the first British aircraft with a retractable undercarriage to go into production.

**12 Sep:** First flight of the Gloster Gladiator, the RAF's last biplane fighter to enter squadron service.

**23 Oct:** A new world speed record was set by a Macchi MC72 racing seaplane in Italy, achieving 440mph (709km/h).

**16 Nov:** First flight of the Savoia-Marchetti S74 three-engined airliner, particularly suited for trans-alpine flights.

**Nov:** The Junkers Ju 86 made its first flight. It was the first passenger aircraft designed for heavy oil (diesel) engines.

**30 Dec:** First flight of the Martin 130, a large strut-braced metal flying-boat with four engines. It was one of the first flying-boats to feature sponsons, or sea wings, instead of wingtip floats. The Martin Clippers made it possible for Pan Am to commence air services from America to China.

*John Young's painting shows de Havilland's famous winning DH88 Comet Racer* Grosvenor House, *one of three built specifically for the MacPherson Robertson race from Mildenhall, England to Melbourne, Australia in October 1934.*

*Winner, Mildenhall to Melbourne* by John Young VPGAvA, VPASAA

# 1935

Long over-water flights over the Pacific became a reality in 1935. Amelia Earhart became the first woman to make a solo flight from Honolulu to California in a Lockheed Vega with a Pratt & Whitney Wasp engine, in a flight time of 18 hours 15 minutes over the distance of 2,408 miles. This route that had cost many airmen their lives. The flying-boat was proving to have a significant advantage over the landplane for long distances. In April, a Pan American Airways System Sikorsky S-42 *Oriental Clipper* completed a proving flight from Alameda, California to Hawaii, the first stage in a trans-Pacific route from the US to the Philippines, and the start of a boom in flying boats. During November, Pan Am operated the first scheduled trans-Pacific airmail service, flying the Martin M130 *China Clipper* from San Francisco to Manila in the Philippines via Honolulu, Midway Island, Wake Island and Guam.

On 17 December the prototype Douglas DST (Douglas Sleeper Transport) made its first flight at Santa Monica. The DC-3, a direct development of the DC-2, was one of the most important transport aircraft ever built. The type probably did more than any other to establish air transport as a normal means of transport and to open up communications in remote areas. The aircraft initially appeared in two versions, the DST with 14 berths, and the DC-3 (day plane) with 21 seats. It was the basis for the growth of airlines all over the world, and became the first transport aircraft capable of making a profit without a subsidy. The DC-3 inspired imitations everywhere. Russia and Japan simply cloned the DC-3, and

companies in France (the Bloch 220) and Italy (the Fiat G18V) copied its lines very closely.

From 11-13 November, Jean Batten in her Percival Gull Six *Jean* (the Gull having made its first flight on 14 March) became the first woman to complete a solo flight across the South Atlantic. She flew from Lympne, Kent to Natal, Brazil via Senegal in a flight time of two days, 13 hours and 15 minutes.

In May, blind-landing radio equipment, developed by a USAAC team, was installed at all major airports between New York and Los Angeles. A group of British research scientists carried out a successful experiment with radio direction finding equipment. Secretly tested in a Hawker Hart, it enabled aircraft in flight to be traced on a cathode-ray tube, where aircraft were mirrored as 'blips'. A Lorenz blind-landing system was installed at Croydon Airport.

Britain caught up with the monoplane fighter trend when the Hawker Hurricane, powered with the new Rolls-Royce PV-13 engine, made its maiden flight on 6 November. This brought Britain up to date with the latest designs, followed by the USSR with the Polikarpov I-16; the USA with the Boeing P-26 and Curtiss-Wright 75; France with the Morane-Saulnier MS405 and Germany with the Messerschmitt Bf 109.

During this vintage time, in patriotic zeal, Britain's Lord Rothermere demanded a high-speed six-seat passenger transport, the Bristol Type 142. This flew on 12 April and he named it *Britain First*. When it outperformed contemporary RAF front-line fighters, Rothermere donated the design to the country and it became the basis for the Bristol Blenheim bomber.

---

**5 Jan:** A radio-controlled target version of the DH82A Tiger Moth, known as the Queen Bee, first flew. A total of 380 was built for the RAF.

**14 Jan:** United Airlines became the first airline to equip its fleet with a de-icing system for aircraft wings, following successful tests on a Boeing 247.

**29 Jan:** A Sikorsky S-39 amphibian established a world altitude record of 18,642ft flying from Miami, FL.

**24 Feb:** The Heinkel He 111a, ostensibly a civil airliner, but in reality intended as a bomber for the still secret Luftwaffe, made its first flight.

**27 Feb:** Latécoère's grand seaplane Santos-Dumont made a record mail flight from Natal to Brazil (with two stops en route) of 53 hours 4 mins.

**22 Mar:** First flight of the Grumman XF3F-1 naval fighter, dubbed 'the Flying Barrel' because of its portly fuselage.

**24 Mar:** The prototype Avro Type 652A flew for the first time. It was built to meet an Air Ministry requirement for a twin-engined coastal patrol landplane. This military version of Imperial Airways'

airliner later became known as the Anson.

**1 Apr:** Swissair inaugurated a regular service from Zurich to Croydon, operated by DC-2s.

**12 Apr:** A through passenger air service, between Brisbane, Australia and London, commenced with QANTAS Empire Airways flying the initial stages. The trip took $12^1/_2$ days.

**1 May:** The Gloster Gauntlet, the last of the open-cockpit fighter biplanes to serve in the RAF, entered service with No 19 Squadron at RAF Duxford.

**9 May:** The German Government announced the establishment of a new national air force, the Luftwaffe.

**28 May:** Perhaps the most important type to make its début in 1935 was the Messerschmitt Bf 109V1 fighter, powered by a Rolls-Royce Kestrel. More than 33,000 Bf 109s were subsequently produced over the next ten years.

**29 Jun:** Consolidated Aircraft Corp was awarded a contract of $6m by the US Government for 60 PBY-1 (subsequently called Catalina) flying boats. This was the largest official order for aircraft since the end of WWI.

**Aug:** Prototype Seversky 1XP made its maiden flight, the first US monoplane fighter with an enclosed cockpit and retractable undercarriage.

**8 Aug:** Morane-Saulnier MS405 fighter made its first flight, numerically the most important French fighter when war broke out in autumn 1939.

**17 Sep:** Junkers Ju 87 Stuka dive-bomber made its first flight, Germany's deadliest weapon in the early stages of WWII.

**29 Oct:** British Airways, to complement Imperial Airways, was created by the amalgamation of Hillman, Spartan and United Airways.

**18 Nov:** British Air Forces in the Middle East were strengthened by the transfer of 12 squadrons from the UK. They were brought to a state of heightened readiness following Italian aggression in Ethiopia.

*An American Airlines DC-3, one of a number flown by the airline before the war, outbound from La Guardia Airport. Robert Watts pictures it over Manhattan, New York.*

*Flagship over Manhattan* by Robert Watts

On the record front, Amy Mollison, flying a Percival Gull Six, set a new record of three days six hours and 26 minutes in May, for a flight from England to Cape Town, when she followed a new route down the west coast of Africa. The German airship *Hindenburg* made a round trip from Germany to New Jersey, also in May. This, and its sister the *Graf Zeppelin II*, were the last two rigid airships to be built.

In October, Imperial Airways introduced its Short S23 'C' Class flying-boat into service on the route between Alexandra, Egypt and Brindisi in Italy. *Canopus* was the first of a fleet of 28 on order. During March, it had inaugurated a weekly London-Hong Kong air service. Imperial Airways made the first scheduled flight between Hong Kong and Penang, Malaysia (via Saigon) on 23 March, using a de Havilland DH86A.

Jean Batten made her longest solo flight, to her home in New Zealand. Leaving Lympne, Kent on 5 October, she took 11 days and 56 minutes to reach Auckland, thereby achieving the first direct flight from England to New Zealand, and becoming the first woman to fly the Tasman Sea. This brought Britain into direct air contact with its furthermost dominion. Beryl Markham, a South African, flew Percival Vega Gull *The Messenger* from England to achieve the first east-west solo transatlantic flight by a woman pilot.

On the light aircraft scene, the Taylor Brothers Aircraft Manufacturing Co introduced the Taylor Cub monoplane in the US, the boast of the firm being: "So easy, even a child could fly it". A simple and easy to maintain aircraft, it became a success in the marketplace.

Aeronca, Porterfield and Rearwin soon followed with similar designs. In August, the diminutive French Pou du Ciel (Flying Flea) was designed by Henri Mignet, and is regarded as the first aircraft intended for amateur construction.

The Spanish Civil War presented an unrivalled opportunity for Germany, Italy and the Soviet Union to test their military aircraft and tactical theories about air power in combat. Olley Air Services, a British airline, flew a secret mission to transport Spanish rebel leader General Franco from the Canary Islands back to Spain on 1 July. By August, the German government had sent six Heinkel He 51 fighters to support Franco and the Nationalists. A consignment of Soviet Polikarpov I-15 fighters were despatched by Stalin's government to support Republican forces in the Spanish Civil War. The war in Abyssinia (Ethiopia) was a victory for numerically inferior forces, who owed their success to the command of the air.

A grass aerodrome beside the London to Brighton railway was officially opened as Gatwick Airport, London's second airport. USAAC Major Ira C. Eaker (later General in WWII) flew entirely by instruments from New York to Los Angeles in a Boeing P-12.

The Supermarine Type 300 Spitfire prototype, designed by R. J. Mitchell and powered by a Rolls-Royce Merlin engine, made its maiden flight on 5 March. This classic single-seat fighter, more than 22,000 of which were built, saw front-line service throughout WWII. Featuring a stressed-skin construction, it had elliptical wings, which had a battery of eight machine guns clear of the propeller arc.

---

**1 Jan:** The US Army Air Corps signed a contract with Boeing Airplane Company for the delivery of 13 YB-17s.

**13 Feb:** Imperial Airways commenced an air mail service to West Africa. De Havilland DH86 *RMA Daedalus* flew from Khartoum, Sudan to Kano, Nigeria.

**17 Feb:** Ansett Airways commenced a Hamilton-Melbourne service in Australia with a Fokker Universal.

**2 Mar:** Frank Whittle, a serving RAF officer, set up Power Jets with a capital of £10,000, to develop a turbojet aircraft engine.

**3 Mar: The** British Government announced proposals for an increase from 1,500 to 1,750 front-line aircraft for home defence.

**4 Mar:** Zeppelin LZ129 *Hindenburg* made its maiden flight, the largest rigid airship in the world.

**14 Mar:** Imperial Airways opened a weekly service to Hong Kong.

**15 Apr:** Development of a turbojet engine began at the German Heinkel plant.

**Apr:** The Fieseler Fi 156 Storch (Stork) STOL aircraft made its first flight in Germany.

**6 May:** The London-Brisbane service was increased to a twice weekly service by Imperial Airways/QANTAS.

**12 May:** First flight of the Messerschmitt Bf 109 fighter.

**27 May:** Aer Lingus, the new Irish airline, inaugurated a service from Dublin to Bristol using a de Havilland DH84 Dragon.

**15 Jun:** The Vickers Wellington first flew. Its geodetic form of construction was developed by Barnes Wallis and it proved to be the best of all the RAF's bombers in the early years of WWII. Westland's Lysander, designed especially to meet the requirements of the Army co-operation squadrons of the RAF, also flew for the first time.

**21 Jun:** First flight of the Handley Page Hampden, which eventually equipped 15 squadrons of RAF Bomber Command.

**26 Jun:** The Focke-Wulf Fw 61 helicopter took to the air, with twin-rotors mounted on long outrigger struts. Development over the following year established it as the world's first successful helicopter.

**1 Jul:** Australian National Airways formed by the amalgamation of Holyman's Airways, Airlines of Australia, Adelaide Airways and West Australian Airways.

**10 Sep:** Luft Hansa commenced a series of experimental trans-Atlantic flights with a luxury Dornier Do 18 seaplane powered by twin Diesel engines.

**18 Sep:** American Airlines put the new Douglas DST on the continental route between New York and Los Angeles, the flying time between the two cities being 16 hours.

**27 Sep:** Pan Am *Hawaii Clipper* commenced regular passenger flights between the US and the Philippines.

**21 Dec:** The Junkers Ju 88V-1 made its first flight, becoming the most versatile twin-engined bomber operated by the Luftwaffe during WWII.

**27 Dec:** Maiden flight of the ANT-42 (TB-7) prototype, the only four-engined Soviet heavy bomber to see operational service during WWII.

*Edmund Miller's painting depicts the naming of a DH86 Express airliner of Hillmans Airways/British Airways Ltd by Lady Cunliffe-Lister, with Amy Johnson, Capt Geoffrey de Havilland and Edward Hillman and his son and daughter looking on, at Gatwick Airport.*

*Edward Hillman, Gatwick Airport 1936* by Edmund Miller DLC, CEng, MRAeS, GAvA

The flying-boat reached new heights of scheduled passenger operations when Imperial Airways commenced a non-stop service from Southampton to Egypt on 8 February using Short S23s. British Airways introduced the new Lockheed Electra ten-seat airliner into service, in April, on its London-Paris route and during May, Imperial Airways Handley Page HP42 *Heracles* made the airline's 40,000th cross-Channel flight. In June, Imperial Airways S23 flying-boat *Canopus* left Southampton to inaugurate the service to Durban, South Africa. The following month, Imperial Airways and Pan Am opened a joint service between Bermuda and New York with Sikorsky S-42 *Bermuda Clipper*. Survey flights were also made to Australia and New Zealand.

The last and most ambitious flight that Amelia Earhart attempted was to encircle the globe at the Equator. She set out with Capt Fred Noonan on this round-the-world challenge, but on 2 July their Lockheed Electra was lost in the Pacific Ocean between British New Guinea and Howland Island, in unknown circumstances.

The German airship *Hindenburg* was destroyed by fire after being struck by lightning, which caused a static discharge, whilst attempting to land at Lakehurst, NJ. The disaster brought to an end the development of commercial passenger-carrying airships.

On 13 April, unknown to the outside world, RAF officer Frank Whittle tested the new type of engine, the turbojet gas turbine, that he had invented seven years previously. Instead of driving a propeller shaft, it created a high-velocity jet of hot gas, and was the first successful jet engine.

In July, Californians realised they were a mere 6,306 miles away from Moscow, if an aircraft flew over the North Pole. This was achieved by a single-engined Tupolev ANT-25 monoplane, which had been airborne for an amazing two days 14 hours and 17 minutes, the first transpolar flight.

Luft Hansa undertook a remarkable series of seven experimental return flights between the Azores and New York prior to a proposed North Atlantic route which involved a four-engined Blohm und Voss Ha 139 seaplane catapulted from a depot ship on take-off, and hoisted back later. Imperial Airways undertook an experimental commercial crossing of the North Atlantic between Foynes, Ireland and Botwood, Newfoundland.

In July, after a long fight, the Royal Navy took control of the Fleet Air Arm from the RAF. The problem of manning all the new RAF squadrons and providing enough crews for the expanding service was a challenge. To meet this, the RAF Volunteer Reserve was created, drawing upon a new field of entrants. The idea was to train 800 pilots a year at new flying schools near the main centres of population. Called Elementary and Reserve Flying Schools they took over the elementary pilot training for the RAF on weekdays and provided the same facility for Volunteer Reservists at weekends.

Britain's aircraft production had nearly caught up with Germany's. 'Shadow' factories were set up throughout the country. Mostly run by motor manufacturers, production from these factories was initially slow, so Britain placed orders in the USA. These included 200 North American Harvard single-engined trainers and 200 Lockheed Hudsons.

---

**12 Jan:** 'C' Class flying-boat *Centaurus* made Imperial Airways' first all-air trans-Mediterrranean service, Alexandra to Southampton, on the final leg of the India-UK route.

**15 Jan:** First flight of the Beechcraft Model 18 all-metal, twin-engined monoplane.

**16 Jan:** First flight of the Liore et Olivier LeO 45 prototype, the only modern medium bomber in French service at the time of the German attack in 1940.

**7 Feb:** Britain's first dive bomber, the Blackburn Skua, made its first flight and became the first monoplane to enter Fleet Air Arm service.

**1 Mar:** The Second Bombardment Group of the USAAC at Langley Field received the first of its 13 YB-17A Flying Fortresses. It was the Corps' first four-engined, all-weather, long-range bomber.

**18 Feb:** Imperial Airways flying-boat *Caledonia* made a non-stop flight from Southampton to Alexandra (2,222miles/3,576km).

**5 Mar:** Imperial Airways opened a flying-boat base at Hythe on Southampton Water as the terminal for its Empire services.

**2 Apr:** The Swedish aircraft manufacturer Saab was established.

**5 Apr:** The Douglas Aircraft Corporation took over Northrop.

**5 Apr:** Lockheed Electras were introduced on the London-Paris route of British Airways.

**12 Apr:** The Whittle gas turbine was successfully bench tested for the first time.

**16 Apr:** Trans-Canada Airlines (TCA) was formed.

**9 Jun:** South African Airways inaugurated a Johannesburg-Lusaka service using Junkers Ju 52/3Ms.

**30 Jun:** The Bristol Type 138 recaptured the world altitude record for Britain and achieved a height of 53,937ft.

**7 Jul:** Japan initiated a full-scale invasion of China.

**27 Jul:** First flight of the Focke-Wulf Fw 200V-1 Condor, a 26-seat passenger aircraft for Luft Hansa, adapted by the Luftwaffe for shipping-patrols over the North Atlantic during WW2.

**9 Aug:** A London-Berlin night airmail service was inaugurated by British Airways and Luft Hansa.

**11 Aug:** The Boulton Paul Defiant made its first flight, the first two-seat fighter to be used in RAF service with a power-operated four-gun turret.

**22 Aug:** A Heinkel He 112, fitted with both piston and rocket motors, took off and made a flight on the power of the rocket motor only.

**16 Oct:** First flight of the Short Sunderland flying-boat, which the Germans called the 'Flying Porcupine' during WWII.

**18 Oct:** Jean Batten, flying her Gull Six *Jean*, established a new solo record flight time from Darwin, Australia to Lympne, Kent in five days, 18 hours and 15 mins.

**25 Oct:** A Focke-Wulf Fw 61, flown by Hanna Reitsch, established a world distance record for helicopters of 67.71 miles (109km).

*Roger H Middlebrook was the first winner of the newly established E J Riding Memorial Trophy in 2000 with his painting* The Glory Years. *It shows the first Imperial Airways Short C Class flying-boat* Canopus *en route over Africa.*

These pages generously donated by the Hymatic Engineering Company Limited

*The Glory Years* by Roger H Middlebrook GAvA, FSAI

Although Imperial Airways were heavily involved in flying-boat operations, it was taking steps to acquire a modern landplane fleet to assist with the Empire Air Mail Programme, and to cater for increased passenger traffic. It was decided to maintain a landplane route between the Middle East and India, using the Armstrong Whitworth AW27 four-engined high-wing monoplane. It was known as the Ensign class, and 14 were ordered. Britain was being forced to re-arm to meet the German threat, and priority had to be given to Armstrong Whitworth's Whitley bomber, so the first flight of the Ensign was not made until 24 January.

In-flight refuelling trials were made in January by Sir Alan Cobham's Flight Refuelling Ltd. This represented one of the approaches being made by Imperial Airways to establish regular mail/passenger services across the North Atlantic, when the 'C' class flying-boat *Cambria* was refuelled over Southampton Water by the loaned Armstrong Whitworth AW23 prototype.

Despite the rapidly deteriorating international situation of the middle to late 1930s, aircraft manufacturers and commercial airlines were becoming increasingly interested in the establishment of long-range intercontinental passenger/mail flights, particularly over such formidable barriers as the North Atlantic and Pacific Oceans. One of the ideas put forward was for a composite aircraft. Major Robert Mayo, the Technical General Manager of

Imperial Airways, proposed the use of two aircraft, the lower serving to lift its heavily laden upper component into the air before releasing it to continue its journey. Short Bros designed the S20 flying-boat *Maia* as the lower lifting component and the S21 floatplane *Mercury* as the long-distance element. On 6 February, the first in-flight separation was made and *Mercury* was released over Foynes. It was refuelled and flew on to Port Washington, New York.

The world's first pressurised airliner made its maiden flight in December, the Boeing 307 Stratoliner, developed from the B-17 Flying Fortress, with a new fuselage that provided accommodation for 33 passengers. It was able to cruise at 245mph at 20,000ft, well above turbulence and weather encountered by non-pressurised airliners.

A report on civil aviation progress in 1938 showed that British air services had flown 13,556,000 aircraft miles compared with 10,733,00 in 1937. The number of registered civil aircraft in the British Empire had increased from 3,179 to 3,260 during 1938.

Much publicity was received for the new Hawker Hurricane, just entering RAF service, when one flew from Edinburgh to London at an average speed of 408mph, albeit aided by a 50mph tailwind. The work of the RAF's Long Range Flight found fruit in the achievement of the two RAF Vickers Wellesleys which flew non-stop from Ismalia, Egypt to Darwin, Australia between 5-7 November, a distance of 7,158 miles (11,250km)

---

**1 Jan:** First flight of the Aichi D3A carrier-borne dive-bomber, subsequently known as the 'Val'.

**15 Feb:** Six YB-17s of the USAAC 2nd Bombardment Group left Langley Field on a goodwill mission to a number of South American countries.

**23 Feb:** Imperial Airways extended its Empire Air Mail service to India, Burma, Ceylon and Malaya.

**26 Mar:** DH88 Comet *Australian Anniversary* completed a 26,000 mile flight from England to New Zealand and back in a record ten days and 21 hours.

**27 Mar:** A German Luft Hansa flying-boat Dornier Do 18 was catapulted from a seaplane carrier off the Devon coast and flew 5,313 miles non-stop to Caravellas, Brazil in 43 hours 15 mins.

**1 Apr:** The US Navy's most modern combat aircraft, the Northrop BT-1 Devastator entered service. As a predecessor to the excellent SBD Dauntless the BT-1 helped scout-bomber squadrons gain tactical and technical experience, that was to prove decisive in the Pacific War in 1942.

**Jun:** A Heinkel He 118 served as a flying test bed for a turbojet engine, the Heinkel HeS.3.

**7 Jun:** First flight of the Boeing Model 314 flying-boat, built for Pan Am.

**7 Jun:** First flight of the Douglas DC-4, the first of the great US family of metal four-engined transport monoplanes, that doubled the capacity of the DC-3.

**11 Jul:** The Soviet Air Force went into action when fighting broke out against the Japanese over territory on the frontiers of Korea, Manchuria and Siberia.

**14 Jul:** Howard Hughes, in a Lockheed 14, made a 15,432 mile flight around the world, completed in three days, 19 hours and 14 minutes.

**21 Jul:** The Short Mercury, the upper component of the Short-Mayo composite, made the first commercial crossing of the North Atlantic by a heavier-than-air aircraft.

**1 Aug:** The Dornier Do 217 made its first flight. It represented a marked improvement over the Do 17.

**8 Aug:** Luft Hansa's Blohm und Voss Ha 139 seaplane *Nordwind* powered by four 600hp Junkers Jumo diesel engines, flew non-stop from the Azores to New York in 15 hours 50 minutes.

**22 Aug:** The Civil Aeronautics Act became effective in the USA,

co-ordinating all non-military aviation under the Civil Aeronautics Authority (CAA).

**2 Oct:** First flight of the Dewoitine D520, the most advanced French fighter in service with the French Air Force in the early stages of WWII.

**11 Oct:** The Westland Whirlwind made its maiden flight. It became the RAF's first single-seat, twin-engined fighter.

**14 Oct:** The Allison-powered Curtiss XP-40 prototype fighter made its maiden flight.

**24 Oct:** Imperial Airways commenced operations with the AW Ensign on the London-Paris route.

**28 Dec:** First flight of the de Havilland all-metal DH95 Flamingo. Too late to achieve any worthwhile success before the start of the war, it was designed as a response to the import of Lockheed Electras and Model 14s by the pre-war British Airways.

*The 1938 Kings Cup Race was won by Alex Henshaw in Percival Mew Gull G-AEXF at an average speed of 236.25mph (380.2km/h). Seen here in Michael Turner's painting, this single-seat high-speed monoplane is still airworthy today.*

*1938 Kings Cup* by Michael Turner PGAvA, FGMA

# 1939

Pan Am's Boeing Model 314 flying-boat *Yankee Clipper* made a North Atlantic survey flight on 26 March, flown from Baltimore, Maryland, via the Azores, Lisbon, Marseilles, Biscarosse and Southampton to Foynes. The scheduled transatlantic mail service was inaugurated on 20 May, and the first passengers were carried on the route on 28 June. Britain's Imperial Airways joined the fray using Short S30 flying-boat *Caribou*, which made the transatlantic crossing once a week.

In America in the 1930s, radial engines developed for naval aviation aircraft offered considerable advantages in ease of maintenance and reliability over in-line engines. As a result, US aircraft manufacturers used radial engines for the DC-3 and B-17, followed by the P-47, B-24, B-25, B-26 and C-47, amongst others. If it had not been for the Navy, the USAAC would have favoured in-line engines, as did the RAF.

By 1939 American aircraft manufacturers, particularly Boeing, were producing bombers with greater range, load-carrying capacity, speed and survivability. The invention of the Norden bombsight (developed by the US Navy) had a significant effect on the accuracy of hitting targets throughout the war years.

Civil aviation in Europe involved relatively short distances, and therefore the development of airframes and engines was more limited than in the US. This factor really put the Luftwaffe at a disadvantage in developing sufficiently powerful engines for a four-engined bomber in 1939.

The world's first turbojet-powered aircraft, the Heinkel He 178 was flown for the first time at Marienehe, Germany in August. As it was deemed to be underpowered, further development was abandoned in favour of a twin-engined jet fighter, but the diminuative Heinkel had achieved its place in aviation history.

Britain was relying on radar as one of its main lines of defence against German aggression and a 'Chain Home' Radio Direction Finding (RDF) network was set up. It was made up of stations built around the coast which used radio beams to detect enemy aircraft approaching the country. Even after Munich in 1938, the British Government refused to increase defence spending significantly, and hence there was no substantial increase in air defence. It was not until the seizure of Czechoslovakia in March 1939 by the German Army, that additional resources were allocated to Fighter Command. By the summer Dowding had developed an integrated air defence network and as a result in September, only Fighter Command, alone of the RAF forces, was ready for war.

Following the outbreak of war on 3 September, and the initial attack by Germany on Poland, events for a time moved slowly. Limited aerial fighting took place along the French/German border throughout the remainder of 1939, and the RAF carried out reconnaissance and raids on shipping.

Russian-born aircraft designer Igor Sikorsky made the first tethered flight in his VS-300 helicopter at Stratford, Connecticut.

---

**9 Feb:** Alex Henshaw, flying his Percival Mew Gull, made a record flight to Cape Town and back in four days, ten hours and 20 minutes.

**28 Mar:** The Spanish Civil War ended as Madrid and Valencia surrendered to the Nationalist forces of General Franco.

**1 Apr:** The Mitsubishi A6M1 Zero fighter, intended for service with the Imperial Japanese Navy, made its first flight. It was the first Japanese monoplane with a fully enclosed cockpit and fully retractable undercarriage to enter squadron service.

**1 Apr:** Trans-Canada Airlines (TCA) began passenger flights between Montreal and Vancouver using ten-seat Lockheed 14Hs and 14-seat Lockheed Lodestars.

**16 Apr:** A London-Paris service, jointly operated by Imperial Airways and British Airways began.

**28 Apr:** Imperial Airways' British-West African service was extended to Takoradi on the Gold Coast.

**14 May:** The Short Stirling first flew, the RAF's first new four-engined bomber, followed five months later by the Handley Page Halifax bomber, which took to the air on 25 October.

**24 May:** Imperial Airways' Short flying-boat *Cabot* was successfully refuelled in mid-air by a modified Handley Page Harrow.

**1 Jun:** First flight of the Focke-Wulf Fw 190, which went on to be the most successful German fighter of WWII.

**15 Jun:** The French flying-boat *Lieutenant de Vaisseau Paris* flew from Port Washington to Biscarosse in 28 hours.

**16 Jun:** Air France inaugurated flights 'every hour, on the hour' from Paris to London.

**20 Jun:** The Heinkel He 176 rocket-powered aircraft first flew.

**25 Jun:** Luft Hansa opened a Berlin-Bangkok fortnightly service using a Junkers Ju 52/3m.

**1 Jul:** The Commonwealth Wirraway, the first aircraft to be mass-produced in Australia, based on the North American NA 33, was delivered to the RAAF.

**17 Jul:** Initial flight of the Bristol Beaufighter, the RAF's first purpose-built twin-engined nightfighter.

**27 Aug:** The first flight by a jet-propelled aircraft, a Heinkel He 178, powered by the revolutionary HeS-3B jet engine, was made secretly in Germany.

**3 Sep:** With Germany refusing to withdraw its forces from Poland, the UK and France declared war.

**10 Oct:** The Empire Air Training Scheme was set up to train Australian, Canadian and New Zealand aircrew.

**24 Nov:** The BOAC Act, which established the British Overseas Airways Corporation by the merger of Imperial Airways and British Airways came into force.

**30 Nov:** Without prior declaration of war, the Soviet Union launched air attacks on Finland thus marking the beginning of the Russo-Finnish 'Winter War'.

**29 Dec:** First flight of the Consolidated XB-24 Liberator four-engine heavy bomber.

*Sean Thackwray's painting, specially commissioned by EADS Military Aircraft Division, Germany, shows the Heinkel He 178, taking-off at Marienehe airfield.*

These pages generously donated by European Aeronautic Defence and Space Company – EADS Military Aircraft

*First Jet Flight* by Sean M Thackwray

The best of all civil flying-boats ultimately came from the USA, largely because of the peculiar requirements of the American route. Britain's Empire boats were suitable for 'short hops' from England to Gibraltar, Malta and Alexandra on the way to India/Australia. But the American boats had to contend with the long hop of 2,400 miles between North America and Hawaii, the longest overwater leg in the world. The Boeing 314 Clipper proved the greatest of all civil flying-boats. Two things caused the demise of the flying-boat; the increase in performance of four-engined land aircraft and the creation of airfields world-wide over the following five years, making flying-boats unnecessary.

As the Axis powers had control of most western Europe and Mediterranean airspace, the BOAC flying boats opened a weekly service to Australia on the 'Horseshoe Route', flying from Durban, South Africa up the east coast of Africa, then via India and Burma.

The Caproni N1 was flown in Milan to test a method of jet propulsion which had been invented in England. An ordinary piston engine drove a ducted fan which pumped air out of a nozzle in the tail, but it proved slower than if the engine drove an ordinary propeller.

By 1940, the Luftwaffe had begun equipping its aircraft with blind-bombing and bad weather devices. The RAF had no such technology until 1942, while the USAAF had to 'borrow' from the RAF in 1943 and 1944 to support their efforts during bad weather. The

Luftwaffe put considerable effort into the development of a long-range escort fighter, the Messerschmitt Bf 110, but it was incapable of handling the RAF's lighter single-seat interceptors. However, it had attempted to address the problem of supporting its bomber force with a fighter escort.

The German assault on France and the Low Countries on 10 May put an end to the 'phoney war'. The RAF gave maximum support against the advancing German columns but, in the face of overwhelming odds, its efforts achieved little. RAF fighters, based in England, covered the evacuation from Dunkirk but 959 RAF aircraft were lost in the Battle for France, including 477 fighters, mainly Hurricanes.

During the Battle of Britain – the aerial battle that lasted from 10 July to 30 October – it was the German intention to destroy the RAF in the same way as other air forces had been destroyed by *blitzkriegs* from September 1939 to May 1940. However, the large aerial battles showed the Germans that air superiority could not be achieved, and the intended invasion of Britain was postponed, and subsequently cancelled. The price of victory for the RAF was high: 375 pilots were killed and 358 wounded. Fighter Command lost 915 aircraft against the 1,733 fighters and bombers lost by the Luftwaffe, but the aircraft factories continued to function day and night and managed to keep pace with the losses. New versions of the Spitfire (Mark II) and Hurricane (Mark IIA) began to appear in the autumn.

---

**13 Jan:** First flight of the Yak-1, the first Soviet aircraft powered by a 1,100hp Klimov engine, which featured cannon armament.

**24 Feb:** The Hawker Typhoon made its initial flight, the first fighter to be powered by the new Napier Sabre II engine.

**5 Apr:** Prototype of the Mikoyan Guryevich I-200 flew, which was developed into the MiG-3.

**13 May:** The first free flight of the Sikorsky VS-300 helicopter – a single rotor helicopter which introduced a small rotor at the tail of the aircraft to overcome the torque reaction of the main rotor.

**16 May:** President Roosevelt called for the production of 50,000 aircraft a year in the US.

**29 May:** The Vought XF4V-1 Corsair was flown for the first time, which became probably the best carrier-based fighter of WWII.

**8 Jul:** TWA began operating the Boeing 307B Stratoliner on the San Francisco to New York route. The flight took 13 hours 40 minutes, two hours faster than the DC-3.

**19 Aug:** First flight of the North American B-25 Mitchell. It exceeded the USAAF specification for a medium bomber and a total of 9,816 was built.

**1 Sep:** No 71 Squadron was formed at RAF Church Fenton; the

first 'Eagle Squadron', whose pilots were American citizens drawn to Britain's cause.

**13 Sep:** Japan's A6M1 Zero made its combat début, shooting down 27 Chinese and Soviet fighters over China without loss.

**13 Sep:** Pan Am commenced scheduled passenger flights to New Zealand.

**12 Oct:** The first flight of the Ilyushin Il-2 Shturmovik, the most famous Soviet aircraft in this class during WWII. Over 36,000 examples were built.

**26 Oct:** Designed to meet a British requirement, the North American NA-73X single-seat fighter was flown. As the Mustang it was one of the most successful fighters of the war, especially when subsequently powered by the Rolls-Royce Merlin.

**14 Nov:** The Luftwaffe made a devastating night raid on Coventry. The concentrated bombing was achieved by the use of *Knickebein* (crooked leg), a radio beam which guided the pilot to the target by tones heard in his headphones. This enabled him to carry out a 'blind-bombing' raid accurate to within one mile in 180. Another device known as *X-Gerät* informed the pilot when to drop the bombs.

**18 Nov:** Radio detection terminology standardised when the US Chief of Naval Operations authorised the use of the abbreviation RADAR (Radio Detection and Ranging).

**25 Nov:** The highly secret prototype of the wooden de Havilland DH 98 Mosquito was first flown from Hatfield. It was the RAF's first unarmed bomber and arguably the most effective strategic bomber of the 1940s.

**25 Nov:** First flight of the Martin B-26 Marauder medium-range bomber that was widely used by the USAAC.

**18 Dec:** The Henschel Hs 293A radio-controlled guided bomb made its first flight. The rocket motor enabled the missile to be released from low-level.

**18 Dec:** The Curtiss SB2C-1 Helldiver made its maiden flight, a carrier-based scout-bomber which saw extensive service on US carriers in the Pacific theatre.

*A typical Battle of Britain scene is illustrated by Frank Wootton in* Battle over London. *It shows Spitfires and Hurricanes attacking a large formation of Heinkel He 111 bombers.*
© Mrs V.Wootton

These pages generously donated by Robert Stuart plc

*Battle over London* by Frank Wootton OBE, FPGAvA

# 1941

By 1941, British manufacture of aircraft had surpassed that of Germany, and remained so for the rest of the war. The Blitz had revealed that the Luftwaffe's means were inadequate to defeat England from the air. The Heinkel He 111s, supplanted by Dornier Do 17s and Junkers Ju 88s, were not particularly successful. As the RAF could not be eradicated, then Britain would not be invaded.

However, the German forces, acting in combination, were overwhelming the Allies on every front causing defeat after defeat. Distinguished air combat was nowhere more apparent than during the RAF's valiant defence of Malta. This eventually sealed the fate of the Mediterranean and probably North Africa. The RAF did have some success when it launched Operation *Rhubarb*, conducting daylight sweeps over Northern France.

To help protect British shipping in Atlantic convoys, a number of adapted Hawker Hurricane fighters were rocket launched from merchant ships, as a means of defence against marauding Fw 200 Condors. The pilot later had to ditch, and pray.

Britain put a jet aircraft into the air on 15 May. The Gloster E28/39, powered by a Whittle engine, made a 17-minute flight from RAF Cranwell. Basically it was a test bed for the larger production aircraft then being developed, the twin-engined Gloster Meteor.

British Air Staff issued a directive to RAF Bomber Command to commit the Bomber Force for the purpose of dislocating the German transportation system, and destroying the morale of the civilian population. RAF Coastal Command aircraft began to be fitted with the new British-designed air-to-surface (ASV) Mk 1 radar system to assist in target detection. The system was particularly efficient at sea since their were no natural obstacles to give false echoes.

The RAF introduced new navigational aids such as *Gee*, to be followed by *Oboe* and H2S. Target Force 'E' was inaugurated in June 1941 to expand Bomber Command to 250 standard-sized squadrons, under eight operational groups, by the spring of 1943.

On 22 June, Germany launched Operation *Barbarossa*, the invasion of the Soviet Union. By mid-day over 1,200 Soviet aircraft had been destroyed. The fighting fronts in Europe and North Africa had expanded, attrition increased and the air war had gradually spread to a multitude of campaigns.

Japan launched a surprise attack on the US naval base at Pearl Harbor on Hawaii on 7 December, which virtually destroyed all the battleships of the US Pacific fleet and severely depleted the USAAF assets deployed in the region. Fortunately the Japanese failed to destroy any US aircraft carriers, as they were all out on manoeuvres well away from Hawaii at the time. Six Japanese carriers launched 365 bombers, torpedo bombers and fighters, sinking five battleships and severely damaging three others, together with a variety of smaller vessels.

**9 Jan:** First flight of the Avro Lancaster, the best Allied heavy bomber of WWII. It entered squadron service later in the year and a total of 7,300 was eventually built.
**Jan:** First flight of the Kawanishi H8K1 'Emily' long-range flying boat, considered to be one of the best water-based aircraft of WWII.
**8 Feb:** Operation *Sonnenblume* commenced, the transportation of Rommel's Africa Corps to North Africa by a fleet of Ju 52/3ms.
**25 Feb:** Messerschmitt's new Me 321 Gigant glider, with a wing span of 180ft, flew for the first time. Towed by three Bf 110s, it could carry 22 tons of cargo.
**2 Mar:** Under cover of darkness, BOAC restarted secret regular flights from Scotland to Stockholm, using a single Lockheed 14 Lodestar. It conveyed Swedish-made ball bearings that were vital to Britain's armaments industry.
**11 Mar:** US congress passed the Lend-Lease bill, whereby military aircraft were sent to Allied countries.
**2 Apr:** The world's first twin-engined jet aircraft, the Heinkel He 280V-1 fighter made its first flight. It did not enter production as the contemporary Messerschmitt Me 262 proved more successful.
**1 May:** Japan's Nakajima J1N Gekko made its maiden flight, the first purpose-built Japanese long-range night fighter.
**4 May:** The first B-24 Liberator was delivered to RAF Coastal Command.
**6 May:** Igor Sikorsky made a one hour 32 minute flight in his VS-300 helicopter, a world helicopter endurance record.
**6 May:** First flight of the Republic P-47 Thunderbolt. It was regarded as being one of the three best Allied fighters of WWII, and a total of 15,683 was built.
**26 May:** An RAF Catalina found the German battleship *Bismarck*, the greatest threat to the Royal Navy in the German fleet, in mid-Atlantic. Swordfish biplanes from HMS *Ark Royal* were scrambled and made an attack which damaged the *Bismarck's* steering gear. This slowed the battleship, enabling British surface ships to sink it.
**29 May:** The USAAC Ferrying Command was formed to fly US-built aircraft to Britain. An Atlantic Ferrying Organisation (later to be taken over by BOAC) was set up in England to return crews to the USA, and fly war material from the US on the return leg.
**20 Jun:** The USAAC was renamed the United States Army Air Force (USAAF). Its first head was General 'Hap' Arnold.
**1 Aug:** The Soviet Air Force used 'parasite' I-16SPD dive-bombers, carried under the wings of TB-3 heavy bombers, and released near to targets in Romania.
**13 Aug:** First flight of the Messerschmitt Me 163A prototype at Peenemünde, the first time under full rocket power. By October it was achieving a speed of 625mph, then a world speed record.
**17 Sep:** RAF Mosquito PR1 aircraft flew their first operational reconnaissance missions over Brest and Bordeaux to photograph harbour installations.
**Oct:** First flight of the Heinkel He 111Z, a five-engined hybrid, designed to tow the Me 321 glider. It was built by amalgamating two He 111H fuselages by a constant chord wing section on which was mounted the fifth engine.
**Dec:** The Kawasaki Ki-61 'Tony' made its first flight, the only Japanese fighter to feature a liquid-cooled engine in WWII.

*A scene of mayhem at Pearl Harbor on 7 December 1941 is caught in this painting by Robert Taylor. It shows the aircraft attacking anchored US warships to devastating effect.*

These pages generously donated by the Air Training Corps, founded in February 1941

*Remember Pearl Harbor* by Robert Taylor

In early 1942, Japanese carrier aircraft sank HMS *Repulse* and HMS *Prince of Wales* as a prelude to gobbling up the rest of southeast Asia, and they looked forward to victory in Australia, India and Ceylon.

In April, 20 Lancasters of Nos 44 and 97 Squadrons carried out a low-level daylight raid on the MAN factory at Augsburg. Operation *Millennium* was the first 1,000 bomber raid on Cologne on the night of 30/31 May. In the Western Desert, prior to the Battle of Alamein in October, the RAF was able to field 1,200 serviceable front-line aircraft. Fighter Command started to receive the Rolls-Royce Griffon-engined Spitfire XII, which was used to counter German bomb-carrying fighters attacking southern England in daylight.

On 18 April, 16 B-25 Mitchells, led by Colonel James H. Doolittle, were launched from USS *Hornet* to make the first ever air attack on the Japanese home islands. Unable to return to the carrier after dropping their bombs, the B-25s had to fly on to the Chinese mainland.

The Battle of the Coral Sea took place between 4-8 May, followed by the Battle of Midway on 4-7 June, when US Navy aircraft inflicted heavy losses on the Japanese carriers. The Japanese offensive power had been checked. The first phase of the Pacific War was over, and the Japanese threat against Australia was thwarted.

The US was blessed with a two-year delay before entering the war. During those two years there was an infusion of orders from Britain and the knowledge gained from observation made a lot of difference. Though the Soviet Union had begun the war with few modern aircraft, they undertook an industrial expansion similar to that in the USA.

The Lockheed P-38 Lightning, the 'Forked Devil', was the only American fighter in continuous production from before the war until the end of hostilities. The long-range P-38 served in every theatre in a variety of capacities, and was credited with shooting down more Japanese aircraft than any other type.

Although 60% of all German airpower was deployed to the Eastern Front, it mainly concentrated on supporting ground battles at Stalingrad and in the Caucasus, rather than attacking strategic targets. Soviet air units began receiving newer aircraft models from factories relocated to the Ural Mountains, where they were safe from German attack. The Shturmovik ground attack aircraft was one of several machines that could match those of the Germans.

The RAF began striking at targets in Germany. It provided effective air support in the North African campaign, especially with army co-operation. It helped the 8th Army overcome the Afrikacorps by the Battle of Alamein in the autumn of 1942. Bombers had badly damaged Rommel's supply lines across the Mediterranean and fighters were beginning to establish air superiority over the ground battles. In November, Operation *Torch* was launched by the Allies on French North Africa and carrier aircraft were heavily involved.

---

**28 Jan:** The first two RAF Mustangs were delivered to the Air Development Fighting Unit at Duxford. Operational sorties with the type over France began on 5 May.

**30 Jan:** Canadian Pacific Air Lines formed by the amalgamation of numerous small airlines.

**11/12 Feb:** The German battleships *Gneisenau*, *Scharnhorst* and *Prince Eugen* made good their escape from Brest by a dash through the English Channel to German home ports. In air attacks by the RAF and Fleet Air Arm against the ships in very poor weather conditions 42 aircraft were lost. All six aircraft in a formation of Swordfish were shot down.

**22 Feb:** Assam, Burma and China Ferry Command was set up to airlift essential supplies to China, flying over the Himalayan 'Hump' route using C-46 Commandos.

**26 Mar:** First flight of the Northrop XP-61 Black Widow, the USAF's first purpose-built radar-equipped night fighter. It became successfully operational in the Pacific theatre in 1944.

**19 Apr:** First flight of the Macchi C205, regarded as the best Italian fighter of WWII.

**20 Apr:** Malta was re-enforced by 47 Spitfires that took off from HMS *Wasp* some 660 miles west of the island.

**12 Jun:** The first USAAF attack on a strategic target in the Balkans, when B-24s operating from bases in Libya attacked the Ploesti oil refineries in Romania.

**26 Jun:** The Grumman XF6F Hellcat made its maiden flight, and became a significant Allied carrier-borne fighter.

**1 Jul:** The first B-17 Flying Fortress to equip the US Eighth Air Force arrived in England.

**18 Jul:** Messerschmitt's Me 262 prototype made its maiden flight under jet power.

**17 Aug:** The USAAF Eighth Air Force made its first B-17 heavy bomber attack against targets in Western Europe.

**18 Aug:** The RAF's Pathfinder Force was established to mark targets in advance for attacks by mainstream Bomber Command.

**24 Aug:** The first Luftwaffe Junkers Ju 86P-2 was destroyed over Egypt. A very high-altitude pressurised reconnaissance aircraft, it was intercepted at 42,000ft by an unpressurised RAF Spitfire V.

**2 Sep:** First flight of the Hawker Tempest V, a development of the Typhoon. When it entered service with the RAF in April 1944, it was the fastest fighter of WWII.

**21 Sep:** Maiden flight of the Boeing XB-29 Superfortress, the vehicle for the atomic bombs dropped three years later.

**29 Sep:** The RAF 'Eagle' Squadrons were formally taken over by USAAF Fighter Command.

**1 Oct:** Germany launched the first successful V-2 ballistic rocket on the Baltic coast at Peenemünde.

**21 Oct:** BOAC made an experimental non-stop flight, using a converted Liberator 1, from Prestwick, Scotland to Moscow.

**2 Nov:** The US Navy established the Patuxent River Naval Air Station as a test unit for naval aircraft.

**15 Nov:** The Heinkel He 219 twin-engined night fighter was first flown. It was the first German aircraft with retractable tricycle landing gear and also the world's first to be fitted with ejection seats.

**4 Dec:** B-24 Liberators of the USAAF 9th AF in the Middle East made the first bombing attacks on Italy.

*Robert Bailey's painting shows Oberst Hajo Herrman in a Junkers Ju 88 leading his combat group KG30 during an attack on Allied merchantmen in Convoy PQ-17 in the Barents Sea on 5 July 1942.*

*Arctic Encounter* by Robert Bailey ASAA

RAF Lancasters of No 617 Squadron, led by Wg Cdr Guy Gibson, attacked the German dams in the Rhur Valley on 17/18 May. The Möhne, Eder and Sorpe dams were breached by earthquake 'bouncing bombs' designed by Barnes Wallis. Water from the dams flooded the Rhur Valley industrial area, and 75% of the total water available in the area was lost. Eight of the 19 aircraft involved were lost in the action. Gibson subsequently received the Victoria Cross for his role.

The US 8th Air Force became heavily involved in daylight raids. As they went deeper into Germany, they met ferocious opposition from the Luftwaffe. At that time, US fighters, even with drop tanks, could barely reach over the Rhine, and RAF fighters had even shorter range. The Eighth attacked airframe and aircraft component factories by day, while by night RAF Bomber Command pounded urban areas that contained a preponderance of industry orientated to aircraft production. On 17 August, the 8th Air Force lost 59 heavy bombers in one day on raids upon Regensburg and Schweinfurt.

On 1 August, B-24s from Libya attacked the heavily defended Romanian oil refineries at Ploesti in Romania at low-level. This was the longest bombing mission to date and 57 Liberators were lost in the operation.

In June, the 'Window' metal foil anti-radar device was used for the first time, during a major attack on the port of Hamburg. There was a considerable drop in aircraft casualties following its introduction. FIDO (Fog Intensive Dispersal Operation) was instigated by the RAF to effect the safe landing of returning bombers in fog at certain airfields.

Allied bombing strategy gained a new dimension in June when 'shuttle' missions were introduced, whereby crews left England for long-range targets in Southern Germany and flying on to be refuelled in North Africa. The bombers then attacked targets in Italy on the journey home.

During October, RAF photo reconnaissance obtained evidence of a launch site for Hitler's latest secret weapon, the V-1 flying bomb, well within the presumed range for attacking London. The British Government had been aware of a German rocket programme for some months, and Allied reconnaissance was finding increasing evidence of radical new types of aircraft on trial for the Luftwaffe at test establishments throughout Germany. Allied air power in the Mediterranean was growing ever stronger, and although Mussolini was deposed and Italy surrendered, German forces in the country fought on.

In America, the aviation industry had expanded vastly since Pearl Harbor and by 1943 women accounted for 28% of workers. During 1943, the US had doubled the 1942 figure of aircraft delivered, with a staggering 85,898 airframes rolling off the assembly lines.

In America, a new generation of transport aircraft took to the air with flights of the Douglas C-54 Skymaster and Lockheed C-69A Constellation. Innovations of new aircraft in 1943 included the wooden Curtiss C-76 Caravan, all-wing Northrop XP-56 Black Bullet, Fisher XP-75 Eagle, Curtiss CW-24 XP-55, Focke-Wulf Ta 154A night fighter of film-bonded wood, Hughes XF-11 reconnaissance and the Miles M39B Libelle, which tested the aft-wing concept.

**27 Jan:** England-based US 8th Air Force B-17s and B-24s completed their first daylight raid on Germany, attacking Emden and Wilhelmshaven.

**30 Jan:** RAF Mosquitos made the first daylight raid on Berlin.

**30 Jan:** The H2S radar navigation system was used by the RAF for the first time.

**3 Feb:** BOAC began a Mosquito high-speed delivery service between RAF Leuchars and Stockholm on 'ball bearing' flights.

**13 Feb:** The Vought F4U-1 Corsair made its operational début in the Pacific, escorting PB4Y-1 Liberators.

**22 Feb:** The North American Mitchell entered operational service as a day bomber with the RAF.

**10 Mar:** The US 14th Air Force was activated under the command of former Flying Tigers chief Maj Gen C.L.Chennault, operating the Curtiss C-46 Commando.

**13 Mar:** Consolidated Aircraft merged with Vultee Aircraft to form Consolidated-Vultee Aircraft Corporation (Convair).

**16 Mar:** The Luftwaffe commenced the use of Junkers Ju 87G anti-tank aircraft on the Eastern Front.

**18 Apr:** A USAAF P-38 Lightning downed a Mitsubishi G4M1 'Betty' with Admiral Isoroku Yamamoto on board, the head of the Japanese Navy who had planned the attack on Pearl Harbor.

**7 May:** The first successful US helicopter flights were made at sea when a Sikorsky XR-4 underwent trials in conjunction with the tanker *Bunker Hill*.

**1 Jun:** A KLM DC-3 flying from Lisbon to Whitchurch, England was shot down by Luftwaffe Ju 88s, killing all 17 onboard. The film actor Leslie Howard was one of the passengers. German intelligence had suggested Winston Churchill was on the airliner.

**15 Jun:** The prototype Arado Ar 234V-1 jet bomber made its first flight.

**29 Jun:** QANTAS flew its first service from Perth to Colombo, Ceylon using a Catalina flying-boat.

**17 Aug:** First use of the Henschel Hs 293A-1 radio-controlled bomb, when a Dornier Do 217 attacked British shipping in the Bay of Biscay.

**31 Aug:** Combat début of the F6F Hellcat. Operating from USS *Yorktown*, they attacked Japanese positions on Marcus Island.

**8 Sep:** The first operational use of the 12,000lb (5,443kg) bomb by a Lancaster during an attack on the Dortmund-Ems canal.

**26 Oct:** The Dornier Do 335V-1 Pfeil made its maiden flight. This advanced aircraft had pusher and tractor powerplants.

**2 Nov:** The US Navy received the first Martin Mars four-engined flying-boat.

**1 Dec:** Operational début of a P-51 Mustang in USAAF service powered by a Rolls-Royce Merlin.

**2 Dec:** First flight of the Grumman XF7F-1 Tigercat prototype, the US Navy's first twin-engined fighter.

*A representation of one of the famous bombing scenes of World War II, when RAF Lancasters breeched the Möhne and Eder dams on the night of 16-17 May 1943, Robert Taylor's painting shows Lancaster IIIs of No 617 Squadron, led by Wg Cdr Guy Gibson and his 'Dambusters', in Operation Chastise.*

*Operation Chastise* by Robert Taylor

# 1944

An endless supply of planes, crew members, bombs, guns and ammunition continued to arrive in Britain during 1944, especially for the forthcoming invasion plans. England was gradually converted into the most versatile and quite unsinkable aircraft carrier in existence. After mid-1944, RAF Bomber Command and the US Eighth Air Force combined their capabilities and began to attack Germany in earnest.

The long and arduous campaign continued in Italy. While the Allied Tactical Air Forces were able to dominate the skies, the land forces faced stiff resistance. The Mediterranean Air Force was involved in the landings in the South of France in August, and the Balkan Air Force, based in Italy, provided assistance to partisan forces in Yugoslavia.

The success of the Allied invasion of Normandy owed much to the effective application of the air power lessons learnt in the desert and Italy. D-Day saw RAF and USAAF aircraft of all types in action, and they managed to virtually eliminate the Luftwaffe from the area during the landings on the Normandy coast. The Tactical Air force quickly began to deploy across the Channel to give close air support to the ground forces. The Normandy invasion provided the first example of how Allied air superiority could be used. With the hordes of Tempests, Typhoons, Mustangs and Thunderbolts, the Luftwaffe was simply brushed aside.

By September, the target priority for the Allied bombing campaign was the German oil industry. Within a short time, the Luftwaffe found itself short of fuel and had to severely curtail its operational missions. Flying training was also brought to a virtual standstill.

The besieged defenders in Kohima and Imphal in Burma were supplied by air for three months, this being a landmark in the history of air transport. It paved the way for the campaign when the 14th Army reconquered Burma, relying throughout almost entirely on air power as a source of supply and reinforcement.

In October, Japanese suicide (kamikaze) attacks began on US warships in the Pacific, using converted Mitsubishi A6M5 fighter-bombers. Over the following months many attacks were launched, which caused considerable damage to ships. During November, Japan launched its Fu-Gu (balloon bomb) against the US west coast, employing an altitude-keeping device which kept them in the prevailing west-east wind along the 40th parallel. A timing device caused the balloon to crash, whereupon its small bombload detonated. Apart from a scare campaign very little damage was sustained.

In late 1944, the real airpower news was the massive build-up of the B-29 Superfortress effort that would ravage Japan in 1945. The B-29 represented perhaps the most complex aviation engineering achievement in history. Its speed and range were unsurpassed by any other heavy WWII bomber. Japan had yet a little respite before the B-29 raids became effective, but was chronically short of aviation fuel and trained pilots. During 1944, the US produced nearly 100,000 aircraft of the total of 167,654 built by the Allies.

**8 Jan:** First flight of the Lockheed XP-80 at Muroc Dry Lake, the USAAF's second jet-powered aircraft after the Bell XP-59 Airacomet, which flew on 2 October 1942.

**11 Jan:** US Navy TBF-1C Avengers from the USS *Block Island* made the first US attack with forward-firing rockets.

**11 Jan:** The strategic offensive that preceded Operation *Overlord*, the invasion of Normandy, began.

**17 Feb:** The first night-bombing attack from a US aircraft carrier took place. US Navy Avengers from USS *Enterprise* attacked Japanese ships during the battle for the Marshall Islands.

**3 Apr:** Fleet Air Arm Fairey Barracudas attacked and seriously damaged the *Tirpitz* in Alten Fjord, Norway.

**17 Apr:** Howard Hughes flew a TWA Lockheed Constellation from Burbank, California to Washington, DC in just under seven hours, setting a new speed record of 331mph (533km/h).

**6 May:** First flight of the Mitsubishi A7M1 Reppu, the fighter designed to replace the Zero.

**2 Jun:** US bombers flew their first 'shuttle' bombing raids of WWII. They took off from bases in Italy to attack communications targets in Hungary before landing at USAAF bases in the USSR.

**5 Jun:** The B-29 Superfortress made its operational début on a raid on Bangkok operating from bases in India.

**13 Jun:** German V-1 flying bomb operations against London and southern England commenced.

**25 Jun:** The first operational mission of the Mistel (mistletoe) 'piggy-back' system, made up of a Luftwaffe Bf 109 or Fw 190 fighter mounted on top of a pilotless Junkers Ju 88 with its crew section filled with a 8,500lb warhead.

**18 Jul:** The first use of VHF R/T was made to call up direct support from rocket-firing Typhoons at the Falaise Gap, known as the 'cab rank'.

**27 Jul:** RAF Meteor F1 jet fighters, operating from RAF Manston, undertook their first V-1 flying bomb intercept missions.

**28 Jul:** First flight of the de Havilland Hornet. When it entered service in 1946 it was the fastest single-seat twin-engined fighter in the world.

**14 Aug:** Luftwaffe Me 163B Komet rocket-powered interceptors made their first contact with US bombers making daylight raids on German targets.

**16 Aug:** The Junkers Ju 287V-1 prototype jet bomber made its first flight. It was the first aircraft in the world to feature forward-swept wings.

**8 Sep:** The first V-2 rockets fell on Paris and London.

**16 Sep:** First flight of the Fairchild C-82 Packet transport. It was the first aircraft of the war designed solely for cargo, attracting huge orders and led to the more successful C-119 Flying Boxcar.

**12 Nov:** The *Tirpitz* was sunk by RAF Lancasters, using 12,000lb bombs, in the Norwegian port of Tromsö.

**13 Nov:** Croydon Airport was re-opened for civil operations.

**15 Nov:** The prototype Boeing XC-97 made its first flight. As a development of the B-29 it was designed for long-distance transport operations, and as the Stratocruiser made a considerable impact on civil transatlantic operations after the war.

**6 Dec:** The Heinkel He 162 Volksjäger (Peoples Fighter), a wooden-winged jet designed and built in 69 days, first flew.

*Stan Stokes' painting depicts Russian ace Ivan Kozhedub in his Lavochkin La-7 fighter locked in combat with a Luftwaffe Fw 190. Kozhedub was the top scoring fighter pilot on the Allied side during World War II, with 62 victories claimed.*

*Ivan the Terrible* by Stan Stokes

# 1945

The Allied 'push' into Germany reached its peak during the opening months of the year, with little effective resistance from the Luftwaffe, whose combat aircraft inventory had been decimated. The opportunity was therefore now available to bring about the final destruction of German industrial production and its means of communication and transport, and thereby force the beleaguered Nazi leadership into submission.

The bombing of Dresden by the RAF and US Army Air Force on 13-14 February was followed by Operation *Clarion*, a one-day, all-out effort aimed at severing Germany's arteries of supply and communication. Around 9,000 Allied aircraft were involved, with the Luftwaffe unable to hold back the onslaught. Some 79.8% of all aircraft taken on strength by the Luftwaffe had been lost during the course of the war.

The continuation of the war in the Far Eastern theatre saw air power again being used in ways which had never been seen before. The increase in Japanese 'kamikaze' suicide attacks presented a new threat to US Navy operations, over 400 such strikes being carried out on 6 April alone. USAAF B-29s mounted ever more devastating incendiary and conventional attacks against Japanese cities, industrial facilities and airfields that dealt an enormous blow, in the lead-up to the two strikes which effectively brought an end to the whole war: the dropping of atomic bombs on Hiroshima and Nagasaki.

The attack on Hiroshima by B-29 *Enola Gay*, piloted by Col Paul Tibbetts, took place at 09.15hrs on 6 August. Three days later, B-29 *Bock's Car* dropped the second atomic bomb on Nagasaki. In just over a year of operations in the Pacific theatre, Superfortresses had dealt Japan a tremendous blow. B-29s alone were responsible for dropping over 171,000 tonnes of ordnance.

At the lighter end of the spectrum, the maiden flight of the Bell Model 47 helicopter was a major milestone during 1945. The 178hp (239kW) Franklin-engined utility helicopter went on to become a huge success, licence production being undertaken in many countries. In many ways, the Bell 47 was the world's first truly practical helicopter design (and certainly the first to be properly adaptable and commercially successful).

**1 Jan:** A somewhat depleted Luftwaffe attempted to destroy Allied airfields in liberated Europe. Operation *Bodenplatte* was the air arm's final major offensive of the war, and resulted in the destruction of just 150 Allied aircraft against the loss of 270 Luftwaffe aircraft.
**3 Jan:** USAAF B-29 Superfortresses, flying from the Mariana Islands, began a series of incendiary raids with a strike on Nagoya.
**1 Feb:** First flight of the Kawasaki Ki-100, one of Japan's most potent fighter designs of WWII.
**22 Feb:** Operation *Clarion* began, a maximum effort by the Allies to paralyse Germany's remaining means of transportation and communication.
**28 Feb:** The first manned flight of the vertically-launched Bachem Ba349 Natter rocket-propelled interceptor ended in an accident which killed the test pilot.
**10 Mar:** A major incendiary raid on Tokyo was carried out by USAAF B-29s. Some 83,000 people are believed to have been killed, the largest death toll from a single aerial bombing raid.
**18 Mar:** The Douglas XBT2D-1 made its first flight. Named the Skyraider, it later became one of the most successful American combat aircraft ever.
**20 Mar:** The last Luftwaffe air raid on the UK, and the last German aircraft shot down over British soil (a Ju188, claimed by the crew of a Mosquito).

**31 Mar:** Official end of the British Commonwealth Air Training Plan, which had trained 137,739 Allied aircrew (including 54,098 pilots).
**25 Apr:** The US Eighth Army Air Force carried out its last bombing mission of the war, with B-17s and B-24s attacking targets in south-east Germany.
**2 May:** The final RAF Bomber Command raid of the conflict, mounted against Kiel by 126 Mosquitos.
**8 May:** Victory in Europe was celebrated following the signing on the previous day of the German surrender.
**17 May:** Maiden flight of the Lockheed P2V Neptune maritime patrol aircraft for the US Navy.
**22 Jun:** The Vickers Viking short-haul twin-engined airliner took to the air for the first time.
**6 Aug:** B-29 Superfortress *Enola Gay* dropped the first atomic bomb to be used in war, on the Japanese city of Hiroshima.
**9 Aug:** The second, and so far last, atomic bomb to be dropped in anger was released from B-29 *Bock's Car* on the Japanese city of Nagasaki.
**14 Aug:** The final raids against Japan were mounted by the US 20th Air Force's B-29s.
**2 Sep:** Representatives of the Japanese Emperor, the country's government and the Imperial General Headquarters signed a formal surrender aboard the American battleship USS *Missouri*.

This date officially marked the end of World War II.
**5 Sep:** First flight of the Douglas C-74 Globemaster transport.
**20 Sep:** The maiden flight of an aircraft powered by turboprop engines, when a Gloster Meteor fitted with two Rolls-Royce Trents flew for the first time.
**25 Sep:** What was to become one of the most successful British civil aircraft of all time, the de Havilland DH104 Dove, made its first flight.
**4 Oct:** A new record for a round-the-world flight (149hr 4 mins) was set by six USAAF Air Transport Command C-54 Skymasters.
**7 Nov:** A new absolute world air speed record of 606.25mph was set by Gp Capt H.J. Wilson, flying Gloster Meteor *Britannia*.
**3 Dec:** Lt Eric Brown, RN landed a DH Vampire I on the deck of HMS *Ocean*, the first carrier landing by a turbojet aircraft.
**8 Dec:** Maiden flight of the Bell Model 47 helicopter.
**21 Dec:** First flight of America's first turboprop-powered aircraft, the Consolidated-Vultee XP-81.
**22 Dec:** The Beech 35 Bonanza, which became one of the most successful general aviation designs ever, made its first flight.

*By 1945, USAAF 8th Air Force B-17Gs on missions to the German heartland were being challenged by the Luftwaffe's new jet fighters. Robert Taylor's painting shows Messerschmitt Me 262s harassing a formation of Flying Fortresses during a daylight raid.*

*Combat over the Reich* by Robert Taylor

With the restrictions that had been imposed on air travel during the war years lifted, civil aviation began to re-develop in earnest during 1946. Not only were new airlines and routes being established, but a number of new airliners started to enter service. Most notable was the beautiful Lockheed Model 049 Constellation, which first entered scheduled service with Pan American on 3 February. On that date, operations of the type began between New York's La Guardia Airport and Bermuda, while TWA followed up two days later by beginning its own Constellation services from Washington to Paris via New York. One day prior to that, a Pan Am Model 049 undertook a flight between La Guardia and Bournemouth-Hurn Airport in the UK in only 12hr 9min, easily eclipsing the previous benchmark which had been set by a Douglas DC-4 (some 17 hours).

The type's pace had been evident upon the prototype's first flight and subsequent immediate entry into USAAF service as the C-69 in 1943, when it proved faster than some contemporary fighters. Constellation Model 049s built prior to 1945 which had already been ordered by airlines were pressed into military use as C-69s, with an appropriately modified interior for troop transport. When the war ended, Lockheed bought back the USAAF's remaining examples, and turned the production line back over to producing civil Model 049s. The rush to produce the type for military duties had meant that teething troubles with the Constellation's Wright R-3350 Cyclone engines had not been ironed out by the time Pan Am and TWA (for whom the aircraft had originally been conceived) began

regular services, and various incidents ensued. Development of the improved Model 649 thus continued apace, and without military interference.

The most revolutionary first flight of 1946, in terms of the aircraft's configuration, was the Northrop XB-35, an experimental bomber of tailless 'flying wing' design, with a span of some 172 feet. It was powered by four Pratt & Whitney R-4360 Wasp Major turbo-supercharged radial engines, each driving contra-rotating three-blade propellers: this truly was an aircraft ahead of its time, and one which nearly entered operational service. During the war, the USAAF placed an order for 200 production B-35Bs, but the type was rendered obsolete by the advent of jet bombers, and it was decided to pursue the XB-35 as a testbed only. Only two were built, and both were scrapped after the end of their trials programme in 1949. However, the jet-engined YB-49 was to follow in 1947.

In terms of its impact on aviation, perhaps the most significant event of 1946 took place on 24 July when Bernard Lynch became the first person to use an ejector seat in flight. He 'banged out' of the rear cockpit of a modified Gloster Meteor F3 flying at 8,000ft at a speed of 320mph. The ejector seat had been developed by the Martin-Baker company. Founded as an aircraft manufacturer in 1929, Martin-Baker soon diversified into the development of escape systems, and the company decided to concentrate on this business from 1949 onwards, subsequently becoming a world leader in its field. Since the first ejection in 1946, it is estimated that around 7,000 aircrew lives have been saved by Martin-Baker technology.

---

**1 Jan:** Air France was re-established as the country's flag carrier.

**1 Jan:** Wartime restrictions on civil aviation in the UK were lifted by the Air Ministry.

**9 Jan:** First flight of the Soviet Union's first post-war civil airliner, the Ilyushin Il-12. It was not a success, though its re-designed successor, the Il-14, was.

**25 Jan:** The Bell XS-1 rocket-powered research aircraft (later known as the X-1) made its first flight, an unpowered descent after being dropped from its modified B-29 carrier aircraft.

**26 Jan:** Maiden flight of the McDonnell XFD-1 Phantom jet fighter, designed for the US Navy and Marine Corps, and which was designated FH-1 in service.

**15 Feb:** The Douglas DC-6 made its maiden flight.

**28 Feb:** The prototype Republic XP-84 made its inaugural flight from Muroc AFB, CA. As the P-84 (later F-84) Thunderjet in service, it enjoyed a long and successful career with the USAF and many overseas air arms.

**21 Mar:** Formation of the USAAF's Strategic Air Command.

**24 Apr:** The Soviet Union's first jet aircraft, the Mikoyan-Gurevich I-300 (later known as the MiG-9) development aircraft, took to the air.

**5 May:** De Havilland's DH108 tailless research aircraft made its maiden flight from Woodbridge in Suffolk, with Geoffrey de Havilland (son of the firm's founder) at the controls.

**22 May:** First flight of the de Havilland Canada DHC1 Chipmunk ab initio trainer.

**25 Jun:** The Northrop XB-35 piston-engined 'flying wing' experimental bomber made its initial flight.

**27 Jul:** Maiden flight of the prototype Supermarine Attacker, which became the Fleet Air Arm's first jet fighter four years later.

**31 Jul:** A merger was finalised between the major airlines in Denmark, Norway and Sweden which created the Scandinavian Airline System (SAS).

**1 Aug:** British European Airways (BEA) was established, operating a variety of services from London using DC-3s.

**8 Aug:** The prototype Convair XB-36 Peacemaker strategic bomber made its inaugural flight from Fort Worth, TX.

**7 Sep:** A new absolute world air speed record was set by Gp Capt E. M. Donaldson of the RAF's High Speed Flight. At the controls of a Gloster Meteor F4, he reached a speed of 615.78mph.

**27 Sep:** Geoffrey de Havilland was killed when the DH108 Swallow he was flying suffered a structural failure during a dive at Mach 0.875 over the Thames Estuary in Kent, and broke up.

**1 Oct:** A Lockheed P2V Neptune, named *Truculent Turtle*, completed a record-breaking non-stop flight between Perth in Western Australia and Port Columbus, OH after having been airborne for 55hr 17min.

**3 Nov:** An often-forgotten aviation record was broken by the US Navy's non-rigid XM-1 airship: the longest unrefuelled flight duration by any form of craft. Its flight of over 170hr was not beaten until the Rutan Voyager's feat of 1986.

**9 December:** The first powered test flight of the Bell XS-1 was carried out, with test pilot Chalmers 'Slick' Goodlin at the controls.

*A de Havilland DH89A Dragon Rapide of Railway Air Services Ltd is shown landing on a snow covered airfield in Anthony Cowland's painting entitled* The Christmas Mail Arrives.

These pages generously donated by DynCorp International LLC, founded in 1946

*The Christmas Mail Arrives* by Anthony Cowland BA(Hons), MCSD, GAvA, FSAI

One of the most significant milestones that had yet to be reached in the history of flight was finally achieved during 1947 with the breaking of the sound barrier. After the cancellation of the promising Miles M.52 before the aircraft had been completed, the British aviation industry had effectively conceded defeat to the USA in the race to go supersonic. Initial research into the design of a rocket-powered transonic research aircraft by a US Army Air Force team headed by Ezra Kotcher had failed to gain any industry support until late 1944, when the Bell Aircraft Corporation took the programme on. At this stage, NACA (the National Advisory Committee for Aeronautics, NASA's immediate forerunner) was refusing to become involved, as its experts advised that turbojet power was a safer, though less powerful, option.

The Bell research aircraft was initially referred to by the USAAF as project MX-653, though it was soon given the official designation of XS-1 before roll-out on 27 December 1945. Gliding flight trials of the first two examples were undertaken during 1946 when they were launched (as with all subsequent flights) from the belly of a modified B-29 Superfortress carrier aircraft, before powered tests commenced.

The attempt to break the sound barrier took place on 14 October. USAF Maj Charles E. 'Chuck' Yeager and the orange XS-1, now named *Glamorous Glennis* in tribute to the pilot's wife, was flown by the B-29 mother ship to 20,000ft and dropped into free flight. The XLR11 rocket engine was ignited, and the aircraft climbed to 40,000ft from where the supersonic run began. Four minutes later, Yeager and the XS-1 were flying faster than sound, effortlessly reaching a speed of Mach 1.06. After that, the rocket chambers were shut down and the glide back to Muroc commenced. Pilot and aircraft had made aviation history, albeit in secret, as the details were not released until two months later.

A far cry from the little Bell XS-1 and its supersonic exploits, the largest aircraft ever to have flown also took to the air in 1947, albeit only briefly. Design work on an enormous flying boat intended to carry either 750 troops or two Sherman tanks over long trans-ocean routes began early in WWII. It was the idea of Henry Kaiser, whose steel company had produced Liberty ships, and was backed by reclusive multi-millionaire aviation entrepreneur Howard Hughes. Never before had the production of an aircraft of such a size been attempted, and it was decided not to place further demands on scarce and much-needed metal supplies by building the machine, designated as the HK-1, almost entirely from laminated birchwood. Many delays were encountered, the US Government lost interest, the war ended and there was no role left for the HK-1. Kaiser pulled out of the project and the aircraft was re-named the Hughes H-4 Hercules.

The most significant new jet fighter to make its maiden flight in 1947 was the North American XP-86, which as the F-86 Sabre went on to become one of the most significant combat aircraft of all time. Its design benefited greatly from the availability of German wartime research into high-speed flight and, in particular, the value of swept wings in achieving this. Powered by a General Electric J35-C-3 turbojet, the XP-86 took to the air from Muroc on 1 October, and progressed quickly through early flight testing to the point where service evaluation began within two months. By now, the US Air Force had been formed as a separate entity, and the Sabre would soon become a vital operational asset.

---

**11 Jan:** Maiden flight of the McDonnell XF2D-1 carrier-borne fighter prototype, which spawned the US Navy's production F2H Banshee.

**10 Mar:** The long-running line of jet fighters produced by Sweden's Saab concern began with the first flight of the Saab 21R.

**16 Mar:** The Convair 240 twin-piston airliner first flew.

**17 Mar:** First flight of the North American XB-45, which (as the production B-45 Tornado) became the USAF's first all-jet bomber.

**15 Apr:** The Douglas D-558-1 Skyrocket high-speed research aircraft developed by NACA and the US Navy took to the air for the first time.

**17 Jun:** Pan American started to operate the first round-the-world airline service, using Lockheed Constellations.

**19 Jun:** The absolute world air speed record was broken by USAAF chief test pilot Capt Albert Boyd flying a Lockheed P-80, reaching 623.74mph (1,003.6km/h).

**25 Jun:** The Boeing B-50, a more powerful development of the B-29, made its maiden flight.

**16 Jul:** An aircraft of what was at the time a unique type made its maiden flight from Cowes in the UK – the Saunders-Roe SRA/1 jet flying boat.

**25 Aug:** After a successful record-breaking attempt five days earlier, the Douglas D-558-1 Skyrocket raised the world air speed record still higher, to 650.796 mph (1,047km/h).

**2 Sep:** First flight of the prototype Hawker P1040 jet fighter, the precursor to the Royal Navy's carrier-borne Sea Hawk.

**18 Sep:** The US Air Force (USAF) was officially established.

**22 Sep:** The first trans-Atlantic flight to be carried out entirely under autopilot was completed at RAF Brize Norton by a USAF Douglas C-54D.

**1 Oct:** Maiden flight of the North American XP-86, the first swept-wing fighter to fly.

**14 Oct:** USAF Maj Charles E. 'Chuck' Yeager, flying the Bell XS-1, became the first person to fly faster than the speed of sound.

**21 Oct:** The jet-engined Northrop YB-49 'flying wing' experimental bomber made its first flight.

**24 Oct:** First flight of the prototype Grumman XJR2F-1 Albatross amphibian.

**23 Nov:** The maiden flight of the Consolidated Vultee XC-99 transport (based on the B-36).

**30 Dec:** The prototype of the Soviet Union's first truly successful jet fighter, then designated the Mikoyan-Gurevich I-310 but later re-named the MiG-15, made its inaugural flight.

*This painting by Wilfred Hardy is of Capt Charles E 'Chuck' Yeager, USAF, in the Bell XS-1 rocket-powered research aircraft* Glamorous Glennis. *It became the first aircraft to exceed the speed of sound in level flight on 14 October 1947.*

These pages generously donated by Red Admiral Productions

*The Winged Bullet* by Wilfred Hardy GAvA

# 1948

This was the year during which tension between East and West came close to precipitating actual armed conflict, and certainly sparked off the so-called Cold War which would be waged for almost 40 years. It was also the year which demonstrated the peacetime humanitarian value of air transport, in effectively saving the occupants of an entire city. Berlin was the flashpoint, deep within the Soviet Zones of Occupation in Germany, and itself divided into four sectors – between the USA, France, the UK and the USSR. After talks on the future of Germany broke down and a hardening of Western attitudes towards the Soviet Union, Stalin started to tighten his grip over his European 'satellite' states, including the eastern half of Germany. He and the Soviet leadership embarked on a policy of harassment of the western Allies, which included placing restrictions on Allied military and passenger traffic between the Western Zones of Occupation in Germany and their respective sectors in Berlin. On 2 April, the then commander of US Air Forces in Europe (USAFE), Gen Curtis LeMay, was directed to supply the US military garrison in Berlin by air. USAFE C-47 Skytrains flying in from Rhein-Main in Frankfurt began what became known as the 'Little Lift', delivering stocks of essential goods. However, the situation deteriorated still further.

The Soviets responded by blockading the city completely, and all road, rail and barge traffic was halted; only the air corridors remained open. Supplying Berlin and its over two million inhabitants by air alone was a risky, audacious move, and one which the Soviets hoped and believed would lead to the Allies withdrawing from the city completely. By the end of 1948, no fewer than 100,136 Airlift flights had been made into Berlin, and the loads brought in totalled around 663,788 tonnes. The effort was far from over, but enough vital supplies were reaching the Berliners, and the Allies' resolve had not been broken.

Away from the Berlin Airlift, perhaps the most significant event of 1948 was the maiden flight in July of the Vickers Viscount, the first production turboprop airliner. In some respects, its design was based on the company's earlier Viking, but apart from the turboprops, other alterations included the use of a tricycle undercarriage, a different wing and a pressurised fuselage of circular section. The powerplants were four Rolls-Royce Darts, and from the outset the type looked like being a success, but no-one could have envisaged just how successful the Viscount would become. Minor changes, including a fuselage stretch to increase passenger accommodation to 47, were made before production began for BEA in 1950, and sales to many other UK and foreign carriers followed. A total of 444 Viscounts of various types was eventually built, a production run that remained the highest for a British commercial aircraft for many years.

---

**30 Jan:** After a heart attack three days earlier, pioneer aviator Orville Wright died at the age of 76.

**4 Feb:** The swept-wing US Navy/NACA Douglas D-558-II Skyrocket made its first flight, albeit without its intended XLR8 rocket engine.

**22 Mar:** Maiden flight of the Lockheed TF-80C, a two-seat advanced trainer development of the F-80 Shooting Star fighter. The type later achieved considerable success as the T-33.

**23 Mar:** The prototype Douglas XF3D-1 Skyknight night fighter for the US Navy (known in production as the F3D) flew for the first time. It went on to prove itself in the Korean War, shooting down more Communist aircraft than any other Navy type, and later served in Vietnam.

**23 Mar:** A new world altitude record was set by de Havilland test pilot John Cunningham in the third production DH100 Vampire fitted with extended wingtips.

**26 Apr:** The (unmodified) XP-86 became the first turbojet aircraft to go supersonic, in a shallow dive.

**30 Apr:** Maiden flight of the US Navy's prototype Martin XP5M-1 Marlin anti-submarine flying boat.

**18 Jun:** USAF Strategic Air Command's first two Air Refueling Squadrons were activated, both flying Boeing KB-29Ms.

**26 Jun:** Start of the Berlin Airlift, the blockaded German city being supplied entirely by Allied air transport.

**8 Jul:** Inaugural flight of the USSR's first jet bomber, the Ilyushin Il-28 (later codenamed 'Beagle' by NATO).

**14 Jul:** The first trans-Atlantic flight by turbojet-powered aircraft came to an end, when six de Havilland Vampires of No 54 Squadron, RAF landed at Goose Bay in Canada after having set off from Stornoway in Scotland two days earlier.

**14 Jul:** Airborne car ferry services across the English Channel began, when Silver City Airways began operating its Bristol 170 Freighters between Lympne in Kent and Le Touquet, France.

**16 Jul:** First flight of the turboprop-engined Vickers Viscount airliner.

**20 Jul:** Repeating the RAF Vampires' trans-Atlantic flight in the opposite direction, 16 USAF Lockheed F-80s arrived at Stornoway.

**23 Jul:** No 617 Squadron, RAF (the 'Dam Busters') completed the first east-west crossing of the Atlantic by a bomber squadron, with 16 Avro Lincolns. They went on to undertake a goodwill tour of the USA.

**16 Aug:** The Northrop XF-89 Scorpion all-weather interceptor prototype for the USAF made its first flight.

**1 Sep:** Initial flight of the Saab 29, which entered Swedish Air Force service in 1951 and thus became the first operational swept-wing fighter to equip any air arm outside of the USA and USSR.

**3 Sep:** The Fleet Air Arm's prototype Hawker Sea Hawk carrier-borne jet fighter took to the air for the first time.

**9 Sep:** A British aircraft finally exceeded Mach 1 when John Derry took the third prototype de Havilland DH108 through the sound barrier.

**19 Nov:** Maiden flight of the Hawker P1052, a swept-wing research aircraft which in many ways was a precursor of the classic Hunter.

**29 Dec:** The Supermarine Type 510 prototype, the first British jet fighter design to have swept wing and tail surfaces, made its first flight. It was later developed into the Swift for the RAF.

*The Saab 29 was the first swept-wing jet fighter to be put into large-scale production in Western Europe. Roger H Middlebrook's painting illustrates an early example of the 'Flying Barrel' which was initially test flown in September 1948.*

*A Super Swede* by Roger H Middlebrook GAvA, FSAI

During 1949, the British aviation industry was able to celebrate the maiden flights of two aircraft which represented truly great advances in their respective fields. The first, and most enduring, was the prototype English Electric A1 jet bomber, given the name Canberra the following year. Designed by W. E. W. 'Teddy' Petter of English Electric (EE) at Preston, the aircraft met Specification B3/45 issued in September 1945 for a new high-speed, high-altitude bomber, powered by two Rolls-Royce Avons, to replace the RAF's Mosquitos. It was flown from EE's new Warton facility on 13 May, with Wg Cdr Roland Beamont at the controls of the sleek blue machine, serialled VN799. From the outset, the A1 demonstrated outstanding flying characteristics, the only major design modification resulting from the maiden flight being the 'squaring-off' of the tail fin and rudder. Subsequent flights remained trouble-free, and Beamont was able to show the machine off to the world at the Farnborough Air Show during September. This performance greatly impressed everyone who saw it, and helped focus much welcome attention on the qualities of this new British product. By the year's end, three other prototypes of what would become the Canberra B1 had also flown.

The same is undoubtedly true of the de Havilland DH106 Comet, which later became the first jet airliner to see revenue-earning service. It was developed as a result of the wartime Brabazon Committee, which looked into the predicted needs of British civil airlines after the war. One of these requirements was laid down as a jet-engined airliner, able to fly between 700-800 miles at a cruising altitude of 30,000ft at a speed of 450mph. It was also intended that the selected design would be developed for use on the North Atlantic route to the USA. Much interest was expressed by BOAC for such an aircraft, and by de Havilland for its design and production. What emerged was the very sleek, pressurised, 36-seat DH106 (named Comet in December 1947) powered by four of de Havilland's own Ghost turbojets, but specially modified for this design. The prototype was rolled-out at Hatfield on 25 July 1949, and took to the air under the command of John Cunningham two days later. It appeared at Farnborough that September, and the following month carried out a round trip from Hatfield to Castel Benito in Libya, at an average speed of 448mph. This sort of performance was unheard of in an airliner, making the Comet a true ground-breaker. Unfortunately, tragedy was to follow later, but not before the type had proved that jet airliner travel was the way ahead.

The other great achievement of 1949 was the successful conclusion of the Berlin Airlift. The arrival of more C-54s and the instigation of ever more efficient operational practices by the Joint Airlift Task Force meant that daily tonnages continued to rise: the one millionth ton of cargo was delivered on 18 February, and it was decided that 15-16 April would see a special all-out effort to set a new record for 24 hours of operations. This was reached easily, with 1,383 flights delivering 12,849 tonnes of coal to Berlin's airfields, and provided still greater impetus to the operation as a whole, apart from the propaganda victory it represented. With the realisation that the Western Allies were not going to give Berlin up, Stalin lifted the Soviet blockade of the city on 12 May. The Airlift continued until 30 September, when the last USAF C-54 arrived at Tempelhof with its load of coal, in order to ensure an adequate stockpile of supplies. According to USAF figures, since the operation began in earnest during June 1948, some 2,325,509.6 tonnes of cargo had been flown into Berlin (1,783,572.7 tonnes by the American Operation *Vittles*, 541,936.9 tonnes by the British Operation *Plainfare*). It had been a remarkable effort, a tribute to the resilience and determination of the Allies, and to air transport.

---

**28 Feb:** Maiden flight of the Dassault MD450 Ouragan, France's first indigenous fighter since the war.

**2 Mar:** The first non-stop round-the-world flight was completed by Boeing B-50A *Lucky Lady* of the USAF's 43rd Bomb Group. It took 94hr 1min and four in-flight refuellings from KB-29s for the aircraft to make it from Carswell AFB, TX all the way around the globe and back to its start destination.

**9 Mar:** The prototype Avro Shackleton maritime reconnaissance aircraft made its inaugural flight.

**26 Mar:** First flight of the Consolidated Vultee B-36D, the latest version of the Peacemaker family, which used four General Electric J47-GE-19 turbojets under its wings in addition to its six pusher-mounted piston units.

**1 Apr:** The Boeing 377 Stratocruiser entered service with Pan Am.

**26 Apr:** An extremely unusual feat was completed by an Aeronca Chief, which landed after having remained airborne continuously for six weeks and one minute (a record that still stands), as a successful campaign to improve the airfield at Fullerton in Los Angeles. The Aeronca was refuelled using cans passed up by hand from a vehicle on the ground.

**24 Jun:** The third Douglas D-558-II Skyrocket, using both its turbojet and rocket powerplants, exceeded Mach 1, the first in the D-558 series to do so.

**4 Sep:** The largest aircraft ever built in the UK, the eight-engined Bristol Brabazon, was first flown from the company's airfield at Filton (which had been specially enlarged to accommodate it).

**4 Sep:** The first Avro 707 tailless delta-wing research aircraft made its first flight.

**19 Sep:** Maiden flight of the Fairey Gannet turboprop anti-submarine warfare aircraft for the Fleet Air Arm, which was the first aircraft to use a turboprop engine (an Armstrong-Siddeley Double Mamba) with a dual propeller.

**7 Nov:** Inaugural flight of the Sikorsky S-55 helicopter.

**27 Nov:** The prototype Douglas C-124 Globemaster II took to the air for the first time. It was a modified development of the first Globemaster, the C-74, with a double-deck fuselage.

**22 Dec:** First flight of the North American F-86D Sabre, the first all-weather version of the type, thanks to its nose-mounted radar. It was also equipped with an afterburning General Electric J47 turbojet.

*The massive airlift in which the US Air Force and the RAF led the relief of the beleaguered Germans in Berlin brought all manner of transport aircraft into the operation. Wilfred Hardy's painting shows a typical scene at Gatow with Dakotas, Hastings and Yorks.*

These pages generously donated by 4624 (County of Oxford) Movements Squadron RAuxAF

*Airlift – To Save a City* by Wilfred Hardy GAvA

The invasion of the Republic of Korea on 25 June by Communist North Korean forces provided an unforseen early opportunity for many of the new aircraft types, introduced since the end of WWII to be tested for the first time in anger. At the outset, the US Far East Air Force (FEAF) was engaged only in protecting ships and transport aircraft involved in the evacuation of American nationals from South Korea, but this defensive role soon changed to something more aggressive. The first air-to-air combat occurred on 26 June, when a flight of F-82 Twin Mustangs was 'bounced' by a North Korean Lavochkin La-7 fighter; a day later, the crew of another F-82 in a flight of five was credited with the first kill of the war, when a Yak-9 was downed. On 28 June, the UN passed a resolution calling for a military response to the Communist aggression, and bombing raids against North Korean forces south of the 38th Parallel, using USAF B-26 Invaders and B-29s, commenced.

This was the first conflict to see widespread use of jet fighters from the outset, and the first jets to be successful in combat over Korea were Lockheed F-80s of the 35th Fighter Bomber Squadron which destroyed four Ilyushin Il-10s on the first day of the air war proper. On 3 July, the US Navy notched up its first kills, when two Yak-9s were shot down by a pair of Grumman F9F Panthers.

UN air superiority was quickly achieved in the early stages of the campaign, but a new threat emerged at the start of November, when the first MiG-15s being operated in the theatre by the Chinese People's Liberation Army Air Force (PLAAF) appeared on the scene. It was immediately apparent that not only was the MiG considerably faster than both the F-80 and the F9F, but that it had a better rate of climb and could out-turn them. and it was clear that extra steps had to be taken to combat this new Communist menace. A request for the deployment of a Wing each of F-86A Sabres and F-84E Thunderjets was accepted, and they were ready for operations during mid-December.

The early months of the Korean War were also significant for the first use of American military helicopters in any war zone. Later to be immortalised on film and television, US Army MASH (Mobile Army Surgical Hospital) units began operating in Korea during July, evacuating casualties from the front line on the ground using stretcher-bearing USAF Sikorsky H-5 helicopters (the military version of the S-51). On 4 September, an H-5 from the 3rd Rescue Squadron carried out the first rescue of a downed pilot from behind enemy lines. At the year's end, H-5s had transported 618 medical cases, including one 125-mile round trip to recover a Fleet Air Arm Sea Fury pilot. Over the course of the conflict, use of helicopters for ever more varied and demanding military tasks would increase significantly.

Finally, among 1950's maiden flights, Canada's first indigenous jet fighter, the often underrated Avro Canada CF-100. This was a two-seat, all-weather interceptor, though the first prototype which took to the air on 19 January was far removed from the type's main production configurations. It was powered by two Rolls-Royce AJ65 Avons, while all later marks used Avro Canada's own Orenda units. A production order for 124 CF-100 Mk3s was placed by the Royal Canadian Air Force in September 1950, and these (which entered squadron service in the summer of 1953) were fitted with the APG-33 fire-control radar which was key to the aircraft's capability.

**17 Jan:** Maiden flight of the Mikoyan-Gurevich MiG-17, a developed version of the MiG-15 which incorporated a new wing with more acute sweep and an afterburning Klimov VK-1F turbojet of indigenous design.
**27 Jan:** An agreement was signed under the Mutual Defense Assistance Program to supply the RAF with 88 Boeing B-29s, which was known as the Washington in RAF service.
**8 Apr:** A US Navy Consolidated PB4Y Privateer on an unarmed training flight was shot down over the Baltic by Soviet fighters.
**18 Apr:** The prototype Convair R3Y Tradewind turboprop long-range transport flying boat for the US Navy took to the air for the first time. Only eleven were built.
**17 May:** Transcontinental and Western Air changed its name to Trans World Airlines.
**1 Jun:** Flying Sikorsky S-51s, British European Airways started the first scheduled passenger-carrying helicopter service in the world, between Liverpool and Cardiff.

**3 Jun:** The swept-wing Republic YF-96A, a prototype forerunner of the F-84F Thunderstreak, made its first flight.
**25 Jun:** Communist North Korean forces invaded the Republic of Korea south of the 38th parallel.
**26 Jun:** The first air-to-air engagement of the Korean War.
**29 Jun:** The latest operational variant of the Gloster Meteor, the F8, entered RAF service.
**29 Jul:** Scheduled turboprop airline services began, when BEA started using Vickers Viscounts on the Northolt-Le Bourget route.
**23 Aug:** Supermarine's Type 535 fighter prototype, the direct forerunner of the RAF's production Swift, made its first flight. It had been modified from the Type 528 which had flown on 27 March.
**22 Sep:** The first non-stop crossing of the North Atlantic by a turbojet-engined aircraft was completed by a USAF F-84.
**13 Oct:** The Lockheed Model 1049 Super Constellation undertook its initial flight. It was 18ft 5in longer than the standard Constellation, able to carry 102 passengers, and powered by four

2,700hp Wright Double Cyclones in production form.
**1 Nov:** The MiG-15 made its first combat appearance in the Korean War.
**8 Nov:** The first ever jet-to-jet air combat was waged between USAF F-80 Shooting Stars and Chinese MiG-15s.
**10 Nov:** BOAC ended all of its remaining flying-boat services.
**20 Nov:** The Hawker P1072, modified from the P1040 prototype, became the first British aircraft to fly using both turbojet and rocket power.
**17 Dec:** USAF F-86A Sabres of the 4th Fighter Interceptor Wing began offensive operations over Korea.

*Keith Ferris's dramatic painting depicts the first engagement between swept-wing jet fighters that took place on 17 December 1950, and shows Lt Col Bruce Hinton of the 4th Fighter Interceptor Group in his F-86A Sabre shooting down a Russian-built Chinese Air Force MiG-15. © 2001 keithferrisart.com*

These pages generously donated by Tony Finding

*First Swept Wing Encounter* by Keith Ferris ASAA

The Korean War continued throughout the year with no major breakthroughs for either side. Increased numbers of USAF F-86 Sabres allowed B-29s to penetrate deeper into the Communist air defences than before, and a major UN air offensive from June to August was a success. USAF B-26 Invaders, US Marine Corps F4U-5N Corsairs and F7F-3 Tigercats mounted effective night intruder raids against enemy land convoys. However, the Chinese People's Liberation Army Air Force, continuing to operate alongside the North Korean air arm, grew substantially during 1951 with further deliveries of MiG-15s (including the more powerful MiG-15bis).

By the end of 1951, well over 500 MiGs were deployed, and Communist air activity had increased substantially, while corresponding calls for an increase in the UN's fighter strength fell on deaf ears. There had, however, been some new additions to the inventory of aircraft available to the UN. The Royal Australian Air Force supplied 15 new Meteor F8s from No 77 Squadron, which after some delays were able to begin participating in offensive missions on 30 July. Sadly, the type did not prove especially effective as an interceptor, and the unit's first two MiG shootdowns did not occur until 1 December. Rather more successful in their chosen role were the US Army Bell H-13 helicopters, the first military version of the Model 47, which began to operate in Korea during January. They were intended mainly for artillery observation and liaison duties, and could be used for casualty evacuation, though only for one person at a time.

The year 1951 was another good one for the British aircraft industry, which won one of its most prestigious contracts ever when the USAF ordered the English Electric Canberra for the night interdiction strike role. A production RAF Canberra B2 was flown to Andrews AFB, Washington on 21 February, setting a new distance/speed record in the process. Test pilot Roland Beamont took over at the controls for a 'fly-off' against the Martin XB-51 prototype, and gave another outstanding demonstration of the type's qualities. A decision on the victor was not long in coming, with the Canberra's range and agility foremost among its winning qualities. 250 were ordered, to be produced under licence by Martin as B-57s and powered by Armstrong Siddeley Sapphire turbojets, also built in the USA as the Wright J-65. Further production contracts were placed subsequently, and the B-57 went on to serve with great distinction, not least in Vietnam.

Meanwhile, the first flight from Boscombe Down in July of the Hawker P1067 prototype WB188, in the hands of Neville Duke, heralded the appearance of another legendary British aircraft: the Hawker Hunter. It was designed to a specification issued in early 1948 for a single-seat interceptor capable of Mach 0.94. What emerged in the swept-wing P1067, re-named Hunter in early 1952, was one of the most elegant combat jets of all time, thanks to the design genius of Sydney Camm. The first two prototypes were powered by a Rolls-Royce Avon (the third P1067 used an Armstrong-Siddeley Sapphire) and though still some way from production configuration, WB188 immediately showed signs of a classic in the making.

---

**23 Jan:** A fierce air battle ensued when 30 Chinese-operated MiG-15s engaged 33 USAF F-84E Thunderjets over Antung airfield in North Korea.

**23 Jan:** Inaugural flight of the tailless Douglas XF4D-1 prototype, which evolved into the considerably-modified F4D Skyray for production and entered US Navy service just over five years later.

**31 Jan:** US Army Bell H-13s, military variants of the Model 47, began operating in the Korean theatre.

**23 Feb:** The Dassault MD452 Mystère fighter-bomber took to the air for the first time.

**15 Mar:** The first air-to-air refuelling (of a B-47 Stratojet) was undertaken by a modified Boeing C-97A transport, re-designated KC-97C. Various sub-types of KC-97 saw sterling USAF service, with regular units and those of the Air National Guard and Air Force Reserve, for many years.

**11 Apr:** The Douglas DC-6B, the dedicated passenger-carrying variant of the type, entered service with United Air Lines.

**18 May:** William Bridgeman became the fastest man in the world when he piloted the second Douglas D-558-II Skyrocket to a speed of 1,130mph or Mach 1.72. This was the first ever flight to exceed 1,000mph.

**18 May:** Maiden flight of the prototype Vickers Valiant jet bomber, the first of the RAF's triumverate of 'V-Bombers'.

**14 Jun:** North Korean Polikarpov Po-2 training biplanes carried out their first night 'nuisance raid' against a UN military installation. These sorties, by Po-2s and other aircraft types proved a considerable irritant over the months that followed.

**20 Jun:** The variable-geometry Bell X-5 research aircraft made its first flight.

**30 Jun:** Gloster Meteor F8s of No 77 Squadron, Royal Australian Air Force started operations over Korea.

**20 Jul:** Initial flight of the Hawker P1067, which was developed for production as the Hunter.

**5 Aug:** The Supermarine Swift took to the air for the first time, in pre-production form.

**7 Aug:** First flight of the McDonnell XF3H-1 Demon all-weather interceptor prototype for the US Navy.

**10 Aug:** The Short SA4 Sperrin bomber prototype made its initial flight from Belfast's Aldergrove airfield. It lost out to the Valiant in the battle for an RAF production order.

**1 Sep:** A new Communist air offensive began after talks aimed at ending the Korean War failed.

**20 Sep:** The Grumman F9F-6 Cougar, a swept-wing derivative of the Panther, made its first flight.

**26 Sep:** Maiden flight of the de Havilland DH110 night fighter prototype, initially intended for the RAF, but which was later purchased by the Fleet Air Arm as the Sea Vixen.

**26 Nov:** Another new British fighter prototype, the delta-winged Gloster Javelin, made its inaugural flight.

**12 Dec:** The prototype de Havilland Canada DHC3 Otter utility aircraft undertook its maiden flight from Downsview, Toronto.

*In the winter of 1950-51 US Navy F4U Corsairs of VF-113, flying from the USS* Philippine Sea *during the Korean War, made concentrated attacks on the bridges at Sinuiju, spanning the Yalu River. One of these air strikes is portrayed in this painting by Phillip E West.*

*Attack on Yalu Bridges* by Phillip West

Three very different heavy bombers took to the air for the first time during 1952, each of which would form a significant part of NATO's strategic deterrent during the Cold War. The development process which led up to the Boeing YB-52's maiden flight on 15 April had begun with the release of a US military requirement back in 1946. Boeing's initial proposals were for a turboprop-powered aircraft, and these designs went through several re-thinks. The most radical of these had taken place in the spring of 1948, when the company finally became convinced as to the merits of turbojet power, a step which ended up giving birth to the Model 464-67. This was developed in rapid time by the company as a result of the unique experience which it had gained in the field of large jet bombers in creating the XB-47 Stratojet.

With support from Strategic Air Command C-in-C, Gen Curtis E. LeMay, an initial contract between the USAF and Boeing for a first batch of thirteen B-52As was signed on 14 February 1951. Work on the prototypes was centred at Boeing's Seattle facility, but an almost unprecedented number of sub-contractors (over 5,000) was also used, without any problems at all. This was an impressive feat at the time. Sadly, damage caused by a pneumatic system blow-out delayed the XB-52's maiden flight for some months, until 2 October 1952, but in fact the YB-52 was airborne from Boeing Field on 15 April, and this aircraft began the test programme.

In contrast to Boeing, the British aircraft industry did not possess significant knowledge of jet strategic bomber design when a number of manufacturers set about providing submissions to the UK Air Ministry requirement B35/46 to provide the RAF with a new medium-range bomber. The crescent-winged Handley Page HP80 and the Avro 698 (with a tailless delta configuration) were initially selected, though the Vickers 660 also gained an order and went on to become the first to fly (in May 1951) and enter service, as the Valiant B1 (during early 1955). Avro tested its aircraft's design using a series of small delta handling prototypes, the Type 707 family, the first of which took to the air in September 1949. By the time of the 698's maiden flight in the hands of 'Roly' Falk on 30 August, they had had already contributed much useful knowledge to the programme. Unfortunately, the intended Rolls-Royce Olympus engines were not ready in time, so the first 698 (named Vulcan four weeks into flight trials) used four Avon RA3 units instead, but the basic configuration was effectively finalised.

Likewise, Handley Page used a scaled-down research aircraft to try out the radical configuration of its new bomber. The little HP88 tested the aerodynamic characteristics of a crescent wing shape for just over two months in the summer of 1951, but it broke up over Stansted that August and was not replaced. The wing had not been at fault, and in any case the HP80 programme itself was well-advanced, though teething problems pushed the first flight date back to Christmas Eve 1952. On that day, Handley Page chief test pilot Sqn Ldr H. G. Hazelden took off from Boscombe Down in the silver HP80 and undertook a short, if effortless maiden sortie. With 25 production examples on order for the RAF, the aircraft's future was already assured, and the name Victor was confirmed in December.

---

**22 Jan:** The first Certificate of Airworthiness to be awarded to a jet airliner was presented to the de Havilland DH106 Comet 1.

**19 Mar:** Initial flight of the North American F-86F Sabre, using a revised wing for extra combat manoeuvrability, which entered USAF service only nine days later.

**1 Apr:** The tandem-rotor Piasecki H-21 helicopter, often known as the 'Flying Banana', took to the air for the first time.

**2 May:** BOAC began commercial operations with the DH106 Comet 1, between London and Johannesburg, the first ever scheduled service to use a jet airliner.

**19 May:** The world's first variable-geometry fighter, the Grumman XF10F-1 Jaguar, made its initial flight.

**29 May:** Air-to-air refuelling was used in a combat situation for the first time when USAF KB-29s replenished a dozen F-84Es on a mission over Korea.

**17 Jul:** 58 USAF F-84G Thunderjets completed a massed flight from Turner AFB, GA to Misawa and Chitose air bases in Japan, supported by KB-29 tankers.

**23 Jul:** The distinctive butterfly-tailed Fouga CM170 Magister made its inaugural flight. It was the first jet trainer specifically designed for the training role.

**29 Jul:** A USAF RB-45C Tornado completed the first non-stop flight across the Pacific, from Elmendorf AFB, AK to Yokota in Japan.

**31 Jul:** The first crossing of the North Atlantic by helicopters ended. It had been carried out by two USAF Sikorsky H-19s, and took some 16 days.

**9 Aug:** Lt Peter Carmichael of 802 NAS, Fleet Air Arm, at the controls of a Hawker Sea Fury FB11 became the first pilot of a piston-engined aircraft to shoot down a MiG-15 during the Korean War.

**16 Aug:** Maiden flight of the Bristol 175 Britannia airliner, powered by four Bristol Proteus turboprops.

**22 Aug:** The giant Saunders-Roe SR45 Princess flying boat prototype first flew, powered by ten Bristol Proteus turboprops.

**30 Aug:** First flight of the prototype Avro 698 jet bomber, the second of the RAF 'V-Bombers', later named the Vulcan.

**20 Sep:** The sole Bell X-3, intended as a Mach 2 research aircraft, took to the air for its initial flight. Its highest recorded speed was Mach 1.21 in July 1953.

**16 Oct:** The prototype Sud-Ouest SO4050 Vautour all-weather fighter for the French Armée de l'Air made its maiden flight.

**28 Oct:** The first prototype Douglas XA3D-1, later known as the Skywarrior, took to the air.

**3 Nov:** First flight of the Saab 32 Lansen.

**4 Dec:** Maiden flight of the prototype Grumman XS2F-1 anti-submarine warfare platform, produced as the S2F Tracker.

**24 Dec:** The last of the RAF's trio of 'V-Bombers' to fly, the Handley Page HP80 (the prototype of the Victor) took to the air.

*John Young's painting shows the prototype of the world's first jet airliner getting airborne at Hatfield. The production de Havilland DH106 Comet first entered commercial service with BOAC in May 1952.*

These pages generously donated by Breitling

*Jet Age Traveller* by John Young VPGAvA, VPASAA

# 1953

The conclusion of the Korean War, with the ceasefire of 27 July, brought to an end a conflict which had demonstrated beyond any doubt the superiority of jet fighters in aerial combat, and in particular the capabilities of the North American F-86 Sabre. By this stage, two USAF wings operating the type over Korea had re-equipped with F-86E and F-86F versions, and there was no question that the UN air forces had achieved the upper hand. Large numbers of relatively inexperienced Communist pilots now flying MiG-15s tended to remain at over 40,000ft, and the new F-86F proved more than a match for the Soviet fighter at all altitudes. In January alone, 37 Communist aircraft were 'downed' in combat, mostly by F-86Fs in high-altitude engagements. The type also proved to be an effective fighter-bomber, in spite of some initial misgivings as to its suitability for the role.

Even before the last firing of an F-86's guns in anger over Korea had taken place, North American had virtually completed development on the type's successor, the F-100 Super Sabre, which would become the first aircraft capable of going supersonic in level flight to reach operational service. The development period of the Super Sabre was very rapid indeed, and its attainment of the major intended performance milestone even more so. Ten YF-100 prototypes and 110 production F-100As, powered by Pratt & Whitney's new J57 afterburning turbojet, were initially ordered by the USAF in November 1951, and the first example undertook its maiden flight just over eighteen months later, on 25 May 1953. What was so remarkable about the prototype's first flight was that the test pilot took the YF-100 through the sound barrier during the course of it, at the time a unique feat.

In fact, the British aircraft industry could already have started producing its first supersonic fighter, had the Hawker P1083 (a development of the Hunter, powered by an afterburning Rolls-Royce Avon) not have been cancelled in 1953. However, the manufacturer continued to experiment with the use of reheated engines, and in September a new absolute world speed record was set by Neville Duke in the modified first prototype Hunter WB188, now designated as the Mark 3. This used an afterburning Avon RA7R, delivering 9,600lb of thrust with the reheat engaged, which allowed the aircraft to reach 1,107.76km/h (727.63mph) over its 3km course off the south coast of England. This was to be a short-lived record, though the next benchmark kept the 'honours' in Britain as Mike Lithgow flew a factory-fresh Supermarine Swift to 1,183.74km/h (735.7mph) in a record attempt over Libya on 25 September.

The very different capabilities of another new RAF aircraft were demonstrated during October, when Canberra PR3 WE139 of No 540 Squadron set two new records during its victorious participation in the UK to New Zealand Air Race. The aircraft flew from London to Basra in Iraq (a distance of 2,832 miles) in 5 hours 11minutes, and completed the overall race distance in 23 hours 50 minutes. Apart from being an extremely impressive feat in itself, this performance illustrated the fact that the RAF's Canberras would be easily deployable over long distances, if circumstances dictated.

**3 Jan:** First flight of the Cessna 310 twin piston-engined executive aircraft.
**6 Jan:** A new German national airline, Luftag, was established. It was re-titled Deutsche Lufthansa on 6 August 1954.
**30 Jan:** Maiden flight of the Boeing B-47E Stratojet, which was equipped with JATO packs for better take-off performance. It became the most-produced version of the type.
**31 Jan:** The largest rescue operation using helicopters to date – Operation *Canute*, which followed floods across eastern England and the Netherlands.
**21 Feb:** The Bell X-1A made its initial powered flight.
**10 Mar:** Communist jet fighters attacked those of NATO over Western Europe for the first time, when two Czechoslovak Air Force MiG-15s engaged a pair of USAF F-84s over Bavaria.
**27 Mar:** The USAF issued a classified design requirement for a high-altitude 'special reconnaissance aircraft', which led to the Lockheed U-2.
**9 Apr:** An aircraft of unique configuration made its maiden flight: the Convair XF2Y-1 jet seaplane fighter prototype.

**18 Apr:** Scheduled turboprop airline services began when BEA started using the Vickers Viscount between London and Nicosia, Cyprus.
**18 May:** Jacqueline Cochran, at the controls of a Canadair Sabre, became the first woman to officially fly faster than sound.
**18 May:** First flight of Douglas' new DC-7 airliner.
**25 May:** A great line of USAF fighters began, when the North American YF-100 took to the air.
**14 Jun:** Maiden flight of the RAF's Blackburn Beverley transport.
**30 Jun:** A record-breaking month for USAF F-86 Sabre pilots operating over Korea, during which they had shot down 77 Communist aircraft, came to an end.
**20 Jul:** The first Martin B-57A, the licence-built version of the Canberra for the USAF, made its inaugural flight from Baltimore.
**27 Jul:** The final 'kill' of the conflict occurred in Korea, when a 4th FIW F-86F Sabre shot down an Ilyushin Il-12 transport.
**27 Jul:** The last combat mission of the Korean War, a close support sortie undertaken by a B-26C Invader of the 3rd BW.
**27 Jul:** The Korean War officially came to an end when North

Korea signed a ceasefire with the United Nations.
**7 Sep:** A new absolute world air speed record was set by Hawker test pilot Neville Duke at the controls of modified Hawker Hunter prototype WB188. He reached 1,107.76km/h (727.63mph).
**9 Oct:** The London-New Zealand air race was won by an RAF crew flying a Canberra B2.
**24 Oct:** First flight of the prototype Convair XF-102 delta-wing interceptor. It was not immediately successful and had to be modified into the improved YF-102A before performance reached expectations.
**29 Oct:** The first North American YF-100 set a new absolute world air speed record of 1,215.04km/h (755.149mph).
**20 Nov:** The first flight past Mach 2 was undertaken by the second Douglas D-558-II Skyrocket.

Lawrence Hargrave, *one of a pair of Lockheed Constellation Model 749s of the Australian airline QANTAS, looks on as the Wright Cyclones on its neighbour burst into life in this painting by John Young.*

*Kangaroo's Giant Leap* by John Young VPGAvA, VPASAA

Seldom in one year have so many significant new aircraft types made their maiden flights than did so in 1954 and, equally, seldom have the hopes for another been so comprehensively dashed. It is difficult to say which could generally be described as the most significant, but in terms of its subsequent production run the Lockheed C-130 Hercules merits first mention. Its gestation period really began during the Korean conflict, when the USAF began to study the need for a medium tactical transport, able to haul a payload of 30,000lb over some 1,500 miles and to operate from unprepared strips. Only five months after a Request for Proposals was issued to manufacturers, the Lockheed design was declared the winner, with two YC-130 prototypes being ordered. A little more than a year on from that announcement, the first USAF production contract for seven C-130As was signed, with others increasing the totals to 75 by September 1954.

Just as the C-130 went on to serve in roles far removed from that for which it was originally designed, so the Boeing 367-80 jet transport prototype also turned out to be the progenitor of one of the most varied families of aircraft ever produced. The Boeing Company ploughed some $16 million of its own money into the development of this aircraft, commonly known as the Dash 80 (referring to the fact that it was originally conceived as the eightieth design configuration of the Model 367, the C-97/KC-97 family), because it recognised the benefits that jet power could offer for the future of commercial and military transport aircraft, and also military air-to-air refuelling tankers. No backing from airlines or the US military was forthcoming when Boeing began its brave private venture in August 1952, and this was still the case when the Dash 80 made its first flight from Renton Field, Seattle.

In terms of the Dash 80's intended military applications, the aircraft was fitted with a dummy 'flying boom' for air-to-air refuelling early in its test programme, and it was announced only three weeks after its maiden flight that the USAF would be purchasing 29 tanker variants designated KC-135A. A separate procurement programme for a jet tanker was in fact already under way, with the Model 717 (the manufacturer's designation) in contention; it was won by Lockheed, but the USAF decided that the use of two different types to replace the KC-97 was unworkable, and so the KC-135 won the day with a further order of 68 units being placed in early 1955. With production for the US military under way, development of the Model 707 for civilian use could commence in earnest, its first flight occurring three years later (see 1957).

The success of Boeing's jet transport was extremely galling for de Havilland, coming as it did in the period after all DH106 Comet 1s had been permanently grounded due to a series of three fatal accidents. The first of them had seen BOAC's G-ALYV break up in a tropical thunderstorm during climbout from Dum Dum Airport in Calcutta on a flight to Delhi on 2 May 1953 with 43 people on board. At that time, it was not thought necessary to ground the fleet. This took place for the first time after G-ALYP broke up on 10 January 1954 at 26,000ft while flying between Rome's Ciampino Airport and London-Heathrow, the final leg of a service from Singapore. On this occasion, the 35 aboard were killed, and all BOAC Comets were grounded from the following day until 23 March while modifications took place, aimed at preventing engine explosions which were thought to have caused this tragedy. However, on April 7, G-ALYY (crewed by South African Airways, and en route to Johannesburg) disintegrated near Naples after taking off from Rome, with 21 fatalities.

---

**10 Jan:** 35 people on board BOAC DH106 Comet 1 G-ALYP were killed when the aircraft broke up at 26,000ft on climb-out from Rome's Ciampino Airport. All the airline's Comets were grounded a day later.

**13 Feb:** The RAF received its first swept-wing jet fighters, in the shapes of No 56 Squadron's new (but, alas, rather troublesome) Supermarine Swift F1s.

**28 Feb:** Maiden flight of the prototype Lockheed XF-104 interceptor, which became the Starfighter.

**8 Mar:** The Sikorsky S-58 utility helicopter took to the air for the first time in prototype form.

**23 Mar:** The grounding order on BOAC's Comet 1s was lifted and the fleet became operational again.

**7 Apr:** BOAC Comet 1 G-ALYY broke up during its climbout from Rome. Two days later, all examples of the type were permanently grounded.

**1 May:** The USAF's first Airborne Early Warning & Control Division was formed, operating Lockheed RC-121Cs.

**22 Jun:** The Douglas A4D Skyhawk prototype for the US Navy made its first flight.

**26 Jun:** Initial flight of the RAF's new Hunting Jet Provost T1 basic jet trainer.

**15 Jul:** The Boeing 367-80 made its inaugural flight. It became the USAF's KC-135 Stratotanker and the civil 707.

**3 Aug:** Rolls-Royce's Thrust Measuring Rig VTOL test platform made its first flight. It was more popularly known as the 'Flying Bedstead', and remains the only flying machine built by the famous company.

**4 Aug:** Maiden flight of the English Electric P1 interceptor prototype, later developed into the RAF's Lightning.

**27 Sep:** Entry into full operational service of the production North American F-100A Super Sabre, with the USAF's 479th Fighter Day Wing at George AFB, CA.

**29 Sep:** The McDonnell F-101 Voodoo made its maiden flight.

**6 Oct:** Built as a supersonic research aircraft, the delta-winged Fairey Delta 2 took to the air for the first time.

**11 Dec:** The USS *Forrestal* was launched, and became the first new aircraft carrier built since the war.

**20 Dec:** After problems with the YF-102 flown the year before, the modified Convair YF-102A interceptor made its initial flight. The design incorporated the distinctive waisted 'area rule' fuselage configuration developed by Richard Whitcomb of NACA.

*The prototype Vickers Viscount, when first flown in July 1948, was the world's first turboprop airliner. Wilfred Hardy's painting depicts the larger Viscount Type 700, which was ordered in quantity for British European Airways and entered passenger service with the airline in 1953.*

*Turboprop Triumph* by Wilfred Hardy GAvA

Having undergone a lengthy period of reconstruction following the damage wrought on the country's industrial base during the war, France's aerospace industry was already in resurgent mood by 1955. During the course of this year, a number of new products from its aircraft manufacturers took to the air for the first time; types which would go on to significant production runs and lengthy operational careers.

However, a pair of new interceptor prototypes from Dassault were important, not as successful aircraft themselves, but as the progenitors of other, more enduring designs. The Super Mystère B1 was a development of the earlier Mystère IV series, whose design was influenced in a number of ways by close study of the North American F-100 (in particular, the type's new wing, of much thinner section than that of its predecessor). Marcel Dassault's initial choice of powerplant was the Rolls-Royce Avon RA14, but their supply was not forthcoming, and the aircraft which took to the air on 2 March used an older Avon RA7R. No order for the Armée de l'Air was placed at this stage. This had to wait until the Super Mystère B2, which used a SNECMA Atar 101G2, but was otherwise almost identical.

Meanwhile, the MD550 Mirage I prototype never saw series production, but is significant as the first machine to bear the Mirage name. Its initial flight took place in June, but it was too small and had poor lift characteristics due to its wing configuration. However, preparations for what was to become the Mirage III were soon well under way.

The Sud-Est SE210 Caravelle twin-jet airliner required very little adaptation from prototype form before it entered production. In many ways, this was a pioneering design: the first to have its powerplants (initially Rolls-Royce Avons) mounted on the rear fuselage rather than underwing, and also the first jetliner in the short-to-medium-haul sector.

Significant developments to this end had also been occurring in the Soviet Union, where the prototype Tupolev Tu-104 made its inaugural flight on 17 June. Unlike the Caravelle and most other early jetliners, though, this was an adaptation of an existing military aircraft, the Tu-16 'Badger' strategic bomber, first flown in 1952. The initial aircraft was a 50-seater with two Mikulin RD-3 turbojets, though the production Tu-104A had space for 70 passengers and used a pair of Mikulin AM-3M engines, generating considerably more power. Less than a year later, on 22 March 1956, the prototype was the subject of great Western attention when it paid a visit to London-Heathrow Airport, but regular Aeroflot operations did not begin until 15 September of that year. This did however make the Soviet carrier the second in the world, after BOAC with the ill-fated Comet 1, to introduce scheduled passenger-carrying jet airliner services.

The other important Soviet aircraft which took to the air in 1955 were a series of interceptor prototypes by Mikoyan-Gurevich. An official requirement had been issued for a point defence fighter capable of attaining 2,000km/h (1,243mph) with a minimal load of armaments. Work began on such an aircraft in 1953, and the Ye-2 prototype which flew in February 1955 was the initial result. It was a standard swept-wing design, as Mikoyan (along with other Soviet fighter design bureaux) had been relatively slow to realise the advantages of a delta configuration, as was being adopted by many Western manufacturers such as Saab and Dassault. Proposals for a tailed delta represented an acceptable compromise, and thus a second prototype, the Ye-4, was built.

---

**9 Feb:** The first of the RAF's 'V-bombers' entered full operational service when No 138 Squadron declared service readiness with its new Vickers Valiant B1s.

**14 Feb:** Mikoyan-Gurevich's Ye-2 interceptor prototype made its first flight. This was the first in a series of prototypes which gave birth to the production MiG-21.

**26 Feb:** North American test pilot George F. Smith carried out the first supersonic ejection, from an F-100 Super Sabre.

**12 Mar:** The Sud-Est SE3130 Alouette II made its first flight. It became the first turboshaft-engined helicopter to enter production, powered by a Turboméca Artouste II unit, and proved very successful, with over 1,300 being built.

**25 Mar:** The initial flight of the Vought XF8U-1 fighter prototype for the US Navy was made from Edwards AFB.

**10 May:** Admission of the Federal Republic of Germany to NATO, which thereby helped pave the way towards re-establishment of the country's armed services.

**27 May:** First flight of the prototype Sud-Est SE210 Caravelle twin-jet airliner.

**17 Jun:** The USSR's first production jet airliner, the Tupolev Tu-104, took to the air for its initial flight.

**2 Aug:** The Lockheed U-2 high-altitude reconnaissance aircraft took to the air for the first time from Groom Lake, NV.

**20 Aug:** A new absolute world air speed record was claimed by an F-100C Super Sabre, which reached an average 1,323.03km/h (822.135mph).

**22 Oct:** First flight of the Republic YF-105A Thunderchief tactical fighter-bomber prototype for the USAF.

**25 Oct:** The Saab 35 Draken delta-winged interceptor made its initial flight.

**18 Nov:** The Bell X-2 was released by its EB-50A carrier aircraft for its first powered flight, using its Curtiss XLR-25-CW-3 rocket engine.

**24 Nov:** Fokker's twin-turboprop F-27 Friendship regional airliner was flown for the first time.

**Nov:** Mikoyan-Gurevich's Ye-50 interceptor prototype made its first flight. In production as the MiG-21, it went on to become one of the most successful and long-serving of all Soviet-built combat aircraft.

**10 Dec:** Inaugural flight of the Ryan X-13 Vertijet, developed in order to carry out research into vertical take-off and landing techniques by fixed-wing aircraft. It was launched vertically and then made the transition into conventional flight.

**20 Dec:** The prototype de Havilland DH106 Comet 3, immediate precursor to the stretched and improved production Comet 4, completed the first circumnavigation of the globe by a jet airliner.

*A Hawker Hunter F2 of No 263(F) Squadron is featured in this painting by John Young, flying over its RAF Wattisham base in the mid-1950s. The squadron operated the Sapphire-engined F2 from February 1955 to August 1956.*

*Hunter over Wattisham* by John Young VPGAvA, VPASAA

# 1956

There were some major developments within NATO during the year. Most significant was the re-establishment of the German Luftwaffe on 24 September, made possible by the Federal Republic's admission to the Alliance on 10 May 1955. For its first year, the 'new' air arm concentrated on training and support tasks, using a variety of aircraft supplied as a result of the USA's Mutual Defense Assistance Program. Through this funding was made available for the re-equipment of European NATO armed forces. For training, Piper L-18C Super Cubs and CCF-built Harvard IVs were used for basic instruction before Luftwaffe pilots moved on to the Lockheed T-33A. In addition, Douglas C-47s were supplied for transport duties. The build-up continued apace to the point where, the following year, the Luftwaffe's first post-war combat unit was formed in the shape of JBG-31, flying the F-84F Thunderstreak.

The French Armée de l'Air was looking to upgrade its combat potential, and key to this was another Dassault delta – the Mirage III, which made its maiden flight in November and subsequently went on to become one of the most successful European-built jet fighters. The SNECMA Atar 101G-2 turbojet powered the aircraft past Mach 1.52 just over two months after its maiden flight. In fact, the pre-production Mirage IIIA and subsequent full production IIIC had relatively little in common with the prototype aircraft, as an uprated Atar 9 engine was available which delivered enough extra power to merit redesigning the

delta wing and fuselage. Thus equipped, the Mirage IIIA passed Mach 2 within a few weeks of its initial flight on 12 May 1958, becoming the first European aircraft to do so.

One of the aircraft which went on to be almost a symbol of the Cold War began operations in 1956 – the Lockheed U-2. Just eight months after the type's maiden flight, the first examples of this high-altitude reconnaissance aircraft were deployed briefly to RAF Lakenheath in the UK, and then more permanently to Wiesbaden AB in Germany, for operation by WRSP (Weather Reconnaissance Squadron Provisional) 1. This was a cover for the unit's real purpose, which was to undertake photo-reconnaissance over the Warsaw Pact states in Eastern Europe on behalf of the CIA.

The first penetration of the USSR's airspace took place on 4 July, a mission that illustrated the value of employing such a high-flying aircraft when the unarmed U-2 was sighted by a group of Soviet MiGs. However, they were unable to engage it successfully. The intelligence provided by the U-2s of WRSP-1 was, from the outset, extremely valuable, helping, for instance, to dispel the notion that the Soviet bomber force was expanding at a rate which far outstripped that of the USAF's. The one slight cloud hanging over these early missions was the fact that Soviet air defence radars had easily managed to lock on to the overflying U-2s, proving, as would subsequent events, that the aircraft was more vulnerable to attack than had been anticipated.

**20 Jan:** Maiden flight of the Supermarine Type 544 swept-wing fighter prototype, which was developed as the Scimitar for the Fleet Air Arm, and became the Service's first supersonic aircraft.
**25 Jan:** It was announced by the British Ministry of Supply that a joint working group to investigate the possibilities for a supersonic jet airliner had been set up between airlines and manufacturers.
**10 Mar:** Peter Twiss, flying the Fairey Delta 2 research aircraft, set a new absolute world air speed record of 1,821.39km/h (1,132mph). It was the last time that the record would be held by a British pilot flying a British aircraft.
**23 Apr:** Maiden flight of the Douglas C-133 Cargomaster strategic transport for the US Military Air Transport Service (MATS).
**1 Apr:** The Lockheed U-2 was deployed operationally for the first time.
**1 May:** The Bölkow aircraft firm was established in Stuttgart. It later merged with the Messerschmitt and Heinkel companies.
**20 May:** A hydrogen bomb was dropped from an aircraft for the first time, when a USAF B-52 released the weapon near Bikini Atoll.
**7 Jul:** The de Havilland DH106 Comet C2 entered RAF service

with No 216 Squadron at Lyneham, which thus became the world's first military jet transport unit.
**23 Jul:** Maiden flight of the Dassault Etendard II, a swept-wing tactical strike and light reconnaissance aircraft developed to meet a common NATO requirement (eventually won by the Fiat G-91).
**24 Jul:** The naval Etendard IV undertook its initial flight. This version proved successful, entering carrier-borne Aéronavale service in IVM guise during 1962.
**9 Aug:** The Fiat G-91 flew for the first time. It was the successful contender for NATO's NBMR 1 requirement.
**31 Aug:** First flight of the Boeing KC-135A Stratotanker air-to-air refuelling platform.
**15 Sep:** Aeroflot began using the Tupolev Tu-104 on scheduled services, between Moscow, Omsk and Irkutsk. It was the only jet airliner in service at the time due to the grounding of the Comet.
**24 Sep:** Re-establishment of the German Luftwaffe.
**10 Oct:** Inaugural flight of the Lockheed L-1649 Starliner, a substantial re-development of the Super Constellation. It was the first airliner capable of flying across the North Atlantic non-stop.
**30 Oct:** A US Navy Douglas R4D, a ski-equipped C-47, landed

at the South Pole, the first aircraft to do so.
**31 Oct:** RAF and Fleet Air Arm air strikes against Egypt began, after President Nasser had nationalised the Suez Canal on 26 July, and refused to move Egyptian military forces from the region.
**5 Nov:** RAF Hastings and Valetta transports, together with Armée de l'Air Noratlas and C-47s, dropped paratroopers around the Suez Canal. Two days later, a ceasefire was signed to end the crisis.
**11 Nov:** Maiden flight of the Convair XB-58 Hustler nuclear bomber prototype for the USAF, capable of more than Mach 2.
**28 Nov:** The Ryan X-13 Vertijet research aircraft undertook a transition from vertical to horizontal flight for the first time, at 6,000ft over Edwards AFB, CA.
**26 Dec:** First flight of the Convair YF-106A supersonic all-weather interceptor prototype, a much-altered development of the F-102 Delta Dagger.

*In October and November 1956, Canberra B2s operating from Cyprus flew against Egyptian military targets during the Suez campaign. Wilfred Hardy's painting depicts a B2 of No 10 Squadron which carries the distinctive Suez yellow/black bands.*

These pages generously donated by the Coachmakers and Coach Harness Makers

*Suez Stripes* by Wilfred Hardy GAvA

# 1957

The British military aircraft production industry was thrown into turmoil during 1957, when an axe was wielded over planned procurement. On 4 April, the then Secretary of State for Defence, Duncan Sandys, published a Defence White Paper which effectively sounded the death knell for the development and production of any further manned interceptors for the RAF, in favour of the use of surface-to-air missiles. The exception was the English Electric P1B (later developed into the Lightning), which coincidentally made its first flight on the same day. The Conservative Prime Minister, Harold Macmillan, had asked Sandys to 'secure a substantial reduction in expenditure', and this was achieved, albeit with enduring consequences.

An RAF requirement entitled OR337 for a dual turbojet/rocket-powered interceptor was cancelled, not long before the maiden flight of the Saunders-Roe SR53 which had been selected for this purpose. The SR53 had been intended as the prototype forerunner of the production P177, which was also to have been operated by the Fleet Air Arm, but in August Sandys announced that this requirement was also obsolete. Hope for Saunders-Roe's promising fighter lay with the possibility of an order for the German Luftwaffe, who wanted to purchase a supersonic interceptor, but the F-104 Starfighter was selected instead.

Another casualty was the Avro 730, intended as a 'V-bomber' successor and high-altitude reconnaissance aircraft capable of more than Mach 2. Construction of the first prototype had begun when the White Paper appeared, and recommended that the UK's strategic nuclear deterrent should in future not be provided by a potent RAF bomber force, but by the Blue Streak intercontinental ballistic missile – which itself ended up being cancelled.

In the civil field, Boeing was able to celebrate the first flight of its new jet airliner, the 707-100. Developed from the company's private-venture 367-80 prototype, which had first flown three years earlier, this event came over a year after the first KC-135A Stratotanker flew – and just over six months after its entry into USAF service.

Already, Pan Am had shown faith in the 707 by placing an order for twenty (designated 707-121s) during October 1955, when the 367-80 had demonstrated its potential for commercial use by making a round-trip flight between Seattle and Washington DC in just eight hours and eight minutes, considerably faster than propeller-driven machines. Across the Atlantic, Air France, Sabena and Lufthansa followed up with orders. The 707-100 was powered by four Pratt & Whitney JT3C-6 turbojets, and able to cruise some 200mph faster than its piston-engined contemporaries. It was just capable of flying the North Atlantic non-stop, and while the type's range was not quite up to scratch, the 707 could carry up to 179 passengers over that distance.

The Lockheed Model 188 Electra four-turboprop short to medium-haul airliner, powered by four Allison 501D-13 units, had been developed as a result of a specification issued by American Airlines in 1954. It was the first turboprop airliner to be built in the USA, and was capable of carrying 74 passengers in its initial form. Sadly for Lockheed, the advent of the jet age had a profound effect on the civil market that narrowed the Electra's appeal to airlines, and production ceased after just 170 units. The L188 later found a new lease of life as a freighter, and was developed for military use into the P3 Orion anti-submarine warfare and maritime reconnaissance aircraft.

---

**18 Jan:** A trio of B-52B Stratofortresses from the 93rd BW, USAF, completed Operation *Power Flite*, the first non-stop round-the-world flight by turbojet aircraft.
**1 Feb:** Entry into service with BOAC of the Bristol Britannia 102 turboprop airliner.
**19 Feb:** A so-called 'flat-riser' VTOL aircraft flew for the first time, in the shape of the experimental Bell X-14. Unlike previous VTOL machines such as the Ryan X-13, it took off from a conventional attitude, rather than a vertically-pointing position.
**7 Mar:** The USSR's first turboprop airliner, the Antonov An-10, made its maiden flight.
**20 Mar:** Initial flight of the first production de Havilland DH110 Sea Vixen FAW1 all-weather fighter for the Fleet Air Arm.
**25 Mar:** The Vought F-8A Crusader entered operational service with US Navy squadron VF-32 at Cecil Field, FL.
**4 Apr:** First flight of the English Electric P1B interceptor prototype, forerunner of the Lightning, on what was otherwise

an inauspicious day for the British aircraft industry.
**16 May:** The experimental Saunders-Roe SR53 fighter took to the air, powered by a de Havilland Spectre rocket motor and an Armstrong Siddeley Viper turbojet.
**21 May:** The Avro Vulcan B1 entered operational RAF service with No 83 Squadron at Waddington.
**11 Jun:** The USAF's first Lockheed U-2 was delivered to the 4080th Strategic Reconnaissance Wing at Laughlin AFB, TX.
**4 Jul:** Maiden flight of the Ilyushin Il-18 four-turboprop airliner.
**28 Aug:** With its two Rolls-Royce Avons augmented by a Napier Double Scorpion rocket motor, Canberra B2 WK163 set a new world altitude record for a manned aircraft, at 70,310ft.
**31 Aug:** The prototype Avro Vulcan B2 made its first flight.
**1 Sep:** The first post-war Luftwaffe combat aircraft unit came into existence – Jagdbombergeschwader 31, flying F-84F Thunderstreaks.
**1 Sep:** Establishment of the British Army Air Corps (AAC).

**4 Sep:** First flight of the Lockheed CL-329 JetStar prototype. It had been designed for a USAF light transport requirement, but went on to achieve more success as a civil executive jet.
**Sep:** The world's largest helicopter to date, the Russian Mil Mi-6, made its inaugural flight.
**3 Oct:** Another Soviet turboprop airliner, the 220-seat Tupolev Tu-114, made its first flight.
**6 Nov:** Inaugural flight of the Fairey Rotodyne convertiplane, intended for military and civil use.
**19 Dec:** BOAC began using the Bristol Britannia 312 between London and New York – the first trans-Atlantic airline service to use turboprop aircraft.

*The huge Convair B-36 Peacemaker bomber featured six engines with pusher propellers on the wing trailing edge. This painting by Stan Stokes depicts a B-36D version, which had four additional General Electric J47-GE-19 jet engines in underwing pods.*

*Peacekeeper* by Stan Stokes

# 1958

What was to become one of the greatest combat jets of all time made its maiden flight in May 1958. The McDonnell Aircraft Company of St Louis had already developed a reputation for producing very capable all-weather fighters, firstly the F3H Demon, then the F-101 Voodoo. When the US Navy contracted Chance Vought to produce its first supersonic fighter (resulting in the F-8 Crusader), McDonnell decided to go it alone, and designed a private-venture attack aircraft called the AH-1. Some interest was shown, and in April 1955 the Navy approached McDonnell with a more formal request for a design specification – not, however, for an attack aircraft, but for a carrier-borne fleet defence fighter. What resulted was the two-seat F4H-1 Phantom II, to be powered by General Electric's new J79 engine, and armed with four Raytheon Sparrow radar-guided air-to-air missiles. Early aerodynamic tests of the initial design revealed some shortcomings, which would have restricted the aircraft's ultimate performance to below Mach 2, so major changes were made. These led to some of the type's most distinctive design features, with anhedral being applied to the all-flying tailplane, and the wings being given a dog-tooth leading edge and dihedral on their folding portions.

The US Navy placed orders for two prototypes, five pre-production airframes and eleven production F4H-1s. Although the very first XF4H-1 suffered teething troubles and was considerably different from early series aircraft which followed (being fitted with two J79-GE-3A engines rather than the more powerful J79-GE-8s which were not ready, and not being equipped with the intended AN/APG-50 radar), it soon demonstrated impressive performance. In fact, by the time of the aircraft's inaugural flight from St Louis, the US Navy had yet to officially select the F4H-1 for its new fighter requirement, as the Vought F8U-3 Crusader III remained in competition. However, following a fly-off at Edwards AFB, the McDonnell machine was selected in December 1958. It was officially named as the Phantom II during summer 1959, and so was born a truly legendary aircraft.

The Avro Canada CF-105 Arrow, one of the most impressive fighters of the era, also took to the air in 1958. Unfortunately, it fell victim to a political axe less than a year after its first flight. The CF-105 (intended as a successor to the very effective CF-100) was designed to be capable of up to Mach 2.3 in level flight thanks to its two afterburning Orenda Iroquois PS-13-3 turbojets, to have a maximum altitude of 66,000ft and to incorporate an internal missile bay larger than the bomb-bay of a B-29. All this, coupled with a considerable combat radius, amounted to an unprecedented performance for an interceptor, a design ahead of its time in many respects. After three CF-105s had flown and with ten more on the production line in various states of completion, the whole project was cancelled by the Canadian Prime Minister on 20 February 1959, with the order that all traces of the aircraft be destroyed. The perceived effectiveness of surface-to-air missiles in place of manned interceptors and the cost of the CF-105 programme were given as justifications.

Development of the Comet 4, which drew on the lessons learnt from the investigations into the accidents to its predecessors, had been underway for some time thanks to the interim (and record-setting) Comet 3. BOAC had already ordered 19 Comet 4s for services between London and New York, and on 4 October its operation of the type commenced with the first ever simultaneous flights in both directions by jet airliners across the North Atlantic. Thanks to the Comet 4's availability, BOAC became, for a short time, the second most popular provider of trans-Atlantic services after Pan American, and ahead of TWA.

**14 Jan:** QANTAS started its round-the-world service, using Lockheed L-1049G Super Constellations.
**26 Jan:** The Lockheed F-104A Starfighter entered operational USAF service.
**9 Apr:** The last of the RAF's 'V-bombers' to enter operational service, the Handley-Page Victor B1, did so with No 10 Squadron at RAF Cottesmore.
**10 Apr:** First transition from vertical to horizontal flight by the Fairey Rotodyne prototype.
**27 Apr:** The de Havilland DH106 Comet 4 made its first flight.
**30 Apr:** Initial flight of the Blackburn NA39 ground attack aircraft, developed for the Fleet Air Arm. It was later re-named Buccaneer.
**2 May:** A new absolute world altitude record for manned aircraft of 79,452ft was claimed by the hybrid-fuelled Sud-Ouest SO9050 Trident II. It beat the previous record of 18 April

(76,932ft), established by a US Navy Grumman F11F-1 Tiger, but was itself surpassed just five days later by the 91,243ft benchmark established by a USAF F-104A Starfighter.
**30 May:** Maiden flight of the Douglas DC-8 four-jet airliner.
**2 Jun:** The Short SC1 research aircraft made its first flight to involve vertical, horizontal, sideways and backwards travel.
**9 Jun:** London's Gatwick Airport was re-opened.
**20 Jun:** First flight of the Westland Wessex, the British-built version of the Sikorsky S-58 which went on to serve both the RAF and Royal Navy.
**30 Jul:** Inaugural flight of the de Havilland Canada DHC4 Caribou utility transport.
**19 Aug:** Maiden flight of the Lockheed YP3V-1, an aerodynamic development aircraft for the P3V Orion anti-submarine warfare and maritime patrol platform ordered for the US Navy on 24 April.
**31 Aug:** The North American A-5 Vigilante carrier-borne strike

aircraft for the US Navy made its first flight.
**1 Oct:** NASA (National Aeronautics and Space Administration) was established as a replacement for NACA (National Advisory Committee for Aeronautics).
**4 Oct:** Entry into service with BOAC of the new Comet 4.
**26 Oct:** First flight of the Boeing B-52G Stratofortress, the most-produced variant of the type.
**25 Nov:** The prototype English Electric P1B became the first British aircraft to exceed Mach 2 in level flight.

*The Tupolev Tu-104 was first flown in the mid-1950s and formed part of a major programme to modernise the fleet of Aeroflot, the Russian airline. It was basically a new fuselage using the wing, tail unit, undercarriage and engine installation of the Tu-16 bomber. This specially commissioned painting by Edmund Miller shows a Tu-104 over the Ural mountains.*

116

*Tupolev 104 over Mountain Terrain* by Edmund Miller DLC, CEng, MRAeS, GAvA

Just over half a century on from the first controlled powered flight, an aircraft appeared in 1959 which pushed back the boundaries of aviation to an extent which was simply unprecedented: the North American X-15. A combined committee of representatives from NACA, the US Air Force and US Navy (who had each been carrying out their own studies) met in Washington in July 1954 to discuss the development of a hypersonic research vehicle, which would look into the effects of high temperatures and speeds on aerodynamics and structures.

It was soon decided that NACA, which was replaced by NASA on 1 October 1958, would take overall control of the project with funding being provided by the two armed services. Submissions for provision of the aircraft itself were made by Bell, Douglas, Republic and North American, but it was the latter which was deemed the one 'most suitable for research and potentially the simplest to make safe for the mission'. A contract was signed in June 1956 for the construction of three X-15s, as the machine was designated, and production began soon afterwards.

As the X-15 was intended to achieve speeds of up to and over Mach 6, and altitudes of around 250,000ft, North American was taking a huge step into the unknown with the aircraft's construction – these were areas of the flight envelope which had never been explored before. Not only was the field of thermodynamics that of the X-15's intended research, but it was also one of the primary considerations in its construction, without all the necessary data being available. The structure had to be insulated to cope with temperatures of over 2400 deg F. The powerplant was intended to be a single-chamber Thiokol XLR99 liquid-fuelled rocket motor capable of delivering 57,000lb of thrust, but this very advanced unit was not fully-developed when the first X-15 was ready for flight, and therefore a pair of four-chamber Reaction Motors LR8 (formerly XLR11) motors were pressed into service. A number of captive flights, during which the aircraft remained attached to its NB-52 'mother ship', were undertaken before the first glide flight on 8 June 1959. The second X-15 built was used for the first flight to be carried out under the XLR11s' power, on 17 September. A maximum speed of Mach 2.11 and a height of 52,341ft were achieved on that maiden flight, impressive enough figures for a conventional aircraft, but for the X-15 programme, this was just the beginning.

Of great future significance as an enduring success story was the initial flight in March 1959 of the prototype Sikorsky YHSS-2 anti-submarine warfare helicopter, the first of the S-61 family. The US Navy had contracted Sikorsky to produce a new helicopter which would combine the hunter and killer functions of anti-submarine operations, as a replacement for the HSS-1 (the Navy's version of the Sikorsky S-58). The design of the military maritime version included an amphibious capability, afforded by a watertight hull and retractable landing gear, while power was provided by two General Electric T58-GE-8 turboshafts driving a five-bladed main rotor.

The companion civil variant, the 28-seat S-61L (first flown in December 1960) attracted much attention from commercial operators. In the years ahead, both the civil S-61 and military SH-3 Sea King were ordered in large numbers and licence-produced throughout the world.

---

**27 Jan:** Maiden flight of Convair's 110-seat CV-880 jet airliner.

**12 Feb:** USAF Strategic Air Command's bomber force became equipped entirely with jet aircraft when the last Convair B-36J was retired from the 95th Bombardment Wing at Biggs AFB, TX.

**11 Mar:** First flight of the Sikorsky YHSS-2 anti-submarine helicopter.

**10 Apr:** The Northrop T-38A Talon jet trainer first flew.

**14 Apr:** The prototype OV-1 Mohawk for the US Army made its first flight.

**15 May:** The end of an era as No 205 Squadron, RAF retired its Short Sunderlands at Seletar, Singapore. These aircraft were the service's last flying boats.

**1 Jun:** Scheduled airline services between London and Singapore began, courtesy of BOAC with its new Comet 4s.

**4 Jun:** American pilot Max Conrad set a new endurance record for a light aircraft when he arrived in New York in his Piper Comanche, having flown 7,683 miles non-stop from Casablanca in Morocco.

**8 Jun:** First unpowered glide drop of the North American X-15 rocket-powered research aircraft.

**12 Jun:** Entry into service of the Lockheed Hercules, when the USAF's 463rd Troop Carrier Wing received its new C-130Bs.

**17 Jun:** The prototype Dassault Mirage IVA strategic nuclear bomber for the Armée de l'Air made its inaugural flight.

**30 Jun:** The Bell HU-1A utility helicopter entered USAF service, four years before it did likewise with the US Army.

**2 Jul:** Maiden flight of the US Navy's prototype Kaman HU2K-1 Seasprite anti-submarine warfare helicopter, later known as the SH-2.

**30 Jul:** Developed as a private venture, the Northrop N-156 lightweight fighter flew for the first time. It later entered production as the F-5.

**25 Aug:** A US Navy Douglas A3D Skywarrior became the heaviest aircraft ever to be operated from a carrier, namely the USS *Independence*.

**17 Sep:** Inaugural powered drop (from its NB-52 carrier aircraft) of the North American X-15.

**23 Nov:** The maiden flight of the Boeing 720, a shorter-range, shorter-fuselage version of the 707. It entered service with United Air Lines in July 1960, and 154 were eventually built.

**25 Nov:** The prototype Lockheed YP3V-1 Orion anti-submarine warfare and maritime patrol aircraft developed for the US Navy undertook its maiden flight.

**14 Dec:** A USAF F-104C Starfighter became the first aircraft to exceed an altitude of 100,000ft.

**20 Dec:** First flight in Russia of the twin-turboprop Antonov An-24 short-haul military and civil transport.

*The Boeing 707 entered commercial service with PanAm in 1958. Aerolineas Argentinas, featured in Carlos Garcia's painting, was one of the numerous smaller international airlines that subsequently operated the airliner.*

*Aerolineas Argentinas Boeing 707* by Carlos A Garcia

The year 1960 saw the Short SC1 jet-lift vertical take-off and landing (VTOL) research aircraft make its first full transition from vertical to horizontal flight (and vice versa) at RAE Bedford. It was the first aircraft with separate lift and propulsion engines ever to accomplish the transition. The five engines, four for lift and one for propulsion, were all basically the same Rolls-Royce RB 108 engine.

With Britain leading the way in this new mode of flight, the first tethered flight was made on 21 October of the Hawker P1127, which proved the world's first successful take-off and landing (V/STOL) tactical fighter.

An event which was to have unprecedented political and military repercussions occurred on 1 May. A Central Intelligence Agency (CIA) Lockheed U-2 high altitude reconnaissance aircraft was downed by a Soviet air defence SAM whilst overflying Sverdlovsk, at an altitude of over 65,000ft. The U-2 had left Peshawar in northern Pakistan en route to Bodo in Norway, which enabled it to photograph key Soviet strategic airfields and secret industrial sites. Pilot Gary Powers survived unharmed, but was captured by the Soviets. This incident led to a massive breakdown in negotiations at the Paris Summit following Krushchev's denouncement of 'hostile' American spyflights over the USSR.

In April, British European Airways (BEA) inaugurated a turbojet operation with the de Havilland Comet 4B on the London-Moscow route, replacing the Vickers Viscount. The Comet was intended to maintain BEA's dominance of the European market in face of increasing competition from the French Caravelle. The Vickers Vanguard was designed to replace the Vickers Viscount, (but in the event it only complemented it) and BEA introduced the new type on its London-Paris route on 17 December.

During 1960, Britain ended ballistic missile development in favour of the American Skybolt missile, intended to be carried by the RAF's V-bombers. Britain also abandoned a ground-based nuclear deterrent, opting for the use of submarines or air-launched nuclear weapons.

One of the most successful single-engined, four-seater aircraft took to the air for the first time on 14 January, the Piper PA-24 Cherokee, which was designed as the successor to the Piper Tri-Pacer series. During April, the US Court of Appeal upheld the FAA's decision to ban pilots over the age of 60 from flying commercial airliners. RAF Fighter Command moved into the supersonic era when the English Electric Lightning entered service with No 74 (Tiger) Squadron at RAF Coltishall in June. In December, BOAC inaugurated an all-jet round-the-world service with de Havilland Comet 4s connecting with Boeing 707-436s on the London-Hong Kong eastern and western routes respectively.

Consolidation of the British aircraft industry continued when Westland Aircraft took over the interests of the Fairey Company in May. It had already taken over the helicopter division of Bristol Aircraft in March. In the US, the Martin Company ended its 51-year association with aircraft production. It delivered its last P5M-2 Marlin flying-boat to the US Navy, the last of 12,400 aircraft produced.

---

**14 Jan:** Sweden's powerful SAAB J35D Draken, with its unique double delta wing configuration, proved its worth by flying at twice the speed of sound.

**16 Feb:** First flight of the Vought F8U-2N Crusader. This F8D version was an improved all-weather fighter with upgraded radar and AAMs.

**20 Feb:** Air India made the first non-stop flight from Heathrow to Bombay during a delivery flight of a Boeing 707 from Seattle. It began regular India-London flights in May.

**20 Mar:** The US FAA ordered Lockheed Electra airliners to fly no faster than 315mph while the causes of two serious crashes were investigated.

**1 Apr:** Czechoslovak Airlines (CSA) inaugurated a Prague-Heathrow service with the Tupolev Tu-104. This was the first use of a Russian-built jet airliner on regular flights to England.

**19 Apr:** Grumman's A2F-1, the A-6A Intruder carrier-borne aircraft, made its first flight.

**27 May:** BOAC began using the Boeing 707-436 on its London-New York route.

**1 Jun:** Trans-Canadian Airlines commenced North Atlantic operations using jet airliners. It inaugurated a Douglas DC-8 service between Montreal and Heathrow.

**24 Jun:** The Avro 748 (subsequently produced as the HS 748) twin-turboprop airliner made its maiden flight.

**1 Jul:** British United Airways (BUA), a new independent airline, was formed in Britain. It became operational following the merger of a number of smaller units.

**12 Aug:** The North American X-15A research aircraft reached a height of 136,500ft, a new world altitude record.

**19 Aug:** *Sputnik 5*, the Soviet Union's satellite, was launched into Earth orbit carrying two dogs. They were successfully recovered after the completion of 18 orbits.

**15 Sep:** The final flying-boat operation by Tasman Empire Airways. The Short Solent *Aranui* made the last scheduled service from Tahiti to Auckland, New Zealand.

**17 Sep:** East African Airways inaugurated a London-Nairobi service using de Havilland Comet 4s.

**15 Oct:** Mooney Aircraft introduced the first all-metal M-20B.

**5 Nov:** An Alouette III, a seven-seat helicopter, landed on the 19,690ft peak of Deo Tibaa in the Himalayas.

**12 Nov:** A restartable rocket engine was used for the first time when *Discoverer 17* was launched from Vandenburg AFB.

**16 Nov:** Utilising a swing-tail configuration for the first time for cargo loading, the Canadair CL-44D-4 (a Canadian development of the Bristol Britannia) made its initial flight.

**18 Nov:** Aer Lingus received its first turbojet transport, a Boeing 720. It commenced a regular service from Dublin, via Shannon, to New York during the following month.

**19 Nov:** The giant Tupolev Tu-114 set a new world record for propeller-driven aircraft of 545.07mph. It entered Aeroflot service in the following April.

**3 Dec:** Ghana Airways received the first of six Ilyushin Il-18 turboprop airliners for its international services.

*Anthony Cowland's specially commissioned painting shows the Hawker P1127 making its historic first untethered flight, hovering over a grille, on 19 November 1960.*

These pages generously donated by Turner Charles Limited, Engineering and IT Recruitment Consultants

*Liberation Day* by Anthony Cowland BA(Hons), MCDS, GAvA, FSAI

In April, the Soviet Union surprised the Western World when it announced the almost unbelievable news that it had launched its spacecraft *Vostock 1* into Earth orbit, carrying 27-year old cosmonaut Major Yuri Gagarin, the first man in space. He landed safely after one complete orbit, which took a flight time of just under two hours. Gagarin had taken-off from Tyuratan in central Asia and had transmitted the first words from space by radio. A parachute on the re-entry vehicle was used to bring Gagarin safely back to Earth in eastern Kazakhstan. The Soviet Union launched its second man into Earth orbit in *Vostock 2* on 6 August and 17 Earth orbits were completed before a landing after 25 hours in space.

Alan B. Shepard became the first American in space aboard the *Mercury* ballistic capsule *Freedom 7*, following a launch by a Redstone rocket on 5 May. This sub-orbital trajectory reached a height of 116 miles (187km), and a range of 297 miles (478km) was accomplished.

Flight tests by Britain with the first two Hawker P1127 prototypes continued at a commendable pace. The first accelerating and decelerating transitions were made between vertical and horizontal flight in September. It was the only VTOL aircraft to achieve both high speed flight and the ability to hover, all with a single engine. Bristol Aero-Engines (later Rolls-Royce) developed the Pegasus with four nozzles – two cold (from the single large fan) and two hot (from the jet).

There can be no doubt that the subsequent Harrier family of V/STOL combat aircraft and the Rolls-Royce Pegasus series of vectored-thrust turbofans, together formed Britain's most important contribution to post-war military aviation technology. Until the end of the first decade of the 21st Century, the British Aerospace/McDonnell Douglas Harrier would continue to be the world's only high-performance V/STOL combat aircraft to see service on a significant scale, just as its Rolls-Royce Pegasus vectored-thrust turbofan (subsequently substantially upgraded) remained the only series-built V/STOL engine.

The Handley Page HP115 research aircraft, designed to obtain data into low-speed handling of delta-winged aircraft, essential for the development of the forthcoming Anglo-French Concorde, flew in August. The delta wing had an extremely low aspect ratio, being very long from front to rear in relation to its short wingspan. A crucial feature of such a wing was that it generated a strong vortex along the leading edge. The HP115 confirmed that Britain was progressing along the right lines in advocating a slender delta-wing configuration for the supersonic airliner.

The new Convair B-58A Hustler delta-winged supersonic bomber, which could cruise at speeds in excess of 1,300mph (2,095km/h) won the Blériot trophy. This had been created 30 years earlier, for the first aircraft to maintain a speed of more than 2,000km/h for more than 30 minutes in a closed circuit. The aircraft landed at the 1961 Paris Air Show after flying from New York in three hours 19 minutes, at an average speed of 1,103mph.

Boeing revealed the GAM-87A Skybolt air-launched intermediate-range ballistic missile to be carried by the B-52 Stratofortress. The Skybolt, developed by Douglas, was a two-stage solid-propellent powered missile and was originally intended for operational use with the British V-bomber force.

The USAF Military Air Transport Service (MATS) entered the jet age in June when it took delivery of the first of 30 Boeing C-135A Stratolifter transports.

---

**31 Jan:** NASA launched a Mercury space capsule that contained a chimpanzee, which was successfully recovered following a 420 mile (676km) down-range sub-orbital flight.

**1 Feb:** BEA introduced a full Vickers Vanguard service.

**3 Feb:** Operation *Looking Glass*, the constant operation of SAC's airborne command post, began with specially-equipped Boeing KC-135B airborne command post (ACP) aircraft. To provide continuous cover, each aircraft was airborne for eight hours per shift, with a SAC general and personnel who could take over command, should the need arise.

**28 Feb:** Cessna's 336 Skymaster made its first flight, a business aircraft (but also purchased by the USAF) equipped with two engines – one in the nose, the other behind the cabin driving a pusher propeller.

**5 Apr:** First flight of the Dassault Mirage IIIE long-range fighter bomber. This version became the main version of the Mirage to enter service with the Armeé de l'Air.

**21 Apr:** The Thiokol XLR99-RM-2 rocket engine was fitted into the North American X-15A research aircraft to enable it to make the first full-power test flight, when it achieved a speed of 3,074mph (4,947km/h) at 79,000ft.

**28 Apr:** A Mikoyan Ye-166A regained the world height record for the Soviet Union when it achieved an altitude of 113,898ft.

**2 May:** Maiden flight of the Pilatus PC-6A Turbo-Porter.

**1 Jun:** United Airlines took over Capital Airlines, thus becoming the largest civil operator in the Western world. During the year it had a fleet of 267 aircraft serving 116 destinations.

**17 Jun:** First flight of the Hindustan Aircraft HF-24 Marut supersonic fighter in India. The aircraft was designed by Kurt Tank, who created the WWII Focke-Wulf Fw 190.

**21 Jun:** Aviation Trader's ATL 98 Carvair made its first flight. Developed for Laker's Channel Air Bridge it was a converted Douglas DC-4 with a bulbous forward fuselage, incorporating an elevated flight deck and a nose-loading door.

**28 Jun:** Prompted by the collapse of one of its four Goodyear ZPG-3W airborne Early Warning airships, the US Navy ended its airship operations.

**29 Jun:** Launch of the US Navy's *Transit IV* satellite, the first to carry a nuclear power source.

**22 Nov:** A USAF F-4H-1F Phantom established a new world speed record of 1,606mph (2,588km/h).

**25 Nov:** USS *Enterprise*, the US Navy's first nuclear-powered aircraft carrier, was commissioned.

**11 Dec:** NORAD's SAGE system was declared operational following the completion of the 21st, and final, control centre at Sioux City, Iowa.

*The Soviet Union surprised the world when it launched a man into space for the first time. This Keith Ferris painting illustrates Yuri Gagarin launching into Earth orbit in spacecraft Vostock I.*
© 2001 keithferrisart.com

*Vostock I with Yuri Gagarin* by Keith Ferris ASAA

Continuing the space saga, Lt Col John H. Glenn USMC became the first US astronaut to orbit the Earth. He made three orbits in a total flight time of just under five hours in the *Mercury* capsule *Friendship 7*.

France entered the VTOL race when the Dassault Balzac V-001 research aircraft made its first tethered flight on 12 October and made a free flight a week later.

Britain continued to develop experimental aircraft for specific tasks and, on 14 April, the first of two Bristol Type 188 high-speed research aircraft made its maiden flight. The aircraft, constructed of stainless steel, were intended to explore the effects of prolonged kinetic heating.

The world came to the brink of World War III in October during the 'Cuban Missile Crisis' when a Lockheed U-2 reconnaissance flight over Cuba confirmed that launch sites for Soviet medium-range ballistic missiles were being installed there. President John F. Kennedy announced to the world that the offensive missile sites were aimed towards the USA and US carriers took up station in the Caribbean. Lengthy exchanges between Kennedy and Khrushchev eased the situation when the US pledged not to invade Cuba. By the end of November, the Soviet Union agreed to the removal of all Soviet missiles from Cuba, and the World breathed again.

In Vietnam, the USAF began Operation *Ranch Hand*, using Fairchild C-123 Providers to spray defoliating herbicides on vegetation and expose roads and trails used by the Viet Cong. The most common of the defoliants used was known from the metal containers as 'Agent Orange'.

The promising Fairey Rotodyne vertical take-off and landing airliner was cancelled by the British Government because of the costs involved.

In 1962, Britain led the way in developing human-powered aircraft capable of sustained flight. During May, the Hatfield Man-Powered Aircraft Club flew its Puffin monoplane in a straight line for 2,988ft, the first time an aircraft of this type had ever exceeded a distance of half a mile. The balsa-wood aircraft weighed only 265lb at take-off.

On 29 June, the prototype Vickers VC10 long-range jet airliner made its maiden flight at Brooklands. Technically it was very impressive, with an uncluttered high-lift wing and four Rolls-Royce Conway turbofans mounted on pylons on the rear fuselage. BOAC, the VC10's launch customer, cut its initial order. This action enraged BOAC's cynics, who alleged a 'buy US' faction. In October, French President Charles de Gaulle made an impassioned plea for Britain and France to co-operate in building civil aircraft, using the joint resources of their two aircraft industries to counter what he called 'American colonisation of the skies'.

---

**9 Jan:** First flight of the Hawker Siddeley Trident 1. No prototype was involved, and the initial flight was made by the first of 24 Trident 1s ordered specifically for BEA operations.

**10 Jan:** A B-52H Stratofortress established a new world absolute distance record when it flew 12,532 miles (20,169km) from Okinawa to Madrid.

**24 Jan:** The first US Navy McDonnell F4H Phantom IIs were assigned to the USAF's Tactical Air Command for orientation purposes. This was the first step towards the F4H becoming a joint service aircraft.

**31 Jan:** William P. Lear, who had already designed the world's first successful jet auto pilot, set up his own jet aircraft company at Wichita, KA to develop a twin-jet for use by business executives.

**1 Mar:** The world's first multi-engined turbine-powered helicopter service was inaugurated by Los Angeles Airways.

**18 Mar:** The Convair CV-990 airliner was put into service by American Airlines. This was the longer-range turbo-fan powered development of the CV-880.

**30 Apr:** The NASA manned-North American X-15A attained a new height record of 246,700ft. Two months later it attained its highest recorded speed of 4,159mph (6,693km/h).

**9 May:** Initial flight of the Sikorsky S-64A Skycrane, then the most powerful helicopter outside the USSR. It was the only crane-type helicopter in the Western world.

**9 Jun:** First flight of the F-104G Starfighter, assembled by Fiat in Italy.

**29 Jun:** The prototype Vickers VC10 airliner made its maiden flight from Brooklands.

**30 Jun:** US military aircraft were given common designations. These were gradually based on those of the USAF, which meant that aircraft of the US Navy and US Marine Corps had totally new designations.

**7 Jul:** A Soviet Mikoyan Ye-166 set a new world speed record for aircraft at 1,666mph.

**10 Jul:** *Telstar I*, a communications satellite, was placed into Earth orbit by a Delta booster rocket.

**11 Aug:** The Soviet Union spacecraft, *Vostock 3* and *4* made a rendezvous in orbit and TV cameras in the spacecraft gave the first TV transmission from a manned vehicle in space.

**13 Aug:** First flight of the HS125 executive jet prototype, unveiled as the jet successor to the DH Dove.

**30 Aug:** The Nihon Airplane Manufacturing Company's twin-turboprop, medium-range YS-11 made its first flight. It was Japan's first post-war commercial aircraft.

**19 Sep:** First flight of the Conroy 'Pregnant Guppy', a converted 1950s Boeing 377 Stratocruiser, designed to carry outsize loads.

**2 Oct:** The Tupolev Tu-124 entered service with Aeroflot.

**25 Oct:** Developed from the Saunders-Roe P531 for the Royal Navy, the Westland Wasp helicopter had its maiden flight.

**26 Oct:** The USAF received the last Stratofortress, a B-52H.

**2 Nov:** Lockheed's Model 186 research helicopter, which featured a rigid main rotor, made its maiden flight.

**7 Dec:** The Aérospatiale Super Frelon helicopter was first flown.

**14 Dec:** NASA's *Mariner II* approached the surface of Venus, the first man-made satellite to reach another planet.

**21 Dec:** First flight of the Nord 262 Fregate, a French twin-engined light transport which was pressurised. It was developed from the Nord 260 Super Broussard.

*The Douglas DC-8 Series 30 was specially tailored to intercontinental operations. The Japan Airlines aircraft depicted in Douglas Neilson's painting had drooped flaps to improve its take-off performance, in spite of an increased take-off weight.*

*Japan Airlines Douglas DC-8* by Douglas Nielson

# 1963

The Boeing 727 short/medium-range airliner was flown for the first time in February. It had a fuselage similar to the Model 707/720, but it incorporated three rear-mounted engines and a T-tail. The 727 attracted huge sales, especially on the US domestic market, and for many years it was the world's top-selling commercial jet aircraft.

Also with a T-tail, but with two turbofans in a similar rear configuration, the British Aircraft Corporation's BAC One-Eleven was flown for the first time in August. It was the first really modern, short-haul jet airliner and had its origins in the Hunting H107. The aircraft attracted favourable comment from airlines around the world and was seen as the 'jet successor to the Vickers Viscount' (which had secured sales of nearly 450 at that date). Like its turboprop predecessor, the One-Eleven was developed in many different versions.

In March, the Hunting H126 research aircraft was first flown. This was designed to evaluate the jet flap, where the entire efflux from the Bristol Siddeley Orpheus turbojet could be discharged through special heat-resisting flaps. The idea was to achieve an enormous increase in wing circulation by powered lift.

Unilateral declarations were made in October by the United States and the Soviet Union that no weapons would be mounted or used in space. In July, a nuclear test treaty was finalised after some three years of intensive discussion. Subsequently signed by most nations, it brought an end to tests in the atmosphere.

Light aircraft production in the US was in a healthy state, as business was booming for both commercial and pleasure purposes. In January, Piper Aircraft delivered its 1,000th PA-28 Cherokee. An all-metal, low-wing aircraft, it was available in a number of versions.

Several of the biggest firms in the US aerospace industry rushed to take the lead in a gigantic contest to build the SST (Supersonic Transport), which had been launched by the late President Kennedy. The administration set up a special SST Programme Office of the FAA to evaluate bids. Boeing suggested the SCAT-16 variable-sweep Model 733; Lockheed the CL-823 and North American the NAC-60, but the outcome was that the American SST programme faltered.

USAF operations over Vietnam continued to increase, with the number of advisors and air support growing all the time. The air defence task was taken up by the *Candy Machine* deployment of F-102A Delta Daggers from the 509th Fighter Interceptor Squadron based at Tan Son Nhut and Da Nang. For ground support work, the 1st Air Commando Squadron was formed at Bien Hoa, receiving Douglas A-1E/H Skyraiders to supplement its existing B-26 Invaders and T-28 Trojans.

Among the unit's roles was the provision of air support for helicopter operations, which became an ever more important aspect of its tasking, as the US Army's rotary-wing activities grew appreciably. Tactical transport operations also assumed greater importance and more squadrons of Fairchild C-123B Providers were sent to the region. Further intelligence gathering was carried out by Martin RB-57Es.

---

**7 Jan:** Aeroflot commenced a scheduled passenger service between Moscow and Havana in Cuba using the Tupolev Tu-114.

**16 Jan:** Cosmonaut Valentina Terehkova became the first female to travel in space when she was carried in the Soviet Union's *Vostock 6* spacecraft.

**17 Jan:** The prototype of the Short Skyvan light and rugged transport flew with piston engines. It featured a perfectly square section box fuselage and rear-loading ramp. Its first flight with turboprop engines was subsequently made on 2 October.

**29 Jan:** First flight of the Douglas DC-8F Jet Trader, which incorporated side-loading doors and strengthened flooring for the transportation of freight.

**14 Feb:** Introduction of the Soviet-built MiG-21 into Indian Air Force service.

**14 Feb:** The Avro Vulcans of No 617 Squadron, RAF became fully operational with the Blue Steel stand-off bomb.

**25 Feb:** The Franco-German Transall C-160 transport made its first flight. Loading was accomplished via a ramp under the tail.

**18 Mar:** The French Dassault Balzac VTOL research aircraft made its first transition from vertical to horizontal flight, and vice-versa.

**1 Apr:** BEA introduced the first 'stand-by' fares, under which passengers arriving at the airport on the chance of an available seat were given a third off the full fare.

**23 Apr:** First flight of the Argentinean FAMA IA-50 Guarani II 15-seat turboprop transport.

**6 Jun:** Air France inaugurated a non-stop Paris to Los Angeles route with Boeing 707s. It was the longest non-stop stage in the world, 5,660 miles in 12 hours.

**29 Jun:** First flight of the Swedish Saab 105 trainer/light-attack aircraft.

**26 Jul:** *Syncom 2*, the world's first geosynchronous satellite, was launched by the United States, remaining in orbit above the Antarctic.

**20 Aug:** Two Israeli Air Force Mirage IIIs shot down eight Syrian MiG-17 fighters.

**14 Sep:** First flight of the Mitsubishi MU-2 light utility transport. Able to seat seven passengers, it could reach speeds of 350mph.

**20 Sep:** The German EWR-Süd VJ 101C X-1 experimental tilt-rotor VTOL aircraft achieved its first transition from vertical to horizontal flight.

**1 Oct:** A ski-equipped C-130 Hercules made a first trans-polar non-stop flight from Cape Town to the base at McMurdo Sound in Antarctica.

**30 Oct:** A US Marine Corps KC-130 Hercules made the first landing by the type on the carrier USS *Forrestal*, without the aid of an arrester hook.

**17 Dec:** First flight of the Lockheed C-141A StarLifter, a new four-turbofan long-range military transport for service with the USAF's Military Air Transport Service (MATS).

**21 Dec:** First flight of the Hawker Siddeley Andover, the military version derived from the HS 748 for the RAF.

*John Young's painting captures the North American X-15A high performance research aircraft that in the 1960s was flown faster and higher than any other manned aircraft, achieving a speed of Mach 6.72 and an altitude of 354,200ft.*

*Space Beckons* by John Young VPGAvA, VPASAA

# 1964

The existence of the Lockheed A-12 high-altitude strategic reconnaissance aircraft was revealed in February, although the aircraft had been flying since April 1962. Sinister in appearance, it was coated overall with a matt black finish which dissipated heat and helped make the aircraft invisible to radar. Designed to fly unarmed at unprecedented altitudes and speeds in spying missions over hostile territory, it carried special cameras and sensors. The slightly larger SR-71A Blackbird was developed from the CIA's A-12 for USAF service and was first flown on 22 December. The Blackbird, capable of Mach 3.3 at optimum altitudes, became the fastest air-breathing aircraft in service. Intended to succeed the veteran U-2 spyplane, but in the event complementing it, the SR-71A was a product of Kelly Johnson's Lockheed secretive 'Skunk Works' at Burbank, CA.

With flying-boats consigned to aviation's history books, Short Bros turned their skills in large aircraft manufacturing to produce a long-range heavy-lift cargo transport, resulting in the Belfast, which took to the air on 5 January.

The Boeing 727-100 short/medium haul airliner entered passenger carrying service with Eastern Airlines in February and later in the year was introduced by American and TWA.

The Hawker P1127 went to sea in February. During trials on HMS *Ark Royal* the aircraft made many test vertical take-offs and landings, with the ship both underway and at anchor, the P1127 being unique in that it did not need wind over the deck to take off.

The later HS Kestrel 'Jump Jet' vertical/short take-off and landing (V/STOL) aircraft flew on 7 March, produced for the NATO requirement for a V/STOL tactical support aircraft. Developed from the Hawker P1127, the Kestrel formed the basis of the Tripartite Evaluation Squadron (TES) with British, American and West German representatives at Dunsfold in October.

The first operational Blackburn Buccaneer S1B subsonic low-level attack bomber embarked on the *Ark Royal* in February. At the time, the naval Buccaneer had a weapons system that was unique and perhaps many years ahead of its competitors. It featured an integrated navigation and control system, which brought together the function of the navigation and attack avionics, autopilot, radar and instruments.

Distinguished by its striking forward-swept wings, the prototype German HFB 320 Hansa twin-turbojet executive transport made its first flight in April. The forward-swept configuration was pioneered by Germany during WWII, and it enabled strong spars to pass behind the cabin.

Following many delays, BAC's new TSR2 supersonic tactical strike aircraft made its first flight on 27 September. Intended as a supersonic replacement for the English Electric Canberra, the promising aircraft immediately ran into political controversy, and when the incoming Labour Government took office, the project was cancelled in the following April.

During May, BEA Helicopters Ltd opened the first helicopter passenger service in Europe with the multi-engined Sikorsky S-61N, from Penzance in Cornwall to the Isles of Scilly.

---

**20 Jan:** First flight of the Beech King Air 90.

**29 Jan:** The Royal Australian Air Force received its first Dassault Mirage IIIO, as part of an initial licence-built batch of delta-winged fighters.

**29 Jan:** Saturn I SA-5 was launched, being the first flight with a live second stage rocket.

**24 Feb:** The Northrop F-5B, a tandem-seat trainer derivative of the lightweight F-5A Freedom Fighter made its first flight. It entered USAF service as the T-38 Talon.

**1 Mar:** Under a shroud of secrecy, Soviet Union aircraft designers had spent a considerable period developing a long-range jet airliner. This resulted in the launch of the Ilyushin Il-62.

**11 Mar:** BEA introduced the first Trident service on the Heathrow-Copenhagen run.

**8 Apr:** The first unmanned *Gemini* spacecraft was launched into Earth orbit by a Titan II booster.

**9 Apr:** Maiden flight of the de Havilland Canada DHC-5 Buffalo, basically a scaled-up turboprop successor to the Caribou. It was developed for a 1962 US Army STOL transport competition.

**1 May:** First flight of the BAC 221. Developed from the Fairey FD2 high-speed research aircraft, the 221 featured an ogival wing and a drooping nose and was used to gain data for the Concorde project.

**7 May:** The BAC Super VC10 made its first flight. This had a longer fuselage, more powerful engines and an increased fuel capacity, offering an extended range.

**11 May:** Jacqueline Cochran, flying a TF-104F Starfighter, set a new speed record for women at 1,429mph.

**25 May:** The Ryan 43/XV-5A 'fan-in-wing' VTOL research aircraft made its first conventional take off. Its first vertical take-off and landing was achieved two months later.

**28 Jul:** NASA's unmanned *Ranger 7* was launched to land on the moon. It transmitted TV pictures back to Earth prior to its impact on the lunar surface.

**7-9 Aug:** Turkish Air Force attacks by F-84Gs and F-100C/Ds on Greek Cypriot positions in Cyprus were terminated by United Nations intervention.

**21 Sep:** First flight of the North American XB-70 Valkyrie Mach 3 strategic bomber. The programme was subsequently cancelled.

**12 Oct:** *Voskhod 1* spacecraft went into Earth orbit, the first to carry a multiple crew.

**14 Oct:** First flight of the Sikorsky CH-53A Sea Stallion, a heavy assault helicopter developed for the US Marine Corps.

**16 Oct:** The People's Republic of China exploded its first atomic bomb, thus becoming the world's fifth nuclear power.

**18 Nov:** First flight of the Grumman C-2A Greyhound, a carrier on-board delivery transport, developed from the E-2 Hawkeye.

**28 Nov:** The US space probe *Mariner 4* was launched. The following year it passed Mars and transmitted images of the Martian surface.

**21 Dec:** The initial prototype General Dynamics F-111A variable geometry (swing-wing) fighter was first flown.

*The English Electric Lightning was the RAF's first truly supersonic fighter. Keith Woodcock's painting shows a Lightning F1A of No 111 Squadron getting airborne from RAF Wattisham armed with Firestreak missiles.*

*The RAF's First Supersonic Aircraft* by Keith Woodcock GAvA, ASAA, GMA

The heightening tempo of operations in Vietnam led to the US forces involved introducing a number of new aircraft and operational techniques during 1965. With Operation *Rolling Thunder* making available a wider range of targets following the authorisation of strikes against Communist positions in North Vietnam connected with Viet Cong attacks on the South, sortie rates by both USAF and US Navy air assets increased substantially. So too did the likelihood of having to engage enemy aircraft (even though aerial combat was only permitted if it had been initiated by North Vietnamese Air Force action). The first 'kills' by US aircraft (Navy F-4Bs) took place in June, but a new, further danger emerged soon after – that of guided surface-to-air missiles, installed in North Vietnam by the Soviets. A USAF F-4C was destroyed by an SA-2 SAM during an attack sortie south of Hanoi on 24 July, the first such shoot-down of an American combat aircraft.

It was this threat which gave birth to the *Wild Weasel* version of the two-seat F-100F Super Sabre, which began operations in November with the 388th Tactical Fighter Wing. The SA-2 was a radar-guided missile, and it soon became clear that what was needed was a 'hunter-killer' aircraft equipped with radar warning equipment and the weaponry to destroy what it detected. Initial *Weasel* sorties involved the F-100Fs (in limited numbers at first) marking the target with a rocket salvo before F-105s arrived to bomb it. From 1966 onwards the Super Sabres were armed with AGM-45A Shrike anti-radar missiles before being replaced in the role by converted F-105s and F-4s, having pioneered an entirely new combat technique. So too did what was known as the Douglas FC-47 upon its entry into service – the famous gunship conversion of the Skytrain, whose sorties were flown under the callsign 'Spooky'. It had been realised that a very heavily-armed, rugged aircraft flying slowly around concentrations of Communist forces would be able to wreak a lot of damage on the enemy, and the C-47 was both available and ideal. With three GE SUU-11A/A miniguns,

each capable of firing 6,000 7.62mm rounds per minute, mounted in the aircraft's hold, the type was much in demand from the moment it arrived in-theatre with the 4th Special Operations Squadron. The FC-47 fighter designation was soon changed to AC-47A, and the type proved notably successful at night when the sight of its firepower seemingly raining down on North Vietnamese targets led to another nickname: 'Puff the Magic Dragon'. The other very significant new deployment to Southeast Asia was that in February of SAC B-52F Stratofortresses to Andersen AFB on Guam. After a wait of over four months while their exact use was decided upon, the first *Arc Light* raids were flown against pockets of Viet Cong about 40 miles north of Saigon.

In the UK meanwhile, there was decimation of new military aircraft projects on an unprecedented scale. The first two to face the axe (announced in February) were the Hawker Siddeley HS681, a medium-range V/STOL transport, and the Hawker Siddeley P1154, a supersonic V/STOL strike fighter, originally intended for both the RAF and Royal Navy. The latter was effectively scuppered by the need to build two different aircraft for the two services. With Spey-engined F-4s being ordered instead for the RN, it was almost inevitable that the RAF P1154 would also be scrapped. What both ended up with was a Phantom variant which fell some way below the type's par, and the chance to develop an effective supersonic V/STOL combat aircraft was lost.

However, the cancellation of the BAC TSR2 was the most bitter blow. After the two aforementioned programmes were scrapped, the British Government decided to press ahead with TSR2, but opposition to the ever-rising costs involved, when compared with estimates for what turned out to be the extremely costly abortive purchase for the RAF of F-111Ks, spelt doom. On 6 April came confirmation that the programme was to be cancelled, effectively spelling an end to indigenous British combat aircraft production, not to mention the development of an extremely promising and certainly very capable strike aircraft.

---

**26 Jan:** It was confirmed by the UK Ministry of Defence that the RAF's Vickers Valiants were to be withdrawn from service after metal fatigue had been discovered in the wings of some of the fleet.
**25 Feb:** Maiden flight of the Douglas DC-9 twin-jet airliner.
**27 Feb:** What was then the world's largest aircraft took to the air: the Antonov An-22 turboprop freighter, with a 211ft 3in wingspan and a fuselage measuring 189ft 11in.
**15 Apr:** First flight of the Sud Aviation SA330 assault and utility transport helicopter, later named the Puma and also produced in collaboration with Westland.
**18 May:** Initial flight of the Grumman F-111B naval fighter.
**20 May:** Maiden flight of the de Havilland Canada DHC-6

Twin Otter utility aircraft, more than 830 of which were built.
**13 Jun:** The Britten-Norman BN-2 Islander utility transport took to the air for the first time from Bembridge, IoW.
**17 Jun:** The first shoot-down of North Vietnamese aircraft during the conflict there, when two US Navy F-4B Phantoms from VF-21 on the USS *Midway* downed a pair of MiG-17s.
**10 Jul:** The USAF's first combat victories of the Vietnam war. Two MiG-17s were shot down by F-4Cs of the 12th TFW.
**16 Jul:** Maiden flight of the North American YOV-10A, developed as a counter-insurgency aircraft for the USMC.
**31 Aug:** First flight of the Aero Spacelines B377-SG Super Guppy, a Boeing Stratocruiser modified to carry outsize loads.

**7 Sep:** In what is believed to still constitute a record, Pakistan Air Force pilot Sqn Ldr Mohammed Mahmood Alam, flying an F-86F Sabre, shot down four Indian Air Force Hunters within 30 seconds (following a further Hunter 'kill' a few minutes before).
**27 Sep:** First flight of the LTV A-7A Corsair II, developed for the US Navy as its new carrier-borne attack aircraft.

*An Avro Vulcan B2 of No 617 (Dambusters) Squadron is captured in this atmospheric painting by Nicolas Trudgian as it thunders into the air from RAF Scampton. It is painted in the all-white anti-nuclear flash scheme for the bomber's role when it was the mainstay of the RAF's nuclear strike force.*

*Vulcan Thunder* by Nicolas Trudgian

# 1966

One British aviator in particular hit the headlines in 1966. This was Sheila Scott, who set off from London-Heathrow Airport on 18 May for the first leg of what was to be a multi record-breaking flight. Flying her new Piper PA-24-260B Comanche G-ATOY *Myth Too*, she not only set a new record solo time for the 31,000-mile (49,693km) flight (of 33 days 3 minutes, totalling some 189 hours, and at an average speed of 166mph(267km/h)) but also became the first British pilot to complete a round-the-world flight when she landed back at Heathrow on 20 June. Over the next 13 years of its flying career, *Myth Too* went on to complete many more flying feats, ending up in 1979 (when it suffered an accident and was written off) with more than 90 aviation records. This was also the first of a number of records set by Sheila Scott, who, most notably, set the fastest light aircraft time in 1969's *Daily Mail* Transatlantic Air Race and in 1971 became the first pilot to overfly the North Pole in a lightplane, a Piper PA-23 Aztec.

A very significant maiden flight of the year was that by the prototype Bell Model 206 JetRanger, which went on to become the most successful civil helicopter of all time, whilst also seeing extensive military use in many countries. It had its origins in a design intended for use by the US Army, the OH-4A, which had been developed for the service's Light Observation Helicopter (LOH) requirement and first flew in December 1962. This was won by the Hughes OH-6, but after this setback Bell pressed ahead with the five-seat civil Model 206A JetRanger, first flown on 10 January 1966 and which received FAA certification in October. Not only did the type quickly look like a winner in terms of commercial sales, but it also won favour with the US Army again when the LOH

competition had to be re-opened due to the rising costs of the OH-6 programme. This time, the Model 206 won, and production of military OH-58 Kiowas started immediately.

The delivery to the 4200th Strategic Reconnaissance Wing at Beale AFB, CA in January of the USAF's first operational Lockheed SR-71A marked the start of a service career which spanned the whole of the rest of the Cold War, and beyond. An intensive programme of crew testing commenced at Beale, where the operating unit was re-named the 9th SRW in June. Initially, the aircraft were limited to Mach 2.6, but this was raised to Mach 3 by the end of the year as more experience was gained, and thereafter to the SR-71's Mach 3.2 maximum speed.

There was bad news at the end of 1966 for the West German Luftwaffe, as it was forced to ground its entire F-104 Starfighter fleet. Already, the number of accidents involving the newly-delivered jets had caused major political ructions and public outcry in the country, culminating in September with Generalleutnant Johannes Steinhoff taking over as the new Chief of the Air Staff, and establishment of a new Starfighter Task Group to look into safety issues. It made several recommendations, including the fitment of rocket packs to the type's C-2 ejector seats, hastening the retirement of the Luftwaffe's remaining F-84s so as to increase manpower and concentrate resources on the F-104s, and the need for more engineering support from industry. Having seen this report, in December Steinhoff ordered the fleet's grounding for three weeks. Within a year of his appointment, and with the Starfighters flying again, the accident rate had fallen dramatically, in fact into line with other European F-104 operators. The drastic measures had proved successful.

---

**1 Jan:** The USAF's Military Airlift Command was formed out of the former Military Air Transport Service.

**10 Jan:** Maiden flight of the Bell 206A JetRanger helicopter.

**11 Feb:** The USAF's Strategic Air Command retired the last two B-47 Stratojets from the bomber role, these being B-47Es based at Pease and Mountain Home AFBs.

**7 Mar:** President Charles de Gaulle announced that France was to withdraw from the military structures of NATO. This meant that all non-French forces had to withdraw from the country's soil, including many USAF assets, together with NATO Headquarters, which moved to Brussels.

**17 Mar:** Bell Aerospace Textron's four-turboshaft X-22A ducted-propeller VTOL research aircraft took to the air.

**1 Apr:** The USAF began using B-52Ds with their increased weapon capacity for *Arc Light* raids against North Vietnam.

**7 Apr:** The longest ever non-stop flight (Culver City, CA to

Ormond Beach, FL – a total of 2,230 miles) by a helicopter was completed by a US Army Hughes OH-6A.

**13 Apr:** An order announcement by PanAm for 25 aircraft set the Boeing 747 programme on the road to production.

**26 Apr:** When a flight of F-105s they were escorting was attacked, Maj Paul Gilmore and 1st Lt William Smith (flying an F-4C Phantom) became the first USAF crew to down a North Vietnamese MiG-21.

**8 Jun:** The second North American XB-70A Valkyrie prototype was destroyed during an air-to-air photographic sortie over the Mojave Desert, when a NASA F-104N Starfighter, which had been caught in the experimental bomber's vortex, collided with it. NASA test pilot Joseph Walker and the XB-70's co-pilot were killed, but the Valkyrie's pilot survived an ejection at 25,000ft.

**27 Jun:** First flight of the Rolls-Royce Spey-engined F-4K Phantom, developed by McDonnell for the Royal Navy and RAF.

**19 Oct:** The first C-130K Hercules destined for the RAF made its initial flight.

**21 Oct:** Maiden flight of the prototype Yakovlev Yak-40, a tri-jet, 27 to 32-seat airliner for use by Aeroflot and other airlines of Warsaw Pact countries on short-haul services, and as a VIP transport.

**14 Nov:** A USAF C-141A StarLifter became the first jet to land in the Antarctic.

**23 Dec:** The Dassault Mirage F1, the first member of the family not to have a delta configuration, completed its maiden flight.

**31 Dec:** Boeing was declared the winner of the competition to build the USA's first supersonic airliner.

*Robert Taylor's painting shows a formation of USAF McDonnell Douglas F-4 Phantoms making a low-level attack on an industrial complex during the Vietnam War.*

*Phantom Strike* by Robert Taylor

# 1967

At the time of its initial flight on 9 April, it was very far from certain whether or not the Boeing 737 would turn out to be a commercial success. The company's first twin-jet airliner, an 85 to 99-seater in its initial 737-100 form, had been officially launched in November 1964 but struggled to gain any orders. With the BAC 1-11 and DC-9 already on offer in this section of the civil marketplace, competition was stiff, and the announcement by Lufthansa in February 1965 that it was to buy ten 737-100s was hardly a great boost, though the German flag carrier's purchase was subsequently enlarged to 21. Significantly, this was the first time that Boeing had sold a new airliner type to a foreign carrier before doing so to a US airline, and for the 737 to succeed it was very important to get a big American order on the books as soon as possible.

During April 1965, United Air Lines signed up for 40 examples of the stretched 737-200, which was developed in order to meet the carrier's requirements. Adding over six feet to the fuselage length allowed for the carriage of 124 passengers, and the 737-100 and -200 (powered respectively by two Pratt & Whitney JT8D-7 and the slightly more powerful JT8D-15 turbofans) went on to receive FAA certification at the same time, in December 1968. By this stage, six prototype 737s had flown and had carried out a 1,300hr flight test programme. Lufthansa received its first 737-100 on 28 December, and began operating the new aircraft on scheduled services the following February, with United beginning revenue-earning 737 flights two months later.

The year's major military aviation stories centred largely around two conflicts. That in Southeast Asia was still ongoing, and at a heightened tempo. On 6 May, a USAF B-52 undertook the 10,000th mission over North Vietnam by the type since the *Arc Light* raids began in June 1965. Over the course of 1967, SAC doubled the rate of these sorties, which concentrated on hitting North Vietnamese troop positions and supply routes. This was, in effect, tactical bombing – for which the Stratofortress had never been intended. In addition, B-52s were also used as part of Operation *Neutralize,* which began on 11 September as a more concentrated and sustained effort against Communist forces in North Vietnam and Viet Cong located in the South, involving the co-ordination of air power, artillery and naval warships.

Meanwhile, the value of air power to strategists in terms of delivering a sudden, 'surprise' blow was demonstrated in a very different theatre during June, when combat aircraft of the Israeli Defence Force/Air Force (Dassault Ouragans and Super Mystéres) carried out attacks on ten Egyptian military airfields in the Sinai Peninsula, thus starting what became known as the 'Six Day War'. The cause had been Egyptian President Nasser's order for a military build-up on the Sinai and an accompanying blockade of the Straits of Tiran. The air strikes were backed up by an Israeli tank assault across the Sinai, before further IDF/AF attacks against airfields in Egypt itself, including Cairo Airport. By the end of the first day's action, 5 June, the Israelis had destroyed 240 Egyptian aircraft plus 45 Syrian, sixteen Jordanian and seven Iraqi. Twenty IDF/AF aircraft had been lost, but only one of those in air combat. Four days into the war, they had captured the Sinai right up to the Suez Canal, and on 10 June the brief conflict ended after Israel signed a ceasefire with Syria, which it had started attacking directly the day before.

**8 Jan:** The Sikorsky CH-53 transport helicopter went into action for the first time when four US Marine Corps CH-53A Sea Stallions from HMM-463 were deployed to Da Nang in South Vietnam for load-hauling duties.

**8 Feb:** Maiden flight of the 'double-delta' Saab 37 Viggen multi-role combat jet prototype.

**10 Feb:** Dornier's innovative Do31E experimental V/STOL transport took to the air for the first time.

**24 Feb:** United Airlines introduced the stretched DC-8-61 into service. Capable of carrying up to 259 passengers, the variant demonstrated the cost-per-seat advantages of higher-capacity airliners.

**15 Mar:** First flight of the USAF's Sikorsky HH-53B transport and rescue helicopter, which entered service with the 37th Air Rescue and Retrieval Squadron just six months later.

**7 Apr:** The Sud-Aviation SA340 single-turboshaft light utility and training helicopter prototype undertook its initial flight. In conjunction with Westland, it was subsequently developed into the SA341 Gazelle.

**28 Apr:** The McDonnell Douglas Corporation was formed from the merger of the McDonnell Aircraft Corporation and the Douglas Aircraft Company.

**19 May:** Maiden flight of the Dassault Mirage V, intended as an export version of the existing IIIE.

**23 May:** The RAF's new Hawker Siddeley Nimrod MR1 maritime patrol aircraft took to the air. It was the first four-jet type to be used for this role.

**1 Jun:** Two USAF Sikorsky HH-53Es completed the first non-stop helicopter flight across the North Atlantic.

**30 Jun:** First flight of the F-4E Phantom II, the first variant of the type to be cannon-equipped. It became the most-produced of all F-4 derivatives.

**24 Jul:** Launch of the tri-nation (UK, France and West Germany) European Airbus airliner programme.

**3 Oct:** The final absolute world speed record to be set by an X-15 was attained by the second aircraft – 4,520mph (Mach 6.7).

**23 Oct:** The Canadair CL-215 firebomber amphibian was airborne for the first time.

**4 Dec:** US Navy A-7A Corsair IIs of VA-147 aboard the USS *Ranger* made the type's combat début over Vietnam.

**28 Dec:** The RAF's first definitive Hawker Siddeley Harrier GR3 was flown for the first time.

**29 Dec:** The last B-47 Stratojet in service, an RB-47H of the 55th Strategic Reconnaissance Wing, was retired at Offutt AFB, NE and flown to Davis-Monthan AFB for storage.

*Chance-Vought F-8E Crusaders flown by Cmdr Harold 'Hal' Marr USN and his wingman Lt Phil Vamptella are the subject of Philip West's painting. They made a high-speed low-level victory fly-by alongside the deck of the USS* Hancock *in 1967 to celebrate the downing of a North Vietnamese MiG-17.*

*Checkmate-211* by Phillip West

The maiden flight of the Tupolev Tu-144 on the last day of 1968 represented a major coup for the Soviet Union: it had managed to beat the West into the air with a supersonic transport (SST) aircraft, coming as it did just over two months prior to Concorde making its first flight. What was possibly even more impressive was the fact that Andrei Tupolev's team had only begun development work in 1964.

However, one reason for this impressively short gestation is now known to have been the use of espionage, it being subsequently revealed that Aeroflot staff working in Paris and a British aeronautical engineer recruited by the KGB in 1967 (together with other operatives of the Soviet intelligence agency) were among those who were involved in gaining access to and making copies of blueprints and documents relating to the Concorde programme. Armed with this information, and also using experience its designers had gained in the course of studies for two experimental supersonic bombers (Projects 125 and 135, both of which existed only on paper), Tupolev was able to design and build the Tu-144 in very short order – most importantly, in time to beat Concorde into the air.

Although some features were very clearly 'borrowed' from its Anglo-French counterpart, notably the ability to 'droop' the nosecone, Tupolev had managed to overcome many of the potential problems inherent in an SST design: the high aircraft skin temperatures and the requirement for the engine air intakes to be able to operate effectively throughout a very wide speed envelope, being but two. It was also the first Soviet airliner to use hydraulically-boosted flight controls. However, its maximum speed was to be set at 2,500km/h (Mach 2.35), thereby allowing the use of aluminium alloys for a large part of the aircraft's construction. The ogival wing layout, much more angular in configuration than Concorde's, had been evaluated on the modified MiG-21I Analog testbed in order for experience of the design's basic handling characteristics to be gained. Once the primary research phase was over, Tupolev OKB test pilots Elyan and Koslov undertook the maiden flight of Tu-144 prototype CCCP-68001 on 31 December 1968.

This momentous event was only announced to the world after it had occurred, and when pictures became available the extent of the similarity between the Soviet SST and its Western counterpart soon saw the application to the Tu-144 of the nickname by which it remains best known – 'Konkordskii'.

Not only did 1968 see the first flight of the fastest transport aircraft ever seen, but that of one of the largest as well, the prototype of the Lockheed C-5A Galaxy. The then US Military Air Transport Service (MATS) had in 1963 started to look into the potential operation of a very large airlifter for use on strategic taskings, but which would still be able to operate from the same airfields capable of taking the new C-141A StarLifter. This resulted in the CX-HLS requirement, which recognised the need for the US Army to undertake increasingly bigger deployments (including ever larger equipment) all at once.

Development contracts for the vast new aircraft, described by President Johnson as one which would "represent a dramatic step forward in the worldwide mobility of our forces", were awarded to Boeing, Douglas and Lockheed in 1964, and in October 1965 it was announced that the latter had been successful, its proposed aircraft to be powered by four of General Electric's specially-designed TF39-GE-1 turbofans. With a maximum take-off weight of some 769,000lb, the C-5A Galaxy (as the type was named in 1966) did offer an immense jump in capability for what was now the USAF's Military Airlift Command. Following its first flight, service entry occurred in December 1969, and soon C-5s were operating on heavy-lift supply missions to the Southeast Asia theatre.

---

**16 Jan:** British Prime Minister Harold Wilson announced that the order for 50 F-111Ks for the RAF has been cancelled, and that Royal Navy Phantoms and Buccaneers would be transferred to the Air Force to fill the gap.

**27 Feb:** The USAF's AC-130A Hercules gunship went into combat action in Vietnam for the first time.

**25 Mar:** The initial combat sorties by six USAF F-111As which had been deployed to the Southeast Asian theatre.

**28 Mar:** Cancellation of the General Dynamics F-111B programme for the US Navy.

**6 Apr:** Maiden flight of the LTV YA-7D Corsair II prototype, ordered by the USAF for the attack role.

**8 Apr:** End of the North Vietnamese siege of the US Marine Corps base at Khe Sanh.

**30 Apr:** Major command structure changes for the RAF came into effect, as Fighter and Bomber Commands were merged into a new Strike Command.

**25 May:** The Grumman EA-6B Prowler electronic countermeasures platform for the US Navy made its inaugural flight.

**12 Jul:** The US Navy retired its last flying-boat, a Martin SP-5B Marlin. It was presented to the Smithsonian Institution.

**13 Jul:** First flight of the General Dynamics FB-111A, initially ordered by USAF Strategic Air Command as an interim replacement for the B-58 Hustler prior to the B-70 (which was subsequently cancelled) entering service.

**16 Jul:** Commercial airline services between the USA and USSR began with an Aeroflot Ilyushin Il-62 touching down at New York's JFK Airport and a Pan Am Boeing 707 doing likewise at Moscow-Sheremtyevo.

**8 Sept:** The two-seat French-built Jaguar E01 operational trainer prototype, forerunner of subsequent single-seat strike examples, took to the air for the first time.

**24 Oct:** Final flight of NASA X-15 number 1. It was subsequently presented to the Smithsonian Institution.

**1 Nov:** *Rolling Thunder* strikes by US aircraft against North Vietnam were halted.

**31 Dec:** The first of the two supersonic transport aircraft (SSTs) under development, the Soviet Tupolev Tu-144, made its maiden flight from Zhukovsky near Moscow, ahead of the Anglo-French Concorde design.

*This painting by William S Phillips was completed as a tribute to US Army aviators during the Vietnam War. It depicts an 82nd Medical Detachment Bell UH-1 Iroquois escorted by a pair of Bell AH-1 Huey Cobras.*

*Dust Off: Angels of Mercy* by William S Phillips ASAA

Of all the years of controlled, powered flight, there can be no doubt that 1969 saw the greatest concentration of dramatically significant events – none more so than that which occurred at 10:56pm Eastern Daylight Time on 20 July, when man set foot on the Moon for the first time. In so doing, NASA fulfilled the late-President John F. Kennedy's pledge that America would land a man on the lunar surface by 1970.

The crew of the Apollo 11 mission, comprising commander Neil Armstrong, lunar module pilot Edwin E. 'Buzz' Aldrin and command module pilot Michael Collins had begun their flight into history four days earlier, when on the morning of 16 July, a Saturn V rocket carrying the *Eagle* lunar module and the command/service module, named *Columbia*, blasted off from Cape Kennedy. Around three hours after launch, at a speed of some 24,200mph, the craft left the Earth's orbit, the Saturn rocket separated and the 'mated' *Columbia* and *Eagle* carried on towards the Moon.

On 20 July, Aldrin and Armstrong crawled into the lunar module which then separated from *Columbia*, in which Collins was to continue orbiting. The landing craft's descent engines were fired and preparations for touchdown made. It occurred at 4:18pm EDT, whereupon Armstrong told Mission Control: "The *Eagle* has landed." It took over six hours for him to emerge from the module's small hatch, onto the nine-rung ladder which stood between him and a surface upon which no human had set foot. At 10:56pm, he did so, putting his left foot on the dusty ground and declaring "That's one small step for a man, one giant leap for mankind."

He was subsequently joined outside the capsule by Aldrin, and the pair began collecting samples from the Moon's surface. Having flown the United States flag, both astronauts were then addressed by President Nixon, who said: "For every American this has to be the proudest day of our lives. And for people all over the world I am sure they, too, join with Americans in recognising what a feat this is. Because of what you have done, the heavens have become a part of man's world."

Just as the Apollo 11 mission opened up an entirely new realm of manned flight, so too did two very different commercial aircraft which both took to the air within a month of each other in 1969. The first flights of the initial French prototype BAC/Aérospatiale Concorde 001 at Toulouse on 2 March, and the British-built Concorde 002 at Filton on 9 April were spectacular events, watched live by television viewers in both countries in a way that no such happenings had been seen before – or ever would be again. This reflected the level of interest on both sides of the Channel in the Anglo-French SST, whose development had been through so many political tribulations. Intensive flight trials started immediately afterwards, which saw 001 become the first to break the sound barrier when it attained Mach 1.05 on 1 October, during its 45th sortie.

The Boeing 747-100 prototype took off from Paine Field in Seattle on its inaugural flight on 9 February. It was by far the largest-capacity airliner in the world at the time with intended space for up to 490 passengers. There were to be few large difficulties during flight testing, either with the airframe or the specially-developed Pratt & Whitney JT9D turbofans. The 747 was certified by the FAA for commercial use on the penultimate day of the year, paving the way for Pan American to begin scheduled services. PanAm had been the type's launch customer, having announced in April 1966 that it had ordered 25 examples, and by the close of 1969 some 188 747s were on order for 29 operators.

---

**14 Jan:** Grumman was awarded the US Navy's VFX two-seat long-range interceptor order, with its F-14 Tomcat.

**9 Feb:** Maiden flight of the prototype Boeing 747-100.

**2 Mar:** Concorde 001, the first prototype (F-WTSS), undertook its initial flight from Toulouse in the hands of Aérospatiale test pilot André Turcat.

**19 Mar:** The US Department of Defense confirmed an order by the Marine Corps for 12 AV-8A Harrier V/STOL combat jets.

**26 Mar:** The Panavia consortium was established to design and produce the variable-geometry Multi-Role Combat Aircraft (MRCA).

**9 Apr:** The initial British prototype Concorde 002 (G-BSST) made its first flight, piloted by Brian Trubshaw.

**21 May:** A new world maximum take-off weight record of 728,100lb was set by a Lockheed C-5A Galaxy.

**28 May:** The new Airbus consortium formally decided to go ahead with its A300B short to medium-haul airliner programme.

**5 Jun:** The Tupolev Tu-144 became the first of the two new supersonic airliners to fly faster than sound.

**20 Jul:** NASA's *Eagle* lunar module touched down on the surface of the Moon, allowing Neil Armstrong and 'Buzz' Aldrin to become the first humans to set foot on another celestial body.

**21 Jul:** The *Eagle* lunar module lifted off from the surface of the Moon and went on to re-dock with the *Columbia* command/service module before embarking on the journey back to Earth.

**24 Jul:** The Apollo 11 spacecraft with its three crew aboard splashed down in the Pacific Ocean. Armstrong, Aldrin and Collins were recovered by a helicopter from the USS *Hornet*.

**1 Aug:** Inaugural flight of the prototype Lockheed S-3A Viking twin-turbofan, anti-submarine warfare aircraft.

**16 Aug:** American Darryl Greenamyer set a new world air speed record for piston-engined aircraft when he piloted a Grumman F8F-2 Bearcat to an average of 776.449km/h (482.49mph) over a 3km course.

**15 Sep:** The first in a new line of twin-turbofan Cessna business jets, the Model 500 Citation, made its maiden flight.

**1 Oct:** Concorde 001 exceeded Mach 1 for the first time.

**23 Dec:** McDonnell Douglas was declared the winner of the USAF's F-X air superiority fighter order, with the aircraft which became the F-15 Eagle.

*The moment that Neil Armstrong stepped from the* Eagle *lunar module at 10.56pm on 20 July 1969 and declared "One small step for man, one giant leap for mankind" is recorded in this painting by John Young.*

*Giant Leap for Mankind* by John Young VPGAvA, VPASAA

# 1970

The year was largely dominated by civil aviation, in particular the development of ever larger and faster airliners. Having flown for the first time the previous year, the Boeing 747 entered service with airlines in many countries. Following a record-breaking proving flight in January, Pan American World Airlines was the first to carry out a revenue-earning flight with a 747-100, between JFK International Airport in New York and Heathrow on 22 January. TWA followed up with the first 747 service across the continental USA, introducing the aircraft on the Los Angeles-New York route on 25 February. In the USA, the 747 entered service with American Airlines, Continental and Northwest during the year, while Lufthansa became the first European operator. Airlines around the world ordered the Boeing 747 in considerable numbers, securing production well into the 21st century.

The Douglas DC-10 and Lockheed L-1011 TriStar, both tri-jet wide-bodied airliners, took to the air towards the end of 1970. Construction of the prototypes began within a year of each other, the DC-10 in early 1968 and the TriStar a year later, and the pair competed strongly for orders. Financial problems at Rolls-Royce in the UK caused by a severe overspend on development of the RB211 engine used on the TriStar, proved damaging for the Lockheed design in the sales stakes, and orders were lost in favour of the DC-10 which, in the event, remained in production for six years longer than its rival.

On 6 September one of the emerging hazards of civil aviation was brought into sharp focus when the Popular Front for the Liberation of Palestine (PFLP) hijacked a Swissair DC-8, a TWA Boeing 707 and an El Al 707. They took the passengers hostage as a demand for the release of Palestinians imprisoned in West Germany, Switzerland and Israel. The Swissair and TWA aircraft were flown to Dawson's Field, a remote desert airstrip at Zarqa, Jordan. One of the two hijackers aboard the El Al airliner was shot dead by Israeli security guards aboard the aircraft and the other, Leila Khalid, was restrained. The pilot made an emergency landing at London-Heathrow and Khalid was taken into custody. Soon afterwards, a new Pan Am Boeing 747 was hijacked by two more Palestinians, but could not land on the relatively short desert runway at Dawson's Field and was flown to Cairo instead, where it was blown up on the ground. The fifth aircraft to be involved, a BOAC Super VC10, was hijacked on 9 September en route from Bombay to Beirut. It too was landed at Dawson's Field, and the 114 passengers held hostage along with the 114 who had been aboard the TWA and Swissair flights. Six days after the start of the crisis, the PFLP was informed that the Swiss and German governments would be releasing the Palestinians imprisoned in both countries, and that Leila Khalid would be released from custody in London. The passengers remaining on the airliners at Dawson's Field were set free, and the three aircraft were blown up by the PFLP.

**4 Jan:** An air race between England and Australia, held to commemorate the 50th anniversary of Ross and Keith Smith's flight between the two countries, was won by Capts Bright and Buxton flying a Britten-Norman Islander.
**13 Jan:** A Boeing 747 of Pan American on a proving flight from London to New York became the first aircraft to fly across the Atlantic carrying over 300 people (361 in total).
**16 Jan:** The USAF's last two B-58A Hustlers were retired from operational service.
**22 Jan:** Pan American made the first commercial flight of a Boeing 747, between New York's John F. Kennedy International Airport and London-Heathrow.
**16 Feb:** Harrier GR1s from No 1 Squadron at RAF Wittering made a first overseas proving flight to RAF Akrotiri in Cyprus.
**19 Feb:** Canadair's CL-84 tilt-wing turboprop V/STOL development aircraft made its maiden flight.
**27 Feb:** Hawker Aviation Ltd began buying back surplus Hunters and reworking them for further sales.
**13 Mar:** The Aero Spacelines Guppy 101 flew for the first time.
**18 Mar:** BEA inaugurated its new Airtours charter service from London-Gatwick airport.
**19 Mar:** The Martin Marietta X-24 successfully performed its first powered flight after launch from its NB-52B mothership.
**10 Apr:** First production McDonnell Douglas A-4M Skyhawk for the USN and USMC made its maiden flight.
**22 Apr:** Two USAF HH-53 Super Jolly helicopters made the first non-stop rotor flight across the Pacific, landing at Da Nang AB in South Vietnam.
**26 May:** It was reported that the Tupolev Tu-144 had become the first supersonic airliner in the world to exceed Mach 2 in level flight, reaching 1,336mph (2,150km/h) on a test flight.
**1 Jun:** The first production Lockheed C-5A Galaxy was delivered to USAF Military Airlift Command.
**18 Jul:** First flight of the Aeritalia (Fiat) G222 utility transport, of which the Italian Air Force ordered 44 examples.
**20 Aug:** The Sikorsky S-67 Blackhawk private venture attack helicopter made its first flight.
**29 Aug:** Maiden flight of the Douglas DC-10 tri-jet airliner.
**11 Sep:** Britten-Norman's three-engined 'stretched' development of the Islander, the BN-2A Trislander, took to the air.
**12 Sep:** The USAF's first General Dynamics F-111Es to be permanently deployed outside the USA arrived at RAF Upper Heyford for service with the 20th Tactical Fighter Wing.
**4 Nov:** Concorde 001 was flown through Mach 2 for the first time. At the controls for this, the aircraft's 102nd flight, was test pilot André Turcat. UK-built 002 achieved this nine days later.
**16 Nov:** First flight of the second new wide-bodied tri-jet airliner, the Lockheed L-1011 TriStar.
**16 Nov:** The US Marine Corps received its first McDonnell Douglas AV-8A Harrier.
**30 Nov:** British United Airways and Caledonian merged to form British Caledonian Airways.
**1 Dec:** The Dassault Falcon 10, a shortened version of the Falcon 20, made its first flight in France.
**21 Dec:** Maiden flight of the Grumman F-14A Tomcat carrier-based variable-geometry multi-role fighter for the US Navy.

*The Lockheed Hercules was produced for many roles, including US Navy use in the Antarctic during the Deep Freeze operations. Illustrated in Lou Drendel's painting is a ski-equipped LC-130F.*

These pages generously donated by Marshall Aerospace Limited

*Arctic C-130* by Lou Drendel

Flights to the moon were the flavour of the year. At the end of January, NASA's Apollo 14 was launched as the third moon landing, the first mission for three astronauts to land on the moon's highlands. Apollo 15, the fourth moon landing, was made in June and saw the first use of the Lunar Roving Vehicle (LRV). By December, the last moon landing was made, this by Apollo 17, which again made use of the LRV. The 75-hour stay on the lunar service was the longest of any Apollo missions.

By the early 1970s, some remarkable aircraft built by amateur constructors began to emerge. One was the Bede BD-5A, an unusual single-seat pusher-engined monoplane, that first flew in December. Within four months, the company had received orders for some 2,000 plans and kits.

Concorde 001, the UK-built first pre-production aircraft, made its first flight. Five were ordered by British Airways in May 1972. Conversely, the US Supersonic Transport Program was officially terminated by Congress.

In June, the first flight by a light aircraft from equator to equator, via the North Pole, was made by British airwoman Sheila Scott in a Piper Aztec D, which covered an epic 34,000 mile journey. Miss Scott was the first woman to fly over the Pole and the first to fly over it solo. During the flight she conducted research on behalf of British and US organisations.

Diplomatic relations between the US and Israel, which had been strained since the 1967 six-day war, started to ease and the arms embargo was lifted. This enabled 18 A-4 Skyhawk fighters, together with some ex-USAF C-130E Hercules transports to be delivered. However, the French did not lift an embargo on 50 Mirage Vs due to be exported, and these went instead to the Armée de l'Air.

The short and intense Indo-Pakistan War took place between 3 and 17 December, a conflict over the sovereignty of East Pakistan, which subsequently became Bangladesh. The Indian and Pakistan Air Forces were engaged in air battles, with the former losing 72 aircraft and the latter 94 aircraft.

The Arab/Israeli War of attrition in 1970 had seen a dramatic reversal in the trend to high engagement altitudes set during the first 50 years of air combat. The primary reason for this was the SAM (Surface-to-Air-Missile), which had driven combat aircraft down to the treetops and sand dunes, in an attempt to exploit the weaknesses of radar at those levels.

During the year, SNECMA of France sought a partner and in December reached an agreement with General Electric; CFM was formed three years later. Further serious problems with the RB211 aero engine led to Rolls-Royce declaring itself bankrupt on 4 February, but the British government formed Rolls-Royce (1971) Ltd 19 days later. Dr S. G. Hooker had been recalled from retirement to study the RB211, and within two years the engine was certified at 42,000lb st.

---

**22 Jan:** A US Navy Lockheed P-3C Orion set a new world distance record of 7,010 miles (11,282km) in the FAA category for turbo-powered landplanes.

**21 Mar:** First prototype of the Westland/Aérospatiale WG Lynx, the third helicopter covered by the Anglo-French collaboration of 1968, made its first flight at Yeovil.

**25 Mar:** Russia's Ilyushin Il-76 transport first flew. Intended to replace the An-12 in Aeroflot and military service it appeared at the Paris Airshow in May.

**26 Mar:** CASA's C-212 Aviocar twin-turboprop STOL utility transport made its first flight.

**31 Mar:** First flight of the Kaman SH-2D Seasprite to meet the US Navy's LAMPS helicopter requirement for operation from small ships.

**5 Apr:** With a crew of two and up to seven passengers, the Agusta A109 Hirundo (Swallow) twin-engined general purpose helicopter made its first flight.

**19 Apr:** The Soviet Union launched the Salyut 1 into Earth orbit, the world's first space station. It re-entered the Earth's atmosphere after its mission had terminated on 11 October.

**8 May:** The first flight of the twin-engined Dassault G8 variable-geometry experimental fighter.

**13 May:** Concorde 001 made its first fully automated approach and landing at Toulouse.

**25 May:** Maiden flight of the first of two prototypes of the Dassault-Breguet Mercure, a twin-turbofan short-range civil transport. Ten were ordered by Air Inter (the only buyer) in the following May.

**22 Jun:** First production Scottish Aviation Bulldog Series 100 made its maiden flight. It was a military primary trainer developed from the Beagle Pup.

**14 Jul:** The first Fokker VFW 614-G1 prototype short haul transport made its first flight. It featured twin over-wing mounted Rolls-Royce 501s.

**20 Jul:** Japan's first supersonic aircraft of indigenous design and manufacture, the Mitsubishi XT-2 two-seat jet trainer, made its first flight.

**23 Jul:** First flight of Australia's Government Aircraft Factories (GAF) Nomad, suitable for military or civil roles.

**24 Aug:** The second Aero Spacelines Super Guppy was flown, and the two such aircraft were acquired by Airbus Industries to ferry major fuselage components and wings from their production centres to the final assembly line in Toulouse.

**8 Sep:** The Lockheed TriStar powered with Rolls-Royce RB211-22 turbofans made its first flight.

**10 Sep:** The first of three prototypes of the VFW-Fokker VAK 191B experimental V/STOL aircraft made its first free flight, following a series of tethered hovering flights.

**30 Sep:** First flight of the AEW 2 airborne early warning version of the Avro Shackleton.

**6 Nov:** Two new Egyptian Air Force MiG-25s flew with impunity over the Israeli-held Sinai peninsula. Able to operate at over 70,000ft and at Mach 2.3 the MiG was well beyond the capabilities of Israel's F-4 Phantoms.

**30 Nov:** A freighter version of the Boeing 747, the -200F was flown for the first time.

*The Boeing 737 airliner is still in series production in 2003. An early 737-200 model in American Airlines' distinctive livery is depicted in John W Clark's painting.*

These pages generously donated in memory of Jack Cullum, founder of Cullum Detuners Limited

*Commercial Aviation – Boeing 737-200* by John W Clark ASAA

President Nixon announced in January that the US would fund a massive investment for the construction of a 'reusable' space vehicle/shuttle, which was capable of flying both in space and the Earth's atmosphere. In July, NASA disclosed that Rockwell had won the contract to build the space shuttle orbiter.

By 1972, the North Vietnamese had created the most favourable system of air defences in the world, more modern and more concentrated than faced by an air force before. When the North Vietnamese withdrew from negotiations in Paris to take advantage of the weakened condition of the South in 1972, the US Air Forces conducted unrestricted attacks against Hanoi and Haiphong, including strikes by B-52 Stratofortresses and other aircraft, in a furious December campaign that forced North Vietnam back to the peace table.

The addition of the USAF's C-5A Galaxy fleet to the 'air bridge' transporting supplies to the Vietnam theatre, was a major improvement to the assigned transport fleet. Alongside them, C-130 Hercules and C-141 StarLifters had replaced C-124s, C-133s and C-135s used earlier for the long-range missions. Gunship operations by AC-130 Spectres, now including improved AC-130E versions, continued over the Ho Chi Minh Trail in an attempt to slow the stream of enemy movements between the North and the South.

The McDonnell Douglas F-15A fighter, which became the Eagle, made its maiden flight from Edwards AFB, CA, becoming the USAF's foremost interceptor for the remainder of the century (and into the 21st).

Production of small civil aircraft in the USA was progressing at a commendable pace and in May Cessna Aircraft Corporation announced the completion of the company's 100,000th aircraft, Cessna being the first company in the world to achieve such a production figure. The United States, particularly with Boeing, Douglas and Lockheed, had dominated the airliner from the very early days, but Europe began the long haul to make inroads into this lucrative market. The first step was the Airbus A300B1, capable of carrying 300 passengers, which made its first flight at Toulouse in France.

Vietnam helped to maintain the helicopter's search and rescue role, with Sikorsky HH-53C Jolly Green Giants venturing far behind enemy lines to pick up downed crew members. Probably the war's most significant advance in military terms came with the introduction of the attack helicopter, primarily the Bell HueyCobra.

The Cessna Citation twin-jet entered the market in 1972 and deliveries commenced in April. With a flight level of over 33,000ft the aspect of executive transport was altered, particularly with speed increases to over 400mph.

Freddie Laker, aviation entrepreneur and thorn in the side of the large established airlines, took delivery of his first DC-10 in November. Initially it went into service on the 'sunshine' routes flying holiday makers to the Mediterranean area as his 'Skytrain' service, with no frills and no advance booking transatlantic service, still had to gain approval.

A new passenger terminal was opened in Aberdeen, Scotland in November for the growing number of helicopters being used as workhorses in support of oil and gas rigs and the production platforms in the North Sea.

---

**4 Jan:** Bangladesh Biman was founded, the national airline of new Bangladesh, previously East Pakistan.

**21 Jan:** First flight of the Lockheed S-3A Viking, a twin-engined carrier-based anti-submarine warfare aircraft.

**28 Jan:** Jetstream Aircraft, the company which took over the production of the Jetstream feeder airliner following the collapse of Handley Page Aircraft, delivered its first aircraft. The following month the Ministry of Defence announced that the RAF would purchase 25 for use as multi-engined trainers.

**2 Feb:** Aeroflot commenced full commercial operations with the Tupolev Tu-154.

**5 Feb:** Lufthansa and Aeroflot inaugurated passenger services between Frankfurt and Moscow.

**3 Mar:** *Pioneer 10*, the American unmanned spacecraft, was launched. It subsequently sent back the first pictures of Jupiter.

**8 Mar:** *Europa*, the Goodyear non-rigid airship, made its first flight in the UK.

**27 Mar:** *Venera 8*, the Soviet Union probe, was launched, and eventually made the first sun-side landing on Venus.

**25 Apr:** A world sailplane distance record was set by a Schleicher ASW12, which achieved 907.7 miles (1,460.5km).

**26 Apr:** The first Lockheed L-1011 TriStar entered scheduled service with Eastern Airlines on its route to New York.

**29 Apr:** The long-serving YRF-4C Phantom prototype, adapted as the first fly-by-wire control system test bed and known as the F-4PACT (Precision Aircraft Technology) demonstrator, made its initial flight, but it was not until January 1973 that an all-FBW flight was achieved.

**10 May:** First flight of the Fairchild A-10A, one of the contenders for the USAF's close-support requirement.

**26 May:** The USA and USSR signed the SALT 1 (Strategic Arms Limitation Treaty) agreement.

**2 Jun:** First flight of the Aérospatiale Dauphin helicopter.

**11 Aug:** The Northrop F-5E Tiger II, a lightweight, relatively cheap and simple, yet effective multi-role fighter, flew for the first time.

**4 Sep:** First flight of the Beriev M-62.

**27 Oct:** Maiden flight of the Beech C-12/U-21 Super King Air.

**27 Oct:** USAF Systems Command launched the world's largest balloon with an internal volume of 47.8 million cu ft, from Chino, CA. It reached a new altitude record of 170,000ft carrying a 250lb load of scientific instruments.

**29 Dec:** At midnight on day eleven of *Linebacker II*, all USAF bombing operations against North Vietnam were brought to a halt. Over 1,800 sorties, mainly involving B-52s, had been flown during this campaign.

*Ronald Wong's painting shows the unusual Beriev M-62 that made its first flight on 4 September 1972. It was converted to an Ekranoplan in 1976. The Soviet aerospace industry created a remarkable new species of vehicle which combined modern airframes with jet power on a scale previously seen only in shipbuilding.*

*Beriev's Bizarre Behemoth* by Ronald Wong BSc(Hon), GAvA, ASAA, GMA, TWAS

# 1973

USAF B-52 Stratofortresses flew their final mission against targets in North Vietnam. On 27 January, an agreement was signed ending the war and the last operational mission over North Vietnam was flown that day.

It was a very expensive and wholly unsatisfactory conflict from almost all points of view, not least the eventual outcome. On the whole, airpower was not used wisely or effectively, with the exception of helicopters and close-air support, during the USAF's 12 years of heavy involvement in Vietnam. Very often politics had a major influence on the selection of weapons and targets for US raids. There were too many sanctuaries and rules of engagement, which proved costly in terms of aircraft and aircrew, and too many pauses in the bombing, which allowed the Communists to recover and convince themselves that the US was not fully committed to the war.

A number of factors affected aircraft design during the seventies, but perhaps the most important was the great rise in fuel prices following the Arab oil embargo of 1973. This crisis of the global marketplace caught the Western world by surprise. Yet while aircraft prices have since soared, the principal user of an aircraft may actually find that costs have fallen. Aviation's price-cost paradox reflects a complex web of economic and political factors. Deregulation of the airlines has greatly increased competition among the regular carriers. Flying used equipment for the most part, new companies have emerged with pricing practices that have driven older, more famous airlines (eg PanAm) out of business.

In March NASA began testing the new 'supercritical' wing invented by Richard Whitcomb of NASA. Such a wing was fitted to an F-8A Crusader supersonic fighter for appraisal. It had a flatter upper surface than other wings, but a lighter structure, thicker leading edge, bulging underside and down-curved trailing edge.

Also emerging was the use of the new generation of very high-powered turbofans built by Rolls-Royce, General Electric and Pratt & Whitney, using many advanced structural techniques and materials,

Civil airliner production was continuing at a healthy pace. and Boeing announced in November that the 1,000th B727 had rolled off the production line. It had been continually modernised and updated to meet the needs of both airlines and airports.

Concorde originally had an initial reservation of delivery positions for 74 aircraft by 16 airlines, but this options system was abolished in March. Initial firm orders were placed by British Airways and Air France, but the other options were never taken up.

Another war broke out in the Middle East in October, the 18-day Yom Kippur War, the beginning of the Day of Atonement, or Yom Kippur in the Jewish calendar. Egyptian and Syrian movements of the previous three weeks had been intended to reduce tension, and as late as 5 October, Israel and US intelligence had no knowledge of Arab intentions. Mindful of Israel's pre-emptive strikes of the 1967 Six-Day War, Egypt began its attack along the Suez Canal on 6 October. A further 200 aircraft hit Israeli air bases and SAM sites, backed by tactical missions and stand-off bombs for more distant targets. Simultaneously, the Syrian Air Force struck at Israeli positions and armour in the Golan Heights. It was a while before the IDF/AF could respond in force, only to receive an unexpected counter-attack from Soviet-built SAMs, which had claimed 30 Israeli aircraft by nightfall.

**7 Jan:** The world's first hot-air airship made its first flight. This was developed in England by Cameron Balloons of Bristol.
**16 Feb:** The first production Dassault Mirage F1C multi-mission fighter/attack aircraft made its maiden flight.
**17 Apr:** The PZL-106 Kruk (Raven) agricultural aircraft, intended as a replacement for the PZL-101, made its first flight in Poland.
**8 May:** One of the Airbus A300B1 prototypes made the type's first fully automatic approach and landing.
**3 Jun:** The 30th Paris Airshow witnessed the fatal crash of the second prototype Tupolev Tu-144SST. All six crew members, together with eight on the ground, were killed. On the last manoeuvre the aircraft lost a wing and broke apart, plummeting to earth. The exact cause of the crash has never been revealed.
**1 Aug:** A Martin Marietta X-24B lifting-body research aircraft made its first flight, gliding to Edwards AFB, following launch from its NB-52 mother plane at an altitude of over 40,000ft. It made the first flight under rocket power on 15 November.

**15 Aug:** With the end of bombing missions against the Khymer Rouge in Cambodia, US involvement in Southeast Asia was finally concluded.
**22 Aug:** First flight of the Learjet Model 35 executive jet.
**26 Aug:** Sikorsky flew its first prototype S-69 research helicopter, under the Army designation XH-59A. This was designed to test the Advancing Blade Concept (ABC) rotor, in which two co-axial counter-rotating rigid rotors were used. Thus no anti-torque tail rotor was required.
**20 Sep:** Concorde 002 landed at Dallas-Fort Worth Regional Airport, being the first visit of a supersonic airliner to the US. The airliner had limited itself to flying supersonic only over water.
**21 Sep:** First flight of the Beech T-34C, the turboprop version of the Mentor.
**9 Oct:** The Boeing 747SP entered airline service with JAL. This high-density short-haul version incorporated structural changes for high-frequency take-offs and landing cycles. JAL introduced

the new version on the Tokyo-Okinawa route.
**21 Oct:** The Militky MB-E1 became the first electrically-powered manned aircraft to fly when it took-off from Lintz in Austria. Basically it was a modified HB-3 sailplane with a Bosch electric motor driven by rechargeable batteries.
**26 Oct:** The Franco-German Dassault-Breguet/Dornier Alpha Jet basic/advanced trainer made its first flight.
**23 Nov:** The XH-C-1A, AIDC of Taiwan's first aircraft of indigenous design and manufacture, made its maiden flight. The turboprop secondary trainer was built for the Chinese Nationalist Air Force.
**3 Dec:** The unmanned US *Pioneer 10* became the first spacecraft to approach the planet Jupiter.

*Three USAF B-52 Stratofortresses heading for Hanoi at altitude are illustrated in Philip E West's painting, produced as a tribute to the B-52 crews operating from Guam to targets in North Vietnam.*

*Lone Star Lady* by Phillip West

After months of fruitless lobbying, the UK Government opted out of the proposed Hawker Siddeley/Douglas partnership to develop an advanced Harrier, for which both the UK and US forces had expressed a substantial requirement. As a result the project was dropped, thus allowing McDonnell Douglas free rein to exploit the Harrier concept, and the US company became the prime contractor for the later AV-8B.

The prototype Panavia Tornado MRCA, assembled by MBB, was first flown at Manching in southern West Germany on 14 August. The aircraft would eventually become the mainstay of the RAF inventory for the rest of the century. It was to become the RAF's first variable wing strike aircraft, and as the GR1 it was destined to replace the Vulcan, and most of the Buccaneers and Jaguars.

Designed as a replacement for the B-52 Stratofortress, the first of four prototypes of the Rockwell B-1 four-turbofan variable-geometry strategic heavy bomber made its first flight on 23 December. This, the Air Force's new Advanced Manned Strategic aircraft, was intended to be the third main element in the US strategic defence system, alongside land-based and submarine-launched ballistic missiles. With a potential weapons load of some 80,000lb, including such weapons as the Boeing AGM-69A SRAM and air-launched cruise missiles, and with a maximum range of over 6,000 miles, it was the most flexible. Subsequently the development of the type was suspended in 1977, though it was resurrected five years later by President Reagan and evolved into the B-1B Lancer.

The first prototype General Dynamics F-16A Fighting Falcon made its maiden flight on 20 January (albeit a day earlier than expected when the test pilot elected to take-off when the tailplane was damaged during high-speed taxi tests). The F-16 was one of the two entrants in the USAF's lightweight fighter (LWF) competition, the other being the Northrop F-17, which made its first flight on 9 June. With potentially very large orders from NATO's European air forces to replace their F-104 Starfighters, the rewards from whichever company was successful were very rich indeed. Although the F-17 lost out in this competition, Northrop and McDonnell Douglas later developed the twin-engined single-seat fighter into the F/A-18 Hornet, following the design's victory in the NCAF (Naval Air Combat Fighter Competition) project on 2 May 1975.

Another aircraft that first flew this year was the Hawker Siddeley Hawk. The two-seat basic and advanced jet trainer, with close support capability, made its first flight on 21 August. Intended to replace the Gnat and Hunter T7, it was the first British aircraft to be designed using the metric measurements system.

The engine maker SNECMA was formed in 1974 to manage the programme (as agreed with General Electric) for the CFM56. All versions have a single stage fan rotating with a three stage LP compressor driven by a four stage turbine. The first engine ran at GE on 20 June and the CFM56-2 was certificated on 8 November 1979. In 1974 Pratt & Whitney commenced work on the JT10D to fill the gap between the JT8D and JT9D with a modern engine. Following long collaboration, MTU and Fiat were brought in as risk-sharing partners.

---

**1 Mar:** A three-engined development of the S-65A, the Sikorsky CH-53E made its first flight. It was designed to provide the US Navy and US Marine Corps with a heavy-duty multi-role helicopter.

**1 Mar:** The plan for a third London airport at Foulness, Essex was abandoned by the British government.

**1 Apr:** BOAC and BEA amalgamated to form British Airways.

**10 Apr:** A Martin Marietta Titan III-D launched an additional (eighth) Big Bird reconnaissance satellite into Earth Orbit from Vandenberg, CA.

**23 May:** Air France introduced the Airbus A300B2 wide-body airliner into revenue service. The airline initially ordered six A300s.

**24 May:** Long-range strategic reconnaissance was now provided by Vulcan SR2s of the newly formed No 27 Squadron at RAF Waddington, replacing the Victor SR2s with No 43 Squadron. The latter was disbanded at Wyton.

**24 Jun:** The Aérospatiale AS 350 Ecuruil (Squirrel) helicopter made its first flight.

**22 Aug:** First flight of the Shorts 330. Based on the experience in the design and operation of the Skyvan, Shorts developed the larger commuter airliner in the 30-seat category for which there was an emerging market.

**1 Sep:** A Lockheed SR-71A Blackbird crossed the Atlantic in less than two hours on its way to the Farnborough Air Show. The recorded distance of 3,490 miles was accomplished in one hour, 55 minutes and 42 seconds.

**11 Sep:** Bell Helicopters flew the prototype of the Model 206L LongRanger, which was developed from the Model 206B JetRanger II.

**29 Sep:** Japan Air lines (JAL) and the Civil Aviation Administration of China (CAAC) opened services between Tokyo and Peking.

**17 Oct:** The first of three Sikorsky UH-60A prototypes was flown as part of the US Army's UTTAS (Utility Tactical Transport Aircraft System) requirement. It subsequently entered production as the Blackhawk.

**28 Oct:** Developed from the Etendard IVM, the Dassault Super Etendard carrier-based attack prototype made its maiden flight.

**8 Nov:** First flight of the production example of the IA 58 Pucarà twin-turboprop COIN aircraft, developed for the Argentinean Air Force.

**15 Nov:** Launch of INTASTAT, the first Spanish satellite.

**18 Dec:** Europe's first communications satellite, *Symphonie A*, was launched into geostationary orbit from Cape Kennedy using a Delta vehicle.

**22 Dec:** The Dassault Breguet Mirage F1E successfully took to the air for the first time.

**26 Dec:** The Airbus A300B4, a development of Europe's first wide-body airliner with increased range, made its initial flight.

*The Martin-Baker company has more than fifty years experience of developing emergency ejector seats for aircraft. Ray E Layzell's painting shows modified Gloster Meteor T7 Asterix. A pair of modified Meteors continues to be used for ejection flight trials by the company today.*

*Asterix* by Roy E Layzell

Direct involvement by the United States in North Vietnam finally ended during 1975. The North Vietnamese launched a large invasion of the South, resulting in the fall of Saigon on 30 April.

Retirement of the last Lockheed F-104 Starfighter from USAF Air National Guard squadron service on 31 July illustrated the service's changing requirements as far as its front-line fighters were concerned. The type was the perfect example of an interceptor design of the 1950s, when such aircraft were developed simply with their missile-firing capabilities in mind. The Vietnam conflict had reaffirmed the need for dogfighting ability, a primary design feature of the F-15 and F-16. Elsewhere, the F-104 continued to serve with many air arms, including NATO countries, until replacement mainly by F-16s.

An electronic countermeasures (ECM) version of the General Dynamics F-111 was first proposed in 1970, to replace the veteran Douglas EB-66. At one stage, consideration was given to converting the 24 F-111Cs that had been built for the RAAF, but not delivered. In January 1975, Grumman was appointed as prime contractor to convert two F-111As as prototypes of the specialised electronic warfare EF-111A. This new version was capable of undertaking stand-off and penetration escort missions.

The fourth production BAC/Aerospatiale Concorde became the first aircraft to make four transatlantic crossings (two return crossings, on a London-Gander/Newfoundland route) in one day. Later in the year both British and French Concordes received their Certificate of Airworthiness.

The first combined US/USSR space mission took place in July when Apollo ASTP and Soyuz 19 spacecraft docked together in Earth orbit for experiments and crew exchanges.

Technical advances from warfare (or sometimes referred to as 'spinoffs') have enriched commercial aviation and the civilian economy in general. Onboard and ground-based computers were beginning to give pilots far more precise instrumentation. In addition, satellite weather prediction and better communications have become more part of daily life.

In areas such as airframe design, the civil benefits have been somewhat more limited. Several military aircraft employ the swing wing, but its applicability to airliners has not yet been approved. Perhaps the greatest benefit stems from the increased use of composite materials that reduce weight in the mid-1970s.

In 1975 Douglas Aircraft Company (a division of McDonnell Douglas) studied a number of possible derivatives of its DC-9 that would take advantage of uprated versions of the Pratt & Whitney JT89 engine. Market surveys led to the launch, later in the decade, of the DC-9 Super 80.

---

**1 Jan:** Headquarters of the US 8th Air Force was relocated to Barksdale AFB, LA from Andersen AFB, Guam.

**12 Jan:** British Airways introduced a shuttle service between Heathrow and Glasgow. Using the tri-jet DH Trident 1, it was the first no-booking guaranteed seat service in Europe.

**Jan:** Prior to entering front-line service in the USAF, the stripped-down F-15A 'Streak Eagle' broke eight world time-to-height records.

**5 Mar:** The Japanese Maritime Self-Defence Force (JMSDF) took delivery of its first Shin Meiwa US-1, an indigenous four-engined amphibian, for its air-sea rescue role.

**7 Mar:** The Yakovlev Yak-42 short-range transport made its first flight. A development of the Yak-40 it was powered by three Lotarev D-36 turbofans.

**27 Mar:** The de Havilland (Canada) DHC-7 Dash 7 flew for the first time, landing at an angle of 45 degrees, three times the normal angle of approach, achieved by the use of large Fowler flaps.

**1 Apr:** Formation of the Republic of Singapore Air Force, formed by using Bloodhound SAM units that the British Armed Forces had left behind when vacating Singapore.

**10 Apr:** The first air-to-air refuelling of a Rockwell B-1A by a KC-135 Stratotanker was successfully tested.

**14 Apr:** Israeli Aircraft Industries (IAI) Kfir (Lion Cub) was first displayed to the public. The aircraft was derived from the French Dassault Mirage III, but had a US-supplied General Electric J79 engine.

**30 May:** The European Space Agency (ESA) was founded.

**3 Jun:** First flight of the Mitsubishi FS-T2-Kai supersonic single-seat close-support fighter, developed from the T-2. Designated F-1, it entered JASDF service as a replacement for the F-86F Sabre.

**7 Jun:** The Belgian Government chose the F-16 Fighting Falcon, in preference to the Mirage F1E, placing an order for 102 aircraft.

**20 Jun:** Aircraft of the 601st Tactical Control Wing from Sembach AB, Germany, together with the Air Rescue and Recovery Service, evacuated US citizens from strife-torn Beirut.

**18 Jul:** First flight of the Zlin Z50L aerobatic aircraft. The Czech manufacturer drew on the knowledge gained in 40 years of building competitive aerobatic aircraft, but the Z50L had the US-built 260hp Avco Lycoming engine.

**26 Aug:** The Cessna 441 made its maiden flight, a turboprop version of the piston-engined Model 404 Titan. This led to the production of the Conquest II with Garrett TPE331 engines and up to ten seats, and the Conquest I with PTA-112 engines and up to eight seats.

**16 Sep:** First flight of the Mikoyan MiG-31 'Foxhound' long-range interceptor.

**30 Sep:** In order to fulfill the US Army's requirements for an Armed Attack Helicopter (AAH), Hughes and Bell produced designs, both of which entered a fly-off evaluation. The winner (which was not declared until December 1976) was the Hughes AH-64 that made its first flight on this day. Subsequently named the Apache this helicopter is still in production in 2003.

**31 Oct:** Maiden flight of the definitive Boeing AWACS, the E-3A.

**Oct:** RAF VC10s of No 10 Squadron from Brize Norton evacuated 5,700 people and 350,000lb of freight from Angola.

**29 Nov:** The first *Red Flag* exercise held at Nellis AFB, NV.

**6 Dec:** The F-4G *Wild Weasel* Phantom II was flown for the first time. Subsequently 116 were converted from F-4Es for the SEAD and SAM suppression roles.

*A Russian Tu-95 'Bear' shadowing US naval ships, with a US Navy F-14 Tomcat in close attendance, is portrayed in this Wilfred Hardy painting 'Big Bad Bear'.*

*Big Bad Bear* by Wilfred Hardy GAvA

Western Intelligence received a major coup when a Soviet MiG-25 'Foxbat A' landed in Japan following the pilots defection from a Russian base. At that time little was known about the Foxbat's construction, equipment or capabilities and this defection allowed Western intelligence agencies their first look at this new Russian interceptor.

A new era in passenger travel commenced in January with the first scheduled commercial services by Concorde – the supersonic transport (SST). Although there were substantial adverse reactions from economists and environmental protesters, British Airways and Air France inaugurated services on 21 January. Initially these were between London and Bahrain, and Paris and Rio de Janeiro respectively, and both airlines commenced transatlantic services to Washington's Dulles International Airport.

On 9 August, the Boeing YC-14, the second contender for the USAF's advanced medium STOL transport (AMST) requirement, made its first flight. Its competitor, the McDonnell Douglas YC-15, had got airborne for the first time in August the previous year. The original request was for a C-130 Hercules replacement, making use of improvements in aerodynamics and powerplants. Both aircraft were extremely manoeuvrable, demonstrating this alongside each other at numerous international airshows. However, in spite of their use of the latest aerodynamic technology, particularly with advanced wing, engine and flap configurations that delivered good STOL performance, neither aircraft provided advances that were significant enough over the C-130's capabilities to merit the expenditure on progressing with the production of an entirely new type.

The first launch of the Boeing AGM-86A air-launched cruise missile (ALCM), from a B-52 Stratofortress, was also significant. This stand-off weapon, with a range of up to 750 miles, was intended to be procured for B-52s and the new Rockwell B-1A, for which funding was cut back by the US Senate in August, deferring production.

By the mid-1970s, the homebuilt movement was beginning to provide another means of meeting the demand in many countries for sport and working aeroplanes for the general market. Homebuilders used novel construction techniques and materials to create innovative aircraft. This led to a profusion of landplanes, amphibians and helicopters, all of which were beginning to manifest themselves from the fertile minds of homebuilders.

The ultralight aircraft began to take-off after people began putting tiny engines on their hang-gliders. Since then, the evolution of the microlight has reflected the evolution of the aircraft, each generation becoming larger, faster and more complex, with many of the kits available replicating some of the significant shapes of the past.

The UK Ministry of Defence announced that the Tornado ADV was to be developed as a replacement for the air defence Phantom. The last three new-build Buccaneer S2Bs for the RAF left the Brough factory in December with final deliveries being made to RAF Germany.

**10 Feb:** First flight of the production Westland Lynx HAS2 multi-role helicopter for the Royal Navy.
**16 Mar:** First flight of the General Dynamics YF-16 prototype that was re-engineered as a control-configured vehicle (CCV) testbed aircraft for fully-computerised fly-by-wire tests.
**17 Mar:** A JAL Boeing 747 made the first non-stop flight from Tokyo to New York. The 6,300 mile (10,139km) flight was completed in 11 hours.
**24 Mar:** A new non-stop distance record for a civil aircraft was made by a Boeing 747SP on a delivery flight from the US to Cape Town, South Africa, a distance of 10,290 miles (16,560km).
**13 May:** PanAm Boeing 747SP *Clipper Liberty Bell* established a record-breaking round-the-world flight. Flying from Seattle, with refuelling stops in Delhi and Tokyo, it took a total of 46 hours.
**22 Jun:** The USSR launched the unmanned Salyut 5 space station into Earth orbit. Salyut 21 was launched on 6 July for two cosmonauts to dock with Salyut 5 and stayed in space for just over 49 days.
**1 Jul:** A Thorp T-18 Tiger flew solo from Australia to the UK, the first such flight to be made in a homebuilt aircraft.
**27/28 Jul:** Two USAF Lockheed SR-71A Blackbird strategic reconnaissance aircraft were used to set three new absolute world altitude and speed records. A maximum height of 85,068ft and a speed of 2,193mph (3,529km/h) were achieved.
**12 Aug:** Italy's Aeromacchi MB-339 two-seat multi-role trainer/light strike aircraft made its first flight. Derived from the earlier MB-326 jet trainer design, it went into production for the Italian Air Force.
**13 Aug:** The Bell Model 222 light commercial helicopter made its maiden flight, the first twin-turbine helicopter in this class to be built in the US.
**27 Aug:** Poland's PZL-Mielec M-18 Dromader crop-spraying aircraft made its first flight.
**10 Oct:** First flight of the Embraer EMB-121 Xingu, the first pressurised twin-turboprop general purpose transport to be built in Brazil.
**18 Oct:** Maiden flight of the Lockheed JetStar II, a 12-seat executive transport.
**26 Oct:** First overseas deployment of the US Marine Corps AV-8A Harriers. VMA-231 aboard the USS *Franklin D. Roosevelt* was assigned to the US 6th Fleet in the Mediterranean theatre.
**7 Nov:** Dassault's Falcon 50 three-engined executive jet made its first flight. Intended mainly for the US-market it had a large fuel capacity giving it a range of over 3,400 miles at 500mph.
**16 Dec:** The first flight of the Boeing 747-123 Space Shuttle Carrier Aircraft (SSCA), which had been converted from an ex-American Airlines airliner.
**22 Dec:** The Soviet Union's first wide-bodied airliner, the Ilyushin Il-86 made its first flight from Khodinka. It featured three built-in staircases.
**Dec:** C-141 StarLifters of MAC delivered relief supplies (mainly tents and heaters) to Incirlik AB after more than 3,500 people died in an earthquake in eastern Turkey on 24 November.

*Michael Turner's painting depicts a British Airways Concorde at high level over the Atlantic in the first year that the supersonic transport entered scheduled airline service.*

These pages generously donated by BAE SYSTEMS

*Concorde – Superstar across the Atlantic* by Michael Turner PGAvA, FGMA

# 1977

The greatest loss of life in the history of commercial aviation occurred at Santa Cruz airport in the centre of Tenerife in the Canary Islands on 27 March. 579 people were killed when, in conditions of very poor visibility, a Boeing 747 began its take-off while a taxiing 747 was still on the active runway. As a result of this accident a new airport was built on the south coast of the island.

'Concordski', the Tupolev Tu-144, entered limited Aeroflot service on 1 November, albeit five years behind schedule, but only made just over 100 revenue earning services before operations were ended prematurely seven months later.

In an attempt to reduce the cost of transatlantic flights Freddie Laker inaugurated Laker Airway's London-New York Skytrain service using DC-10s. It had taken him six years to get approval from the authorities to commence this service, but almost immediately six scheduled airlines introduced low-cost transatlantic fares, fearing they would otherwise lose business to Laker.

The tilt-rotor appeared on the scene in May, when the Bell Model 301 research aircraft made the type's initial free hovering flight. In July, the second prototype XV-15 made its first transition from hovering to forward flight. This aircraft was the forerunner of the V-22 Osprey, which still has to enter serious operational service in 2003.

Echoes of the B-70 Valkyrie bomber programme were perhaps to be heard during the year, when President Carter cancelled the Rockwell B-1A programme. Instead of pursuing the advanced penetrating bomber route, the new President had decided to keep the B-52 Stratofortress fleet and its stand-off missiles and to expand development of cruise missiles. The three B-1A prototypes already flying were to continue their research and development programme and completion of the fourth went ahead.

When Sweden produced the Saab JA 37 Viggen, which successfully featured the 'double delta' format, it led in-service European technology until the RAF's Panavia Tornado F3 finally became operational over a decade later.

The unusual Edgeley EA-7 Optica made its first flight in December but was to be plagued by problems throughout its life.

In Europe, the arrival of USAFE's first F-15A Eagles, that equipped the 36th Tactical Fighter Wing at Bitburg AB, Germany in April was a very significant event. The type's impressive performance as an air superiority fighter made it the most potent NATO combat aircraft asset in Europe at the time, and the only aircraft with a greater capability than the Soviet MiG-25 'Foxbat', which was then in service in large numbers in the Warsaw Pact states. The Fairchild A-10 entered service with the USAF in June, the Air Force's first purpose-built close-support aircraft. Started originally as a counter-insurgency aircraft it was quickly developed into a 'tank-buster'.

The RAF's Harriers underwent a programme of progressive improvement, updating them to GR3 standard. Weapon carriage and range were improved by fitting more powerful engines. Laser ranging marked target seeking (LRMTS) and passive radar warning receiver (RWR) equipment was also incorporated.

**6 Jan:** First flight of the HAL HPT-32, a single-engined piston engined basic trainer developed to meet an Indian Air Force requirement.

**18 Feb:** First flight of the Boeing 747 Space Shuttle carrier, with the shuttle *Enterprise* mounted above the fuselage, was successfully made by NASA at the Dryden Flight Research Center. For the first six successful flights the *Enterprise* was unmanned. It made its first manned free gliding flight following launch from the carrier on 11 August.

**1 Mar:** The first Boeing E-3A Sentry was delivered to USAF's Tactical Air Command's 552nd Airborne Warning and Control Wing at Tinker AFB, Oklahoma.

**1 Mar:** Nimrod MR1 aircraft from RAF Kinloss and RAF St Mawgan began regular North Sea oil and gas rig surveillance duties, under the code name Operation *Tapestry*.

**10 Mar:** First flight of the EF-111A Raven, after full modification as an electronic warfare aircraft. The conversions introduced a large fin-tip fairing to house the receiver and antennas of the AN/ALQ-99E tactical jamming system, the transmitters for which were installed in a long canoe-shaped radome under the fuselage.

**31 Mar:** The 10,000th Beechcraft Bonanza was completed, more than 31 years after its first flight in December 1945.

**20 May:** The Soviet Sukhoi Su-27 'Flanker' long-range fighter made its first flight. This aircraft remains in production, albeit in limited numbers, 25 years later. Its contemporary, the MiG-29 'Fulcrum', made its first flight on 6 October.

**27 Jun:** The Spanish CASA C101 low-wing, single-engined jet trainer first flew, and was ordered for the Spanish Air Force.

**10 Jul:** The phased array radar to monitor Soviet space activities, known as *Cobra Dane*, became operational.

**31 Aug:** A Mikoyan Ye-266M recorded a height of 123,524ft, a world record for air-breathing, rather than rocket-powered, aircraft.

**22 Nov:** First flight of the Antonov An-72 'Coaler' twin-turbofan STOL transport, which incorporated features similar to that of the Boeing YC-14 prototype.

**28 Nov:** Dassault's Falcon 20G was flown for the first time, and achieved instant export success with a US Coast Guard order for 41 of the type.

**1 Dec:** First flight of the Lockheed XS7 *Have Blue* stealth technology demonstrator at Groom Lake, Nevada.

**13 Dec:** The first Airbus A300B4 entered service in the USA when Eastern Airlines introduced the European wide-bodied jet airliner on its east coast services.

**13 Dec:** The Malay Government banned the supersonic Concorde from its airspace, thus forcing the suspension of the joint British Airways/Singapore Airlines service.

**14 Dec:** The Soviet Mil Mi-26 'Halo' heavy transport helicopter made its maiden flight. It is still the world's largest production helicopter, and features a unique eight-blade main rotor.

*Confronting danger with professional pride, a US Coast Guard Sikorsky HH-3F Pelican helicopter is shown attempting a rescue in high seas in Paul Rendel's painting.*
© www.paulrendel.com

*Coast Guard Rescue* by Paul Rendel ASAA

# 1978

Twenty years after the prototype first flew, McDonnell Douglas delivered its 5,000th F-4 Phantom. Exported to many air arms, the Phantom can be rated as one of the most successful fighters of the Century.

Claimed to be the first flight by an entirely solar-powered aircraft, *Solo One* made its first flight at Lasham, Hampshire. Power was provided by batteries storing electricity generated by 750 individual solar cells, mounted on the inboard section of the wing.

For many years, operators of commuter-style services in the USA (where a large proportion of the market for this type exists) had been limited by the terms of the CAB Economic Regulation 298 to flying aircraft with no more than 30 passenger seats. To fly larger types required the airline to seek authority under a substantially different set of operating regulations, compliance with which frequently imposed extra costs that were necessarily passed on to the traveller – and this served to diminish the numbers of passengers carried. In turn, it reduced viability and often led to financial collapse. The deregulation of the US airline industry in 1978 brought a relaxation of these rules allowing many third-level airlines to contemplate growth of a kind previously not thought possible. This therefore enabled manufacturers to market aircraft of more than 30-seat capacity.

When the new Carter administration put forward its first US Defense Department budget in January, it contained another significant programme cancellation. Funding was provided for the Air Force's new Lockheed TR-1 battlefield reconnaissance aircraft and the big McDonnell Douglas KC-10 Extender tankers. However, the Advanced Medium STOL Transport (AMST) Program was scrapped, leaving the Boeing YC-14 and McDonnell Douglas YC-15 prototypes 'out in the cold'. This confirmed many more years of production for the C-130 Hercules as the USAF's primary and tactical special mission airlifter.

While MAC had now lost its future advanced STOL tactical transport, its existing strategic transport equipment again proved its capabilities during two airlift operations in 1978. The first of these was in May, when Zaïre was invaded from Angola by rebel troops. In December, the collapse of the Shah's government in Iran and the subsequent revolution saw C-5As and C-141As in action again, evacuating 900 American military dependents from Teheran.

By the latter half of the year USAF plans for the Lockheed TR-1A became clearer. Initial funding provided for the production line to be re-opened to produce 25 TR-1s, a new and updated version of the U-2R, which itself was an enlarged U-2. Included in the build were two twin-seat dual control trainers. The mission equipment included a Hughes Advanced Synthetic Aperture radar incorporating a sideways-looking facility. This allowed an aircraft flying over NATO territory to 'look' up to 49 miles into Eastern Europe.

The RAF announced that the capacity of its Hercules fleet was to be considerably enhanced. Nearly half of the C-130Ks, some 30 aircraft in all, were to be 'stretched' by Marshall of Cambridge, the main contractor to Lockheed for the RAF transport fleet. This was to be achieved by inserting two 'plugs' into the fuselage. The lengthened version (designated C3) was 15ft longer, giving it a 40% increase in total payload.

**1 Jan:** British Aerospace (BAe) was formed by the transfer of the British Aircraft Corporation (BAC), Hawker Siddeley Aviation and Scottish Aviation into one corporation.
**1 Jan:** Introduction of the McDonnell Douglas Advanced Concept Ejection Seat II, known as ACES II.
**22 Feb:** The first Global Positioning System satellite (NAVSTAR) was launched into Earth orbit.
**1 Mar:** The Dash 7 airliner made its entry into service when Rocky Mountain Airways introduced it on the Denver-Aspen route.
**10 Mar:** First flight of the Dassault Mirage 2000 prototype, and achieved Mach 1.3 on its initial flight. The air superiority fighter was selected as the primary combat aircraft for service with the French Air Force.
**23 Mar:** Captain Sandra M. Scott became the first woman pilot to perform alert duty in SAC, whilst assigned to the 904th Air Refueling Squadron, Mather AFB,CA.
**9 Apr:** Powered by a pair of Avco Lycoming LTP 101 turboprops, the Dornier 28D-5 made its first flight.

**18 Apr:** The Vickers Viscount became the first turbine-engined aircraft to complete 25 years of regular airline service.
**9 May:** First crossing of the English Channel by a microlight, at that time referred to as a 'powered hang glider'.
**28 Jun:** The first Dassault Super Etendard entered operational service with the French Aéronavale, and went to sea in December.
**1-19 Jul:** Two single-engined Beechcraft Bonanzas were the first aircraft to fly around the world in formation. Take-offs and landings were made in unison, the distance of 23,848 miles (38,380km) being accomplished in a flight of time of 160 hours.
**12 Aug:** Pilatus flew the first prototype PC-7 Turbo-Trainer in Switzerland, a turboprop trainer that would be widely adopted by military air arms.
**17 Aug:** Completion of the first transatlantic balloon crossing.
**20 Aug:** First flight of the BAe Sea Harrier, the Harrier version developed for the Royal Navy shipboard operation.
**1 Sep:** For the first time, B-52 Stratofortresses began to practice conventional weapons delivery missions (as distinct from nuclear weapons) in support of NATO, during Exercise *Cold Fire 78*.
**13 Sep:** The Aérospatiale AS332 Super Puma first flew.
**8 Nov:** The Canadian CL-600 Challenger twin-turbofan business and commuter transport made its first flight.
**9 Nov:** The Advanced Harrier with increased weapons payload and combat radius, the McDonnell Douglas AV-8B, made its first flight.
**18 Nov:** First flight of the McDonnell Douglas F/A-18 Hornet shipboard attack fighter.
**19 Dec:** Soviet's Beriev A-50 'Mainstay', based on an Ilyushin Il-76MD airframe, made its maiden flight.
**30 Dec:** The prototype SIAI-Marchetti SF600TP Canguro made its first flight, powered by a pair of Lycoming TIO-540-I flat-six piston engines.

*The Dassault Mirage 2000 made its first flight in March 1978. Ronald Wong's painting shows a pair flying over the French coastline after the jet had entered service with the Armeé de l'Air.*

These pages generously donated by Pilatus Aircraft

*Birds of Picardie* by Ronald Wong BSc(Hons), GAvA, ASAA, GMA, TWAS

Sixty years after Blériot flew his aircraft across the English Channel, another unique single-seater made the flight across the water. This was the *Gossamer Albatross* a British man-powered aircraft, with pedal power being used to complete the journey.

The McDonnell Douglas F-15, then widely acknowledged as the world's best fighter, made its combat début in the hands of the Israeli Air Force when a unit shot down four Syrian MiG-21PFMAs with Shafir missiles.

The end of 1979 in the US saw continuing mass production of small aircraft for the civilian market. The four-seat Mooney was the world's fastest single-piston engined production aircraft, and Mooney Aircraft produced its 1,500th example in May.

Development of the stretched version of the Boeing 737 began in 1979, when market studies began to show the need for what Boeing was later to describe as 'a longer-bodied version of the popular 737 twin-jet'. It was designed to burn less fuel per passenger and provide reduced noise levels for the short haul markets of the 1980s and beyond. Military Airlift Command (MAC) received the first of 270 'stretched' C-141B StarLifters later in the year, the prototype having flown in March 1977. In order to utilise the original C-141A's full potential, Lockheed added fuselage 'plugs' 23ft 4in long, fore and aft of the wing, giving a total aircraft length of 168ft 4in and a 35% increase in load-carrying capacity. The addition of an air-to-air refuelling receptacle above the cockpit was to further enhance the StarLifter's strategic capability. In effect, the 'stretch' programme provided MAC with the equivalent of some 90 additional aircraft, for a much cheaper outlay.

The first production F-16A Fighting Falcon was delivered to an operational USAF unit. This marked a significant milestone as the advances provided by the F-16 when compared with its predecessor, the F-4 Phantom, were considerable, given that the new aircraft was lighter and cheaper to operate. The new type's abilities as an air-combat fighter were unrivalled, thanks to its advanced fly-by-wire control system and radar. The expanded range of stores that production examples could carry, combined with its 'dogfighting' capabilities, made it an immediate favourite with pilots.

Although *Red Flag* exercises in Nevada provided excellent training, the weather conditions were very different from those usually encountered over the North German Plain. Therefore, in 1979, the RAF became involved in exercises hundreds of miles to the north, at the Canadian Forces base at Cold Lake in Alberta. This offered more appropriate and realistic weather conditions. Exercise *Maple Flag* became an annual deployment where the flying was done over almost uninhabited forest and lakeland; and where snow, low cloud, rain and other familiar European meteorological conditions prevailed. RAF Jaguars participated in *Maple Flag* for the first time, with Harriers the following year.

New weapons to maximise the Tornado GR1's potential were under development. In the anti-airfield role, it would be armed with the Hunting Engineering JP233, an area denial weapon which distributed cratering sub-munitions and anti-personnel mines, the latter designed to seriously disrupt repair operations on a target airfield. Studies continued into guided anti-armour and anti-radiation weapons to replace BL-755 and Martel.

---

**1 Jan:** The E-3A Sentry assumed an air defence role, after NORAD personnel began augmenting TAC crews on missions flown from Tinker AFB, OK.

**26 Feb:** Russia launched *Soyuz 32* with two cosmonauts on board, which then docked with space station *Soyuz 6*.

**10 Mar:** Two E-3A Sentry AWACS aircraft were deployed to Riyadh, Saudi Arabia to monitor hostilities between North and South Yemen.

**1 Apr:** The go ahead was given for British Aerospace to convert nine second-hand VC10s and Super VC10s into air-to-air refuelling tankers. These were to equip a new squadron to be based at RAF Brize Norton.

**20 Apr:** The 16th and last production Concorde flew.

**11 May:** Boeing Vertol's CH-47D Chinook made its first flight, a development of the original CH-47A.

**5 Jun:** The first production Panavia Tornado IDS was rolled out at Warton. It was an RAF GR1 trainer version, and was followed 17 days later by a West German aircraft.

**10 Jul:** The first full production standard Tornado GR1 made its initial flight at Warton.

**11 Jul:** The US Skylab space station re-entered the Earth's atmosphere, breaking up over Australia and the Indian Ocean.

**17 Jul:** Start of a fly-off between the General Dynamics AGM-109 Tomahawk cruise missile and the Boeing AGM-86B air-launched cruise missile for SAC.

**27 Jul:** The first air-dropped free flight of the Rockwell Highly Manoeuvrable Aircraft Technology (HiMAT) unmanned research aircraft was made from a B-52 carrier aircraft at 45,000ft over the Edwards AFB, CA test range.

**27 Oct:** The Tornado ADV prototype made its first flight at Warton. Eighteen production F2s were eventually built, eight of them being dual-control trainers.

**1 Dec:** It became necessary to despatch a Commonwealth monitoring force, with a sizeable RAF contingent, to Rhodesia (later renamed Zimbabwe) to oversee the ceasefire and subsequent election. During the next four months, the RAF was involved in

a major tactical airlift (Operation *Agila*) with seven Hercules and Puma helicopters.

**12 Dec:** First flight of the Sikorsky SH-70B, the winner of the US Navy's LAMPS system, later named the Seahawk.

**12 Dec:** NATO agreed to the deployment of cruise and Pershing II missiles to Europe.

**21 Dec:** The NASA/Ames AD-1 oblique-wing research aircraft made its first flight. It was designed so that after take-off with the wing in a conventional position, the wing could be slewed to a max angle of 60deg in flight, so as to investigate potential drag reduction/fuel economies.

**22 Dec:** The Aérospatiale TB30 Epsilon standard primary trainer for the Armée de l'Air made its maiden flight.

*This specially commissioned painting by Timothy O'Brien shows pedal power matching Blériot's feat of flying the English Channel. Here the* Gossamer Albatross, *flown by Bryan Allen, is seen being shadowed by a support boat.*

These pages generously donated by the RAF Cosford Airshow

*The Channel Bike Ride* by Timothy O'Brien GAvA

Civil airline growth continued at a healthy pace in the early '80s when Delta Airlines placed the largest order to date of a single jetliner type, when a total of 60 Boeing 757s was ordered. Derived from the Douglas DC-10-30CF, the KC-10A Extender was ordered to fulfill the USAF's advanced tanker/cargo aircraft (ATCA) requirement and a total of 60 was eventually delivered. The aircraft's primary role was the in-flight refuelling of fighter and attack aircraft, although it could carry up to 169,000lb (76,658kg) of freight over a distance of 4,370 miles (7,030km). It was not intended as a replacement for the KC-135 Stratotanker, but to complement the type.

In the year, Learjet delivered its 1,000th aircraft and made the first flight of the Longhorn 50. Also in 1980, Piper delivered its 500th Cheyenne. The company was continuing to improve the range of its models, for comfort as much as safety. The Beechcraft C99 flew on 20 June, marking the return of Beech into the regional traffic sector from which it had withdrawn over five years earlier. The twin-turboprop 19-seat aircraft had a cruising speed of 285mph. Demand was forthcoming because of the gradual withdrawal from service of ageing Douglas DC-3s. This had meant that many provincial towns in the US had lost their connection into the main air traffic network, and the 'feederliner' would be their salvation.

According to Greek mythology, Icarus (the son of Daedalus) was the earliest aviation casualty, through flying too near the sun. In August, the sun brought triumph again, as the *Gossamer Penguin*, a solar-powered monoplane, flew for two miles at Edwards AFB in California, the first sustained flight using solar power. This was a scaled down model of the *Gossamer Albatross*, which had made the first man-powered crossing of the English Channel in 1979. The solar cells provided sufficient power to drive the 3hp engine that drove a seven-foot propeller.

PanAm Boeing 747 *China Clipper* completed the first official flight between the US and China in December, this being the first since the 1949 Communist take-over. In February, Japan Air Lines introduced the first of seven Boeing 747SRs. Able to seat 550 passengers, they were to be used on short-range high-density internal routes.

In November it transpired that Concorde would only be operated by British Airways and Air France, and the service to Singapore was withdrawn. At great financial risk, a BA Concorde stewardess chartered her aircraft to sell short flights to her friends. This was an immediate success which became big business, and many organisations have continued to charter Concorde over the years – a move that no doubt helped the supersonic transport to be financially viable during the next two decades.

The advent of new technology again played a major part in the USAF's year. The service completed its competitive evaluation of the General Dynamics AGM-109 Tomahawk and the Boeing AGM-86B ALCMs in February. Getting the ALCM into service (to equip the B-52 Stratofortress fleet) was a major priority after President Carter's cancellation of the Rockwell B-1A in favour of improved cruise missile technology.

---

**7 Jan:** A single-engined Mooney set a non-stop coast-to-coast record in the USA, using only 105 gallons of aviation fuel in an eight hour and four minute flight.

**18 Jan:** The Danish Air Force received its first F-16B, which was built at the SABCA production facility at Gosselies in Belgium.

**1 Feb:** An Aeroflot Il-18D flew the first Moscow-Antarctic air route (18,642 miles/30,000km) - linking Moscow with the Molodezhnaya Antarctic observatory.

**23 Mar:** Thirty-three Boeing Chinook HC1s were ordered for the RAF. The first flew on this date and production examples followed in December.

**28 Mar:** First flight of the Jetstream 31 feeder airliner.

**May:** The Royal Air Force aerobatic team, the *Red Arrows*, gave its first public display with the BAe Hawk T1, with which it had been re-equipped at the end of the previous season.

**4 Jun:** First US-built F-16J pattern aircraft for the JASDF was flown and delivered to Japan on 15 July.

**5 Jun:** British Airways Helicopters began using the Sikorsky S-76 on its services to North Sea oil and gas platforms.

**5 Jun:** The Soviet Union's first manned *Soyuz T* capsule, incorporating an automatic docking system, was launched into Earth orbit.

**6 Jun:** The first of eight BAe Hawk T53s was handed over to the Indonesian Air Force.

**24 Jun:** A French Microturbo Microjet 200 made its first flight. A two-seat aircraft of wooden construction it was powered by two tiny 243lb st (1.09kN) Microturbo TRS 18-046 turbojets.

**16 Jul:** First flight of the ill-fated BAe Nimrod AEW3. Mounting the radar at the extremities of the airframe ensured all-round coverage with potential for detection of both airborne and maritime targets. After trials in 1982 the project was abandoned and the RAF opted for the Boeing E-3A Sentry.

**17 Jul:** Cathay Pacific inaugurated a Hong Kong-Heathrow route operated by Boeing 747s.

**23 Jul:** The Aérospatiale AS 366G Dauphin II helicopter made its maiden flight. It was subsequently ordered by the US Coast Guard as the HH-65A Dolphin.

**7 Aug:** The MacCready *Gossamer Penguin* made its first straight solar-powered flight of two miles (3km).

**16 Aug:** First flight in Brazil of the EMBRAER EMB-312 Tucano prototype.

**5 Oct:** The McDonnell Douglas DC-9 Super 81 entered Swissair service on its Zurich-Heathrow route.

**11 Oct:** First flight of the two-seat Dassault Mirage 2000 B prototype. A company-funded aircraft it achieved supersonic flight on its first flight.

**11 Nov:** NASA's *Voyager 1* spacecraft flew past Saturn's largest moon Titan, passing below Saturn's rings before travelling on out of the solar system.

**14 Nov:** The SOCATA TB20 Trinidad touring aircraft made its first flight in France.

**26 Dec:** Aeroflot commenced Moscow-Tashkent service with the new Ilyushin Il-86.

*Edmund Miller's painting illustrates RAF Aérospatiale/Westland Pumas and Boeing Chinooks providing Army support during an exercise, deploying troops and equipment.*

These pages generously donated by CAE

*Deploying Troops* by Edmund Miller DLC, CEng, MRAeS, GAvA

# 1981

America's NASA Space shuttle orbiter *Columbia*, the first re-usable space vehicle, was launched on its first mission (STS-1) on 12 April. The re-usable delivery system was designed and developed by NASA to reduce the massive cost of putting objects into space. The forward section of the shuttle had a two-man cockpit, while mission specialists sat behind. A large payload bay amidships would be used to carry satellites and other equipment. The roof of the bay opened out like bomb doors, enabling a powerful manipulator arm to extract the payload. *Columbia* returned after two days, having orbited the Earth 36 times. It re-entered the Earth's atmosphere as an aircraft, complete with aerodynamic controls, for a controlled landing at Edwards AFB, CA. Previous launch vehicles had been destroyed on their one-way missions.

With the introduction of newer airline types, British Airways operated its last VC10s. With a small fleet of 12 VC10s and 17 Super VC10s, the airliner had carried over 13 million passengers without a single fatality. McDonnell Douglas produced its 1,000th DC-9 airliner, a Super 80 (subsequently redesignated MD-80) which was delivered to Swissair.

One of the most daring attacks of the 20th Century took place on 7 June, during a non-war period, when in a very complex operation, Israeli Air Force F-16s with cover provided by F-15s, crossed over Jordan and Saudi Arabia to Iraq. The target was the nuclear reactor at Osirak, near Baghdad, which was destroyed by eight F-16s armed with pairs of Mk 84 iron bombs. The F-16s all returned safely to their base at Etzion in Israel.

The aircraft which revolutionised aerial warfare in the late 20th Century took to the air on 18 June. Shrouded in immense secrecy, the Lockheed F-117, with its multi-faceted 'stealth' design, flew from Groom Lake, Nevada. The Defense Advanced Research Projects Agency (DARPA) had been studying 'stealth' technology since the 1970s, leading to the *Have Blue* programme that developed a flying prototype to test low-observable technology. The F-117 was produced at the famous 'Skunk Works' at Burbank, CA. Virtually all sorties were conducted at night.

The first Lockheed TR-1A, the latest member of the U-2 family (the first of which had flown in the early 1960s), made its first flight at Palmdale, CA. The TR1A featured 'superpods' – modular sensor-carrying containers up to 24ft in length, mounted under each wing to house different forms of antenna for many tasks, alongside the photo-recce and signals intelligence (SIGINT) equipment that could still be carried in the TR-1A's Q-bay, behind the cockpit. Its extended nose-cone carried the sideways-looking surveillance radar, used to provide information on the disposition of forces.

The *Solar Challenger* became the first solar-powered aircraft to fly the English Channel. On 7 July, it reached 12,000ft and cruised across at 37mph (59km/h).

In December, Hughes flew its NOTAR (no tail rotor) experimental helicopter for the first time. The anti-torque tail rotor was replaced by a jet of pressurised air released through adjustable slits. This innovation proved successful and commercial development of the new concept followed.

The BAe 146, nicknamed 'Whisper Jet' made its first flight at Hatfield. The high-wing four-engined airliner was the final outcome of a design dating back to the Hawker Siddeley 146 of 1973. As a 80 to 100 seat short-range transport, the 146 was specially designed to operate from runways that are short or difficult to get into, and immediately proved it could overfly urban areas near airports without causing excessive noise.

---

**1 Jan:** The Russian *Progress 12* unmanned cargo spacecraft docked with and refuelled *Salyut 6* in Earth orbit and then raised the space station's orbit.

**9 Jan:** Laker Airways received the first of its Airbus A300s.

**18 Jan:** Bell delivered its 25,000th helicopter, a Bell 222.

**6 Feb:** First flight of the Sikorsky H-60B army reconnaissance helicopter, a development of the USAF UH-60A Blackhawk.

**28 Mar:** The Dornier 228 commuter transport first flew.

**9 Apr:** First flight of the Transall C160 Second Series military transport, which featured a reinforced wing, larger fuel capacity and enhanced avionics.

**10 Apr:** Italy's SIAI-Marchetti S.211 first flew. It was a private venture jet trainer which later took part in the JPATS competition during the 1990s.

**12 Apr:** NASA's Space Shuttle *Columbia* was successfully launched from Cape Kennedy on Mission STS-1, under the power of its own rocket engines and two jettisonable boosters.

**20 Apr:** Initial flight of the first production Sukhoi Su-27 'Flanker'.

**26 Jun:** The first production EF-111A made its maiden flight.

**19 Aug:** Two US Navy F-14A Tomcats, from USS *Nimitz* intercepted two Libyan Air Force Su-22 'Fitters'. In claimed international waters, the Libyans had approached the USS *Forrestal*, which was conducting exercises off the Gulf of Sidra. The Tomcats launched AIM-9 Sidewinder missiles, which downed both Su-22s.

**15 Sep:** The 494th TFS at RAF Lakenheath became the first USAF squadron to be equipped with the Pave Tack weapons delivery system.

**26 Sep:** Designed by Boeing to challenge the European Airbus A300 and A310, the 767 – a medium-range, 210-seat airliner – was first flown. The classic dials of the cockpit instrument panel gave way to six computer screens showing the key flight parameters.

**6 Oct:** The Airbus A310, with a two-man Forward Facing Crew (FFC), first flew, thereby making it possible for a flight crew of two to operate the wide-body airliner.

**5 Nov:** The first of four Full-Scale Development AV-8B Harriers made its first flight.

**13 Nov:** First manned crossing of the Pacific by balloon *Double Eagle V*.

**19 Dec:** Tupolev's Tu-160 'Blackjack' made its first flight. It was Russia's supersonic heavy bomber equivalent of the American B-1B, initially intended to carry cruise missiles.

*NASA's Space Shuttle* Columbia *on mission STS-1 was launched successfully on 12 April 1981 from Cape Canaveral under the power of its own rocket engines, and the jettisonable boosters. It is shown in Terry Wofford's painting* Spirit of Discovery.

These pages generously donated by Rockwell Collins (UK) Ltd

*Spirit of Discovery* by Terry Wofford

# 1982

After withdrawing from the turbulent Middle East, it was widely assumed that the days of British involvement outside the European theatre were over. So it was something of a shock to conventional defence thinking when Argentine forces seized the Falkland Islands in an unexpected coup on 2 April. A swiftly assembled South Atlantic Task Force set sail from Portsmouth on 5 April. This included HMS *Hermes* with a complement of Sea Harrier FRS1s, and included RAF pilots on exchange duties with the Royal Navy. In the absence of any friendly land base nearer than 3,900 miles away at Wideawake Airfield on Ascension Island, it seemed that the RAF would make little contribution to Operation *Corporate* – other than by lifting men and equipment between the UK and Ascension.

It was soon appreciated that the Argentine threat to the British Task Force and its operations to re-occupy the Falklands required extreme measures to bring at least some land-based air power to bear. The use of the Victor tanker force made this possible. With air-to-air refuelling having been rapidly improvised for Vulcans, Nimrods and Hercules, a series of remarkable sorties was carried out. Vulcan strikes (the *Black Buck* raids) were carried out against targets at Port Stanley airfield. Sorties were also flown by a Vulcan against radar installations using AGM-45A Shrike anti-radar missiles.

Nimrods provided maritime surveillance of the region during certain stages of the operation and Hercules undertook long-range supply-dropping missions to the task force. The four Vulcans which took part in the Falklands Conflict were only three months away from the date when they were due to be scrapped.

Between 20 May and 14 June, constant air attacks by Sea Harriers were a prelude to the landing of UK forces in strength on the Falklands, provoking heavy air attacks by mainland-based Argentinean aircraft. Casualties among ships was heavy, but recapture of the islands was achieved on 14 June. Among the most potent Argentine weapons was the French Exocet missile launched by Argentinean Navy Dassault Super Etendard aircraft.

In 1982, Lockheed decided to drop out of the commercial airline market after existing orders for the TriStar had been completed. McDonnell Douglas fared better with its DC-10, from which was developed the KC-10A Extender.

One of the USAF's longest serving workhorses, the KC-135 Stratotanker, started a new lease of life during 1982, when the programme for the conversion of many of the active-duty fleet to KC-135R standard started. The programme, that had been announced in 1980, involved replacing the original J-57 turbojets with four CFM International CFM-56 turbofans (military designated F108-CF-100). The new powerplants offered considerable advantages over the KC-135A's Pratt & Whitney J-57s, being far quieter, cleaner and more fuel efficient.

There was something of a setback for MAC's new jet transport programme in January, when the US Defense Department cancelled the McDonnell Douglas C-17, that had been ordered the previous year, in favour of the purchase of 50 new C-5B Galaxy variants. However, a great deal of lobbying by the US Air Force, that was in favour of continuing development of the C-17, was successful and in July a $31.6 million contract was placed with McDonnell Douglas by the USAF for the type.

---

**1 Jan:** As part of the *Peace Victor* programme, Egypt received the first of 40 F-16A/Bs from the United States, as replacement aircraft for the obsolete interceptors of Russian and Chinese origin that equipped the country's air force.

**8 Jan:** The Airbus A300 became the world's first wide-bodied airliner to be certificated for commercial operation by a flight crew of two.

**10 Jan:** Gulfstream III *Spirit of America* set a round-the-world record for an executive jet, in 43 hours and 39 minutes.

**3 Feb:** A Soviet Mil Mi-26 'Halo' set a world helicopter lifting record, when it took 125,153lb to a height of 6,562ft.

**5 Feb:** The Northrop *Tacit Blue* stealth technology demonstrator was flown for the first time. A further 135 test flights were made with the highly classified aircraft.

**19 Feb:** First flight of the Boeing 757 – the first Boeing aircraft to fly with non-American engines – powered by two Rolls-Royce 535C turbofans. For the 757 to be profitable, sales had to reach

300 within five years, a figure that was comfortably achieved.

**3 Apr:** First flight of the Airbus A310. Slightly shorter than the A300, it had a new wing to provide fuel economy thus permitting a highly competitive payload and range.

**5 May:** Two British Airways L-1011 TriStars made safe touch-downs at Heathrow in totally blind conditions. The landings were made with an absence of runway visual range and reference height measurements.

**17 May:** First launch of a satellite from an orbiting space station. Salyut 7 placed an amateur radio satellite *Iskra 2* in Earth orbit via an airlock in the space laboratory.

**10 Jun:** The first all-female SAC crew, from the 924th Air Refueling Squadron at Castle AFB, CA completed a KC-135 Stratotanker mission.

**1 Jul:** The 501st Tactical Mission Wing (TMW) was established at RAF Greenham Common, to operate Gryphon ground-launched cruise missiles.

**3 Jul:** The single-seat General Dynamics F-16XL was flown for the first time. It featured a 'cranked arrow' composite wing and a lengthened fuselage, together with a greater weapon-carrying capability.

**30 Sep:** A Bell 206L LongRanger II *The Spirit of Texas* completed the first round-the-world helicopter flight in 29 days and three hours. It made 29 landings in 23 different countries.

**4 Nov:** PanAm inaugurated the longest non-stop commercial service in the world, from Los Angeles to Sydney. The long-range Boeing 747SP was used for the 7,847 mile flight.

**26 Dec:** The prototype Antonov An-124 'Condor' made its maiden flight, then the world's largest aircraft.

*In the 1982 Falklands Conflict, the BAe Sea Harrier FRS1 played a vital role by providing air cover for the British Task Force that was sent to regain control of the islands. Ronald Wong's painting depicts two FRS1s above HMS Hermes in the South Atlantic.*

These pages generously donated by the Directorate of Corporate Communications (Navy)

*Southward Bound* by Ronald Wong BSc(Hons), GAvA, ASAA, GMA, TWAS

The Boeing 757 short/medium range commercial transport entered revenue service in January. Eastern Air lines was the first to introduce the type. British Airways had ordered 21 examples and they went into service on 9 February. These examples were 757-200s powered by Rolls-Royce RB211-535C turbofans, the 757 being the first Boeing airliner to be launched with non-US powerplants, although later variants could be offered with Pratt & Whitney engines. In March, a Boeing 767 set a distance record for a twin-jet airliner in commercial service with a 5,499 mile flight from Lisbon to Seattle.

1983 was a good year for Boeing, especially as the 747-300 entered service, initially with Swissair. The extended upper deck of this version increased the economy-class capacity on this deck from 32 to 91. Alternatively it could provide 26 first-class 'sleeper' units. Japan Air Lines became the launch customer for the long-range Boeing 767-300 airliner, and on 9 December Boeing rolled out its 1,000th Model 737 twin-jet airliner. Boeing took the 727 out of production in 1983, but gradually the 737 eclipsed the DC-9 to become the best-selling airliner of all time, in succession to the 727.

Production of the F-16 Fighting Falcon was progressing at a high rate and by July, the 1,000th production F-16 was rolled out at Fort Worth, and at that date anticipated procurement was just under 3,000.

In the RAF, the extensive modernisation programme, which began in the early 1980s, added the Tornado GR1, VC10 K2/K3, Nimrod MR2 and Chinook HC1 to its inventory. The Falklands War underlined the urgent need for the RAF to possess an adequate air-to-air refuelling capability, not only as a 'force multiplier' for its air defence fighters, but also for long-range deployments by strike/attack, maritime patrol and even transport aircraft. The VC10 K2 and K3 cruised at 560mph and were capable of refuelling large receiver aircraft, such as the Nimrod, from the centre hose and smaller aircraft, such as the Harrier, Jaguar and Tornado, from either the centre hose or, simultaneously, from the two wing hoses. The first of six HS125 Series 700s was introduced in 1983 for use in the communications role.

During October, trouble flared up on the island of Grenada when its Premier was first placed under house arrest and later killed, in a coup that was viewed as having been inspired by Cuba. Coupled with this Communist threat was Grenada's location, north of the coast of Venezuela, which made it an ideal 'staging post' for Soviet aircraft flying to Latin America and as a base for international terrorists. Operation *Urgent Fury* commenced on 24 October and MC-130E Hercules of the 8th Special Operations Squadron (SOS) were used to drop parachute troops from the US Navy's SEAL units and the US Army's elite Delta Force.

More attacks on enemy barracks and defence positions followed, and the operation was eventually successful with all US citizens on Grenada being evacuated, and the possibility of terrorist attacks on the US being launched from the island was removed.

---

**25 Jan:** The SAAB-Fairchild 340 twin-turboprop airliner made its first flight.

**3 Feb:** First flight of the Dassault Mirage 2000N, the all-weather nuclear-attack version of the Mirage 2000.

**9 Apr:** Piper's PA-48 Enforcer 'tank killer' made its maiden flight. A turboprop-powered development of the WW2 P-51 Mustang it was to have been an economical complement to the ultra-powerful A-10 Thunderbolt, but it did not enter production.

**25 Apr:** First flight of the Dornier Do 24TT three-turboprop amphibian. It was built incorporating Do 31 and Fokker F27 components.

**22 May:** A French Aviasud Sirocco made the first flight across the Mediterranean by a microlight.

**26 May:** The BAe 125 Series 800, one of the world's most successful mid-sized business jets, made its first flight. It featured a new wing and more powerful US-built Garrett TFE-731 turbofans.

**17 Jun:** First flight of the Robin ATL (Avion Très Leger – very light aeroplane). A tiny two-seater, with fixed undercarriage, slender rear fuselage and butterfly tail, it only weighed 700lb empty.

**18 Jun:** Space Shuttle mission STS-7, using *Challenger*, began its six-day mission, which included the first night launch and landing.

**20 Jun:** First flight of the de Havilland Canada DHC-8-100 fuel-efficient short haul transport.

**8 Jul:** Prototype of the Airbus A300-600 series first flew.

**12 Jul:** The first Zlin 37T single-engined turboprop agricultural aircraft made its maiden flight. This was derived from the basic Z-37A Cmelak, of which more than 700 had been produced.

**27 Jul:** Brazil's EMBRAER EMB-120 Brasilia made its first flight, a twin-turboprop general purpose 30-seat transport development of the Bandeirante.

**31 Jul:** First flight of the Slingsby T67M Firefly 160.

**9 Aug:** The Mitsubishi T-2CCV made its first flight after conversion as a control configured vehicle. It featured triplex digital FBW computers, manouevring flaps and carbon fibre composite canard surfaces.

**29 Aug:** A dramatic new shape appeared in the sky when the Beech StarShip made its first flight. The twin-turboprops were positioned at the rear of the aircraft, mounted above the aft-positioned swept-wing and driving four-blade pusher propellers.

**15 Sep:** The Italian Agusta A129 Mangusta light anti-tank and attack helicopter first flew. Its design configuration was influenced by the larger AH-64 Apache.

**26 Oct:** PanAm celebrated the 25th anniversary of its inaugural Boeing 707 flight from New York to Paris, the first American international commercial jet service.

**11 Nov:** First flight of CASA's CN-235 in Spain, the first Indonesian-built example making its first flight on 30 December.

**28 Nov:** Space Shuttle mission STS-9/41-A began Space Lab 1 flight.

**4 Dec:** Twenty-eight US Navy attack aircraft from the USS *Independence* and USS *John F. Kennedy* made a raid on Syrian positions, in reprisal for an attack against a US military base in Beirut in October.

*The Pitts S-1 Special single-seat sporting and aerobatic biplane was originally designed by Curtis Pitts in 1944 and has been used with great success in national and international competitions. John C Page's painting shows a Pitts giving a display enhanced with plenty of white smoke.*

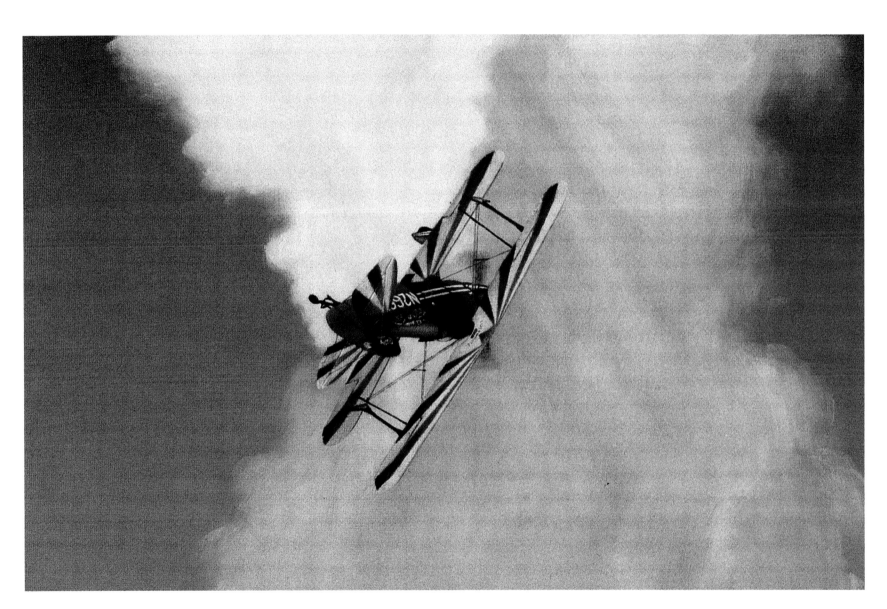

*Pitts Special* by John C Page

The largest single order in the history of commercial aviation was announced by American Airlines in February, when it ordered 67 McDonnell Douglas MD-80 transports, plus options for a further 100 aircraft.

On 24 February, the larger Boeing 737-300 took to the air, aimed at the new emerging market for short-range airliners with around 150 seats. With two CFM56 engines, it provided 20% better fuel economy than the Pratt & Whitneys in the 737-200. Carbon fibre was used for the rudder, flaps and engine nacelles, which were closer to the wing. In March, Airbus Industrie was given the go-ahead for the Airbus A320, presenting a serious challenge to Boeing. In the US, orders for the fuel-efficient MD-80 series made the airliner division of McDonnell Douglas more financially stable.

A remarkable transatlantic collaboration between Italian and Brazilian aircraft manufacturers succeeded in producing an all-weather, fly-by-wire AMX attack aircraft, which made its first flight on 15 May in Rio de Janeiro. Aeritalia and Aermacchi in Italy joined up with EMBRAER in Brazil to build the single-seat AMX.

On 22 June, amid considerable hype, Virgin Atlantic joined the cut-price airlines competing over the North Atlantic route. Initially it commenced with a single Boeing 747-200 leased from the manufacturer, but the airline soon went from strength to strength.

Up to 1984 the North Atlantic (and indeed the South Atlantic) was off-limits to twin-engined commercial aircraft. Piston engines and the first jets had lacked the power and reliability to permit transatlantic flights by twin-engined airliners. With much improved powerplants, the FAA extended to two hours the time that such aircraft were within reach of a diversion airfield, thus allowing the introduction of almost direct transatlantic flights.

The first production Tornado F2 long-range interceptor was delivered to Boscombe Down for development flying. The Tornado ADV was urgently needed to bolster the UK's air defence, intercepting Soviet aircraft at long range and countering modern types such as the Sukhoi Su-24 'Fencer' and Tupolev Tu-22 'Backfire'. The operational requirements demanded an interceptor capable of undertaking combat air patrols (CAPs) in all weathers some 350 miles away from base, at high or low altitudes. It would also be able to function in hostile ECM environments and employ the new Sky Flash missile, which had a look-down, shoot-down capability and a range of over 25 miles. To achieve this, a new technology radar, appropriately named Foxhunter – with a range of over 100 miles – was specified for the Tornado ADV.

The first flight of the latest C-5B Galaxy in September signalled the start of a big increase in US Military Airlift Command's total airlift capability. A shortfall had previously been envisaged, with the number of long term and emergency operations in which the Command had been so heavily involved.

---

**1 Jan:** The USAF's *Seek Igloo* programme was completed, forming a chain of radar stations from Cape Lisburne AFS in the north down to Cold Bay AFS in the south. The 13 radar sites fed information into both the Regional Operations Center and NORAD Headquarters in Cheyenne Mountain.

**9 Jan:** Hughes helicopters flew the first production example of the AH-64A Apache twin-engined attack helicopter. The US Army initially ordered 515 of these combat aircraft.

**12 Jan:** The US Marine Corps received its first McDonnell Douglas/BAe AV-8B Harrier II.

**6 Feb:** First flight of the production AIDC AT-3 jet trainer for the Chinese Nationalist Air force.

**15 Feb:** The first of 15 T-47As for the US Navy, a trainer version of the Cessna Citation II, made its maiden flight.

**24 Feb:** The F-15E Strike Eagle was selected as the USAF two-seat, dual-role fighter rather than the General Dynamics F-16XL. The USAF's stated requirement was for a total of 392 aircraft.

**2 Mar:** Eighteen Shorts 330-200/C-23A Sherpas, together with ten year's maintenance and support, was approved by the USAF.

**6 Mar:** First flight of the British Airship Industries Skyship 600.

**8 May:** The first Hughes 530MG Defender took to the air. Designed as a multi-mission version of the 500 Defender, it had the powerplant of the civil 530F.

**1 Jun:** Schweizer TG-7A motorgliders were delivered to the 94th Air Training Squadron, part of the USAF Academy at Colorado Springs. The TG-7As were for use as powered gliding trainers.

**22 Jun:** Burt Rutan's uniquely-configured 110ft 10in (33,78m) span *Voyager* was flown for the first time. The aircraft was designed and built to attempt a non-stop and unrefuelled 25,000 mile (40,234km) round-the-world flight.

**3 Jul:** Maiden flight of the first VC10 K3 tanker conversion for the RAF.

**16 Aug:** The ATR 42 twin-turboprop transport first flew, a joint project between Aérospatiale of France and Aeritalia of Italy.

**4 Sep:** The USAF's first production Rockwell B-1B strategic bomber, reborn under President Reagan's build up of the US military, made its first flight and 100 were ordered.

**14-18 Sep:** First solo non-stop balloon flight across the North Atlantic. The *Rosie O'Grady* took off from Carbon, Maine and landed at Savona in Italy.

**2 Oct:** Soyuz T-10B returned to Earth after setting a new space duration record of 237 days.

**6 Oct:** The Argentinean FMA IA Pampa basic and advanced trainer made its first flight.

**12 Oct:** First flight of the Polish PZL-130 Orlik radial-engined primary trainer.

**18 Oct:** Maiden flight of the variable-geometry Rockwell B-1B strategic bomber, later to be officially known as the Lancer.

**Nov:** RAF Hercules from Lyneham assisted in the distribution of famine-relief supplies in Ethiopia under Operation *Bushell*.

**7 Dec:** The Boeing 737-300 flew the first revenue service of the type, Southwest Airlines being the launch customer.

**14 Dec:** The Grumman X-29A forward-swept wing (FSW) demonstrator first flew at Edwards AFB.

**Dec:** The McDonnell Douglas MD-83 made its maiden flight, the longer-range version of the MD-80 series.

*The Rockwell B-1B Lancer is the biggest aircraft to feature variable-wing sweepback. This Wilfred Hardy painting has a Lancer flying a high-speed low-level mission with its wings fully swept.*

These pages generously donated by A1 Hire & Sales

*Unstoppable on the Deck* by Wilfred Hardy GAvA

Powerplant development increased in the mid-1980s, when the computerised control of the aircraft's engines in flight by means of full-authority digital systems were becoming more common. These small software-controlled 'black box' systems were designed to operate engines at maximum safety and economy levels.

During the early 1980s, there appeared to be little demand for the 'jumbo' size of airliner carrying around 500 passengers. But Boeing kept its Model 747 in production, and therefore gained considerably when the market for high-capacity transports revived after the middle of the decade. Boeing had invested considerable effort in the continued development of the 747, and the introduction of improvements and updated models saw the company benefit from an increase in orders.

Several of the medium-capacity airliners of the 1970s were still in production into the mid-1980s, but an increased proportion of this market was moving to Airbus and Boeing – the former offering the wide-body A310 as a short/medium-range transport for some 250 passengers, and the latter bracketing the target market with the narrow-body 757 as a short/medium airliner for around 225 passengers, together with the wide-body 767 as a medium-range transport with a seating capacity of up to 300. All these aircraft were variants of the same basic design philosophy – a low-set wing with moderate sweep and improved high-lift devices; a swept tail-unit with a low-set tailplane, and a pair of high-efficiency turbofans installed in pods, pylon-mounted below and ahead of the wings.

At the smaller end of the air transport market, low-capacity airliners continued to sell with modest vigour in the mid-1980s. It ensured the continued production of well-established aircraft such as the twin-turboprop Fokker F27 Friendship (which led to the improved Fokker 50) and the twin-turbofan Fokker F28 Fellowship (subsequently developed into the Fokker 70 and 100).

Still further down the capacity spectrum, the middle of the decade witnessed a small, but significant boom in commuter airliners, which led to new aircraft such as the ATR-42/72, Saab 340 and the de Havilland Canada DHC-8 Dash 8. This was a market in which the superiority of the turboprop became well established and a new generation of turboprops, using core turbines, was introduced.

The latest version of the Fighting Falcon, the F-16C, began to enter service, replacing the earlier F-16A. The two-seat F-16D followed shortly afterwards, superseding the F-16B. The initial 'Block 25' examples of the F-16C were powered by the improved Pratt & Whitney F100-PW-200 engine, and equipped with the Hughes APG-68 multi-mode radar, offering increased range and clarity. The F-16C was the first of the type to have provision to carry the AGM-65D Maverick missile, and included various improvements to the avionics system.

The Shorts Tucano was selected as the RAF's new basic trainer to replace the Jet Provost from 1987. To give the Tucano the performance demanded by the RAF's exacting training syllabus, a Garrett engine was substituted for the original Pratt & Whitney PT6A. Modifications to the cockpit layout were made to harmonise with the Hawk T1, and other improvements included a vertical air-brake and a strengthened airframe to increase load factors and extend fatigue life. The Tucano was the first new tandem-seat trainer for the RAF since the Chipmunk was introduced in 1950.

**27 Jan:** Space Shuttle mission 51-C began, using *Discovery*.
**1 Feb:** TWA was the first US airline to fly a twin-jet engined airliner across the Atlantic when scheduled Boeing 767 services commenced to Paris and Zurich.
**13 Feb:** The British Aerospace ALARM defence suppression missile was flown for the first time on a Tornado GR1.
**27 Feb:** The first of four Boeing EC-18Bs modified as Advanced Range Instrumentation aircraft (AIRAs) had its maiden flight.
**15 Mar:** American Eagle, a new US commuter airline, began operations with the Jetstream 31.
**24 Apr:** LOT, the Polish airline, inaugurated a Warsaw-New York service with the Ilyushin Il-62M.
**30 Apr:** The first flight of the Harrier GR5 took place at Dunsfold.
**11 May:** An RAF Tristar C2 made its first flight to the Falklands. It set a record of 8hr 22min for the Brize Norton-Ascension leg, 8hr 19min for the Ascension-Mount Pleasant leg, and 18hr 28min elapsed time for the whole flight.

**21 May:** First flight of the Dassault Breguet Falcon V 10F business jet. It was the first civil aircraft to be made of composite materials, carbon fibre and epoxy resin.
**9 Jul:** The first flight of the Tristar K1 took place at Cambridge after conversion to dual-role tanker-transport configuration by Marshall of Cambridge.
**29 Jul:** First flight of the Kawasaki T-4 intermediate jet trainer, the successor to the JASDF's T-33 and Fuji T-1.
**13 Aug:** In the worst catastrophe involving a single aircraft, a JAL Boeing 747SR suffered a complete structural failure of the tail during a flight from Tokyo to Osaka. A total of 520 people were killed in the accident.
**10 Sep:** The Lockheed C-5B Galaxy made its maiden flight.
**13 Sep:** An F-15 Eagle launched an anti-satellite missile (AST) from an altitude of over 40,000ft to destroy the inert P78/1 Solwind research satellite that was launched into Earth orbit in 1971.

**18 Oct:** The first flight was made by the AFTI General Dynamics F-111A fitted with the mission adaptive wing (MAW).
**18 Nov:** Cessna, the US's last independent general aviation company, became a subsidiary of the General Dynamics Corporation.
**20 Nov:** The first production Panavia Tornado F3 air defence variant for the RAF made its first flight, fitted with RB199 Mk 104 turbofans with extended nozzles.
**5 Dec:** The Soviet Union launched the *Admiral Kuznetsov*, its first nuclear-powered aircraft carrier.

*The RAF Aerobatic Team, the* Red Arrows, *flying BAe Hawk T1s performs more than 100 displays each year around the UK and overseas. Gerald Coulson's painting shows nine scarlet Hawks over the Royal Naval College Britannia at Dartmouth, Devon during a summer display.*
© Solomon & Whitehead Limited

These pages generously donated by Highworth Press Limited, Swindon

*Red Arrows over Dartmouth* by Gerald Coulson VPGAvA

# 1986

urt Rutan's Voyager completed the task for which it was designed. His brother Dick, with Jeanna Yeager, completed a non-stop navigation of the globe, that took an amazing nine day, three minute flight. Referred to as 'the last major event in atmospheric flight' the weather demanded frequent route detours. The fuselage pod of Voyager was unpressurised and was only two feet in width. It took off from Edwards AFB with the tips of the fuel-laden wings scraping the runway. The epic flight was plagued by weather problems, which included thunderstorms and strong headwinds. Fuel was almost exhausted when it returned to Edwards after an accredited circumnavigation of 26,678miles (43,934km). Solid Magnamite graphite main spars had given Voyager's long wings immense strength and similar composite materials were used throughout the aircraft.

An inducted fan engine was flown for the first time when a Boeing 727 testbed flew with a General Electric GE-36 installed on its starboard engine pylon. A Westland Army Lynx demonstrator set a new helicopter world speed record of 249mph (400km/h) fitted with special British Experimental Rotor Programme (BERP) III main rotor blades.

The Lockheed C-130 Hercules achieved 32 years of continuous production and the 1,800th example was rolled out in late 1986. Following success with the 767-200ER, Boeing introduced the 767-300ER, which featured even greater range and increased weights.

Due to lack of funds, BAe's EAP technology demonstrator was mothballed, but tests had produced useful data for the forthcoming Eurofighter. In April, British Airports Authority (BAA) opened the much-needed fourth terminal at Heathrow, the world's busiest international airport. Initially it was used by British Airways (BA) long-haul flights.

Mid-April saw the biggest air strikes undertaken by the USAF for some years, with attacks on Libya. For the previous five years, terrorism on the part of the Palestine Liberation Organisation (PLO) and direct Libyan aggression against the West, had gradually been escalating, encouraged by the country's leader, Colonel Gadhafi (who was being supplied with arms by the Soviet Union). The USAF was involved in co-ordinated air strikes on Libya, mounted from air bases in England under Operation *El Dorado Canyon*. Eighteen General Dynamics F-111Fs from the 48th TFW at RAF Lakenheath and five EF-111As from the 42nd Electronic Combat Squadron at RAF Upper Heyford made the 5,500-mile round-trip. They were refuelled by 28 KC-10As and KC-135s. One F-111F was lost in unexplained circumstances.

Aircraft from RAF Mildenhall were committed to another important operation later in April, but of a very different kind. The explosion at the nuclear power station at Chernobyl in the Ukraine occurred on the 26th of the month, first being detected by Sweden, whose air force carried out the initial monitoring flights to check on amounts and types of radioactive fall-out, along with an RC-135U of the 55th SRW. Two days later, an EC-135H from the 10th ACCS at RAF Mildenhall confirmed that the explosion had occurred by 'listening-in' to Soviet communications. This was followed by the start of flights by a WC-135B of the 55th Weather Reconnaissance Squadron – this specialist aircraft flew through the easterly airstream, collecting air samples. Had not this independent evidence not been gathered, the Soviets might well have covered-up the facts about this major nuclear accident, which posed a great threat to many Western countries.

---

**11 Jan:** The first MiG-27M, built under licence by Hindustan Aeronautics, entered service with the Indian Air Force.

**28 Jan:** The Space Shuttle *Challenger* was lost in a disastrous launch accident. The crew of seven, including one female, was killed in an explosion 73 seconds after lift-off.

**31 Jan:** De Havilland Canada was purchased from the Canadian Government by Boeing.

**31 Jan:** The first Dornier 228-201 assembled by HAL in India completed its maiden flight.

**19 Feb:** Boeing flew the first of eight KC-3A tanker aircraft for the Royal Saudi Air Force.

**3 Mar:** The Cessna 208B Caravan I made its first flight, a stretched version of the 208A in response to a specific request from parcel carrier FederalExpress.

**8 Mar:** Lockheed delivered the first production C-5B Galaxy to the USAF, thus redressing a shortfall in the USAF airlift capacity.

**13 Mar:** The British satellite *Giotto* intercepted Halley's Comet when it passed within 375 miles of the comet's nucleus.

**1 Apr:** A Boeing 767-200ER established a new distance record of 7,892miles (12,700km) for a twin-engined airliner, flying from Seattle to Kuwait.

10 May: A USAF Boeing B-52H flew for the first time with a maximum load of 20 AGM-86B air-launched cruise missiles.

**19 May:** First flight of the BAe Hawk 200 prototype.

**4 Jul:** First flight of the Dassault Rafale A, an experimental advanced combat aircraft that achieved Mach 1.3+.

**1 Aug:** Schafer, an American company, flew the first of its Douglas DC-3 tri-motor conversions. The rejuvenated aircraft were powered by PT-6A-65AR turboprops.

**6 Aug:** First flight of the BAe Advanced Turboprop (ATP), which was subsequently marketed as the Jetstream 61.

**23 Sep:** Powered by two pusher turboprops, Piaggio's P180 Avanti made its first flight in Italy.

**1 Oct:** The 96th Bombardment Wing at Dyess AFB, TX reached initial operating capability (IOC) with its new Rockwell B-1Bs.

**21 Oct:** McDonnell Douglas flew the first prototype of the two-seat Harrier TAV-8B. The RAF's Harrier T10 was subsequently based on this version.

**30 Nov:** A successor to its F28 Fellowship, Fokker flew the 100 with redesigned wings and had Rolls-Royce Tay engines.

**4 Dec:** First flight of the McDonnell Douglas MD-87, a shortened version of the MD-80 with a seating capacity of 130.

**11 Dec:** Initial flight made by the first 'production' McDonnell Douglas F-15E Strike Eagle, a two-seat ground attack aircraft and air superiority fighter version of the basic Eagle. The aircraft was capable of operating on long-range deep interdiction missions in bad weather, day or night.

*Craig F Kodera's atmospheric painting shows the Rutan Voyager, piloted by Dick Rutan and Jeanna Yeager, during its epic non-stop flight around the world.*

*Voyager: The Skies Yield* by Craig F Kodera ASAA

London City Airport, in the heart of the city's old docklands, was officially opened in November. This was a bold concept, watched closely by many other cities around the world to assess the impact, both economically and environmentally, and the benefits of flying short/medium range airliners into the heart of a conurbation. The environmental battle was won only by the quietness of the STOL de Havilland Canada DHC-7 Dash 7, 50-seat four turboprop. Despite a slow start, the project eventually became a success story, especially when the BAe 146 was allowed to operate from there.

In August, United Airlines opened the world's largest single-airliner hub at Chicago's O'Hare International Airport. The hub had 48 gates and was able to handle up to 18 wide-bodied airliners at a time. This helped relieve congestion at O'Hare, which was originally designed to handle 20 million passengers a year, but in 1986 it had escalated to 55 million.

The latest Airbus Industries development, the Airbus A320, flew for the first time on 22 February. The airliner owed both its existence and its performance to the latest information technology. It was the first airliner to make extensive use in its development of not only computer-assisted design (CAD) but also computer-assisted manufacture (CAM). The A320 made extensive use of composites, and was the first commercial aircraft to make full use of the all electronic 'fly-by-wire' concept, the pilots having 'sidesticks' instead of the time-honoured 'joystick' control columns. The Airbus A300-600R also flew in 1987, an extended-range version with a tailplane trim tank and increased maximum weights.

The F-15 Strike Eagle's flight test and development programme progressed well, with the start of night flying trials at Edwards AFB, CA. These evaluated the dual-role fighter's cockpit displays in night-time conditions, for their brightness and clarity. McDonnell Douglas fitted prototype Martin Marietta LANTIRN (Low altitude Navigation and Targeting Infrared for Night) pods to the first F-15Es in February, which gave the aircraft a long-range interdiction capability at night or in poor weather.

The formation on 1 June of Air Force Special Operations Command (AFSOC) coincided with developments on two new aircraft that it would operate. Rockwell was awarded a contract in July to convert new-build C-130Hs to AC-130U Hercules gunship configuration, with 12 such aircraft scheduled for delivery. The new aircraft was to utilise a single 25-mm GAU-12 cannon with 3,000 rounds, as opposed to the 20-mm cannon of the AC-130H, whilst retaining the 40-mm L-60 cannon and 105-mm M102 Howitzer. For the Combat Rescue role, the new Sikorsky MH-53J Pave Low III was first delivered to AFSOC in July. With more powerful T64 turboshaft engines, and better AN/APQ-158 terrain-following radar, the MH-53J had more advanced avionics equipment than earlier H-53 derivatives used for these operations and the new helicopter soon became a very important Special Operations asset.

In November, No 29 Squadron at RAF Coningsby became the first front-line air-defence unit to become operational with the Tornado F3. It was simultaneously declared to NATO. The F3 was designed to combat the bomber threat in an intense ECM environment and in all weathers.

---

**21 Jan:** The Massachusetts Institute of Technology (MIT) Michelor Light Eagle human-powered aircraft set a world distance record in a straight line, distance in a closed circuit and duration record for women pilots.

**6 Feb:** Aérospatiale's Super Puma II made its first flight. It had a new rotor head, larger blades and a lengthened fuselage.

**13 Feb:** The first production Fokker 50, an improved derivative of the F27, made its first flight in Holland.

**19 Feb:** Initial flight of the first of 15 Boeing E-6As for the US Navy.

**22 Feb:** The Airbus A320 made its maiden flight, the first of a new family of single-isle airliners.

**2 Apr:** An RAF VC10 K3 made a new non-stop flight from the UK to Perth, Western Australia in 16 hours and one minute. It was refuelled twice en route by another VC10 and a Tristar.

**30 Apr:** The Belgian Promavia Jet Squalus trainer made its maiden flight.

**3 May:** Martin-Baker was awarded an important US Navy contract for the development and production of the Navy Aircrew Common Ejection Seat (NACES).

**5 May:** The last LAM-25C Titan II ICBM was taken off alert at Little Rock AFB, AK.

**16 Jul:** The British Airports Authority (BAA) was privatised.

**31 Jul:** Development of the E-8A J-STARS system began when the first Boeing 707-320 to be converted was delivered to the Grumman facility at Melbourne, FL.

**11 Aug:** First flight of the Phantom 2000, an upgrade of the F-4, was flown in Israel. All existing Israeli F-4 Phantoms then received a comprehensive update of structure and equipment.

**24 Sep:** The first unrefuelled transatlantic crossing was made by a British fighter. Returning to the UK after completing successful hot weather trials in Arizona, a Tornado F3 covered the 2,200 nautical miles from Canada in 4.75 hours.

**9 Oct:** The first pre-production EH Industries EH 101 helicopter made its maiden flight at Yeovil.

**14 Oct:** The new London City Airport opened to its first passenger carrying aircraft when a Brymon Dash 7 flew from the airport to Paris-Charles de Gaulle.

**20 Oct:** The Swiss Air Force received approval to purchase 20 BAe Hawk Mk 66 aircraft, procured to replace the veteran Vampire in the advanced training role.

**21 Oct:** British Airways took on its first female pilots.

**28 Nov:** The Handley Page Victor celebrated 30 years of operational service with the RAF.

**29 Dec:** Scaled Composites flew the Rutan-designed ATTT (Advanced Technology Tactical Transport) concept demonstrator.

**29 Dec:** A Russian cosmonaut returned to Earth in *Soyuz TM3* after a 326-day stay in space.

*The Lockheed SR-71 was the first Mach 3 aircraft to enter service with the USAF, remaining in operational use for over 30 years. Keith Woodcock's painting captures the Blackbird, which could operate at altitudes above 85,000ft and at speeds approaching Mach 3.5 for sustained periods, on a reconnaissance mission.*

These pages generously donated by Mike Brennan of Main Event Concessions

*Faster and Higher* by Keith Woodcock GAvA, ASAA, GMA

In November, the US Department of Defense ended years of speculation on its use of 'stealth' aircraft, when the Lockheed F-117 was finally revealed. The fighter had been flying since 1981 and had been operational since 1983. Its primary task was to avoid detection by radar and penetrate enemy defences to destroy high-value targets, such as command posts. The Air Force had worked very hard to keep the F-117 hidden from view by only flying it at night from the Tonapah Test Range airfield in a remote part of Nevada.

The latest 'Jumbo' variant from Boeing made its first flight in April. The 747-400 series carried additional fuel in the tailplane and its extended wingtips featured upturned winglets. With more efficient engines it offered range performance with a full passenger load in the region of 7,250 miles. The increased range was particularly attractive to operators to fly non-stop from Europe to the Far East, thereby eliminating the previously required fuel stops. The two-crew digital avionics flight cabin was the same as that developed for the 757 and 767, thus allowing 60% fewer gauges and instruments on the flight deck. It was the heaviest commercial airliner at the time of its début. The largest of the second generation Boeing 737s, the 400 Series, that could seat up to 168 passengers, was flown in 1988.

In the Soviet Union, a new Ilyushin four-engined airliner made its first flight in September, the Il-96-300, which sported longer-span wings with winglets and a shorter fuselage, derived for Aeroflot from the reasonably successful Il-86.

On the military front, the S/MTD (STOL Manoeuvring Technology Demonstrator) version of the F-15 Agile Eagle took to the air. Equipped with large canard foreplanes (adapted from the tailplane of an F/A-18 Hornet) fly-by-wire controls and two-dimensional thrust vectoring, the S/MTD was used to provide research data on the use of thrust vectoring to reduce take-off and landing runs.

A modern age Daedalus recreated Greek mythology by flying by human muscle power from Crete to Santorini, powered by pedal action. Constructed of advanced and exceedingly light materials, the aircraft flew 74 miles in just under four hours.

Russian space missions had a change of emphasis when the *Buran* Shuttle Orbiter made its first flight unmanned, under control from the ground. It was transported on the new Antonov An-225 *Mirya* (Dream) which was derived from the original An-124 Ruslan, with a stretched fuselage, two extra engines and end-plate tailfins.

Improved 'Block 40/42' F-16C/D Fighting Falcons began to roll off General Dynamics' Fort Worth production line. These aircraft were fitted with two LANTIRN pods, a global positioning navigation system, APG-68(C) radar, an advanced gunsight, together with a strengthened airframe. They were known as Night Falcons.

The BAe Harrier GR5, developed jointly by Britain and the United States, entered operational service during the year. Derived from the McDonnell Douglas/British Aerospace AV-8B, the GR5 had a new wing, a more powerful Rolls-Royce Pegasus engine, increased bird strike protection, a new 25mm cannon, additional electronic countermeasures equipment, increased range and load-carrying capabilities, and a moving map display. It has since been upgraded to undertake low-level missions at night, as the GR7.

---

**1 Jan:** The Canadian airline industry was deregulated.

**26 Jan:** The Dassault Rafale was formally approved for production for the Armeé de l'Air and Aéronavale following trials with four development aircraft.

**27 Feb:** Last Convair F-106 Delta Dart was taken off air defence alert with the New Jersey Air National Guard at Atlantic City, NJ. The type had served in the role since 1959. A number of surviving aircraft were subsequently converted as drones.

**28 Jan:** Initial flight of the Sukhoi Su-35, Russia's advanced air-superiority fighter and ground attack aircraft.

**25 Feb:** India launched the Prithvi, a tactical surface-to-surface missile of its own development.

**1 Mar:** The USAF ordered six Fairchild Swearingen C-26A Metros (later increased to 13) to meet the ANGOSTA (Air National Guard Operational Support Transport Aircraft) requirement.

**30 Mar:** The French Air Force received its first Dassault Mirage 2000N, the version for use in the sub-strategic nuclear role with ASMP missiles.

**16 Apr:** Maiden flight of the McDonnell Douglas/BAe T-45 Goshawk. This was a modified Hawk for service in the US Navy's advanced training role.

**23 May:** The first of six prototype Bell/Boeing V-22A Osprey tilt-rotor transport aircraft was rolled out at Arlington, TX. It had been designed for use by all four US armed services.

**24 May:** British Airways took over its main rival, British Caledonian. Among the inherited fleet were DC-10s and the newly-introduced Airbus A320.

**14 Jun:** The Schweizer 330 made its first flight at Elmira, New York.

**14 Jul:** The TBM 700 made its first flight in France. Developed jointly by Mooney in the US and SOCATA in France, it was a pressurised single-turboprop business aircraft with a capacity of up to eight seats.

**8 Aug:** The BAe 146STA (Small Tactical Airlifter) made its first flight. It was marketed as the military variant of the already successful 146 STOL airliner, but it did not receive the necessary orders to warrant the new type entering production.

**19 Sep:** The prototype of the BAe Sea Harrier FRS2 was flown for the first time. Its Blue Vixen radar gave the aircraft beyond-visual range engagement capability, combined with the ability to launch AIM-120 AMRAAM active-radar missiles, but it was six years before it was delivered to the Royal Navy's front-line squadrons.

**16 Oct:** First flight of the MBB Bo 108 helicopter, which was subsequently developed as the Eurocopter EC 135.

**27 Oct:** Maiden flight of the ATR 72, a stretched version of the ATR 42.

**11 Nov:** Two Soviet cosmonauts set a new space endurance record of 326 days.

**9 Dec:** The prototype Saab JAS39 Gripen made its initial flight in Sweden.

*John Pittaway shows a British Antarctic Survey de Havilland Canada DHC-6 Twin Otter in his painting aptly titled* Ice Bound.

*Ice Bound* by John Pittaway GAvA

McDonnell Douglas, having previously tested the General Electric GE-36 engine, flew the MD-80 UHB (Ultra High Bypass) demonstrator, fitted with a Pratt & Whitney-Allison 578-DX propfan on its rear-port engine pylon.

With seating for 108-132 passenger, the latest and smallest version of the veteran Boeing 737, the 500 Series, made its maiden flight.

The future potential of US global power was demonstrated by the first flight on 17 July of the Northrop Grumman B-2A strategic stealth bomber. The aircraft represented a return to the concept of the flying wing and was the most expensive aircraft in aviation history. It was subsequently named Spirit and had been under secret development since 1978.

Soviet aircraft were in the limelight at the Paris Air Show. The Sukhoi Su-27 'Flanker' stole the show with the novel 'Cobra' manoeuvre. Slowing to just under 300mph in level flight, the pilot switched off the electronics, heaved back the control column and the aircraft abruptly reared up. The full expanse of the underside was applied to bring it to a halt before, just as abruptly, the pilot lurched the fighter into forward flight once again.

A MiG-29 'Fulcrum A' got into difficulties during the show when an engine suddenly cut out whilst undertaking a low-level manoeuvre, and the aircraft dived into the ground. The pilot, anxious to prevent the aircraft from crashing into the crowd, ejected only at the last moment (fortunately safely) just 400ft above the ground, a mere 2.1 seconds before impact.

After successfully completing its vertical-flight tests, the Bell/Boeing V-22 Osprey began a series of tests of its horizontal flying capabilities in September. The two engines, which tilt from vertical to horizontal and back, drive large 'proprotors', each 38 feet in diameter. This allows the tilt-rotor to take-off vertically, and then, when the engines have tilted forward, to fly like a normal aircraft to a maximum of 300mph.

In October, the Beech Super King Air 350 business aircraft was introduced. Powered by two Pratt & Whitney Canada PT6A-60A engines, it was nearly three feet longer than the previous version with an extended wingspan. With a crew of two and seating for up to 11 passengers, it was advertised as 'the most comfortable and capable Super King Air ever built'.

The first operational Cruise Missile Wing at RAF Molesworth closed under the terms of the Intermediate Range Nuclear Forces Treaty of December 1987. The last massive bunkers for the 60 ground-launched cruise missiles were closed.

It was confirmed in July that, for the first time since the RAF was formed on 1 April 1918, women were to be recruited to the service as pilots and navigators. One of the world's largest military hangars was opened at RAF Waddington for the servicing of the RAF's new Boeing E-3D Sentry.

---

**2 Jan:** First flight of the Tupolev Tu-204, designed to replace Aeroflot's ageing Tu-154s. It was the first Russian-built airliner to incorporate a fly-by-wire control system.

**4 Jan:** Two US Navy F-14 Tomcats shot down two Libyan MiG-23 'Floggers' off the Libyan coast. The Navy claimed that the Tomcats acted in self-defence.

**1 Mar:** The first flight of the Yakovlev Yak-141 'Freestyle' supersonic V/STOL fighter intended for Russian naval carrier operations.

**18 Mar:** The last Hercules Airbridge sortie was flown from RAF Lyneham to the Falklands. Since 1982, a total of 650 flights, each involving a round trip of 14,600 miles and 30 hours flying, had taken place. The task was taken over by Tristars of No 216 squadron at RAF Brize Norton.

**22 Mar:** The prototype Antonov An-225 *Mriya* set 106 world and class records. The six-engined aircraft was designed to transport the *Buran* Space Orbiter, but this made only a handful of space missions.

**3 Apr:** Grumman's A-6E Intruder carrier-based aircraft made its first test flight with Boeing-manufactured composite wings.

**25 Apr:** The first Beechcraft Starship I production aircraft made its initial flight. Though of attractive advanced design it failed to attract many orders.

**23 May:** First flight of the Boeing 767 powered by Rolls-Royce RB211 turbofans.

**28 May:** Initial flight of the Taiwanese AIDC Ching-Kuo fighter. It was developed in Taiwan in close co-operation with a number of US aerospace companies.

**1 Aug:** C-5B Galaxies and C-141B StarLifters of MAC started to fly into RAF Greenham Common to airlift the based cruise missiles back to the US.

**18 Aug:** QANTAS Boeing 747-400 *Spirit of Australia* made the longest non-stop flight by an airliner – 11,156 miles(17,950km) from Sydney to Heathrow in 20 hours and eight minutes.

**21 Aug:** A Grumman F8F Bearcat, with a 3,800hp (2,834kW) Wright R-3350 radial engine set a new world speed record for landplanes with piston engines, when it achieved over 528mph (850km/h).

**14 Sep:** The Bell/Boeing V-22 Osprey made its first transition from propeller to wingborne flight.

**22 Sep:** First flight of the Beechcraft Beechjet 400A twin-jet business aircraft.

**4 Oct:** The first C-5B Galaxy to land in Antarctica delivered 168,000lb of cargo and 72 passengers on a re-supply mission.

**26 Oct:** Maiden flight of the Tornado ECR, the Panavia version built specifically for the Luftwaffe.

**22 Nov:** It was announced that the Lockheed SR-71A Blackbird was to be grounded after all funds for continued operations were deleted from the FY 1990 US Defense Department budget.

**20/21 Dec:** The first operational use of the F-117A stealth aircraft when two dropped two 2,000lb laser-guided bombs on the Rio Hato barracks in Panama under Operation *Just Cause*. They had flown non-stop from their base at Tonopah Test Range.

**22 Dec:** First flight of the McDonnell Douglas MD530N NOTAR civilian version, which had originally been developed for military purposes.

**30 Dec:** Maiden flight of the Sukhoi Su-30 'Flanker', the two-seat long-range interceptor development of the Su-27.

*The improved Boeing 747-400 entered service with the world's airlines in 1989. Cathay Pacific in Hong Kong is a long-time operator of the 'Jumbo' and Ronald Wong's painting illustrates one of its 747-400s approaching the former Kai Tak Airport.*

These pages generously donated by Jade Productions

*Return to Kai Tak* by Ronald Wong BSc(Hons), GAvA, ASAA, GMA, TWAS

The huge military build-up in the Middle East, following the surprise Iraqi invasion of Kuwait on 2 August, demonstrated to great effect the speed at which expeditionary air power elements could now be deployed, and in greater strength than ever before. Just four days later, King Fahd of Saudi Arabia requested the presence of foreign military forces on his country's soil, as a safeguard against the threat posed by Iraq to both the nation itself and its oil resources. This led to Operation *Desert Shield*, which became the largest ever deployment of its kind. A record was set only two days after President Bush confirmed the American military commitment, when the last of 48 F-15C Eagles from the USAF's 1st Tactical Fighter Wing completed the longest ever operational fighter deployment. Each aircraft's flight from Langley AFB, VA to Dhahran in Saudi Arabia lasted between 14 and 17 hours and included multiple air-to-air refuelling.

Over the days and weeks that followed, many more deployments were made. The highest-profile arrivals were the Lockheed F-117A Nighthawks of the USAF's 37th Tactical Fighter Wing, the first of which touched down at Khamis Mushait in Saudi Arabia on 21 August. This base had been chosen partly because it was the newest in the region, the 'Stealth Fighters' being protected while stationed there by an extensive network of hardened shelters. The US Marine Corps and Navy also undertook massive operations to get air assets to the Gulf region, the latter committing the USS *John F Kennedy*, and the former sending a number of Marine Expeditionary Forces (each ready to arrive 'in-theatre' within ten days of being assigned) involving up to a total of 560 aircraft and helicopters. The latter, together with vast numbers of US Army helicopters, either sailed to the Gulf on fast transport ships or were flown in on USAF C-5s.

The whole airlift effort required by all the Coalition forces during the build-up phase was immense. It began by moving the US Army 82nd Airborne Division to Saudi Arabia within a day of the *Desert Shield* build-up being authorised, along with equipment and personnel in support of the 1st TFW F-15 deployment, and continued at an unprecedented rate. Military Airlift Command pressed almost its entire C-5 Galaxy and C-141B StarLifter fleets into use, while the first Air Force Reserve and Air National Guard elements to be called-up comprised three squadrons of C-141Bs and two of C-5As. Also 'in action' were the aircraft of operators belonging to the Civil Reserve Air Fleet which was mobilised at an early stage. After just 22 days, this airlift had exceeded the total capacity hauled during the Berlin Airlift in 1948-49. USAF strategic airlifters alone (also including C-130s and KC-10As) flew 20,500 missions during *Desert Shield*, involving the carriage of around 542,000 tons of cargo and 534,000 passengers. This excludes the RAF strategic missions to and from the UK and Germany, for which Hercules, Tristars and VC10 C1Ks were used, and also in-theatre transport.

Away from the Gulf, 1990 was most significant for the maiden flights of the two prototypes of the contenders for the USAF's Advanced Tactical Fighter requirement. The first to take to the air was that which ended up being unsuccessful, the Northrop/McDonnell Douglas YF-23A which flew on 27 August. Just over a month later, on 29 September, the Lockheed/General Dynamics/Boeing YF-22A followed. Two prototypes of each (which would differ substantially from the intended production examples) were to fly, one of each being equipped with experimental versions of one of the two competing powerplants, the Pratt & Whitney YF119-PW-100 and General Electric YF120-GE-100. Both fighters were designed to be capable of achieving 'supercruise', this being the ability to cruise supersonically without the use of afterburner, but only the YF-22 was fitted with thrust vectoring for additional manoeuvrability. The test programme, culminating in a validation fly-off, was to last through to the following April.

**5 Jan:** Maiden flight of the first Boeing E-3D Sentry for the RAF.
**10 Jan:** The McDonnell Douglas MD-11 wide-bodied tri-jet airliner made its initial flight.
**19 Feb:** Boeing 737 production exceeded that of any previous commercial airliner, when the 1,833rd example was rolled out of the Renton plant in Washington.
**28 Feb:** The first Boeing 737-500 (a 108-seater, shorter than the -400 model) was delivered, to Southwest Airlines.
**6 Mar:** Four new speed records were set by USAF Lockheed SR-71A 64-17972 on its last flight.
**10 Mar:** Boeing delivered its 10,000th airliner, a 767-200 for service with Britannia Airways in the UK.
**21 Apr:** The USAF put the Lockheed F-117A on public display for the first time, at an airshow at Nellis AFB.

**24 Apr:** The civil version of the EH Industries EH101 helicopter, named the Heliliner, took to the air for the first time.
**23-24 Jun:** The RAF Aerobatic Team, the *Red Arrows*, made an historic appearance in Kiev as part of 'British Days in the USSR'.
**12 Jul:** Delivery of the USAF's final Lockheed F-117A, the 59th production example.
**2 Aug:** Iraqi troops entered Kuwait, during which operation a number of combat and support aircraft of the Kuwait Air Force were either destroyed or flown to Saudi Arabia and Bahrain.
**8 Aug:** The US military build-up following the Iraqi invasion of Kuwait began.
**11 Aug:** Tornado F3s became the first RAF combat aircraft to arrive in the Gulf region as the international military build-up began to gather pace. They were followed by Jaguar GR1As,

Tornado GR1s and GR1As together with Nimrod MR2s and support elements including VC10, Tristar and Victor tankers and Hercules transports.
**15 Sep:** The 50th anniversary of the Battle of Britain was commemorated by a 168-aircraft flypast over London, led by two Hurricanes and five Spitfires from the RAF's Battle of Britain Memorial Flight.
**11 Oct:** First flight of the Rockwell/MBB X-31A, developed to evaluate the boundaries of fighter aircraft manoeuvrability.

*The F-16 Fighting Falcon made its first flight in early 1974 and is still in production nearly 30 years later. Roger H Middlebrook's painting shows two Royal Norwegian Air Force F-16s that were assembled by Fokker in Holland, the first being delivered in 1980.*

These pages generously donated by Aitch Design

*Like Sharks Lurking* by Roger H Middlebrook GAvA, FSAI

# 1991

Ever since the beginning of the Coalition military build-up (the largest such operation since the end of WWII) in response to the Iraqi invasion of Kuwait the previous August, it had been clear that if the situation was not resolved by political means, a force would be unleashed the like of which had never previously been to war.

With diplomatic avenues exhausted, this was exactly what happened early on the morning of 16 January. Tomahawk missiles launched against Baghdad from three US Navy battleships positioned in the Persian Gulf began Operation *Desert Storm*, striking their targets in the Iraqi capital shortly after 2:37am local time. The first aircraft to be involved were eight US Army AH-64A Apaches, which were used to hit a pair of important Iraqi air defence radars west of Baghdad. This created a 'corridor' through to the city for the strike packages which followed, while Lockheed F-117As from the 37th Tactical Fighter Wing (which had deployed from their base at Tonopah to Khamis Mushait in Saudi Arabia) knocked out a number of other air defence installations such as communications centres in order to do likewise. At the end of the first day, 2,107 sorties had been flown by Coalition air assets, for the loss of six aircraft (eight Iraqi aircraft having been destroyed).

*Desert Storm* represented a 'baptism of fire' for numerous aircraft and weapons systems. Most attention was focused on the inaugural major combat deployment of the F-117A, of which some 45 examples were present at Khamis Mushait in readiness for the first night of the war. Over its course, the 37th TFW's 'Stealth Fighters' were to fly 1,271 offensive sorties, a third against Baghdad, and all in complete radio silence. Perhaps the type's greatest advantage was its ability to loiter undetected over targets, leading to an 80-85% bomb hit rate (the primary weapon used being the GBU-27 Paveway III LGB) against some very small targets. The footage of ordnance dropped by F-117s entering ventilation shafts and windows remains among the most potent memories of the conflict. On its combat début,

the F-15E Strike Eagle (48 of which had been deployed by the 4th TFW) proved invaluable thanks to their all-weather and night attack capability provided by LANTIRN pods. Even with only five laser designation pods available until near the end of *Desert Storm*, the Strike Eagle demonstrated outstanding effectiveness in hitting targets such as 'Scud' missile sites and Iraqi Republican Guard positions with 'dumb' bombs. Perhaps the most revolutionary, and certainly the newest, type to be deployed was the E-8A J-STARS which provided real-time surveillance of ground forces operating well inside Iraqi territory. The two prototype aircraft converted (and still owned) by Grumman arrived in-theatre during January 1991, and flew about 600 combat hours in 54 missions before being returned to the USA, having demonstrated quite clearly that the J-STARS concept worked.

This was also to be the last action for several much more venerable types. Two squadrons of US Navy A-7E Corsair IIs (VA-46 and VA-72) aboard the USS *John F. Kennedy* were participating in their last cruise when the call to arms came. They proved highly effective in both the strike and SEAD (Suppression of Enemy Air Defences) roles, completing 731 combat sorties. Meanwhile, the RAF committed Jaguars and twelve veteran Buccaneer S2Bs, initially as laser target designators for Tornado GR1s, but which were subsequently also used on strike sorties themselves.

The start of the ground war on 24 February brought the campaign into its short final phase. With the Iraqi Air Force effectively grounded, a rapid advance into Kuwait was possible, led by the largest ever helicopter assault. Just two days later, and in the face of an unstoppable ground onslaught, Iraqi President Saddam Hussein announced that his forces would be withdrawing from Kuwait, and a ceasefire was declared on 28 February. The whole campaign had lasted just six weeks, with air power having undoubtedly been the deciding factor to an extent which had never been the case in any previous war.

**19 Jan:** After 62 years, Eastern Airlines ceased operations due to bankruptcy.
**8 Mar:** Air Europe, the second largest scheduled and charter airline in the UK, collapsed.
**26 Mar:** Handover of the RAF's first Boeing E-3D Sentry AEW1.
**1 Apr:** The Royal Aircraft Establishment (RAE) and other UK Ministry of Defence research facilities were merged into the new Defence Research Agency (DRA).
**5 Apr:** The team consisting of Boeing Helicopters and Sikorsky was announced as the winner of the US Army's Light Helicopter (LH) competition. It was named the RAH-66 Comanche later in the year.
**10 Apr:** The German Navy received its first Dornier 228-212LM for the pollution control surveillance role.

**23 Apr:** After 54 months of evaluation, it was announced that the Lockheed/Boeing/General Dynamics YF-22 had been selected for the USAF's Advanced Tactical Fighter (ATF) requirement.
**29 Apr:** Cessna's new Model 525 CitationJet made its first flight.
**10 May:** Maiden flight of Canadair's prototype Regional Jet.
**18 May:** Piper Aircraft Corporation suspended all production due to financial difficulties.
**19 May:** First flight of Dassault's initial prototype Rafale C, the single-seat production variant.
**24 May:** The Israeli airline El Al attained a new record passenger load for any aircraft, when 1,200 people were crammed into a Boeing 747-200C (with the seats removed). They were Ethiopian Jews, being evacuated from Addis Ababa to Israel.
**1 Jul:** The RAF retired its last Avro Shackleton AEW2s from

service with No 8 Squadron, following the start of E-3D Sentry deliveries.
**15 Sep:** The prototype of the USAF's new McDonnell Douglas C-17A heavy-lift tactical transport made its first flight. It was subsequently named Globemaster III.
**2 Oct:** The RAF ended its 24-hour Quick Reaction Alert (QRA) air defence commitment in Germany when two Wildenrath-based Phantom FGR2s carried out a final ceremonial 'scramble'.
**25 Oct:** Maiden flight of Airbus Industrie's first four-engined airliner, the prototype A340.

*Mark Postlethwaite's painting depicts two RAF Jaguars, in a desert paint scheme, taxiing out fully armed prior to a mission in the Gulf during Operation* Desert Storm.

These pages generously donated by Harris Signs Group

*Cats in the Midday Sun* by Mark Postlethwaite GAvA

Much of 1992 proved to be a rather difficult period for the European Fighter Aircraft (EFA), but there was optimism at the year's end. It was already clear that the non-completion of various items of equipment was going to delay the prototype's maiden flight, which had been scheduled for March, but more importantly the German government announced on 30 June that it was to withdraw from the EFA programme at the end of its development phase threw its whole future into very serious doubt. In particular, the cost per aircraft was expected to rise by around 12%, while a complete re-organisation of the project was now necessary. Germany suggested that a 'lightweight' version of EFA might be acceptable to them, and even stated that France might wish to return to the programme's fold, though this was undoubtedly rather fanciful given the progress of its own Rafale's development.

This all came at a time when the German MoD was re-thinking its participation in several collaborative efforts including the Eurocopter Tiger and NH90. However, a so-called 'New EFA' proposal, whereby aircraft of varying levels of cost and sophistication would be tailored for each nation's needs, re-kindled Germany's interest, and was deemed acceptable by the other partner countries. In December, it announced that Germany would be completing the development phase of what was now to be referred to as Eurofighter 2000 – and, as it turned out, such drastic measures as opting for a different radar were not taken.

This was also a busy year for Airbus Industrie, with its prototype A330 taking to the air at the beginning of November, to become the world's largest twin-engined airliner. The initial aircraft was an A330-301, powered by General Electric CF6s, while the Pratt & Whitney PW4168-engined version followed on 14 October. There were many structural similarities between the two (their respective -300 variants shared the same fuselage, for example), while the practically identical nature of their cockpits and their similarity to that of the A320 led to the FAA certifying crew cross-cockpit qualification between the three Airbus variants, at the time a unique step.

On the military front, the new and burgeoning détente between old foes reached previously unimaginable levels in 1992 when CIS Air Force and USAF strategic bombers carried out visits to each other's bases. A pair of B-52Gs from the 2nd Bomb Wing and a support KC-10A arrived at the CIS Long-Range Aviation aircrew training centre at Ryazan on 4 March and stayed for four days, a deployment which involved some 60 personnel. This was followed up by two Tu-142K 'Bears' and an An-124 visiting Barksdale AFB, LA from 9 May onwards. Who would have believed just a few years earlier that such a thing would ever happen? In the field of arms control, the Open Skies agreement was signed by 22 NATO and former Warsaw Pact members on 20 April. This made the provision for overflights of each other's military installations, in order to ensure that the terms of the Conventional Forces in Europe (CFE) treaty were being complied with. A Belgian Air Force C-130H, specially equipped with recce pods, made the first 'trial run' overflights on 7 April, and Open Skies verification sorties by aircraft from both East and West began in earnest once the treaty officially came into force during 1993.

---

**20 Feb:** The Polish Air Force retired its last SBLim-2Ms (MiG-15UTIs) and Lim-6bis (MiG-17Fs) from service.

**21 Feb:** The USAF's 48th Fighter Wing at RAF Lakenheath received its first F-15E Strike Eagle.

**26 Mar:** Maiden flight of the new Saab 2000 twin-turboprop regional airliner, a stretched development of the Saab 340.

**1 Apr:** The shorter-fuselage, longer-range Airbus A340-211 prototype got airborne from Toulouse.

**15 Apr:** The prototype McDonnell Douglas AH-64D Apache Longbow made its first flight from Mesa, AZ.

**25 Apr:** The second Lockheed/Boeing/GD YF-22A prototype was destroyed in a non-fatal crash landing at Edwards AFB, caused by flight control software problems.

**9 May:** The USAF started the transfer of its Lockheed F-117A fleet from its existing base at Tonopah Test Range to Holloman AFB, NM.

**20 Jul:** Another setback for the Bell-Boeing V-22 Osprey programme, when the fourth prototype crashed into the Potomac

River. All seven on board were killed in what was the second accident to befall the type.

**14 Aug:** First flight of a Rolls-Royce-engined Tupolev Tu-204, developed by the British/Russian Aviation corporation (BRAVIA).

**24 Aug:** Hurricane *Andrew*, with winds of up to 168mph, devastated Homestead AFB, FL, several civilian airfields, and caused significant damage to exhibits at the Weeks Air Museum.

**27 Aug:** Establishment of a 'no-fly zone' south of the 32nd Parallel in an effort to protect the Shi'ite Muslim population in southern Iraq. Some 300 US military, RAF and French Air Force aircraft were deployed as a result.

**22 Sep:** Maiden flight of the AV-8B Harrier II Plus, developed by McDonnell Douglas as a AN/APG-65 radar-equipped derivative of the standard AV-8B.

**4 Oct:** A Boeing 747-258F freighter of El Al crashed into a block of flats in Amsterdam after its number 3 and 4 engines detached from the starboard wing shortly after take-off from Schipol Airport. A total of 51 people were killed.

**31 Oct:** The RAF retired its last Phantoms, these being No 74 Squadron's Spey-engined FGR2s.

**2 Nov:** The Airbus A330-301 prototype made its first flight.

**9 Nov:** Continental Airlines, which had been operating under Chapter 11 bankruptcy protection since 3 December 1990, was purchased by a consortium led by Air Canada.

**9 Dec:** It was announced that Lockheed had purchased the Fort Worth Division of General Dynamics, thereby making the F-16 a Lockheed product and giving the company the role of prime contractor in the F-22 programme.

**18 Dec:** McDonnell Douglas Helicopters' latest product, the twin-turboshaft, eight-seat, NOTAR-configured MD900 Explorer took to the air for the first time.

*Michael Rondot's painting depicts a NATO Boeing E-3A Sentry getting airborne for operational duties over Bosnia. NATO has a total of 17 E-3A AWACS in service at Geilenkirchen in Germany, with forward operating bases in a number of countries.*

*Boeing E-3A Sentry* by Michael Rondot GAvA

Two new aircraft which would form important cornerstones of the USAF's 'Global Reach' ability entered service during 1993, the first of these being the McDonnell Douglas C-17A Globemaster III. The sixth production example had the honour of being the first delivered to the 437th Airlift Wing at Charleston AFB, SC by the Air Force's Chief of Staff Gen Merrill McPeak on 14 June, whereupon it was officially handed over to Air Mobility Command. Thereafter, the 437th AW began the process of converting its aircrews onto the new type, with the first of its squadrons scheduled to achieve initial operating capability on the C-17 within two years, as its C-141 fleet began to be phased out. This all followed an arduous test programme, with 405 flights totalling over 1,450 hours being logged since the aircraft first flew on 15 September 1991.

Delivery to Edwards AFB on 2 February of the sixth and final Northrop B-2A of the development batch signalled the fact that its entry into full Air Combat Command service was not long in coming. The 509th Bombardment Wing was re-formed at Whiteman AFB, MS on 1 April as the initial operating unit. The USAF had spent $460 million on facilities at Whiteman, which had not seen regular fixed-wing operations since the last based B-47 Stratojets left in 1963. In mid-December, the 509th BW's 393rd Bomb Squadron received the second production B-2A, heralding a new era for the USAF's strategic bomber force.

What a contrast with the RAF, as its last 'V-bombers', which had been synonymous with the NATO strategic deterrent of the Cold War, were retired in October. At Marham, No 55 Squadron had retained seven Victor K2s as air-to-air refuelling tankers, but with the conversion of Super VC10s into 'new' VC10 K4s for this role, the classic crescent-winged Handley Page design became surplus to requirements. This was over 36 years after the first Victor B1s entered RAF service and 18 years on from initial use of the K2. In addition, earlier in the year Vulcan B2 XH558, which had been preserved by the RAF as a salute to the type's service, also undertook its final flight as a military aircraft. It had been sold to collector David Walton, and was ferried to Bruntingthorpe in Leicestershire on 23 March for preservation and a hoped-for eventual return to airworthiness.

There were vivid illustrations during 1993 of the great changes which had swept through the CIS armed forces and its aerospace industry, in terms of military co-operation and collaborative projects. Typical of the latter was the Ilyushin Il-96M, a 'westernised', stretched 350-seat version of the wide-bodied airliner. This finally achieved Russian certification late the previous year in its original Perm PS-90A-powered form after over four years of testing. The Il-96M used four Pratt & Whitney PW2337 turbofans and incorporated Rockwell Collins avionics. Meanwhile, it was announced at the Paris Air Show that Aermacchi was to join with Yakovlev in developing the new Yak-130 advanced jet trainer, designed as an Aero L-39 replacement.

---

**1 Jan:** The Slovak Air Force was established as a separate entity from its Czech counterpart after Czechoslovakia was divided.
**19 Jan:** The last Canadian Armed Forces McDonnell Douglas CF-188 Hornets left Baden-Sollingen AB in Germany, marking the end of the Canadian military presence in Europe.
**2 Feb:** The first Airbus A340 was handed over to Lufthansa.
**22 Feb:** Maiden flight of the 153-seat McDonnell Douglas MD-90-30 airliner.
**4 Mar:** Dassault's new Falcon 2000 corporate jet took to the air for the first time.
**11 Mar:** The Airbus A321-130 undertook its inaugural flight.
**23 Mar:** The last USAF A-10As to be based in the UK, with the 81st Fighter Wing at RAF Bentwaters, left for a new home at Spangdahlem in Germany.
**31 Mar:** A United Nations resolution formally enforced a 'no-fly zone' over Bosnia-Herzegovina.
**2 Apr:** First flight of the Fokker 70 twin-jet regional airliner, a shorter version of the 100.
**6 Apr:** The Pratt & Whitney PW2337-powered Ilyushin Il-96M took to the air in Moscow.

**30 Apr:** The two-seat Dassault Rafale B carried out its initial flight.
**11 Jun:** USAF AC-130s and US Army AH-1 Cobras attacked targets in Mogadishu, Somalia after 23 UN troops there were killed by the forces of rebel leader Gen Mohammed Farah Aidid.
**14 Jun:** The USAF received its first C-17A Globemaster III.
**15 Jun:** A further three CIS Air Force bases in Germany (Falkenberg, Welzow and Demin/Tutow) were closed, and their based MiG-29s, Su-24MRs and Su-25s returned to the CIS.
**1 Jul:** A new package of US defence cuts was announced, including the withdrawal of USAF F-15s from Bitburg AB in Germany and Soesterberg in the Netherlands.
**14 Jul:** NATO initiated operations to enforce the 'no-fly zone' over Bosnia.
**19 Aug:** The last CIS military aircraft (Antonov An-26s) left Legnica in Poland, bringing the Russian presence in the country to an end after 48 years.
**23-26 Aug:** Russia undertook its first trial Open Skies flights, using an Antonov An-30 from its Nuclear Risk Reduction Centre. A range of installations in Germany were photographed.
**1 Oct:** The USAF's 55th Wing at Offutt AFB received a new

Boeing C-135 variant, the first of three OC-135Bs modified for Open Skies monitoring flights.
**6 Oct:** The Royal Netherlands Air Force announced an order for 17 Eurocopter AS532U-2 Cougar tactical transport helicopters. 20 were ordered by the Turkish Air Force two days later.
**15 Oct:** The RAF retired its last 'V-bombers', the Victor K2 tankers used by No 55 Squadron at Marham.
**15 Oct:** Eight MiG-29s were delivered to the Hungarian Air Force, providing a substantial boost to its capabilities.
**7 Dec:** Departure of the last USAF F-111s from Europe, when the remaining F-111Es of the 20th Fighter Wing at RAF Upper Heyford left for the USA.
**17 Dec:** The USAF's 509th BW received its first B-2A.
**20-21 Dec:** Two new Cessna aircraft made their maiden flights – the Model 526 CitationJet candidate for the USAF/USN JPATS trainer contract, and the Model 750 Citation X corporate jet.

*The Panavia Tornado GR1 was the first swing-wing aircraft to enter RAF service. Derek Bunce's painting illustrates an RAF Tornado GR1 of No 27 Squadron operating at very low level.*

These pages generously donated by Impact Image

*Low-level* by Derek Bunce

# 1994

The draw-down of forces in Europe following the end of the Cold War reached something of a climax during 1994, as aircraft from a number of bases, which had been at the forefront of the military commitments of both NATO and the Warsaw Pact during those long years of tension, departed for the last time. The USAF quit two of what had been its most important European installations, namely Soesterberg AB in the Netherlands, from where the last of the 32nd Fighter Squadron's upgraded F-15A Eagles departed on 15 January, and Bitburg AB in Germany, which had been home to USAFE fighters for 42 years, from where the F-15Cs of the 36th Fighter Wing left on 18 March.

In addition, USAFE Phantom operations ended in February after three decades when the 52nd Fighter Wing at Spangdahlem retired its *Wild Weasel* F-4Gs. However, the most whole-scale changes occurred in the eastern half of Germany as the last Russian forces were withdrawn from the unified country. Remaining fixed-wing combat aircraft in East Germany (Su-17Ms from Templin and MiG-29s from Wittstock) departed back to the CIS in April, and were followed by the helicopter units. The last airfield to be vacated was Sperenberg, home to Mil Mi-24s and Mi-8s, and a ceremony in Berlin on 31 August attended by Russian President Boris Yeltsin marked the final withdrawal of his country's forces from what had been the Cold War front line.

Unfortunately, there were new tensions in the Balkans in what turned out to be a very significant year for NATO. The first ever offensive action in the Alliance's 45-year history took place on 28 February, when two F-16Cs from USAFE's 526th Fighter Squadron shot down four Yugoslav Air Force Soko G-4 Super Galebs which had been involved in an attack on targets in the UN 'no-fly zone' over Bosnia. On 10 April, NATO undertook its first air strikes against Serbian ground positions to protect under-fire UN forces, when another pair of USAFE F-16s hit an artillery command centre near the town of Gorazde, which was being shelled. These operations effectively opened the way towards more direct NATO action in the conflict, and thereby what became a long-term commitment for its air arms.

Meanwhile, there were also two very important maiden flights during 1994. The first of these (albeit some two years later than originally planned) was the Eurofighter 2000, when prototype DA1 took to the air from the DASA airfield at Manching in Germany on 27 March. The first British example, DA2, followed in the hands of BAe's Chris Yeo on 6 April. Although both of these aircraft were far from being of production standard (notably being equipped with Rolls-Royce RB199 turbofans rather than the new EJ200 units, which were still under development), they immediately embarked upon a programme aimed firstly at expanding the EF2000's flight envelope and exploring its agile handling.

In spite of an ongoing recession in the aerospace industry, Boeing was confident about the prospects for its new twin-engined, wide-bodied 777, which made its inaugural flight on 12 June. The first aircraft was a PW4084-powered 777-200. This was just the beginning of an arduous flight test programme for the type, scheduled to involve around 4,800 flights by eight 777s, which would include two each powered by General Electric GE90s and Rolls-Royce Trent 800s.

---

**3 Feb:** The final flight of a NASA-operated F-104 Starfighter (an ex-Luftwaffe F-104G) from the Dryden Research Center.
**15 Feb:** First flight of the new Eurocopter EC135 twin-turbine light utility helicopter.
**19 Feb:** Four Tu-95MS 'Bear-Hs' were transferred from Kazakhstan to Russia, leaving only Ukraine among the former Soviet republics as having strategic nuclear-capable bombers.
**28 Feb:** NATO's first ever 'shoot-down', when two USAFE F-16Cs destroyed a quartet of Yugoslav Air Force Super Galebs over Bosnia.
**24 Mar:** Research and development flying by the Defence Research Agency (previously the RAE) at Farnborough came to an end when all operations were transferred from there (and also from the other DRA airfield at Bedford) to Boscombe Down.
**27 Mar:** Long-awaited maiden flight of the first Eurofighter 2000 took place in Germany.
**31 Mar:** The RAF's No 208 Squadron disbanded, ending the service career of the Buccaneer S2B.
**4 Apr:** It was announced that Northrop had taken over the

Grumman Corporation, thereby creating the new Northrop Grumman concern.
**16 Apr:** A Royal Navy Sea Harrier FRS1 from HMS *Ark Royal* was shot down near Gorazde in Bosnia by a Serbian SA-7 SAM. Its pilot ejected safely and was rescued.
**20 Apr:** The Italian Navy received its first AV-8B Harrier II of sixteen ordered for operations from its new carrier, the *Guiseppe Garibaldi*.
**1 Jun:** The first sale of US military aircraft to Eastern Europe was announced at Berlin's ILA 94 airshow – five Bell 412EPs and two Bell 206B-3 Jet Rangers for the Slovenian Territorial Forces.
**12 Jun:** Maiden flight of the first prototype Boeing 777-200.
**1 Jul:** The prototype Saab 340 AEW&C airborne early warning platform ordered by the Swedish Air Force, incorporating Ericsson's Erieye radar mounted atop the fuselage, took to the air for the first time.
**3 Aug:** The South African Air Force retired its last veteran Douglas DC-4/C-54 Skymasters.

**13 Sep:** Inaugural flight of the Airbus-SATIC A300-608ST Super Transporter, popularly known as the Beluga and designed to replace the veteran Boeing 377SGT-201 Super Guppies, which had transported large Airbus airframe components between the consortium's factories.
**28 Oct:** The USAF received its first three re-engined Lockheed U-2Ss, fitted with the General Electric F118-GE-101 unit instead of the previous Pratt & Whitney J75.
**21 Nov:** The heaviest NATO air strikes against Bosnian Serb forces to date, when 39 aircraft hit the Serb airbase at Udbina.
**16 Dec:** Confirmation that the RAF would be ordering 25 C-130J Hercules and 50 Future Large Aircraft to meet its upcoming transport requirements.

*This Wilfred Hardy painting of a Sukhoi Su-27 'Flanker' belongs to the Russian Gromov Flight Institute and is located at Zhukovsky Airfield, near Moscow. It shows Su-27 '597' being flown inverted over a Russian airfield during a display by Anatoly Kvotchur.*

These pages generously donated by the Daily Mail

*597 – Instant Aerobatics* by Wilfred Hardy GAvA

The start of NATO's Operation *Deliberate Force* at the end of August was important both politically and militarily. It marked not only the most aggressive attempt yet to force the Bosnian Serb military to halt its continuing campaign of aggression in Bosnia-Herzegovina, but also the first occasion on which the Alliance had mounted such a large aerial offensive. *Deliberate Force* began with F/A-18Cs and EA-6B Prowlers from the USS *Theodore Roosevelt* knocking out the Serb air defence network around the Bosnian capital, after which five separate strike packages were sent to hit important military installations. The use of laser-guided weapons ensured a high level of accuracy over those first two nights, and their resumption on 5 September saw the campaign's scope being widened to include command posts and supply routes, especially bridges, all around Bosnia.

*Deliberate Force* was spearheaded by the large US military contingent which had been deployed to bases in Italy and on carriers. F-16Cs from the 31st and 52nd Fighter Wings were heavily involved, the former being equipped with LANTIRN pods for all-weather target designation, the latter with new AGM-88 HARM anti-radiation missiles which were used to destroy hostile radar sites. This was the first time that the 48th FW's F-15Es from RAF Lakenheath had been used in anger, and they were employed on two different strike taskings: during the early attacks near Sarajevo, they dropped Paveway LGBs, but when the range of targets widened they switched to hitting air defence sites with GBU-15 bombs.

More peacefully, Boeing's new 777 began revenue-earning service during 1995. The granting to the Pratt & Whitney PW4084-engined variants of certification by the US and European authorities on 19 April followed 3,000hr of flight testing by nine aircraft since the type's maiden flight just over ten months before. Shortly after certification, United Airlines' first 777-222 (the third aircraft built) completed a three-week worldwide sales tour by setting a new record time of 13hr 36min for a flight between Bangkok and Seattle. Further emphasising its abilities, the 777 was the first ever aircraft to receive FAA approval for extended range twin-engine operations (ETOPS) on its entry into service, this occurring on 30 May. United then introduced the type to commercial service on 7 June, operating the London-Heathrow to Washington-Dulles route.

However, the record-breaking did not stop there, as the third example for United set a new benchmark time between Seattle and Paris four days later, prior to appearing at the Paris Air Show. Variants using engines other than the PW4084 were also being readied for commercial use, the first Rolls-Royce Trent 800-powered aircraft flying on 26 May, while that using General Electric GE90s gained certification in November. This allowed British Airways to become the second airline to use the type, and its initial 777-236 arrived on 12 November with operations (from Heathrow to Dubai and Muscat) commencing five days afterwards.

---

**8 Feb:** France's Sécurité Civile received its first Canadair CL-415 turboprop firebomber. Twelve had been ordered as replacements for the radial-engined CL-215s.

**10 Feb:** The first prototype Antonov An-70 collided with its An-72 chase aircraft and was destroyed, with the loss of the seven people on board the new transport.

**9 Mar:** It was announced that the RAF had placed an order for 22 EH101 transport helicopters and fourteen further Chinook HC2s to satisfy its support helicopter requirement.

**17 Mar:** Maiden flight of Canadair's latest Challenger derivative, the CL604 with General Electric CF34-3B turbofans.

**31 Mar:** The largest all-composite aircraft ever built, the twin-turboprop Grob Strato 2C high-altitude atmospheric and meteorological research aircraft, took to the air for the first time.

**7 Apr:** The Dutch Government announced that the AH-64D Apache Longbow had been selected as the Royal Netherlands Air Force's new attack helicopter.

**2 Jun:** An F-16C from USAFE's 31st Fighter Wing was shot down by a Bosnian Serb SAM-6 missile while carrying out a patrol at 20,000ft near Banja Luka in Bosnia. The pilot evaded capture by

Serb forces for six days before being rescued by a US Marine Corps CH-53E operating from the USS *Kearsage*.

**22 Jun:** It was announced that the Raytheon Beech MkII, a modified version of the Pilatus PC-9, had been selected for the USAF/US Navy's very long-running JPATS (Joint Primary Aircraft Training System) contract.

**30 Jun:** The German Bundestag voted in favour of allowing the country's armed forces to deploy outside NATO territory.

**7 Jul:** The Italian Air Force received the first of 24 Tornado F3s which it leased from the RAF as Eurofighter 'stop-gaps'.

**13 Jul:** The UK Ministry of Defence confirmed an order for 67 Westland-built WAH-64 Apache Longbows, to be operated by the Army Air Corps.

**1 Aug:** First flight of the stretched Ilyushin Il-76MF, powered by four Aviadvigatel/Perm PS-90AN turbofans in place of the D-30 units used on previous variants.

**11 Aug:** Embraer's prototype EMB-145 regional jet took to the air for the first time.

**17 Aug:** The first production Northrop Grumman E-8C J-STARS undertook its initial flight after conversion from a Boeing 707.

**25 Aug:** Maiden flight of the 124-seat Airbus A319 prototype.

**7 Oct:** Mitsubishi's indigenous FS-X (later F-2) multi-role fighter prototype made its first flight from Komaki AB near Nagoya. The Japanese Air Self Defence Force had 141 examples on order.

**7 Oct:** Maiden flight of the Learjet 45, exactly 32 years after the first aircraft in this famous family.

**2 Nov:** The Royal Netherlands Air Force's first Fokker 60UTA-N transport, a stretched derivative of the Fokker 50, took to the air from Amsterdam-Schipol.

**17 Nov:** Official retirement by the South African Air Force of its last 55 North American Harvards, which had been in use with the SAAF's Central Flying School at Langebaanweg.

**29 Nov:** The first McDonnell Douglas F/A-18E Super Hornet took to the air for its inaugural flight.

**18 Dec:** First flight of the multi-national NH Industries NH90 multi-purpose helicopter prototype.

*Ian Bott's painting shows a Cessna 152 training aircraft belonging to the Golden State Flying Club, Gillespie Field, El Cajon, California, some ten miles east of San Diego, on the occasion of* My First Solo.

These pages generously donated by Orion Security Print

*My First Solo* by Ian Bott

This was a year which saw very significant upheavals in the global aerospace industry, most notably the announcement in December of the intended merger between Boeing and McDonnell Douglas, which was confirmed the following year after claims that it would create an unfair monopoly were rejected by the US Federal Trade Commission. The enlarged Boeing company thus became the world's largest aerospace and defence concern by some margin, with over 200,000 employees at the time of the takeover. Its headquarters remained in Seattle and Boeing had been pursuing a possible bid for some time, the move being hastened by MDC's loss of a contract to provide one of the Joint Strike Fighter demonstrator prototypes and its decision not to pursue its MD-XX airliner project.

Definitely not a profitable proposition, unfortunately, was Fokker. The famous Dutch manufacturer lost the financial support of its majority shareholder Daimler-Benz Aerospace in January, whereupon the Netherlands Government made a substantial loan package available to keep the company afloat. It also paid in advance for the four new Fokker 60UTA-N utility transports ordered by the Royal Netherlands Air Force, deliveries of which began in June, and hastened an order by the air arm for two Fokker 50 VIP transports. This was not enough to save the concern, and after last-minute negotiations with Samsung of South Korea about a possible takeover fell through, Fokker was declared bankrupt on 15 March.

In contrast, the Lockheed Martin C-130J Hercules was already on course for success by the time of its long-awaited maiden flight from Marietta on 5 April. The aircraft which carried this out was a stretched C-130J-30, destined for the RAF as a Hercules C4, while the first standard-length C-130J for the USAF followed up with the second flight on 4 June. Various delays had set the programme back a little by this stage, the first flight having been delayed by some three months due to problems with the computer systems which were one of the features making the J-model more of an entirely new aircraft than just another Hercules. Among the major changes were the use of a head-up display for the first time in a transport aircraft, the four Rolls-Royce Allison AE2100-D3 turboprops (delivering 30% more power compared with the T56s of earlier C-130s while burning 15% less fuel) allied with six-blade propellers and a FADEC (Full Authority Digital Engine Control) system, and a digital 'glass' cockpit. Unfortunately, this degree of advancement over any previous C-130 would continue to bring its own difficulties, not least due to the requirement for the aircraft to gain FAA certification prior to delivery to its military customers. Much to the frustration of the USAF, RAF and other purchasers, it was still some time before the C-130J was ready for service, but at least the important milestone of the first flight had been reached and intensive flight testing began.

---

**4 Jan:** Maiden flight of the prototype Boeing Sikorsky YRAH-66 Comanche attack helicopter for the US Army.

**22 Feb:** The French Government announced sweeping intended changes to the country's defence industry, including a proposed merger of Dassault and Aérospatiale.

**16 Mar:** The prototype MiG-AT advanced jet trainer made its first flight from Zhukovsky.

**29 Mar:** Details were announced of bi-lateral military agreements between Russia and Ukraine, which included long-awaited plans to transfer Tu-95MS and Tu-160 strategic bombers from Ukraine to Russia, with various types (among them MiG-29s and Su-27s) going in the other direction as compensation.

**2 Apr:** The Sukhoi Su-37 thrust-vectoring control (TVC) version of the 'Flanker' took to the air for the first time.

**16 Apr:** Cessna undertook the first flight of a new-build 172 since production ceased in 1986. A new 182S followed exactly three months later.

**25 Apr:** The Yak-130 advanced jet trainer, jointly developed by Yakovlev and Aermacchi, took to the air.

**30 Apr:** The Northrop *Tacit Blue* stealth technology demonstrator, kept secret since its first flight in 1978, was revealed.

**5 Jun:** It was announced that Fairchild Aircraft was to take an 80% stake in Dornier, creating the new Fairchild Dornier concern.

**10 Jun:** Delivery to the Royal Netherlands Air Force of its first new Fokker 60UTA-N utility transport.

**17 Jun:** The first jet to have been used by the USAF as the Presidential Air Force One transport, Boeing C-135B 58-6970, was retired by the 89th Airlift Wing and went on display at Boeing's Seattle museum.

**25 Jul:** It was announced that BAe's Nimrod 2000 rebuild proposal had been selected for the RAF's Replacement Maritime Patrol Aircraft requirement.

**27 Jul:** Retirement of the USAF's last two F-111Gs from service, with the 27th Fighter Wing at Cannon AFB. The type had officially been named Aardvark just before this event.

**9 Aug:** First flight of the initial Boeing E-767 AWACS for the Japanese Air Self-Defence Force since fitment of its APY-1 radar and rotodome.

**9 Aug:** The man behind the first turbojet engine to power an aircraft, Sir Frank Whittle, died at his home in Maryland.

**31 Aug:** Eurofighter DA6 became the first two-seat example of the type to take to the air, and also the first Spanish prototype.

**10 Sep:** Aeroflot announced that it was purchasing ten new Boeing 737-400s as Tu-134 replacements, much to the irritation of the Russian aircraft industry.

**13 Oct:** Maiden flight of Bombardier's new Global Express long-range, high-speed business jet.

**25 Oct:** The Romanian Air Force received the first two of four surplus USAF C-130B Hercules. These were the first aircraft to be supplied by the USAF to a former Warsaw Pact air arm.

**29 Oct:** The USAF re-commenced Lockheed SR-71A operations following re-activation of the type.

**29 Nov:** Upgraded and re-engined Tupolev Tu-144LL RA-77114 took to the air from Zhukovsky. This heralded the start of the type's use by NASA and various aerospace companies for research in preparation for the next generation of supersonic airliners.

**19 Dec:** The US Navy's last A-6E Intruders, in service with VA-75, completed their final carrier deployment (on the USS *Enterprise*).

*The Canadair CL-415 amphibian was designed from the outset for aerial firefighting. This later model twin-turboprop was officially launched in the early 1990s and is depicted here in Paul Tuttle's painting dumping water on a forest fire.*

*Containing the Front* by Paul Tuttle

# 1997

In the year of the US Air Force's 50th anniversary, an occasion marked by some spectacular aerial celebrations both in the USA and overseas, it was appropriate that Air Combat Command's most potent strategic asset should have achieved initial operating capability (IOC) during the year. The Northrop Grumman B-2A Spirit reached this milestone on 1 April, at which time some 13 examples had been delivered to the 393rd Bomb Squadron, 509th Bomb Wing at Whiteman AFB. Under the existing order for the type, eight more were then still to be delivered. The USAF confirmed that all B-2A sorties would be undertaken directly from Whiteman without landing elsewhere, though by the autumn it was countering this statement by announcing that it would be deploying Spirits to unspecified locations for two-week periods around the turn of the year.

1997 also saw some very significant milestones being achieved by the Lockheed Martin/Boeing F-22A programme. The first of seven engineering and manufacturing development (EMD) pre-production examples was rolled out at Marietta on 9 June, on which occasion the type was officially named Raptor. Unfortunately, the F-22A's maiden flight, which had been scheduled for 29 May, had to be delayed due to a fuel leakage problem. This was resolved and the aircraft got airborne for the first time on 7 September. A week later, however, the second flight ended prematurely when the aircraft's telemetry signal failed and a planned third test was cancelled in order to get the programme back on schedule, which involved maintenance and modification at Edwards AFB.

On the civil front, Boeing got its first two 'New Generation' 737 models into the air during 1997, some four years after the programme had been launched. These new aircraft, beginning with the 737-700 (flown on 9 February) and the -800 (which followed just under six months later) incorporated a new advanced-technology wing for greater aerodynamic and fuel efficiency, and thereby increased range. The new variants were designed to be powered by the new CFM-56-7 turbofan, which themselves offered advantages of lower fuel consumption and noise levels. Improvements to the cockpit and interior environments drew heavily on advancements incorporated into the 777. Before their respective maiden flights, both aircraft had achieved healthy sales figures, the 126 to 149-seat 737-700 first being ordered upon its launch by Southwest Airlines who received its initial examples in December 1997. The -800 programme had officially begun during 1994, with German carrier Hapag-Lloyd being the first to sign up.

While these new Boeing 737s represented the evolution of a successful design rather than revolutionary change, one flying machine which took to the air for the first time in 1997 was definitely an example of the latter, although it did revive a very famous name. The immense Zeppelin LZ N-07 airship had been designed to demonstrate the myriad commercial possibilities of a truly modern blimp, equipped with fly-by-wire controls, powered by three Textron Lycoming IO-360 engines and capable of quite astonishing agility for such a large craft (75m long).

**27 Feb:** US Air officially changed its name to US Airways.
**14 Mar:** The final Eurofighter 2000 prototype to fly, BAe's two-seat DA5, did so from Warton.
**27 Mar:** The British armed forces retired the de Havilland Canada Chipmunk T10 from service as a basic trainer. Its last user was the Army Air Corps Basic Fixed Wing Flight at Middle Wallop.
**11 Apr:** The first prototype McDonnell Douglas YC-15 was re-flown for the first time since 1978, in preparation for a research programme by its former manufacturer.
**23 Apr:** It was announced that the BAe Hawk 100 had been selected for the advanced training segment of the NATO Flying Training in Canada (NFTC) programme.
**24 Apr:** The second prototype Antonov An-70 took to the air, just over two years after the initial example had been lost.
**25-26 Apr:** The USAF's oldest active aircraft, highly-modified Lockheed NT-33A 51-4120 (delivered in 1951) which had mainly been used for research into flight control systems, made a final public appearance (at Nellis AFB for the Golden Air Tattoo,

celebrating the Air Force's 50th anniversary) before being retired to the USAF Museum.
**8 May:** The Indian government stated that the country's two national carriers, Air India and the purely domestic Indian Airlines, would be merged in an effort at cost-cutting following large losses.
**29 May:** BAe announced that production of the Jetstream 41 would cease at Prestwick, and with it both aircraft manufacturing in Scotland and building of the Jetstream family.
**11 Jun:** British Airways revealed its controversial new corporate identity, incorporating international 'ethnic' tail fin artwork on many aircraft.
**25 Jun:** First flight of the Kamov Ka-52 Alligator attack helicopter, a two-seat derivative of the existing Ka-50.
**30 Jul:** For the first time, approved photographic sorties by a Russian military survey aircraft, an Antonov An-30B, were undertaken over military bases in the USA. This took place under the Open Skies treaty.
**2 Aug:** First flight of the Aero Vodochody L-159 ALCA (Advanced Light Combat Aircraft), ordered by the Czech Air Force.

**7 Sept:** Maiden flight of the first pre-production F-22A Raptor.
**12 Sept:** The Israeli Defence Force/Air Force's first F-15I Ra'am (Thunder) version of the Strike Eagle carried out its inaugural flight from St Louis.
**17 Sept:** Antonov's 50-seat twin-turboprop An-140 airliner took to the air for the first time.
**25 Sep:** First flight of what was then referred to as the Sukhoi S-32, the company's next-generation fighter research aircraft. It was later re-named the S-37 Berkut.
**19 Dec:** The first three surplus USAF KC-135A Stratotankers out of seven ordered by the Turkish Air Force were delivered to Incirlik AB.

*NASA's long-serving Lockheed ER-2s were re-engined with the General Electric F118 non-afterburning turbofan in the early 1990s to give weight reduction and greater fuel efficiency. Nixon Galloway's painting was specifically commissioned by NASA and shows the ER-2 which achieved a new world altitude record over Edwards AFB that resulted in the award of the Collier Trophy.*

These pages generously donated by Thompson and Wilson Communications Ltd

*High Altitude ER-2* by Nixon Galloway ASAA

Seldom in one year, for a considerable period, had so many new commercial aircraft taken to the air for the first time than was the case in 1998, and most of them were produced by Boeing. In spite of being a new product, one of them marked the end of an era, namely the 717-200, which was the last airliner to be designed by McDonnell Douglas (as the MD-95) prior to the company's merger with Boeing. As such, and with 106 seats and a range of some 2,867km (1,545nm), the type had been developed as a smaller version of the MD-90 which would compete with the Airbus A319 and Boeing 737-600. One thing which definitely set the 717 apart from its rivals was its extreme quietness, thanks to the use of two BMW Rolls-Royce BR715 turbofans, specially designed for the aircraft and built at a state-of-the-art plant at Dahlewitz near Berlin. First deliveries took place to US low-cost domestic carrier AirTran Airways (formerly ValuJet) in September 1999, and since then the 717 has proved popular with all its customers, if somewhat slow-selling overall.

The Boeing 737 range expanded still further in 1998, with the addition of further New Generation variants. The smallest of them, the 737-600, with seating for between 110 and 132 passengers, took to the air on 22 January and entered a test programme which culminated in its entry into service with SAS in September after FAA certification had been achieved. During April, the 737-800 also began earning its keep with launch customer Hapag-Lloyd of Germany. The Next Generation 737s thus began to build on the great popularity of this most successful of all jetliners ever, the scale of this success being emphasised on 26 January when the 3,000th 737 'Classic' (a 737-400 destined for Alaska Airlines) was rolled out in Seattle, some 31 years and six days after the first 737-100 had been unveiled. That initial aircraft was of course a very different machine from those of three decades later, and in particular the Boeing Business Jet (BBJ), the opulent new corporate version of the 737-700 and -800 which made its maiden flight on 4 September, with 29 examples then on order.

Definitely unique, though, was the most distinctive new aircraft of 1998: the Scaled Composites Proteus, designed by Burt Rutan as a high-altitude, long-operation (HALO) multi-mission research platform. In terms of its configuration, the Proteus was, and is, like nothing else in the air, with its tandem-wing, twin-boom design incorporating two Williams/Rolls-Royce FJ-44-2 turbofans mounted on the aft fuselage. Its construction is modular, allowing easy changes of payload depending on the desired role. The aircraft's main function was conceived as being broadband telecommunications relay, but it was also intended to be ideal for many other tasks including atmospheric research and remote sensing.

---

**19 Jan:** The Israeli Defence Force/Air Force took delivery of its first two F-15I Ra'ams out of 25 ordered.

**30 Jan:** British Airways officially announced that its new low-cost offshoot would be named Go. Scheduled services began on 22 May.

**31 Jan:** The stretched Dash 8Q-400 prototype made its maiden flight from Bombardier's Downsview factory airfield.

**11 Feb:** First flight of the Boeing C-32A, the USAF's VIP transport version of the 757-200. Four entered service with the 89th Airlift Wing as replacements for its C-137Bs and Cs.

**20 Feb:** US Navy aircraft operations in Antarctica ended after 42 years when the US Naval Antarctic Support Unit was disbanded at Christchurch, New Zealand. Ski-equipped LC-130R Hercules of VXE-6 had been the last USN aircraft used but their role had gradually been taken over by USAF LC-130Hs.

**28 Feb:** The Teledyne Ryan (later Northrop Grumman) RQ-4A Global Hawk high-altitude surveillance UAV undertook its maiden flight.

**31 Mar:** The RAF's nuclear strike capability came to an end when its last WE177 tactical freefall nuclear bomb was decommissioned at RAF Marham.

**27 Apr:** Confirmation that the USAF would be permanently retiring the Lockheed SR-71A, of which it still held six examples.

**2 May:** The USAF's last two EF-111As were withdrawn from service with the 429th Electronic Combat Squadron at Cannon AFB, NM.

**12 Jun:** The AH-64D Apache Longbow entered US Army service at Fort Hood, TX.

**24 Jun:** The Rolls-Royce Trent 700-powered Airbus A330-200 took to the air on its maiden flight.

**2 Jul:** Official opening by Chinese President Jiang Zemin of Hong Kong's new international airport at Chek Lap Kok. Three days later, commercial flights out of Kai Tak ceased.

**4 Jul:** First flight of the Embraer ERJ-135 regional jet.

**26 Jul:** The Scaled Composites Proteus high-altitude research aircraft made its initial flight from Mojave, CA.

**18 Aug:** First flight of Aero Vodochody's new single-seat L-159A lightweight fighter.

**24 Sep:** Maiden flight of the Beriev Be-200 twin-turbofan amphibian.

**25 Sep:** The first WAH-64 Apache Longbow for the British Army Air Corps made its initial flight from Mesa, AZ, prior to production starting at GKN Westland's Yeovil plant.

**22 Oct:** NATO's Operation *Eagle Eye* began over Kosovo, providing surveillance of Yugoslav troop and weapon withdrawals from the province which had been agreed just before a deadline passed which would otherwise have seen the Alliance taking military action. USAF U-2s and RQ-1A Predator UAVs, US Navy P-3Cs, RAF Canberra PR9s, French AF Mirage IVPs and Navy Atlantiques were involved at the outset.

**18 Nov:** South African President Thabo Mbeki announced orders totalling $5.2 billion for 28 Saab JAS39 Gripens, 24 BAe Hawks, 40 Agusta A109s and four GKN Westland Super Lynx 300s, as the country's armed forces continued their gradual re-equipment.

**16-17 Dec:** Air strikes against Iraq resumed in earnest under Operation *Desert Fox*, after the country's government refused to comply with UN weapons inspectors. The strikes continued for four nights.

*High battlefield survivability was a particularly important feature of the Fairchild A-10 Thunderbolt's design from the outset, with emphasis on low-level agility than on outright performance. Ronald Wong's painting shows USAF A-10s in action over Kosovo in 1998.*

*Target Marking in Kosovo* by Ronald Wong BSc(Hons), GAvA, ASAA, GMA, TWAS

Fifty years on from its establishment, 1999 was a highly-significant year for NATO in other ways. It had been intended that this would be a year of celebration, particularly as the Czech Republic, Hungary and Poland became the first former Warsaw Pact states to join the Alliance. However, these events were overshadowed by the need for its member states to again go into action in the Balkans, this time as a result of the refusal of Yugoslav President Slobodan Milosevic to withdraw his forces from the province of Kosovo. Air strikes had narrowly been averted the previous year when NATO demands began to be adhered to at the last moment, but on 23 March the Organisation's Secretary-General, announced that efforts at negotiation at Rambouillet near Paris had failed, and that offensive operations were the only remaining option.

Operation *Allied Force* began on 24 March, with eight USAF B-52H Stratofortresses operating out of RAF Fairford taking part in the first wave, alongside two B-2A Spirits from the 509th Bombardment Wing at Whiteman AFB making the type's combat début. They dropped Boeing GBU-29/30 Joint Direct Attack Munitions (JDAMs) on important military targets near the Yugoslav capital of Belgrade during a mission mounted directly from Whiteman. The second wave of strikes was carried out by NATO combat aircraft operating from bases in Italy and the USS *Enterprise* in the Adriatic, with participation by eleven nations, including Germany. This latter involvement, by Tornados stationed at Piacenza, was significant as it was the first time that the Luftwaffe had participated in offensive missions since the end of WWII. On that very first night, three Yugoslav Air Force MiG-29s were shot down by NATO aircraft, two by USAF F-15C Eagles, the third by a Royal Netherlands Air Force F-16A Fighting Falcon.

Less certain at the time was the reason why a USAF F-117A came down 26nm north-east of Belgrade in the early morning of 28 March, as no confirmation of the cause was given, but it was almost certain to have been due to a Serbian SAM which was able to track the Nighthawk after it descended to 15,000ft in order to get below cloud. However, the pilot ejected and was rescued successfully by an MH-53J Pave Low III combat SAR helicopter, after what had been the first combat loss of a 'stealth' aircraft.

As at 24 May, some 62 days into the campaign, NATO had no fewer than 922 aircraft deployed in the theatre, with over 300 more scheduled to arrive during the following weeks. By now, this total included US Army AH-64A Apaches based at Rinas in Albania in readiness for their possible involvement in any ground offensive. A much more significant event occurred on 5 May, when (after a vote in the country's Parliament approved it) Hungary saw one of its military airfields being used by NATO aircraft on operations for the first time, eight USAF KC-135Rs, based at Ferigehy Airport in Budapest. On 23 May, 18 US Marine Corps F/A-18D Hornets arrived at Taszar AB in south-western Hungary and soon became combat-ready at their forward location. The fact that NATO combat aircraft were using a former Warsaw Pact military airfield as their base for offensive missions did not go overlooked.

The conflict came to an end on 10 June as Yugoslav forces began to withdraw from Kosovo as agreed under a Technical Agreement (TMA) signed the previous day. Thereafter, NATO forces in the theatre began the task of peacekeeping under the new KFOR operation, with RAF Pumas and Chinooks joining the US Army AH-64s in providing support to the first contingents of Allied troops crossing over from the Macedonian border.

---

**18 Jan:** With delivery to the Royal Navy of the last new-build BAe Sea Harrier FA2, production of all-British fighter aircraft ended.

**28 Jan:** The USAF received its first six C-130J Hercules.

**8 Feb:** First flight of Tupolev's medium-haul Tu-334 airliner, intended as a replacement for the now obsolete Tu-134.

**24 Mar:** After the Yugoslav Government failed to withdraw its troops from Kosovo or halt its offensive against the Kosovar Albanians, NATO air arms began air strikes against Yugoslavia under Operation *Allied Force*.

**25 Mar:** The EH Industries EH101 entered commercial service when an Agusta-built example was delivered to the Tokyo Metropolitan Police Air Wing.

**3 Apr:** Operation *Shining Hope*, a humanitarian airlift of supplies into Albania to aid Kosovar refugees there, began with the first USAF C-17A flights to Tirana.

**22 Apr:** On the 30th day of Operation *Allied Force*, NATO announced that some 9,300 sorties had been flown to date, of which 2,750 were strike missions.

**30 Apr:** The first production Bell/Boeing MV-22B Osprey for the US Marine Corps made its maiden flight.

**24 May:** NATO now had over 1,000 aircraft committed to *Allied Force* in-theatre.

**27 May:** Bombardier's new 70-seat CRJ700 airliner first flew.

**10 Jun:** Air strikes against Yugoslav forces ceased as they began to withdraw from Kosovo. The KFOR peacekeeping force officially came into being.

**15 Jun:** It was announced that Raytheon had been selected to supply the RAF with the aircraft platform for its ASTOR (Airborne Stand-Off Radar) programme, using five Global Express long-range business jets.

**10 Aug:** A Pakistan Navy Breguet Atlantic was shot down by an Indian Air Force MiG-21 when it entered Indian airspace, causing another upsurge in tension between the two countries.

**25 Sep:** The C-27J Spartan, developed by Lockheed Martin Alenia Tactical Transport Systems, made its maiden flight.

**8 Oct:** The USAF decided to ground its Slingsby T-3A Firefly fleet permanently, after plans to get them back into the air after engine problems had ensued took longer than originally thought.

**9 Oct:** First flight of the Boeing 767-400ER.

**5 Nov:** A Tu-160 'Blackjack' became the first of eleven Ukrainian Air Force strategic bombers (eight Tu-160s and three Tu-95MS 'Bear-Hs') to be returned to Russia

*The Lockheed F-117A Nighthawk stealth strike fighter dropped many precision-guided weapons during the Gulf War and was again deployed to Europe for use in the Balkans campaign. Here Ronald Wong portrays an F-117A bombing Belgrade in March 1999.*

These pages generously donated by DKA

*Storm over Belgrade* by Ronald Wong BSc(Hons), GAvA, ASAA, GMA, TWAS

The fatal accident to an Air France Concorde on 25 July was the first such catastrophe to hit the world's only successful supersonic airliner in the 31 years since the first prototype took to the air. F-BTSC, the oldest operational Concorde, had just taken off on a charter flight from Paris-Charles de Gaulle bound for New York's JFK airport, with nine crew (led by Capt Christian Marty) and 100 German tourists on board, when a major fire started in its two port Olympus engines and along the wing trailing edge. The aircraft struggled to gain height, power from numbers 1 and 2 engines disappearing, before control was lost which resulted in a pitch-up. Two minutes after take-off, the Concorde crashed into a hotel in the Paris suburb of Gonesse, killing a further four people on the ground.

All Air France and British Airways Concordes were grounded, but BA's started flying again 24 hours later. However, operations were curtailed again on 15 August, as it had been advised by the UK's Civil Aviation Authority that its French counterpart was to recommend the following day that the type's Certificate of Airworthiness should be withdrawn. This was in the light of initial investigations which showed that a tyre blow-out on takeoff, caused by contact with a small metal strip on the runway, had resulted in what were described as 'catastrophic consequences in a short period of time'.

When the detailed report on the accident was released in 2001, it was confirmed that debris from the exploded tyre had ruptured a wing fuel tank. In the meantime, the only operational supersonic transport remained grounded, albeit with much well-founded confidence being expressed by Air France, British Airways, industry and politicians as to the aircraft's future after the incorporation of a number of safety-related modifications.

2000 was unfortunately a bad year for another revolutionary aircraft. The loss on 8 April of a US Marine Corps Bell/Boeing MV-22B Osprey engaged in operational evaluation flying from MCAS Yuma, AZ, was a further blow to the ongoing development of the tiltrotor machine which was now entering service (this was the fourth series example, two prototypes having already been lost, in 1991 and 1992). Then, the start of low-rate initial production was delayed indefinitely when an aircraft in service with VMMT-204, the first unit operational on type, crashed on approach to its base at MCAS New River on 11 December. The signing of contracts for the production of further USMC MV-22Bs and Special Operations-optimised USAF CV-22Bs hung in the balance, as a program review panel appointed by Defense Secretary William Cohen began to address its problems.

At the end of the year, Airbus Industrie was able to announce the official launch of its 555-seat A380, development of which was expected to cost the consortium some $12 billion. Emirates announced its intention on 30 April to become the launch customer, citing a shortage of capacity on some of its popular routes, and the lack of slots now available at many international airports, as its prime reasons for purchasing a larger airliner. Confirming this potential market, once Airbus received approval from its shareholders to offer the A380 to potential customers, Emirates put down its deposit, and by the end of the year Singapore Airlines, International Lease Finance Corporation (ILFC), Air France, QANTAS and Virgin Atlantic had done likewise. With 50 firm orders and 42 more on option, plus others 'on the stocks', the A380 programme was secure.

---

**22 Jan:** A Boeing 747-4G4 freighter was flown to Boeing's Wichita plant for conversion to become the prototype YAL-1A airborne attack laser platform for the USAF.

**21 Feb:** Transfer of the Ukrainian Air Force's remaining strategic bombers to Russia was finally completed when two Tu-160 'Blackjacks' left Priluki Air Base.

**25 Feb:** Boeing handed the last two 'Classic' 737s to be produced, both 737-45Ss, to CSA Czech Airlines.

**29 Feb:** The first flight of RSK-MiG's 1.44 next-generation research fighter took place at Zhukovsky.

**1 Mar:** The first Raytheon Beech T-6A Texan II was delivered to USAF Air Education and Training Command at Randolph AFB, TX, in preparation for operational testing and evaluation.

**8 Apr:** A US Marine Corps MV-22B Osprey crashed with the loss of 15 Marines and four crew aboard.

**14 Apr:** First flight of the Boeing C-40A Clipper, the variant of the 'convertible' passenger/cargo 737-700C ordered by the US Navy as a C-9 Nightingale replacement.

**28 Apr:** Lockheed Martin handed over its 4,000th F-16, a Block 40 F-16C for the Egyptian Air Force.

**16 May:** The British Government confirmed that four C-17As would be leased to fulfill the RAF's Short-Term Strategic Airlift needs, and that 25 Airbus A400Ms would be purchased for the longer-term Future Transport Aircraft requirement.

**30 Jun:** Production contracts totalling 6.6 billion Euros ($6.4 billion) for the NH90 helicopter were signed between the participating countries and NH Industries.

**18 Jul:** The first GKN Westland-assembled WAH-64 Apache Longbow for the British Army Air Corps was flown.

**26 Jul:** Agusta and GKN Westland formally merged their helicopter businesses into the new AgustaWestland concern.

**27 Jul:** Signing of a joint declaration of commitment to the A400M programme by defence ministers of the participating nations.

**3 Aug:** Maiden flight of the 177-seat Boeing 737-900.

**18 Sep:** The Boeing X-32A made its inaugural flight, thereby becoming the first of the JSF prototypes to take to the air.

**24 Oct:** Initial flight of the Lockheed Martin X-35A, first prototype of the second JSF contender.

**24 Oct:** Czech aircraft manufacturer Let was declared bankrupt.

**11 Dec:** Another fatal V-22 Osprey crash, again involving a US Marine Corps MV-22B.

**19 Dec:** Airbus Industrie officially confirmed the launch of the A380, previously known as the A3XX.

*Patricia Forrest's painting shows a British Midland Airbus A321, finished in the airline's then new blue and silver livery, flying over its Castle Donington-East Midlands base on delivery.*

*Showing her New Plumage to Castle Donington* by Patricia Forrest GAvA

# 2001

During the course of the history of powered flight, the power of aircraft as weapons of destruction has been demonstrated on many occasions. However, the events in the United States of September 11, 2001, involving four airliners hijacked during domestic flights, were unprecedented in terms of the form that these attacks took, and their symbolic potency in having been directed at the twin hearts of the United States' financial and political might, New York and Washington, as the world looked on. In the months afterwards, an unprecedented coalition of nations formed to combat international terrorism, and in particular Osama bin Laden's al-Qa'eda terrorist organisation, which was behind the September 11 attacks. From October onwards, military air power was unleashed against the Taleban régime in Afghanistan, which had refused to surrender bin Laden and other senior al-Qa'eda figures, while airlines and civil aircraft manufacturers worldwide suffered immediate and hard-hitting economic hardships, with many airliners flown into storage as a result.

Operation *Enduring Freedom* began on 7 October, and commenced with a series of strikes aimed at a total of 31 targets, comprising Taleban military installations and al-Qa'eda training camps. Among the aircraft involved were six B-2A Spirits of the USAF's 509th Bomb Wing, which departed their home base at Whiteman AFB, MS, each dropped 16 JDAMs on targets in Afghanistan, and then made a quick refuelling stop on Diego Garcia (also the operating base for B-1Bs and B-52s) after 44 hours in the air – a new record. Humanitarian aid drops using C-17As of the 437th Airlift Wing flying directly out of Ramstein AB, Germany, commenced later that night.

The impact of September 11 on civil aviation proved to be the straw which broke the camel's back, and the Swiss Government had to step in with a rescue bid involving regional carrier Crossair taking over a proportion of Swissair's assets and services. An even worse fate befell Sabena as a result of all this, as Swissair had a 49.5% stake in the Belgian flag carrier. Sabena was forced to file for bankruptcy on 7 November, and its entire fleet was grounded. Regional carrier Delta Air Transport, previously a wholly-owned Sabena subsidiary, was 'hived off' from its parent by two businessmen and slightly expanded to cover some of the gaps in European services out of Belgium left by Sabena's demise.

In industry terms, BAE Systems was forced to end all regional jet production, and with it the Avro RJ programme (which had only recently spawned the new Avro RJX variant) that followed on from the BAe 146, first flown back in 1981.

**10 Jan:** American Airlines announced that it was to acquire the assets of the collapsed TWA.
**18 Jan:** An Air France Concorde (F-BVFB) took to the air for the first time since the accident of the previous July, flying from Paris-CDG to the French military test centre at Istres, in preparation for high-speed taxiing trials.
**16 Feb:** A missile was live-fired from a UAV for the first time, when an AGM-114 Hellfire-C was launched by a specially-configured USAF RQ-1A Predator near Nellis AFB.
**5 Mar:** Balkan Bulgarian Airlines was forced to terminate its operations following financial difficulties.
**29 Mar:** Boeing unveiled its Sonic Cruiser concept, a near-supersonic airliner of extremely futuristic design.
**1 Apr:** A US Navy EP-3E Aries II electronic surveillance aircraft, engaged in a routine patrol mission, and a Shenyang J-8 II 'Finback-B' fighter of the Chinese Naval Air Arm collided over the South China Sea. In spite of almost rolling inverted, the Aries II was able to reach the Chinese military airfield at Lingshui for an emergency landing. The crew were released ten days later.
**23 Apr:** Maiden flight of the stretched 380-seat Airbus A340-600 from Toulouse-Blagnac, the company's largest airliner to date.
**23 May:** The RAF received the first of four leased C-17As, which entered service with No 99 Squadron at Brize Norton.
**17 Jul:** British Airways Concorde G-BOAF took off from London-Heathrow for a successful test flight with modified fuel tanks and undercarriage assembly.
**13 Aug:** NASA Dryden's solar/electric-powered Helios research craft set a new altitude record for a non rocket-propelled aircraft (previously set at 85,068ft by an SR-71A in 1976) when it reached a height of 96,500ft.
**21 Aug:** After 56 years, the RAF's presence in Germany came to a close when No 31 Squadron's Tornado GR1/4s departed for a new home in the UK at RAF Marham. The other two resident Tornado units, Nos 14 and 9 Squadrons, had left earlier in the year. Bruggen was then transferred to the British Army.
**5 Sep:** The British and French authorities reinstated Concorde's Certificate of Airworthiness. Crew refresher training commenced soon afterwards, and BA undertook a flight with 100 engineering staff aboard on 11 September.
**10 Sep:** It was confirmed that the Hungarian Air Force would be leasing fourteen Saab JAS39 Gripens from Sweden.
**19 Sep:** In response to the terrorist attacks eight days earlier, 100 additional US combat aircraft were deployed to the Persian Gulf region.
**7 Oct:** The start of air strikes against Taleban-held targets in Afghanistan, as part of Operation *Enduring Freedom*, the so-called 'war against terrorism'.
**26 Oct:** Lockheed Martin, in partnership with Northrop Grumman and BAE Systems, was announced as the winner of the $19 billion competition against Boeing to build the Joint Strike Fighter.
**12 Nov:** New York suffered another terrible air disaster, when an American Airlines Airbus A300B4-605R (N14053) crashed into the Queens district shortly after take-off from John F Kennedy Airport. 246 passengers and six crew on board were all killed, but thankfully casualties on the ground were light.
**13 Dec:** The Royal New Zealand Air Force's entire combat force was officially disbanded.
**18 Dec:** The eight nations participating in the Airbus Military A400M transport aircraft programme signed a Memorandum of Understanding, paving the way towards production.

*A USAF Northrop-Grumman B-2A Spirit is featured in Ronald Wong's painting making its longest mission to date, when it flew from the US to drop JDAMs on targets in Afghanistan during Operation Enduring Freedom.*

These pages generously donated by Northrop Grumman Corporation

*The Longest Mission* by Ronald Wong BSc(Hons), GAvA, ASAA, GMA, TWAS

# 2002

The ceremony at the Farnborough International Air Show in July which formally named the Eurofighter 'Typhoon', provided one of the few certainties in relation to the aircraft which emerged during the year. The other major milestone was the start of test flying by the five Instrumented Production Aircraft (IPAs), which began when the two-seat, Alenia-built IPA2 took to the air from Caselle in Turin on 5 April. However, concerns still remained about the level of Typhoon procurement by the partner nations, in particular Germany and the UK. In the case of the RAF's planned purchase, there were unconfirmed reports that the UK Ministry of Defence would end up reducing its total as part of plans to free up funding for other projects, including a proposed new aircraft carrier. The welcome announcement that Austria was to purchase 24 Typhoons as replacements for its ageing J-35Ö Drakens ended up in uncertainty, firstly when it was revealed that some of the Eurofighters in question would come out of Germany's first production tranche, thus reducing its procurement commitment 'by the back door', and then after an Austrian public petition in opposition to the order gained enough signatures to force a Parliamentary debate about the proposed purchase.

There was generally better news for the Lockheed Martin JSF/F-35 programme, with several new partner nations making commitments to the development phase, which looked likely to lead to firm orders. Following Canada and the UK, confirmations of participation by Denmark and the Netherlands added the third and fourth international partners, and these were closely followed by similar announcements from Norway, Italy, Australia and Turkey. Italy was keen to stress that this in no way affected its Typhoon buy, with the Eurofighters having air defence and air superiority as their primary tasks, while the F-35s would be used for defensive air power, operating both from land bases and aircraft carriers. Perhaps the most surprising announcement came from Australia, whose competition for an F-111 and F/A-18 replacement had been expected to continue with the F-35 up against the F/A-18E Super Hornet, Dassault Rafale and Typhoon. The country's Defence Minister stressed that a final purchase decision would not be made until 2006, but also stated that none of the other options 'will meet our capability requirements'.

On the civil scene, the after-effects of the events of September 11 2001 continued. Fairchild Dornier unveiled its prototype 728-100 twin-jet airliner at Oberpfaffenhofen on 21 March, but less than two weeks later (on 2 April) the company filed for court protection from its creditors, the German equivalent of US Chapter 11 proceedings. There were also major problems for US Airways, the sixth largest airline in the USA, which filed for Chapter 11 protection on 12 August after incurring losses of $2.1 billion during the previous financial year. Operations were due to continue while new financial arrangements were implemented.

**15 Jan:** Maiden flight of Airbus Industrie's smallest airliner to date, the A318-121.

**11 Feb:** The long-range Airbus A340-541 was first flown.

**19 Feb:** First flight of the 70-78-seat Embraer 170 twin-jet regional airliner.

**20 Feb:** Exactly two decades since the first Boeing 757 flew, the latest Pratt & Whitney PW2040-powered 757-300 was airborne.

**28 Feb:** The British Government announced that the Royal Navy's Sea Harrier FA2s would be withdrawn from service between 2004-06, several years earlier than previously planned.

**4 Mar:** Ansett Australia officially ceased operations, after bids to rescue what had been the country's largest domestic airline came to nothing.

**29 Mar:** It was announced that the USAF had decided to negotiate exclusively with Boeing for the lease of 100 new air-to-air refuelling aircraft. The 767TT Tanker/Transport will initially replace the oldest KC-135s. A further order for tanker transports will follow.

**5 Apr:** First flight of a production-standard Eurofighter Typhoon, an Alenia-built two-seater.

**9 May:** US Navy Secretary Gordon England confirmed that the Bell/Boeing V-22 Osprey was ready to resume flight testing after two fatal accidents during 2000 had led to the grounding of the tilt-rotor aircraft.

**22 May:** Maiden flight of the Boeing X-45A prototype Unmanned Combat Air Vehicle (UCAV), the first unmanned aircraft designed from the outset for combat functions.

**Jul:** Aviation entered the era of the hypersonic jet after an air-breathing engine exceeded 5,000mph in Australia. 'Hypersonic' ignition by the scramjet is potentially one of the most important milestones in aviation since the sound barrier was broken in 1947.

**1 Jul:** The new Pilatus PC-21 advanced turboprop trainer made its first flight from Stans, Switzerland.

**2 Jul:** The Austrian Government announced an order for up to 24 Eurofighter Typhoons.

**22 Jul:** Virgin Atlantic took delivery of the first Airbus A340-600 to enter airline service. It was then flown from London-Heathrow to make its public début at Farnborough International 2002.

**27 Jul:** 83 people were killed in the worst airshow accident ever, when a Ukrainian Air Force Su-27UB 'Flanker-C' crashed during an aerobatic display at Skryliv AB near the city of Lviv near the Polish border in western Ukraine. Two more casualties died in hospital in the days after. A quickly-completed investigation concluded that pilot error and the event organisation had been to blame for the accident.

**16 Aug:** The UK MoD announced that the replacement transport aircraft for the C-130K Hercules fleet would be based at RAF Brize Norton later in the decade.

**16 Aug:** The first BAE Systems Nimrod MR4 was rolled out at the Woodford site.

**20 Aug:** The Kova Aerospace Industries (UKAI) Lockheed Martin Golden Eagle supersonic advanced trainer was first flown in South Korea.

*Declared winner of the US Joint Strike Fighter (JSF) competition in 2002, the Lockheed Martin F-35 is being developed in an international programme as a replacement for the F-16 Fighting Falcon, F-15E Strike Eagle, and AV-8 Harrier. In this specially commissioned painting, Wilfred Hardy is looking ahead to the RAF receiving F-35s to replace its Harriers early in the next decade.*

These pages generously donated by Lockheed Martin

*Burning Blue* by Wilfred Hardy GAvA

# AMERICAN SOCIETY OF AVIATION ARTISTS

Founded in 1986, by five renowned American aviation artists – Keith Ferris, Jo Kotula, Robert McCall, Robert G. Smith and Ren Wicks – the ASAA has grown in 16 years from a charter membership of 25, to include today, 155 Artists and Artist Fellows and 136 Associate members. Artists and Artist Fellows are juried into the ASAA by a review panel consisting of the remaining two founding members, Keith Ferris and Robert McCall, and three Founder Chairs; John Clark, Gil Cohen, and Nixon Galloway, all of whom are Artist Fellows. Artist Fellows are those whose aviation/aerospace art is widely recognized for its consistent high standards of professionalism, authenticity, and artistic quality as recognized by the membership committee. Many Associates are artists themselves, while others are gallery owners, museum curators, or collectors of aviation art.

The ASAA is proud to count among its membership a number of artists from other countries, including Canada, Great Britain, Pakistan, Switzerland, South Africa, Australia, Argentina, Brazil, Hungary and the Philippines. The ASAA has chosen as its primary objective, the raising of standards of aviation art and the promotion of aviation art as a major means of preserving aviation/aerospace history. Its efforts include publication of a quarterly newsletter and other educational documents, an annual Aviation Art Forum, regional meetings, and an annual juried exhibition at a major museum or other appropriate venue, usually in conjunction with our Annual Forum. ASAA also helps in soliciting works for other exhibitions and for publications.

The members have one book of ASAA art in print – *Aviation, a History Through Art*. A scholarship programme helps to finance the participation of young artists in mentoring programmes and in our forums. Works by ASAA members appear in many museums, corporate offices, military installations and private collections throughout the world. ASAA members frequently win top honours in aviation art contests sponsored by various corporations.

Enquiries about the ASAA may be made to:
John Sarsfield, Membership Secretary,
6541 St. Vrain Rd,
Longmont, CO 80503, USA
Web: *www.asaa-avart.org*

# THE GUILD OF AVIATION ARTISTS

The Guild of Aviation Artists, founded in 1971, incorporates the Society of Aviation Artists, which had held its first exhibition in 1954 at London's Guildhall. However, by 1958, a number of professional members had become somewhat disenchanted with the new society and turned their attention to a small social club catering for light flying and gliding enthusiasts called the Kronfeld Club, which was keen to put on an exhibition of aviation art at its Victoria premises. So it was that top professionals like Wootton, Turner and Young hung their work alongside artists who actually flew the aeroplanes.

It is the same today, and from these small beginnings the Guild now has over 450 members and a like number of 'Friends' who are mostly artists as well. An annual open exhibition entitled 'Aviation Paintings of the Year' is sponsored by, amongst others, BAE Systems and Rolls-Royce. It attracts a prize of £1,000 for the artist of what is judged to be the best exhibit.

Other exhibitions are organised to commemorate many of the important events in our aviation history and members' work continues to be sought by historians, publishers and collectors alike. Their paintings are hanging in service messes and clubs, museums, galleries and aviation offices throughout the world.

Enquiries regarding paintings, exhibiting or membership of the Guild should be made to:
The Secretary,
The Guild of Aviation Artists,
Unit 418, Bondway Business Centre,
71 Bondway,
London SW8 1SQ
Telephone: UK (0)207 735 0634
Email: *admin@gava.org.uk*
Web: *www.gava.org.uk*

*Wilfred Hardy's painting* New Century Defender *illustrates the Eurofighter Typhoon that is entering RAF service in 2003. It will also equip German, Italian, Spanish, Austrian and other European air arms in the years ahead.*

These pages generously donated by BAE SYSTEMS

*New Century Defender* by Wilfred Hardy GAvA

# THE CONTRIBUTING ARTISTS

### COLIN J ASHFORD GAvA FCIAD

A diploma student at Wakefield and Glasgow Schools of Art in the 1930s, Colin Ashford served in camouflage development units during World War II in the Middle East. After the war, he exhibited paintings in London galleries and produced illustrations for magazines and advertising. He is one of the full and founder members of the Guild of Aviation Artists, specialising mainly in historical aviation subjects. He is also a member of the Canadian Historical Aviation Society. His paintings are in a number of national and private museums, as well as military bases in Britain, Canada and the USA, including the RAF Museum at Hendon, the Shuttleworth Trust at Old Warden, the Greenwich National Maritime Museum, the Ashmolean Museum at Oxford and the Guild Hall in London.

### ROBERT BAILEY ASAA

Robert Bailey is an Artist Fellow with the American Society of Aviation Artists (ASAA) and a member of the Canadian Aviation Artists' Association, although he was born and raised in Staffordshire. He attended Longton College of Art and for some years worked in television as a photographer and show host, then in newspapers as a designer, photographer and writer. Robert has an extensive collection of World War II uniforms and airplane models for use as reference when creating a project. He produces an average of three or four new limited edition print projects each year. He feels privileged to have made many friends who once flew for the air forces of the United States, Britain, Canada and Germany.

### IAN L BOTT

Ian Bott was born in St Helens in 1960. He has been an aviation enthusiast since the age of five, when he was given some aircraft recognition books from World War II by his father. After graduating with a degree in graphic design in 1983, he began working as a professional illustrator and has produced a wealth of work for magazines, books, newspapers, design companies and advertising agencies worldwide. He recently spent six years living in California, where he fulfilled a lifelong ambition to gain his private pilot's licence.

### DEREK BUNCE

Derek Bunce's love of painting and drawing aircraft began in the late 1930s when, at a very early age, he drew countless World War One dogfights. Most of his working life was spent as an illustrator and Art Director at the Davis Gibson Advertising Agency. The Tornado has featured prominently in his work. Derek worked for many years on the Tornado account from its start as the Multi-Role Combat Aircraft through to its full service with the RAF. This included work on bulletins and promotional work. Derek belonged to the Guild of Aviation Artists for some years and was a regular exhibitor. He has illustrated aviation books and his artwork was used by MATRA/BAe Dynamics for the new METEOR air-to-air missile.

### JOHN W CLARK ASAA

At the age of six, John Clark became interested in aeroplanes. From his home in Chicago, he spent many hours watching them fly overhead on their landing approach to Midway Airport. This interest in aeroplanes expanded to include spacecraft and the astronomical universe. By the 1960s, John had served in Southeast Asia with the US Air Force as an aircraft mechanic. He holds a Bachelor of Fine Arts, Master of Arts and Master of Fine Arts degree in drawing and painting. For 30 years his efforts have been directed toward commissioned works for Astronomy magazine, NASA and the US Air Force Art Program. John is a past president of the American Society of Aviation Artists.

### GERALD COULSON VPGAvA

Born at Kenilworth, Warwickshire, Gerald Coulson is a self-taught artist. He began drawing at around 16 or 17 years of age, but professionally trained and qualified as an aircraft engineer. He served in the RAF for eight years and later used his technical knowledge and drawing ability for a successful career illustrating technical manuals for civil and military aircraft and associated equipment. Gerald qualified for a pilot's licence in 1960, fulfilling a boyhood ambition, and is still active, flying mostly vintage aircraft. A love of flying and anything connected with aviation motivated the desire to put on canvas the sky and all its

various moods. He became a full-time artist in 1969 and his paintings have featured many times in the Fine Art Group top ten best-selling prints, three of which have been number ones for his landscape and aviation subjects. They can be seen in many establishments and collections around the world, and quite naturally in RAF stations, museums and exhibitions. He is a founder member of the Guild of Aviation Artists and four times winner of the *Flight International* Trophy for aviation painting.

### JAMES COX

James Cox was born in Hackney, London in 1943. He started work in 1959 in the studio of transport illustrator R Granger Barrett, at New Court, Carey Street, Holborn. Throughout the 1960s he worked in various London studios and advertising agencies, becoming freelance in 1971. During the latter half of the 1970s, James worked as a professional jazz musician, whilst also painting and selling occasional works in oils of marine and aviation subjects. In the 1980s, by this time married with a family, he returned to full time commercial and fine art work.

### TERENCE CUNEO CVO, OBE, RGI (1907-1996)

Terence Cuneo was born in London on 1 November 1907. He first made his mark as a racing artist in the 1920s, with his 'Pitwork' series depicting Le Mans and other racing circuits. He was a sapper in the Royal Engineers at the start of World War II and became one of the most well known British military artists of the 20th century. His artistic talents were soon recognised and he began a career as a wartime artist. Such was his reputation that in 1953 he was chosen as the official artist for the coronation of Queen Elizabeth II. He was later commissioned by the Queen to paint regal equestrian portraits and was elected to the Society of Equestrian Artists as its first president. He had a passion for powerful machines of any type including cars, jet engines, aircraft, tanks and any other military machines, but especially railway locomotives and the railway as a whole. He designed the set of stamps issued to commemorate the 150th anniversary of the Great Western Railway in 1985. A mouse was always included in his paintings, by way of a trademark.

## LOU DRENDEL

Lou Drendel is a world-renowned aviation artist whose fascination with aeroplanes was fostered by his father, who built solid models of combat aeroplanes during World War II. Lou joined the US 82nd Airborne Infantry and become a paratrooper. He briefly entered the world of sports car racing and then skydiving before gaining his pilot's certificate in 1965. He is a founding member of the *Lima Lima* Flight Team, flying as both the team lead and solo lead for this formation aerobatics team. He has logged over 3,800 hours in the T-34 Mentor and is the current President of the national T-34 Association. His paintings have appeared in the *Chicago Tribune* and *Time-Life* publications as well as more than 50 books authored by him on military aviation. His continuing 'Flyers Series' of paintings for American Flyers celebrates famous aviators and famous aircraft.

## KEITH FERRIS ASAA

Keith Ferris has worked as a freelance aviation artist serving the needs of the aerospace industry, aviation trade publications, aviation museums and the USA's military for 55 years. Amongst his best-known works are the two huge murals at the National Air and Space Museum. His 41 years of flying with the US Air Force have included the documentation of the missions of most jet aircraft types in the USAF inventory. Keith Ferris has had many honours bestowed upon him, as well as being an inductee into the Aviation Hall of Fame in New Jersey. He is a life member of the Society of Illustrators in New York and a founding member and past president of the American Society of Aviation Artists. Keith is also an honorary vice-president of the British Guild of Aviation Artists. Over 40 of his paintings have been published as fine art limited edition prints. In addition, he is also an inventor, holding five US and four foreign patents in the field of deceptive aircraft paint systems.

## PATRICIA FORREST GAvA

Patricia Forrest was born in London in 1933. Her parents moved to Newport in Monmouthshire in 1939, but returned to London in 1947. She studied at St Martin's School of Art in London and then at the Royal College of Art where she obtained her degree. For many years she was a freelance graphic designer. She started painting in 1982 and quickly gained a reputation as a floral and landscape painter. Her 'one-man' shows have proved successful and she has also exhibited collectively. An interest in aircraft was generated in 1987, when she exhibited for the first time with the Guild of Aviation Artists and made a sale on the first day. She is now a full member of the Guild and exhibits every year at 'Aviation Paintings of the Year'. Much of her time is spent painting aircraft, with commissions for her work from individuals and companies.

## THEO FRASER GAvA

Theo Fraser was born on 8 February 1933. He was educated at Dorking County Grammar School and afterwards attended Epsom and Ewell School of Art and Crafts. He completed National Service in the RAF as a leading aircraftman clerk. After this he worked in the printing and security industries, retiring in the spring of 1998. He joined the Guild of Aviation Artists during 1974 and was recently elected to full membership. His paintings are exhibited in galleries, and many are in private collections. In 1985 he won the Aviation Painting of the Year Award.

## NIXON GALLOWAY ASAA

Nixon (Nick) Galloway is an experienced professional who is well known for the broad scope of work he has produced for corporations, and more recently, the prints and the paintings he has created for galleries and individual commissions. He has an extensive background in aviation and over 50 years experience as an artist and for many of those years he worked as a freelance illustrator. His paintings are held in many private collections and have been exhibited at the Air Force Museum, Smithsonian Air & Space Museum, Kennedy Space Center, EAA Museum, RAF Museum in Hendon, and the White House. He has had major one-man shows in Savannah and Dallas and over 30 of his paintings are in the US Air Force Art Collection. He is an Artist Fellow member and a past president of the American Society of Aviation Artists.

## CARLOS A GARCIA

Carlos Adrian Garcia was born in Buenos Aires, Argentina on 20 November 1960. Since his youth, he has been interested in drawing and aviation. In 1984 he was employed as an illustrator by *Aeroespacio*, the Argentine Air Force magazine. He illustrated the Spanish edition of the *Malvinas War Encyclopedia*. He also began to study aeronautical engineering, but left in order to continue his work as an illustrator. Carlos has a diploma in design and ran his own editorial business between 1994 and 1996. He was commissioned by Aerolineas Argentinas and Pegasus Aviation Inc to produce aircraft paintings for them, as well as by the Argentine Post Office to design several celebratory stamps. His paintings are exhibited at many locations including the Argentine Air Force Headquarters, the Argentinean Army Museum of Aviation and the Argentine Post Office, as well as in private collections.

## HOWARD GERRARD GAvA

Howard Gerrard studied art and design at Wallasey School of Art and Merseyside and Liverpool College of Printing, afterwards going on to gain a National Diploma in Art and Design at Leeds College of Art. He started his career as a designer for the Metal Box Company in London and later became a senior designer with leading designer groups in London. He became a freelance designer and illustrator in 1979. A full member of the Guild of Aviation Artists, who is a regular exhibitor at the Guild exhibitions, Howard is now a full-time artist and illustrator. In 1998 he was winner of the Society of British Aerospace Companies Trophy. He followed this by winning the Wilkinson Sword Trophy in 1999 and the Pooley Airtour Sword in 2001.

## WILFRED HARDY GAvA

Wilfred Hardy was born in London on 7 July 1938. Both his father and uncle were artists. He had no formal art training and went straight from school into a series of London art studios, eventually specialising as an illustrator. He became a freelance in 1966, working mainly in magazines and advertising. In 1975 he did his first painting for the RAF Benevolent Fund and has been associated ever since with the Fund and its Royal International Air Tattoo organisation. He has also worked with the RAF Association and is proud of his involvement with the RAF and its charities. His work is to be found in military and civil establishments and museums in many parts of the world. A Full Member of the Guild of Aviation Artists, in 1991 he was awarded the prestigious Roy Nockolds Trophy for the most popular painting by public vote. In recent years he has had considerable success with collectors' plates. His series depicting the legendary No 617 Squadron 'Dambusters' is one of the bestsellers of all time.

## CRAIG KODERA ASAA

Craig Kodera was born in Riverside, California in 1956. He started to paint at 14, and by the time he was 17, he had earned his private pilot's licence. He attended UCLA, where he obtained a Bachelor's degree in mass communications and completed the equivalent of a minor in art history. He became a life member of the Sigma Chi fraternity and served in the Air Force ROTC for three of his four years at UCLA. After graduation, he worked as a commercial artist for several small advertising/design firms, and also for McDonnell Douglas Aircraft, where he was employed as a production/design artist and illustrator. Following a year of commercial art, Craig spent more than seven years in the US Air Force Reserve where he was assigned to the Air Rescue Service and stationed at March AFB. He flew the Lockheed HC-130H Hercules and also served with the Strategic Air Command, where he flew the McDonnell Douglas KC-10A Extender. He began flying for Air California in 1986, staying on when the airline was acquired by American Airlines as a First Officer. He is the Charter Vice President of the American Society of Aviation Artists and is a member of the Air Force Art Program and the Los Angeles Society of Illustrators. His work hangs in several museums and is part of the permanent collection of the Smithsonian Institution's National Air and Space Museum in Washington, DC. He was winner of the 2001 R G Smith Excellence in Naval Aviation Art Award.

### ROBERT LAVIN (1919-1997)

Robert Lavin was born in New York City. His education included Townsend Harris, a prep school in New York, followed by college at City College of New York. He also attended the National Academy of Art, where he studied as a painter. Studying the social realists of the 1930's, Robert Lavin, a former US Marine pilot, portrayed steelworkers, roughnecks and trainmen. His paintings were often used to illustrate magazine advertisements. The Smithsonian Institution and other museums collected his original paintings. He was for a number of years an Associate Professor of Art at City College of New York, a position he left in the mid-1960s in order to devote himself full time to his painting. His commissions took him around the world, from the North Sea to the coast of Africa, from the slopes of Alaska to the Sea of Japan. Another portrait, of one of the early American astronauts, appeared on the cover of *Time*

magazine. Other major commissions during these years included *Readers Digest* books, *Life* magazine and *Fortune* magazine.

### ROY E LAYZELL

Roy Layzell was born on 20 January 1962 in Rochester, Kent. He studied Technical Illustration at Gloucester Art College between 1979 and 1983. After leaving college he worked for industry as a technical illustrator, producing technical manuals and airbrush illustrations. He worked on site and in studio for customers such as Dowty's, BAe, Rover Group, Alvis, Ricardo and the Ministry of Defence. He joined the Guild of Aviation Artists in 1992 as a Friend, exhibiting his painting 'Asterix' in 1993. This became Aviation Painting of the Year, making Roy the Aviation Artist of the Year. He enlisted into the RAuxAF in 1993 as a movements operator with 4624 Squadron, giving him practical experience of aircraft such as Tristars, VC10s, C-17 Globemaster IIIs and Chinooks. Now a movements controller, he is involved in operations throughout the world, which give him a unique insight and source of subject matter for his work.

### KENNETH McDONOUGH GAvA (1921-2002)

Born in February 1921, Kenneth McDonough studied at Regent Street Polytechnic, London. He served for five and a half years in the Army during World War II in North Africa, Italy, France and Germany. He was the last regular artist working on the *Illustrated London News*. He painted in oils and gouache and preferred the impressionistic approach to painting. This can clearly be seen in his work exhibited at the RAF Museum at Hendon, the Fleet Air Arm Museum at Yeovilton, and other collections. Many of Kenneth's paintings have been reproduced as greeting cards and prints. Kenneth's interest was mainly in the dawn of aviation, World War I and the aircraft of the 1920s and '30s. He died on 16 January 2002, shortly before his 81st birthday.

### ROGER H MIDDLEBROOK GAvA, FSAI

Roger Middlebrook studied at the Slade School of Fine Art in London. After completing his studies, he lived and worked in Sweden for 13 years. During this period he painted landscapes, townscapes and portraits. Marriage to a Swedish girl required a more permanent income, and he became a technical illustrator with Volvo cars. Back in England, he eventually became self-employed, and technical illustration gave way to architectural

illustration and illustration work dealing with all forms of air, land and sea transport. He is a full member of the Guild of Aviation Artists and winner of many awards and trophies. These include the Guild's SBAC Trophy (twice), the Guild's Wilkinson Sword Trophy (three times), the E J Riding Memorial Trophy, the Westland Helicopter Trophy and the Guild of Aviation's Painting of the Year Award in 1999 and 2001.

### EDMUND MILLER DLC, CEng, MRAeS, GAvA

Born in July 1929, Edmund Miller was educated at Sale Grammar School. He served two years' National Service in the RAF, then studied Aeronautical Engineering at Loughborough College of Technology, qualifying in 1954. He joined the de Havilland Aircraft Company as an Aircraft Structural Designer and worked on the Comet 4, Trident, Airbus and BAe146 aircraft before joining the Airworthiness Department in 1970, taking early retirement as Principal Airworthiness Engineer in 1988. He has been involved in aviation art since the mid-1950s, exhibiting with the Society of Aviation Artists and then with the Kronfeld Aviation Art Society until the formation of the Guild of Aviation Artists. He served as Chairman of the Guild from 1983 to 1985. He has paintings on permanent exhibition in museums, airports and private collections. His other interests include aviation history, vintage transport, portraiture and gliding.

### FRANK MUNGER AMRAeS, GAvA, MGMA

Frank Munger was invalided out of the RAF just before the end of World War II. Despite having no formal art training, he obtained a post in 1945 as editorial artist with the publishers of the aviation magazine *Flight*, becoming internationally known for his illustrations of aircraft, engines and related subjects. He retired in 1985. He first exhibited aviation paintings in 1965 with the Kronfeld Aviation Art Society and he won the award for the Best Watercolour in 1966. On its formation in 1971, he joined the Guild of Aviation Artists. He has since won the awards for Best Oil, Best Watercolour, Best Sporting Aviation, Flight Trophy and Aviation Painting of the Year in 1991. His main interest is in early aviation. As well as painting marine and wildlife subjects, Frank is also a founder member of the Guild of Motoring Artists. He keeps 'hands on' experience alive as a long standing member of the Rolls-Royce Heritage Trust workshop, restoring historic aero engines.

## DOUGLAS NIELSEN ASAA

Douglas Nielsen was born in Syracuse, New York in 1957, the son of a commercial airline pilot. He worked as an aircraft mechanic for Eastern, Midway and American Airlines and flew as a flight engineer on Boeing 727s for Key Air, an international charter airline. He specialises in commercial aircraft, and has provided paintings for airlines, advertising agencies, model box art, book covers and private collections. He paints in oils, and each image is based on dozens of photos and technical drawings to ensure a high degree of detail and accuracy. He is a trustee and life member of the American Association of Aviation Artists and an active member of the US Air Force Art Program. He is also an advisor for the Poplar Grove Wings and Wheels Museum.

## TIMOTHY O'BRIEN GAvA

Timothy O'Brien was born in Nottingham in 1970, and since childhood has pursued a passion for art. After working in several commercial art studios, he became a full-time freelance artist and illustrator at the age of 22. A former ATC cadet, Tim has flown in a range of aircraft including the Tiger Moth, Chipmunk, Junkers Ju 52, C-130 Hercules, HS125 and the BBMF's Lancaster and Dakota, gathering first hand knowledge for his paintings. Now accepted as one of the youngest full members of the Guild of Aviation Artists, Tim's work can be seen on prints published by Lincolnshire's Lancaster Association, Kestrel Publishing and in occasional magazine articles for *Aeroplane Monthly* and the re-launched *Wingspan*.

## JOHN PAGE

John Page was born in Sussex in 1947. He was encouraged by his mother to draw and paint and by the age of ten his first drawings of horses and portraits began to show his natural talent. At this time John emigrated to Canada where he won numerous prizes with his work and this culminated in one exhibit being hung in the Canadian National Exhibition Centre in Toronto. Upon returning to England, he went into engineering, maintaining his love for art by joining a local art society. Attracted to aircraft, John joined the Guild of Aviation Artists, where he quickly became an associated member. It was not long before his paintings were exhibited at annual exhibitions in London. In the late 1980s, he won the coveted 'John Pooley Sword Award' for a painting of a large landscape, depicting hang gliders. John's success has gone from strength to strength with his paintings of aircraft being published in the Guild of Aviation Artists' book *Five Ages of Aviation*. British Airways has two of John's paintings hanging in its executive boardroom, and the airline's Chairman, Lord Marshall, commissioned John to complete a series of works for other international locations. 1995 saw his first international print launched in England. John has also had paintings on show in the Middle East, and is now again living in Canada, where he is working to establish his art in this part of the world.

## WILLIAM S PHILLIPS ASAA

William S Phillips has had a fascination with aviation for as long as he can remember. His love of flight led him into the US Air Force, where he spent much time sketching various aircraft. On discharge from the service, he studied law, but upon selling some of his paintings, he decided to pursue a career in art. His original paintings hang in museums and public and private collections throughout the world. William is also a member of the US Air Force, NASA, and Navy Art Programs. He has had numerous one-man shows at various locations including the Smithsonian's National Aviation and Space Museum, Naval Aviation Museum, and Airmen Memorial Museum. He was chosen by the US Postal Service to complete a full sheet of stamps on Classic American Aviation. He has received many awards including the Naval Museum Foundation's R G Smith Award and the Art History Award for the Art in the Parks competition. He is an Artist Fellow of the American Society of Aviation Artists.

## JOHN PITTAWAY GAvA

John Pittaway studied at Birmingham School of Art before gaining a three-year scholarship to Birmingham College of Art. He gained plenty of experience in several art studios before starting a career as a freelance illustrator. His work covers a wide spectrum, ranging from landscape figures, aircraft, ships, cars and tanks. He has always been fascinated by aircraft and he served with the Royal Observer Corps during his youth, which doubtless fuelled his desire to paint them in later years. He opened an art gallery in Stratford-upon-Avon, where he made many contacts and friends through exhibitions. Alvis of Coventry commissioned him to illustrate the Scorpion tank. This took several years, culminating with a large eight-foot presentation oil painting, which now hangs at Bovington Camp in Dorset. He also did work for Land Rover Military Vehicles. On the closure of RAF Pendeford, he was asked to paint a presentation painting of a Tiger Moth as used by trainees during World War II, which was presented to RAF Cosford. With his son Marc, John formed a limited edition print company called 'Moving Images' specialising in world speed records, which led to a contract with Richard Noble and his successful Thrust SSC project.

## MARK POSTLETHWAITE GAvA

Born in Enderby, Leicestershire on 11 August 1964, Mark started to paint aircraft on canvas at the age of 17 as a hobby. A lifelong interest in flying and aviation history, together with his professional career as a photographer, soon combined to produce work of the highest standards in this exacting field. In 1987, he became the first ever Artist in Residence at the RAF Museum at Hendon, in what was the first major exhibition of his work. In 1991, Mark was elected to full membership of the Guild of Aviation Artists, thereby becoming the youngest artist ever to receive this distinction. He turned professional as an artist in February 1992, and has worked with numerous RAF squadrons including the RAF Aerobatic Team, the *Red Arrows*. Worldwide, his originals and prints can be found in many major museums and collections, especially in Norway where he is acclaimed for his ability to capture the 'Norwegian light'. In 2001, Mark won the Wilkinson Sword Trophy and the Nockolds Trophy at the Guild of Aviation Artists' annual exhibition.

## PAUL E RENDEL ASAA

Paul E Rendel, a professional freelance artist who lives in Pittsburgh, Pennsylvania, is well known for the artistry of both his commercial work and his aviation paintings. His aviation paintings have been featured at museums and shows in both the US and Europe. Most recently, his work has won awards at the Experimental Aviation Center Museum and the Pensacola Naval Air Museum. He is a past president of the American Society of Aviation Artists, and a member of the New York Society of Illustrators and the US Air Force Art Program. His early training at the Detroit Institute of Arts and Crafts, his 30 years of experience in art studios and his work as a freelance artist have enabled him to excel in combining technical knowledge with artistic quality. He built and flies a Thorpe T-18, and for many years flew sailplanes in competitive soaring events.

## MICHAEL RONDOT GAvA

Michael Rondot was born in Windsor, Ontario and spent his first six years in Canada. He now lives in Norwich, but his formative years were spent in Peterborough, where he studied art 'A' level at King's School. He was in the RAF for 25 years from August 1967 to July 1992 and flew Canberras, Hunters and Jaguars, achieving over 5,000 flying hours before retiring to become a professional aviation artist, when he formed Collectair Limited Editions. Michael's experiences in the Gulf War have given rise to some of the best war art of that conflict. He became a founder associate member of the Guild of Aviation Artists in 1971 and his first limited edition print was published in 1980. Since then he has continued to paint in oils a wide variety of both modern and veteran military aircraft, with occasional commissions for commercial jets. His paintings are in private, corporate and military collections and museums worldwide.

## ROBIN SMITH GAvA

Robin Smith was born in Louth in Lincolnshire in December 1949. He served as an apprentice at Rolls-Royce in Derby from 1966 to 1971 and learned to fly with the Merlin Flying Club, taking an interest in catching aircraft in paint despite no formal education in art, starting with water colours, but now painting in oils. He joined the Guild of Aviation Artists in 1987. He works from his studio at home in Grimoldby, Lincs, specialising in aviation, but also painting landscapes. His particular interest is the older types of aircraft and all aspects of sport aviation, from microlights to Sopwith Camels. His work has been reproduced as fine art prints, greeting cards and video programmes.

## STAN STOKES

Stan Stokes is a California native who developed a passion for vintage cars, trains and aeroplanes at an early age. After studying art at Junior College in Southern California, Stan decided to pursue a career as a professional artist. More than 25 years ago, a friend suggested that Stan combine his passion for aviation history and flying with his artistic talents. Winner of the prestigious Smithsonian National Air and Space Museum's award for his painting of Jimmy Mathern's Lockheed 12A in 1984, Stokes' originals are now in the collections of all the major aviation museums in the US. Stan has also completed several impressive murals for these museums as well, including a 106-feet long life-size scene depicting the Battle of Britain, which was displayed at the Planes of Fame Museum in Minnesota. In 1997 Stan completed the entrance mural for the new Palm Springs Aviation Museum. He was the recipient of the R G Smith award for excellence in naval aviation painting in 2000.

## DOUGLAS SWALLOW GAvA

Douglas Swallow has had a lifelong interest in aviation starting in boyhood during World War II. He served in the RAF between 1946 and 1949 as a radar mechanic. Afterwards he took up a career in the life assurance industry and painted as a hobby when time permitted. On his retirement in 1988 he was able to combine his interest in art and aviation and has exhibited at the Guild of Aviation Artists exhibitions since 1989. In 1988 he joined the staff of the RAF Museum at Hendon as a volunteer where he works part time in the research department.

## ROBERT TAYLOR

The name Robert Taylor has been synonymous with aviation art for over a quarter of a century. Robert's early career was devoted to maritime paintings, and he achieved early success with his prints of naval subjects, one of his admirers being Lord Louis Mountbatten. He exhibited successfully at the Royal Society of Marine Artists in London. He was invited to appear in a BBC Television programme which led to a string of commissions for the Fleet Air Arm Museum. This was the start of Robert's career as an aviation artist. His aviation paintings are instantly recognisable, his trade mark being flying machines that are battle scarred and worse for wear. He has exhibited throughout the US and Canada, Australia, Japan and in Europe. His one-man exhibition at the Smithsonian's National Air and Space Museum in Washington DC was hailed as the most popular art exhibition ever held there.

## SEAN THACKWRAY

Sean Thackwray was born in 1967 into a South African Air Force family, his father being a pilot and his mother an artist. Aviation art was a natural extension of Sean's background and he sold his first aeroplane painting at 12 years of age to a German Air Force pilot. He received his wings in the South African Air Force in 1987 and completed his service flying Atlas Cheetah fighters with No 2 Squadron in 1996. After obtaining commercial pilot qualifications he flew for Cathay Pacific Airlines in Hong Kong for two years, but moved back to South Africa, where he currently flies as a Boeing 737-800 co-pilot with South African Airways. He is an associate member of the Guild of Aviation Artists and has held exhibitions of his work in South Africa and Hong Kong. Currently he has commissions from EADS, BAE Systems and the South African Air Force, as well as numerous private aviation enthusiasts. Sean flies Harvards in his spare time and is a keen aviation modeller.

## CHARLES J THOMPSON GAvA, ASAA, MGMA, EAA

Charles J Thompson was born in Poona, India, the son of a British Army sergeant. He was educated at La Martiniere College, Lucknow and returned with the family to England in 1949 where he joined Briggs Motor Bodies as a trainee draughtsman. Charles served as an airframe mechanic in the RAF for his National Service from 1955 to 1957 before returning to Briggs, which became part of the Ford Motor Co, and took early retirement in 1986. A lifelong aviation enthusiast, he began painting in 1979. Charles became an Associate Member of the Guild of Aviation Artists in 1982 and was elected a full member in 1984. He has won several awards in the Guild's annual London exhibitions including the Wilkinson Sword Poignard in 1983, the Roy Nockolds Trophy in 1989, the QANTAS Trophy in 2000 and commendations in 1998 and 1999. He is also a founder member of the Guild of Motoring Artists.

## NICOLAS TRUDGIAN

Nicolas Trudgian was born in Plymouth, and it was from his father, himself a talented artist, that he acquired his love of drawing. After leaving school, he took a one year foundation course at Plymouth College of Art, later going on to Falmouth College of Art where he specialised in technical illustration and paintings of machines and vehicles for industry. Nicolas spent many years as a professional illustrator working firstly for a design studio in Wiltshire, producing detailed artwork for such companies as Rolls-Royce, General Motors, Volvo trucks, Alfa Romeo as well as the aviation and defence industries. Towards the end of the 1980s, Nicolas was given the opportunity to work for the Military Gallery. After completing a series of aviation posters, including a gigantic painting to commemorate the 75th anniversary of the RAF, his first aviation scene to be published as a limited edition was launched with immediate success.

### MICHAEL TURNER PGAvA, FGMA

President of the Guild of Aviation Artists, Michael Turner was born in Harrow in March 1934. Fired with a boyhood enthusiasm for aircraft and the RAF, he studied at the Heatherley School of Fine Arts in London. This was followed by two years National Service with the REME, and three years working in advertising. His continuing fascination with aviation found expression through his painting, specialising also in motor sport and associated mechanical subjects after turning freelance in 1957. He has flown in a wide variety of service aircraft from Tiger Moth to Tornado, and flies his own ex-RAF Chipmunk. A founder member and twice chairman of the Guild of Aviation Artists, Michael is also a founder member of the International Racing Press Association and a member of the Guild of Motoring Writers. His paintings hang in permanent collections at the Science Museum, the Fleet Air Arm Museum and many more collections in Britain and around the world.

### PAUL TUTTLE

Paul Tuttle was born in Truro, Nova Scotia in 1958. He is employed as an rescue firefighter by the Halifax International Airport Authority. Paul began drawing and sketching at an early age and began painting seriously in the early 1980s. He has painted a variety of subjects over the years, but has concentrated mainly on wildlife and aviation. Paul won Second Prize and was Best of Show Artists Award winner at the 1997 Artflight competition held by the National Aviation Museum in Ottawa, and has had his work exhibited at various shows.

### ROBERT WATTS

After a formal training in design and painting at the Pratt Institute in New York, Robert Watts went on to study at the Art Center School in Los Angeles. He began his career in 1966 when he was appointed lead illustrator for the Ryan Aeronautical Company. His job involved painting aircraft that did not exist. Working from engineering drawings, and making use of a vivid imagination, he had to visualise how these aeroplanes would look in flight even before prototypes were built. In 1971, Robert was asked to join the Naval Art Program, and served as a naval combat artist during the Vietnam years. By 1974, he was working on his own as a professional illustrator and painter, gaining commissions from many of the leading aviation manufacturers, including Hughes, Teledyne, General Dynamics and Northrop. Though most paintings completed by Watts have been concerned with aviation, he also has a talent for painting ships and the sea, and this has led to a commission from the Naval Academy Ships Museum for six oils depicting famous World War II ships. However, his first love is painting aircraft.

### PHILIP E WEST ASAA

Philip West is recognised as one of the world's finest aviation artists. Collectors of his original oil paintings are to be found worldwide. He has produced in excess of 30 limited editions. Noted for his passion for detail, Philip has won many accolades for his paintings, not the least of which was the prestigious Duane Whitney Award for Excellence at the 1997 American Society of Aviation Artists Exhibition. His work is inspired by and reflects his fascination for aircraft through the ages. Philip's knowledge of aircraft and the accuracy of his work combine to record a moment in history perfectly.

### IAN WILSON-DICK GAvA, ASAA

Born in London, Ian Wilson-Dick showed an early interest in drawing and aviation. He attended Tottenham County School during the war years and in 1945 joined Fairey Aviation Company as an engineering apprentice. This led to helicopter flight test engineering and in 1963, to Boeing-Vertol and later Lockheed. His painting interests during those years were primarily seascapes. When Lockheed left the helicopter field, he turned to forensic engineering and later formed a consultancy. During this time he learned to fly. He joined the American Society of Aviation Artists and participated in a Keith Ferris workshop at the 1999 Forum. He returned to England later that year. He is a member of the Guild of Aviation Artists where he regularly exhibits.

### TERRY WOFFORD NDD, ASAA

Terry Wofford was born in England. Her formal art education began at the age of twelve at Moseley Road Art School. From here she went to Birmingham College of Art where she obtained a degree in art and design. She worked for a Finnish textile company before moving to the United States for three years. Her next destination was the Orient where she travelled to many remote regions, flying into all types of terrain on all types of aircraft. On returning to the US, she decided to specialise in aviation and space art. Terry is an Artist Fellow and charter member of the American Society of Aviation Artists, a member of the US Air Force Art Program and the NASA Art Program. Her work is in the US Air Force Art Collection, the NASA Art Collection and she has exhibited at the Smithsonian's Air and Space Museum, the Galaxy Center in Florida and the EAA Museum in Oshkosh, amongst others.

### RONALD WONG BSc(Hons), GAvA, ASAA, GMA, TWAS

Ronald Wong is a long-standing member of the Guild of Aviation Artists. He gained his BSc Degree (Honours) in Biochemistry at Hatfield Polytechnic and subsequently worked in the health service in London. At that stage, painting was a self-taught hobby which was quite separate from his other interests, which included aviation and aircraft modelling. Aviation had made an indelible impression when growing up close to the flight path in Hong Kong. In 1974, one of his early aviation paintings won the SBAC Trophy. Two years later, he left his scientific career and embarked on an artistic one. In 1987 he gained the Nockolds Trophy as well as the Wilkinson Sword Poignard, both for oils. As well as the Guild of Aviation Artists, he has exhibited with the Royal Society of Marine Artists and the Society of Wildlife Artists in London. His work sells through prominent galleries in London and the US. He has worked very closely with the RAF, and in particular with US personnel in this country, and his work can be seen at many military bases.

### KEITH WOODCOCK GAvA, ASAA, GMA

Keith Woodcock was born in April 1940 and educated at Belle Vue Grammar School, Bradford, and Salford College of Art. After pursuing a career in industry, he became a freelance graphic designer and illustrator in 1969. A lifetime enthusiasm for aircraft persuaded him to devote his entire time to aviation art in 1982. He has also added motoring subjects to his repertoire and is now a full member of the Guild of Motoring Artists. Keith is a past winner of the Aviation Painting of the Year Award organised annually by the Guild of Aviation Artists, of which he is a former Chairman. Painting in both gouache and oils, his work is frequently used for fine art prints, book jackets, magazines and cards. His paintings have been commissioned by companies and individuals worldwide. Keith also gives lectures and workshops, not only on his speciality subjects, but on art in general.

**FRANK WOOTTON OBE FPGAvA (1911-1998)**

Eminent among aeronautical artists, Frank Wootton was a Sussex man born and bred, and was, in the words of a leading art critic, 'destined to become the first artist to be inspired by the awe and wonder of aviation and by the transcendent beauty of the element that is its challenge'. Frank, who volunteered for the RAF in 1939, flew in most of the aircraft that he has so vividly painted. At the invitation of the then Air Commodore Peake, Director of Public Relations at the Air Ministry, he toured RAF stations in 1940 and 1941 to record the endeavours of those critical years. Later he served as an official war artist in France and Belgium and in Southeast Asia. Frank continued from those days, until his death in April 1998, to express on canvas his love for aircraft and, in 1979, was awarded the much-prized trophy of the Air Public Relations Association. He donated his 'Bader Bail Out' painting to the RAF Benevolent Fund and it now hangs in the Smithsonian Institution in Washington, DC.

**CLAUS FRIEDL WUELFING**

Claus Friedl Wuelfing was born in Cologne, Germany in December 1937 and has had a keen interest in aviation since he first visited his uncle, who was serving in the Luftwaffe, in 1942. Having studied as a graphic designer, Friedl joined the Ford Werke AG in Germany as an automobile designer. In 1968, Ford Design Europe was formed and he was promoted to Design Manager, responsible for the exterior design of large and medium cars. During this time he made the acquaintance of Charles Thompson (a member of the Guild of Aviation Artists). Friedl was greatly influenced by the aviation paintings produced by Charles and by 1986 had taken up painting aircraft himself as a serious hobby. After early retirement in 1992, he was able to devote more time to painting. Friedl's large paintings hang in permanent display at the Luftwaffen-Museum in Berlin, and messes belonging to the German Federal Luftwaffe, as well as in other private and business collections throughout Germany.

**JOHN YOUNG VPGAvA, VPASAA**

John Young was born in Bristol in 1930 and educated at the Royal Grammar School and the School of Art in High Wycombe. Inspired by the visit of Sir Alan Cobham's National Aviation Day air display near his home in Chesham, his love affair with flying machines began, his interest furthered by the operations of the US Eighth Air Force B-17s and B-24s from nearby Bovingdon during WW2. John has painted professionally since 1950, when employment in the studio of an advertising agency enabled him to translate his interest in aviation into a style of painting which combined portrayal of technical subjects with natural, atmospheric situations. John went freelance in the early 1960s in order to expand his capabilities. He is a founder member of the Guild of Aviation Artists and completed a term as Chairman. John has flown in over 60 different types of aircraft, military and civilian, giving his artwork an 'I was there' flavour. He was awarded the Guild of Aviation Artists Medal in 1983.

# ACKNOWLEDGEMENTS

**The Royal Air Force Benevolent Fund is grateful to the following companies and organisations for their most generous support of the Fund by sponsoring these pages:**

1908   Pages 16 & 17 donated by BAE SYSTEMS.

1909   Pages 18 & 19 donated by the Air League, founded in 1909.

1912   Pages 24 & 25 donated by the Royal International Air Tattoo, commemorating the first UK air display at Hendon in 1912.

1913   Pages 26 & 27 donated by Shell Aviation.

1917   Pages 34 & 35 donated by Mitsubishi Motors, to recognise the production of its first passenger car in 1917.

1918   Pages 36 & 37 donated by the Directorate of Recruitment (RAF) and the Directorate of Corporate Communications (RAF).

1919   Pages 38 & 39 donated by the Royal Air Force Benevolent Fund, founded in 1919.

1923   Pages 46 & 47 donated by AgustaWestland, in recognition of Juan de la Cierva's defining moment in rotorcraft development, from which the modern helicopter has evolved.

1929   Pages 58 & 59 donated by Marshall of Cambridge, which started its world renowned aviation business in 1929.

1930   Pages 60 & 61 donated by the Western Daily Press, commemorating Amy Johnson's pioneering solo flight across Australia.

1937   Pages 74 & 75 donated by the Hymatic Engineering Company Limited.

1939   Pages 78 & 79 donated by European Aeronautic Defence and Space Company – EADS Military Aircraft.

1940   Pages 80 & 81 donated by Robert Stuart plc.

1941 Pages 82 & 83 donated by the Air Training Corps, founded in February 1941 and still developing an aviation interest among young people today.

1946 Pages 92 & 93 donated by DynCorp International LLC, founded in 1946.

1947 Pages 94 & 95 donated by Red Admiral Productions, in celebration of supersonic flight.

1949 Pages 98 & 99 donated by 4624 (County of Oxford) Movements Squadron RAuxAF, whose motto is *Ready to Move*.

1950 Pages 100 & 101 donated by Tony Finding, in celebration of the year 1950.

1952 Pages 104 & 105 donated by Breitling, to celebrate the 50th anniversary of the 'Old Timer' classic timepiece.

1956 Pages 112 & 113 donated by the Coachmakers and Coach Harness Makers, who wish to recognise the achievements of No 10 Squadron, RAF.

1960 Pages 120 & 121 donated by Turner Charles Limited, Engineering and IT Recruitment Consultants, founded in June 1960.

1970 Pages 140 & 141 donated by Marshall Aerospace Limited, sister design authority for the RAF Hercules and world-wide C-130 support centre.

1971 Pages 142 & 143 donated in memory of Jack Cullum, founder of Cullum Detuners Limited, who died on 13 May 1971.

1975 Pages 150 & 151 donated by Imperial Tobacco Limited.

1976 Pages 152 & 153 donated by BAE SYSTEMS.

1978 Pages 156 & 157 donated by Pilatus Aircraft – turboprop training leader, from the PC-7 in 1978 to the latest generation PC-21.

1979 Pages 158 & 159 donated by the RAF Airshow at Cosford, commemorating its first show in 1979.

1980 Pages 160 & 161 donated by CAE, operator of the Medium Support Helicopter Aircrew Training Facility at RAF Benson.

1981 Pages 162 & 163 donated by Rockwell Collins (UK) Ltd.

1982 Pages 164 & 165 donated by the Directorate of Corporate Communications (Navy).

1984 Pages 168 & 169 donated by A1 Hire & Sales, founded in 1984.

1985 Pages 170 & 171 donated by Highworth Press Limited, Swindon – design and print working together.

1987 Pages 174 & 175 donated by Mike Brennan of Main Event Concessions.

1989 Pages 178 & 179 donated by Jade Productions.

1990 Pages 180 & 181 donated by Aitch Design – creative graphic design solutions.

1991 Pages 182 & 183 donated by Harris Signs Group.

1993 Pages 186 & 187 donated by Impact Image, supporting the Royal Air Force in film and video.

1994 Pages 188 & 189 donated by the Daily Mail, celebrating a long association with the Royal Air Force Benevolent Fund Enterprises.

1995 Pages 190 & 191 donated by Orion Security Print, working with RAFBFE protecting ticket revenue since 1995.

1997 Pages 194 & 195 donated by Thompson and Wilson Communications Ltd.

1999 Pages 198 & 199 donated by DKA, celebrating its association with the Royal Air Force Benevolent Fund Enterprises.

2001 Pages 202 & 203 donated by Northrop Grumman Corporation.

2002 Pages 204 & 205 donated by Lockheed Martin.

2003 Pages 206 & 207 donated by BAE SYSTEMS.

**The Royal Air Force Benevolent Fund would like to extend its sincere thanks to the following companies for their exceptional support with the production of this book:**

INTERFOR

INTERFOR LIMITED of HONG KONG
for kindly donating the paper

玉 JADE PRODUCTIONS of HONG KONG
for overseeing all aspects of production

# WRIGHT TO FLY

## CELEBRATING 100 YEARS OF POWERED FLIGHT

Publishing Director: Paul A Bowen
Managing Editor: Peter R March
Editorial Research: Ben Dunnell & Brian Strickland
Editorial Assistant: Robby Robinson
Art Consultant: Wilfred Hardy GAvA
Art Research & Publishing Co-ordinator: Bob Dixon OBE
Art Research Assistant (USA): Wayne Pittman
Book Design: Graham Finch
Publishing Manager: David Higham
Sponsorship Manager: Heidi Standfast
Administration: Helen Airdrie

First published in Great Britain in 2002 by the Royal Air Force Benevolent Fund Enterprises
Douglas Bader House, Horcott Hill, Fairford, Glos GL7 4RB, UK

Text copyright © Peter R March 2002
Design and layout copyright © the Royal Air Force Benevolent Fund Enterprises 2002

Produced in China by Jade Productions

First edition 2002 (hardback) – ISBN 1 899808 76 0
First edition 2002 (softback) – ISBN 1 899808 81 7

SOLD IN SUPPORT OF THE ROYAL AIR FORCE BENEVOLENT FUND

Cover painting: *Wright to Fly*, specially commissioned and painted for this book by Wilfred Hardy GAvA